T0283417

Theoretical Computer Science

Theoretical Computer Science

Edited by Lara Briggs

Larsen & Keller
www.larsen-keller.com

Theoretical Computer Science
Edited by Lara Briggs
ISBN: 979-8-88836-002-6 (Hardback)

Larsen & Keller

Published by Larsen and Keller Education,
5 Penn Plaza,
19th Floor,
New York, NY 10001, USA

Cataloging-in-Publication Data

Theoretical computer science / edited by Lara Briggs.
    p. cm.
Includes bibliographical references and index.
ISBN 979-8-88836-002-6
1. Computer science. 2. Computers. I. Briggs, Lara.
QA76 .T44 2023
004--dc23

For more information regarding Larsen and Keller Education and its products, please visit the publisher's website www.larsen-keller.com

Contents

Preface

Theoretical computer science (TCS) refers to a subset of computer science that deals with algorithmic and computational interactions and processes. It emphasizes on theoretical foundations of computer science and commonly depends on rigorous mathematical proofs. The goal of TCS is to understand the nature of computation and use this understanding to develop more effective methodologies. The primary uses of TCS are quantum computation and algorithm design. It encompasses a wide range of topics such as program semantics and verification, computational economics, computational number theory and algebra, machine learning, cryptography, algorithmic game theory, computational geometry, and computational biology. TCS has also played a vital role in the formation of various fields including algorithmic privacy, quantum computation, algorithmic fairness and algorithmic economics. This book contains some path-breaking studies in the field of theoretical computer science. It presents researches and studies performed by experts across the globe. This book is a complete source of knowledge on the present status of this important field.

The information contained in this book is the result of intensive hard work done by researchers in this field. All due efforts have been made to make this book serve as a complete guiding source for students and researchers. The topics in this book have been comprehensively explained to help readers understand the growing trends in the field.

I would like to thank the entire group of writers who made sincere efforts in this book and my family who supported me in my efforts of working on this book. I take this opportunity to thank all those who have been a guiding force throughout my life.

Editor

1

The Bernays-Schönfinkel-Ramsey Class of Separation Logic on Arbitrary Domains

Mnacho Echenim[1], Radu Iosif[2], and Nicolas Peltier[1(✉)]

Univ. Grenoble Alpes, CNRS, LIG, 38000 Grenoble, France
Nicolas.peltier@imag.fr
Univ. Grenoble Alpes, CNRS, VERIMAG, 38000 Grenoble, France

Abstract. This paper investigates the satisfiability problem for Separation Logic with k record fields, with unrestricted nesting of separating conjunctions and implications, for prenex formulæ with quantifier prefix $\exists^*\forall^*$. In analogy with first-order logic, we call this fragment Bernays-Schönfinkel-Ramsey Separation Logic [$\mathsf{BSR}(\mathsf{SL}^k)$]. In contrast to existing work in Separation Logic, in which the universe of possible locations is assumed to be infinite, both finite and infinite universes are considered. We show that, unlike in first-order logic, the (in)finite satisfiability problem is undecidable for $\mathsf{BSR}(\mathsf{SL}^k)$. Then we define two non-trivial subsets thereof, that are decidable for finite and infinite satisfiability respectively, by controlling the occurrences of universally quantified variables within the scope of separating implications, as well as the polarity of the occurrences of the latter. Beside the theoretical interest, our work has natural applications in program verification, for checking that constraints on the shape of a data-structure are preserved by a sequence of transformations.

1 Introduction

Separation Logic [10,14], or SL, is a logical framework used in program verification to describe properties of the dynamically allocated memory, such as topologies of data structures (lists, trees), (un)reachability between pointers, etc. In a nutshell, given an integer $k \geq 1$, the logic SL^k is obtained from the first-order theory of a finite partial function $h : U \rightharpoonup U^k$ called a *heap*, by adding two substructural connectives: (i) the *separating conjunction* $\phi_1 * \phi_2$, that asserts a split of the heap into disjoint heaps satisfying ϕ_1 and ϕ_2 respectively, and (ii) the *separating implication* or *magic wand* $\phi_1 \twoheadrightarrow \phi_2$, stating that each extension of the heap by a heap satisfying ϕ_1 must satisfy ϕ_2. Intuitively, U is the universe of possible of memory locations (cells) and k is the number of record fields in each memory cell.

The separating connectives $*$ and $\twoheadrightarrow$ allow concise definitions of program semantics, via weakest precondition calculi [10] and easy-to-write specifications of recursive linked data structures (e.g. singly- and doubly-linked lists, trees with linked leaves and parent pointers, etc.), when higher-order inductive definitions are added [14]. Investigating the decidability and complexity of the satisfiability problem for fragments of SL is of theoretical and practical interest. In this paper, we consider prenex SL formulæ with prefix $\exists^*\forall^*$. In analogy with first-order logic with equality and uninterpreted predicates [12], we call this fragment Bernays-Schönfinkel-Ramsey SL [BSR(SL^k)].

As far as we are aware, all existing work on SL assumes that the universe (set of available locations) is countably infinite. This assumption is not necessarily realistic in practice since the available memory is usually finite, although the bound depends on the hardware and is not known in advance. The finite universe hypothesis is especially useful when dealing with bounded memory issues, for instance checking that the execution of a program satisfies its postcondition, provided that there are sufficiently many available memory cells. In this paper we consider both the finite and infinite satisfiability problems. We show that both problems are undecidable for BSR(SL^k) (unlike in first-order logic) and that they become PSPACE-complete under some additional restrictions, related to the occurrences of the magic wand and universal variables:

1. The infinite satisfiability problem is PSPACE-complete if the positive occurrences of $-\!\ast$ (i.e., the occurrences of $-\!\ast$ that are in the scope of an even number of negations) contain no universal variables.
2. The finite satisfiability problem is PSPACE-complete if there is no positive occurrence of $-\!\ast$ (i.e., $-\!\ast$ only occurs in the scope of an odd number of negations).

Reasoning on finite domains is more difficult than on infinite ones, due to possibility of asserting cardinality constraints on unallocated cells, which explains that the latter condition is more restrictive than the former one. Actually, the finite satisfiability problem is undecidable even if there is only one positive occurrence of a $-\!\ast$ with no variable within the scope of $-\!\ast$. These results establish sharp decidability frontiers within BSR(SL^k).

Undecidability is shown by reduction from BSR first-order formulæ with two monadic function symbols. To establish the decidability results, we first show that every quantifier-free SL formula can be transformed into an equivalent boolean combination of formulæ of some specific patterns, called *test formulæ*. This result is interesting in itself, since it provides a precise and intuitive characterization of the expressive power of SL: it shows that separating connectives can be confined to a small set of test formulæ. Afterward, we show that such test formulæ can be transformed into first-order formulæ. If the above conditions (1) or (2) are satisfied, then the obtained first-order formulæ are in the BSR class, which ensures decidability. The PSPACE upper-bound relies on a careful analysis of the maximal size of the test formulæ. The analysis reveals that, although the boolean combination of test formulæ is of exponential size, its components (e.g., the conjunctions in its dnf) are of polynomial size and can be enumerated in polynomial space. For space reasons, full details and proofs are given in a technical report [8].

Applications. Besides theoretical interest, our work has natural applications in program verification. Indeed, purely universal SL formulæ are useful to express pre- or post-conditions asserting "local" constraints on the shape of the data structures manipulated by a program. Consider the atomic proposition $x \mapsto (y_1, \ldots, y_k)$ which states that the value of the heap at x is the tuple $(y_1, \ldots, y_k)$ and there is no value, other than x, in the domain of h. With this in mind, the following formula describes a well-formed doubly-linked list:

$$\forall x_1, x_2, x_3, x_4, x_5 \ . \ x_1 \mapsto (x_2, x_3) * x_2 \mapsto (x_4, x_5) * \top \Rightarrow x_5 \approx x_1 \wedge \neg x_3 \approx x_4 \quad (1)$$

Such constraints could also be expressed by using inductively defined predicates, unfortunately checking satisfiability of SL formulæ, even of very simple fragments with no occurrence of $-\!\!*$ in the presence of user-defined inductive predicates is undecidable, unless some rather restrictive conditions are fulfilled [9]. In contrast, checking entailment between two universal formulæ boils down to checking the satisfiability of a $\mathsf{BSR}(\mathsf{SL}^k)$ formula, which can be done thanks to the decidability results in our paper.

The separating implication (magic wand) seldom occurs in such shape constraints. However, it is useful to describe the dynamic transformations of the data structures, as in the following Hoare-style axiom, giving the weakest precondition of $\forall \mathbf{u} \ . \ \psi$ with respect to redirecting the i-th record field of x to z [10]:

$$\{x \mapsto (y_1, \ldots, y_k) * [x \mapsto (y_1, \ldots, y_{i-1}, \mathbf{z}, y_{i+1}, \ldots, y_k) -\!\!* \forall \mathbf{u} \ . \ \psi]\} \ x.i := z \ \{\forall \mathbf{u} \ . \ \psi\}$$

It is easy to check that the precondition is equivalent to the formula $\forall \mathbf{u} \ . \ x \mapsto (y_1, \ldots, y_k) * [x \mapsto (y_1, \ldots, y_{i-1}, \mathbf{z}, y_{i+1}, \ldots, y_k) -\!\!* \psi]$ because, although hoisting universal quantifiers outside of the separating conjunction is unsound in general, this is possible here due to the special form of the left-hand side $x \mapsto (y_1, \ldots, y_{i-1}, \mathbf{z}, \ldots, y_k)$ which unambiguously defines a single heap cell. Therefore, checking that $\forall \mathbf{u} \ . \ \psi$ is an invariant of the program statement x.i := z amounts to checking that the formula $\forall u \ . \ \psi \wedge \exists \mathbf{u} \ . \ \neg[x \mapsto (y_1, \ldots, y_k) * (x \mapsto (y_1, \ldots, y_{i-1}, \mathbf{z}, \ldots, y_k) -\!\!* \psi)]$ is unsatisfiable. Because the magic wand occurs negated, this formula falls into a decidable class defined in the present paper, for both finite and infinite satisfiability. The complete formalization of this deductive program verification technique and the characterization of the class of programs for which it is applicable is outside the scope of the paper and is left for future work.

Related Work. In contrast to first-order logic for which the decision problem has been thoroughly investigated [1], only a few results are known for SL. For instance, the problem is undecidable in general and **PSPACE**-complete for quantifier-free formulæ [4]. For $k = 1$, the problem is also undecidable, but it is **PSPACE**-complete if in addition there is only one quantified variable [6] and decidable but nonelementary if there is no magic wand [2]. In particular, we have also studied the prenex form of SL^1 [7] and found out that it is decidable and nonelementary, whereas $\mathsf{BSR}(\mathsf{SL}^1)$ is **PSPACE**-complete. In contrast, in this paper we show that undecidability occurs for $\mathsf{BSR}(\mathsf{SL}^k)$, for $k \geq 2$.

Expressive completeness results exist for quantifier-free SL^1 [2,11] and for SL^1 with one and two quantified variables [5,6]. There, the existence of equivalent boolean combinations of test formulæ is shown implicitly, using a finite enumeration of equivalence classes of models, instead of an effective transformation. Instead, here we present an explicit equivalence-preserving transformation of quantifier-free SL^k into boolean combinations of test formulæ, and translate the latter into first-order logic. Further, we extend the expressive completeness result to finite universes, with additional test formulæ asserting cardinality constraints on unallocated cells.

Another translation of quantifier-free SL^k into first-order logic with equality has been described in [3]. There, the small model property of quantifier-free SL^k [4] is used to bound the number of first-order variables to be considered and the separating connectives are interpreted as first-order quantifiers. The result is an equisatisfiable first-order formula. This translation scheme cannot be, however, directly applied to $\mathsf{BSR}(\mathsf{SL}^k)$, which does not have a small model property, being moreover undecidable. Theory-parameterized versions of $\mathsf{BSR}(\mathsf{SL}^k)$ have been shown to be undecidable, e.g. when integer linear arithmetic is used to reason about locations, and claimed to be PSPACE-complete for countably infinite and finite unbounded location sorts, with no relation other than equality [13]. In the present paper, we show that this claim is wrong, and draw a precise chart of decidability for both infinite and finite satisfiability of $\mathsf{BSR}(\mathsf{SL}^k)$.

2 Preliminaries

Basic Definitions. Let $\mathbb{Z}_\infty = \mathbb{Z} \cup \{\infty\}$ and $\mathbb{N}_\infty = \mathbb{N} \cup \{\infty\}$, where for each $n \in \mathbb{Z}$ we have $n + \infty = \infty$ and $n < \infty$. For a countable set S we denote by $||S|| \in \mathbb{N}_\infty$ the cardinality of S. Let Var be a countable set of variables, denoted as x, y, z and U be a sort. Vectors of variables are denoted by $\mathbf{x}, \mathbf{y}$, etc. A *function symbol* f has $\#(f) \geq 0$ arguments of sort U and a sort $\sigma(f)$, which is either the boolean sort Bool or U. If $\#(f) = 0$, we call f a *constant*. We use $\bot$ and $\top$ for the boolean constants false and true, respectively. First-order (FO) terms t and formulæ φ are defined by the following grammar:

$$t := x \mid f(\underbrace{t, \ldots, t}_{\#(f)}) \qquad \varphi := \bot \mid \top \mid t \approx t \mid p(\underbrace{t, \ldots, t}_{\#(p)}) \mid \varphi \wedge \varphi \mid \neg\varphi \mid \exists x \, . \, \varphi$$

where $x \in \mathsf{Var}$, f and p are function symbols, $\sigma(f) = U$ and $\sigma(p) = \mathsf{Bool}$. We write $\varphi_1 \vee \varphi_2$ for $\neg(\neg\varphi_1 \wedge \neg\varphi_2)$, $\varphi_1 \rightarrow \varphi_2$ for $\neg\varphi_1 \vee \varphi_2$, $\varphi_1 \leftrightarrow \varphi_2$ for $\varphi_1 \rightarrow \varphi_2 \wedge \varphi_2 \rightarrow \varphi_1$ and $\forall x \, . \, \varphi$ for $\neg\exists x \, . \, \neg\varphi$. The size of a formula φ, denoted as $\mathsf{size}(\varphi)$, is the number of symbols needed to write it down. Let $\mathsf{var}(\varphi)$ be the set of variables that occur free in φ, i.e. not in the scope of a quantifier. A *sentence* φ is a formula where $\mathsf{var}(\varphi) = \emptyset$.

First-order formulæ are interpreted over FO-structures (called structures, when no confusion arises) $\mathcal{S} = (\mathfrak{U}, \mathfrak{s}, \mathfrak{i})$, where $\mathfrak{U}$ is a countable set, called the *universe*, the elements of which are called *locations*, $\mathfrak{s} : \mathsf{Var} \rightharpoonup \mathfrak{U}$ is a mapping of variables to locations, called a *store* and $\mathfrak{i}$ interprets each function symbol f by a function $f^{\mathfrak{i}} : \mathfrak{U}^{\#(f)} \rightarrow \mathfrak{U}$, if $\sigma(f) = U$ and $f^{\mathfrak{i}} : \mathfrak{U}^{\#(f)} \rightarrow \{\bot^{\mathfrak{i}}, \top^{\mathfrak{i}}\}$ if $\sigma(f) = \mathsf{Bool}$.

A structure $(\mathfrak{U}, \mathfrak{s}, \mathfrak{i})$ is *finite* when $\|\mathfrak{U}\| \in \mathbb{N}$ and *infinite* otherwise. We write $\mathcal{S} \models \varphi$ iff φ is true when interpreted in $\mathcal{S}$. This relation is defined recursively on the structure of φ, as usual. When $\mathcal{S} \models \varphi$, we say that $\mathcal{S}$ is a *model* of φ. A formula is [finitely] *satisfiable* when it has a [finite] model. We write $\varphi_1 \equiv \varphi_2$ when $(\mathfrak{U}, \mathfrak{s}, \mathfrak{i}) \models \varphi_1 \Leftrightarrow (\mathfrak{U}, \mathfrak{s}, \mathfrak{i}) \models \varphi_2$, for every structure $(\mathfrak{U}, \mathfrak{s}, \mathfrak{i})$.

The Bernays-Schönfinkel-Ramsey fragment of FO, denoted by BSR(FO), is the set of sentences $\exists x_1 \ldots \exists x_n \forall y_1 \ldots \forall y_m . \varphi$, where φ is a quantifier-free formula in which all function symbols f of arity $\#(f) > 0$ have sort $\sigma(f) = \mathsf{Bool}$.

Separation Logic. Let k be a strictly positive integer. The logic SL^k is the set of formulæ generated by the grammar:

$$\varphi := \bot \mid \top \mid \mathsf{emp} \mid x \approx y \mid x \mapsto (y_1, \ldots, y_k) \mid \varphi \wedge \varphi \mid \neg\varphi \mid \varphi * \varphi \mid \varphi \mathbin{-\!\!*} \varphi \mid \exists x . \varphi$$

where $x, y, y_1, \ldots, y_k \in \mathsf{Var}$. The connectives $*$ and $-\!\!*$ are respectively called the *separating conjunction* and *separating implication* (*magic wand*). We write $\varphi_1 \multimap \varphi_2$ for $\neg(\varphi_1 \mathbin{-\!\!*} \neg\varphi_2)$ ($\multimap$ is called *septraction*). The size and set of free variables of an SL^k formula φ are defined as for first-order formulæ.

Given an SL^k formula ϕ and a subformula ψ of ϕ, we say that ψ *occurs at polarity* $p \in \{-1, 0, 1\}$ iff one of the following holds: (i) $\phi = \psi$ and $p = 1$, (ii) $\phi = \neg\phi_1$ and ψ occurs at polarity $-p$ in ϕ_1, (iii) $\phi = \phi_1 \wedge \phi_2$ or $\phi = \phi_1 * \phi_2$, and ψ occurs at polarity p in ϕ_i, for some $i = 1, 2$, or (iv) $\phi = \phi_1 \mathbin{-\!\!*} \phi_2$ and either ψ is a subformula of ϕ_1 and $p = 0$, or ψ occurs at polarity p in ϕ_2. A polarity of $1, 0$ or -1 is also referred to as positive, neutral or negative, respectively. Note that our notion of polarity is slightly different than usual, because the antecedent of a separating implication is of neutral polarity while the antecedent of an implication is usually of negative polarity. This is meant to strengthen upcoming decidability results, see Remark 2.

SL^k formulæ are interpreted over SL-*structures* $\mathcal{I} = (\mathfrak{U}, \mathfrak{s}, \mathfrak{h})$, where $\mathfrak{U}$ and $\mathfrak{s}$ are as before and $\mathfrak{h} : \mathfrak{U} \rightarrow_{fin} \mathfrak{U}^k$ is a finite partial mapping of locations to k-tuples of locations, called a *heap*. As before, a structure $(\mathfrak{U}, \mathfrak{s}, \mathfrak{h})$ is finite when $\|\mathfrak{U}\| \in \mathbb{N}$ and infinite otherwise. We denote by $\mathrm{dom}(\mathfrak{h})$ the domain of the heap $\mathfrak{h}$ and by $\|\mathfrak{h}\| \in \mathbb{N}$ the cardinality of $\mathrm{dom}(\mathfrak{h})$. Two heaps $\mathfrak{h}_1$ and $\mathfrak{h}_2$ are *disjoint* iff $\mathrm{dom}(\mathfrak{h}_1) \cap \mathrm{dom}(\mathfrak{h}_2) = \emptyset$, in which case $\mathfrak{h}_1 \uplus \mathfrak{h}_2$ denotes their union. A heap $\mathfrak{h}'$ is an *extension* of $\mathfrak{h}$ by $\mathfrak{h}''$ iff $\mathfrak{h}' = \mathfrak{h} \uplus \mathfrak{h}''$. The relation $(\mathfrak{U}, \mathfrak{s}, \mathfrak{h}) \models \varphi$ is defined inductively, as follows:

$$
\begin{aligned}
(\mathfrak{U}, \mathfrak{s}, \mathfrak{h}) &\models \mathsf{emp} & &\Leftrightarrow \mathfrak{h} = \emptyset \\
(\mathfrak{U}, \mathfrak{s}, \mathfrak{h}) &\models x \mapsto (y_1, \ldots, y_k) & &\Leftrightarrow \mathfrak{h} = \{\langle \mathfrak{s}(x), (\mathfrak{s}(y_1), \ldots, \mathfrak{s}(y_k)) \rangle\} \\
(\mathfrak{U}, \mathfrak{s}, \mathfrak{h}) &\models \varphi_1 * \varphi_2 & &\Leftrightarrow \text{there exist disjoint heaps } h_1, h_2 \text{ such that } h = h_1 \uplus h_2 \\
& & & \quad\text{and } (\mathfrak{U}, \mathfrak{s}, \mathfrak{h}_i) \models \varphi_i, \text{ for } i = 1, 2 \\
(\mathfrak{U}, \mathfrak{s}, \mathfrak{h}) &\models \varphi_1 \mathbin{-\!\!*} \varphi_2 & &\Leftrightarrow \text{for all heaps } \mathfrak{h}' \text{ disjoint from } \mathfrak{h} \text{ such that } (\mathfrak{U}, \mathfrak{s}, \mathfrak{h}') \models \varphi_1 \\
& & & \quad\text{we have } (\mathfrak{U}, \mathfrak{s}, \mathfrak{h} \uplus \mathfrak{h}') \models \varphi_2
\end{aligned}
$$

The semantics of equality, boolean and first-order connectives is the usual one. Satisfiability, entailment and equivalence are defined for SL^k as for FO formulæ.

The Bernays-Schönfinkel-Ramsey fragment of SL^k, denoted by $\mathsf{BSR}(\mathsf{SL}^k)$, is the set of sentences $\exists x_1 \ldots \exists x_n \forall y_1 \ldots \forall y_m \ . \ \phi$, where ϕ is a quantifier-free SL^k formula. Since there is no function symbol of arity greater than zero in SL^k, there is no restriction, other than the form of the quantifier prefix defining $\mathsf{BSR}(\mathsf{SL}^k)$.

3 Test Formulæ for SL^k

We define a small set of SL^k patterns of formulæ, possibly parameterized by a positive integer, called *test formulæ*. These patterns capture properties related to allocation, points-to relations in the heap and cardinality constraints.

Definition 1. *The following patterns are called* test formulæ*:*

$$x \hookrightarrow \mathbf{y} \stackrel{\text{def}}{=} x \mapsto \mathbf{y} * \top \qquad\qquad |U| \geq n \stackrel{\text{def}}{=} \top \multimap |h| \geq n, \ n \in \mathbb{N}$$

$$\mathsf{alloc}(x) \stackrel{\text{def}}{=} x \mapsto \underbrace{(x, \ldots, x)}_{k \ times} \mathbin{-\!\!*} \bot \qquad |h| \geq |U| - n \stackrel{\text{def}}{=} |h| \geq n+1 \mathbin{-\!\!*} \bot, n \in \mathbb{N}$$

$$x \approx y \qquad\qquad |h| \geq n \stackrel{\text{def}}{=} \begin{cases} |h| \geq n - 1 * \neg\mathsf{emp}, & \textit{if } n > 0 \\ \top, & \textit{if } n = 0 \\ \bot, & \textit{if } n = \infty \end{cases}$$

where $x, y \in \mathsf{Var}$, $\mathbf{y} \in \mathsf{Var}^k$ *and* $n \in \mathbb{N}_\infty$ *is a positive integer or* ∞.

The semantics of test formulæ is very natural: $x \hookrightarrow \mathbf{y}$ means that x points to vector $\mathbf{y}$, $\mathsf{alloc}(x)$ means that x is allocated, and the arithmetic expressions are interpreted as usual, where $|h|$ and $|U|$ respectively denote the number of allocated cells and the number of locations (possibly ∞). Formally:

Proposition 1. *Given an* SL-*structure* $(\mathfrak{U}, \mathfrak{s}, \mathfrak{h})$, *the following equivalences hold, for all variables* $x, y_1, \ldots, y_k \in \mathsf{Var}$ *and integers* $n \in \mathbb{N}$:

$$(\mathfrak{U}, \mathfrak{s}, \mathfrak{h}) \models x \hookrightarrow \mathbf{y} \Leftrightarrow \mathfrak{h}(\mathfrak{s}(x)) = \mathfrak{s}(\mathbf{y}) \qquad (\mathfrak{U}, \mathfrak{s}, \mathfrak{h}) \models |h| \geq |U| - n \Leftrightarrow \|\mathfrak{h}\| \geq \|\mathfrak{U}\| - n$$

$$(\mathfrak{U}, \mathfrak{s}, \mathfrak{h}) \models |U| \geq n \Leftrightarrow \|\mathfrak{U}\| \geq n \qquad\qquad (\mathfrak{U}, \mathfrak{s}, \mathfrak{h}) \models |h| \geq n \Leftrightarrow \|\mathfrak{h}\| \geq n$$

$$(\mathfrak{U}, \mathfrak{s}, \mathfrak{h}) \models \mathsf{alloc}(x) \Leftrightarrow \mathfrak{s}(x) \in \mathsf{dom}(\mathfrak{h})$$

Not all atoms of SL^k are test formulæ, for instance $x \mapsto \mathbf{y}$ and emp are not test formulæ. However, by Proposition 1, we have the equivalences $x \mapsto \mathbf{y} \equiv x \hookrightarrow \mathbf{y} \wedge \neg|h| \geq 2$ and $\mathsf{emp} \equiv \neg|h| \geq 1$. Note that, for any $n \in \mathbb{N}$, the test formulæ $|U| \geq n$ and $|h| \geq |U| - n$ are trivially true and false respectively, if the universe is infinite. We write $t < u$ for $\neg(t \geq u)$.

We need to introduce a few notations useful to describe upcoming transformations in a concise and precise way. A *literal* is a test formula or its negation. Unless stated otherwise, we view a conjunction T of literals as a set[1] and we use the same symbol to denote both a set and the formula obtained by conjoining the elements of the set. The equivalence relation $x \approx_T y$ is defined as $T \models x \approx y$ and we write $x \not\approx_T y$ for $T \models \neg x \approx y$. Observe that $x \not\approx_T y$ is not the complement of $x \approx_T y$. For a set X of variables, $|X|_T$ is the number of equivalence classes of $\approx_T$ in X.

---

[1] The empty set is thus considered to be true.

Definition 2. *A variable x is* allocated *in an* SL-*structure $\mathcal{I}$ iff $\mathcal{I} \models \mathsf{alloc}(x)$. For a set of variables $X \subseteq \mathsf{Var}$, let $\mathsf{alloc}(X) \stackrel{\text{def}}{=} \bigwedge_{x \in X} \mathsf{alloc}(x)$ and $\mathsf{nalloc}(X) \stackrel{\text{def}}{=} \bigwedge_{x \in X} \neg\mathsf{alloc}(x)$. For a set T of literals, let:*

$$\mathsf{av}(T) \stackrel{\text{def}}{=} \{x \in \mathsf{Var} \mid x \approx_T x', \, T \cap \{\mathsf{alloc}(x'), x' \hookrightarrow \mathbf{y} \mid \mathbf{y} \in \mathsf{Var}^k\} \neq \emptyset\}$$
$$\mathsf{nv}(T) \stackrel{\text{def}}{=} \{x \in \mathsf{Var} \mid x \approx_T x', \, \neg\mathsf{alloc}(x') \in T\}$$
$$\mathsf{fp}_X(T) \stackrel{\text{def}}{=} T \cap \{\mathsf{alloc}(x), \neg\mathsf{alloc}(x), x \hookrightarrow \mathbf{y}, \neg x \hookrightarrow \mathbf{y} \mid x \in X, \mathbf{y} \in \mathsf{Var}^k\}$$

We let $\#_a(T) \stackrel{\text{def}}{=} |\mathsf{av}(T)|_T$ be the number of equivalence classes of $\approx_T$ containing variables allocated in every model of T and $\#_n(X, T) \stackrel{\text{def}}{=} |X \cap \mathsf{nv}(T)|_T$ be the number of equivalence classes of $\approx_T$ containing variables from X that are not allocated in any model of T. We also let $\mathsf{fp}_a(T) \stackrel{\text{def}}{=} \mathsf{fp}_{\mathsf{av}(T)}(T)$.

Intuitively, $\mathsf{av}(T)$ [$\mathsf{nv}(T)$] is the set of variables that must be [are never] allocated in every [any] model of T, and $\mathsf{fp}_X(T)$ is the *footprint* of T relative to the set $X \subseteq \mathsf{Var}$, i.e. the set of formulæ describing allocation and points-to relations over variables from X. For example, if $T = \{x \approx z, \mathsf{alloc}(x), \neg\mathsf{alloc}(y), \neg z \hookrightarrow \mathbf{y}\}$, then $\mathsf{av}(T) = \{x, z\}$, $\mathsf{nv}(T) = \{y\}$, $\mathsf{fp}_a(T) = \{\mathsf{alloc}(x), \neg z \hookrightarrow \mathbf{y}\}$ and $\mathsf{fp}_{\mathsf{nv}(T)}(T) = \{\neg\mathsf{alloc}(y)\}$.

3.1   From Test Formulæ to FO

The introduction of test formulæ (Definition 1) is motivated by the reduction of the (in)finite satisfiability problem for quantified boolean combinations thereof to the same problem for FO. The reduction is devised in such a way that the obtained formula is in the BSR class, if possible. Given a quantified boolean combination of test formulæ ϕ, the FO formula $\tau(\phi)$ is defined by induction on the structure of ϕ:

$$\tau(|h| \geq n) \stackrel{\text{def}}{=} \mathfrak{a}_n \qquad\qquad \tau(|U| \geq n) \stackrel{\text{def}}{=} \mathfrak{b}_n$$
$$\tau(|h| \geq |U| - n) \stackrel{\text{def}}{=} \neg\mathfrak{c}_{n+1} \qquad\qquad \tau(\neg\phi_1) \stackrel{\text{def}}{=} \neg\tau(\phi_1)$$
$$\tau(x \hookrightarrow \mathbf{y}) \stackrel{\text{def}}{=} \mathfrak{p}(x, y_1, \ldots, y_k) \qquad \tau(\mathsf{alloc}(x)) \stackrel{\text{def}}{=} \exists y_1 \ldots \exists y_k \, . \, \mathfrak{p}(x, y_1, \ldots, y_k)$$
$$\tau(\phi_1 \wedge \phi_2) \stackrel{\text{def}}{=} \tau(\phi_1) \wedge \tau(\phi_2) \qquad \tau(\exists x \, . \, \phi_1) \stackrel{\text{def}}{=} \exists x \, . \, \tau(\phi_1)$$
$$\tau(x \approx y) \stackrel{\text{def}}{=} x \approx y$$

where $\mathfrak{p}$ is a $(k+1)$-ary function symbol of sort Bool and $\mathfrak{a}_n, \mathfrak{b}_n$ and $\mathfrak{c}_n$ are constants of sort Bool, for all $n \in \mathbb{N}$. These function symbols are related by the following axioms, where $\mathfrak{u}_n, \mathfrak{v}_n$ and $\mathfrak{w}_n$ are constants of sort U, for all $n > 0$:

$$P : \forall x \forall \mathbf{y} \forall \mathbf{y}' \, . \, \mathfrak{p}(x, \mathbf{y}) \wedge \mathfrak{p}(x, \mathbf{y}') \rightarrow \bigwedge_{i=1}^{k} y_i \approx y_i'$$

$$A_0 : \mathfrak{a}_0 \qquad A_n : \left\{ \begin{array}{l} \exists \mathbf{y} \, . \, \mathfrak{a}_n \rightarrow \mathfrak{a}_{n-1} \wedge \mathfrak{p}(\mathfrak{u}_n, \mathbf{y}) \wedge \bigwedge_{i=1}^{n-1} \neg \mathfrak{u}_i \approx \mathfrak{u}_n \\ \wedge \, \forall x \forall \mathbf{y} \, . \, \neg \mathfrak{a}_n \wedge \mathfrak{p}(x, \mathbf{y}) \rightarrow \bigvee_{i=1}^{n-1} x \approx \mathfrak{u}_i \end{array} \right\}$$

$$B_0 : \mathfrak{b}_0 \qquad B_n : \left\{ \begin{array}{l} \mathfrak{b}_n \rightarrow \mathfrak{b}_{n-1} \wedge \bigwedge_{i=1}^{n-1} \neg \mathfrak{v}_i \approx \mathfrak{v}_n \\ \wedge \, \forall x \, . \, \neg \mathfrak{b}_n \rightarrow \bigvee_{i=1}^{n-1} x \approx \mathfrak{v}_i \end{array} \right\}$$

$$C_0 : \mathfrak{c}_0 \qquad C_n : \forall \mathbf{y} \, . \, \mathfrak{c}_n \rightarrow \mathfrak{c}_{n-1} \wedge \neg \mathfrak{p}(\mathfrak{w}_n, \mathbf{y}) \wedge \bigwedge_{i=1}^{n-1} \neg \mathfrak{w}_n \approx \mathfrak{w}_i$$

Intuitively, $\mathfrak{p}$ encodes the heap and $\mathfrak{a}_n$ (resp. $\mathfrak{b}_n$) is true iff there are at least n cells in the domain of the heap (resp. in the universe), namely $\mathfrak{u}_1, \ldots, \mathfrak{u}_n$ (resp. $\mathfrak{v}_1, \ldots, \mathfrak{v}_n$). If $\mathfrak{c}_n$ is true, then there are at least n locations $\mathfrak{w}_1, \ldots, \mathfrak{w}_n$ outside of the domain of the heap (free), but the converse does not hold. The C_n axioms do not state the equivalence of $\mathfrak{c}_n$ with the existence of at least n free locations, because such an equivalence cannot be expressed in $\mathsf{BSR(FO)}$[2]. As a consequence, the transformation preserves sat-equivalence only if the formulæ $|h| \geq |U| - n$ occur only at negative polarity (see Lemma 1, Point 2). If the domain is infinite then this problem does not arise since the formulæ $|h| \geq |U| - n$ are always false.

Definition 3. *For a quantified boolean combination of test formulæ ϕ, we let $\mathcal{N}(\phi)$ be the maximum integer n occurring in a test formula θ of the form $|h| \geq n$, $|U| \geq n$, or $|h| \geq |U| - n$ from ϕ and define $\mathcal{A}(\phi) \stackrel{\text{def}}{=} \{P\} \cup \{A_i\}_{i=0}^{\mathcal{N}(\phi)} \cup \{B_i\}_{i=0}^{\mathcal{N}(\phi)} \cup \{C_i\}_{i=0}^{\mathcal{N}(\phi)+1}$ as the set of axioms related to ϕ.*

The relationship between ϕ and $\tau(\phi)$ is stated below.

Lemma 1. *Let ϕ be a quantified boolean combination of test formulæ. The following hold, for any universe $\mathfrak{U}$ and any store $\mathfrak{s}$:*

1. *if $(\mathfrak{U}, \mathfrak{s}, \mathfrak{h}) \models \phi$, for a heap $\mathfrak{h}$, then $(\mathfrak{U}, \mathfrak{s}, \mathfrak{i}) \models \tau(\phi) \wedge \mathcal{A}(\phi)$, for an interpretation $\mathfrak{i}$;*
2. *if each test formula $|h| \geq |U| - n$ in ϕ occurs at a negative polarity and $(\mathfrak{U}, \mathfrak{s}, \mathfrak{i}) \models \tau(\phi) \wedge \mathcal{A}(\phi)$ for an interpretation $\mathfrak{i}$ such that $\|\mathfrak{p}^{\mathfrak{i}}\| \in \mathbb{N}$, then $(\mathfrak{U}, \mathfrak{s}, \mathfrak{h}) \models \phi$, for a heap $\mathfrak{h}$.*

The translation of $\mathsf{alloc}(x)$ introduces existential quantifiers depending on x. For instance, $\forall x \, . \, \mathsf{alloc}(x)$ is translated as $\forall x \exists y_1 \ldots \exists y_k \, . \, \mathfrak{p}(x, y_1, \ldots, y_k)$, which lies outside of the $\mathsf{BSR(FO)}$ fragment. Because upcoming decidability results (Theorem 2) require that $\tau(\phi)$ be in $\mathsf{BSR(FO)}$, we end this section by delimiting a fragment of SL^k whose translation falls into $\mathsf{BSR(FO)}$.

Lemma 2. *Given an SL^k formula $\varphi = \forall z_1 \ldots \forall z_m \, . \, \phi$, where ϕ is a boolean combination of test formulæ containing no positive occurrence of $\mathsf{alloc}(z_i)$ for any $i \in [1, m]$, $\tau(\varphi)$ is equivalent (up to transformation into prenex form) to a $\mathsf{BSR(FO)}$ formula with the same constants and free variables as $\tau(\varphi)$.*

Intuitively, if a formula $\mathsf{alloc}(x)$ occurs negatively then the quantifiers $\exists y_1 \ldots \exists y_k$ added when translating $\mathsf{alloc}(x)$ can be transformed into universal ones by transformation into nnf, and if x is not universal then they may be shifted at the root of the formula since $y_1, \ldots, y_k$ depend only on x. In both cases, the quantifier prefix $\exists^* \forall^*$ is preserved.

---

[2] The converse of C_n: $\forall x \, . \, (\neg \mathfrak{c}_n \wedge \forall \mathbf{y} \, . \, \neg \mathfrak{p}(x, \mathbf{y})) \rightarrow \bigvee_{i=1}^{n-1} x \approx \mathfrak{w}_i$ is not in $\mathsf{BSR(FO)}$.

4 From Quantifier-Free SL^k to Test formulæ

This section states the expressive completeness result of the paper, namely that any quantifier-free SL^k formula is equivalent, on both finite and infinite models, to a boolean combination of test formulæ. Starting from a quantifier-free SL^k formula φ, we define a set $\mu(\varphi)$ of conjunctions of test formulæ and their negations, called *minterms*, such that $\varphi \equiv \bigvee_{M \in \mu(\varphi)} M$. Although the number of minterms in $\mu(\varphi)$ is exponential in the size of φ, checking the membership of a given minterm M in $\mu(\varphi)$ can be done in PSPACE. Together with the translation of minterms into FO (Sect. 3.1), this fact is used to prove PSPACE membership of the two decidable fragments of $\mathsf{BSR}(\mathsf{SL}^k)$, defined next (Sect. 5.2).

4.1 Minterms

A *minterm* M is a set (conjunction) of literals containing: exactly one literal $|h| \geq \min_M$ and one literal $|h| < \max_M$, where $\min_M \in \mathbb{N} \cup \{|U| - n \mid n \in \mathbb{N}\}$ and $\max_M \in \mathbb{N}_\infty \cup \{|U| - n \mid n \in \mathbb{N}\}$, and at most one literal of the form $|U| \geq n$, respectively $|U| < n$.

A minterm may be viewed as an abstract description of a heap. The conditions are for technical convenience only and are not restrictive. For instance, tautological test formulæ of the form $|h| \geq 0$ and/or $|h| < \infty$ may be added if needed so that the first condition holds. If M contains two literals $t \geq n_1$ and $t \geq n_2$ with $n_1 < n_2$ and $t \in \{|h|, |U|\}$ then $t \geq n_1$ is redundant and can be removed – and similarly if M contains literals $|h| \geq |U| - n_1$ and $|h| \geq |U| - n_2$. Heterogeneous constraints are merged by performing a case split on the value of $|U|$. For example, if M contains both $|h| \geq |U| - 4$ and $|h| \geq 1$, then the first condition prevails if $|U| \geq 5$ yielding the equivalence disjunction: $|h| \geq 1 \wedge |U| < 5 \vee |h| \geq |U| - 4 \wedge |U| \geq 5$. Thus, in the following, we assume that any conjunction of literals can be transformed into a disjunction of minterms [8].

Definition 4. *Given a minterm M, we define the sets:*

$$M^e \stackrel{\text{def}}{=} M \cap \{x \approx y, \neg x \approx y \mid x, y \in \mathsf{Var}\} \quad M^a \stackrel{\text{def}}{=} M \cap \{\mathsf{alloc}(x), \neg\mathsf{alloc}(x) \mid x \in \mathsf{Var}\}$$
$$M^u \stackrel{\text{def}}{=} M \cap \{|U| \geq n, |U| < n \mid n \in \mathbb{N}\} \quad M^p \stackrel{\text{def}}{=} M \cap \{x \hookrightarrow \mathbf{y}, \neg x \hookrightarrow \mathbf{y} \mid x, \mathbf{y} \in \mathsf{Var}^{k+1}\}$$

Thus, $M = M^e \cup M^u \cup M^a \cup M^p \cup \{|h| \geq \min_M, |h| < \max_M\}$, for each minterm M. Given a set of variables $X \subseteq \mathsf{Var}$, a minterm M is (1) *E-complete* for X iff for all $x, y \in X$ exactly one of $x \approx y \in M$, $\neg x \approx y \in M$ holds, and (2) *A-complete* for X iff for each $x \in X$ exactly one of $\mathsf{alloc}(x) \in M$, $\neg\mathsf{alloc}(x) \in M$ holds.

For a literal ℓ, we denote by $\overline{\ell}$ its complement, i.e. $\overline{\theta} \stackrel{\text{def}}{=} \neg\theta$ and $\overline{\neg\theta} \stackrel{\text{def}}{=} \theta$, where θ is a test formula. Let $\overline{M}$ be the minterm obtained from M by replacing each literal with its complement. The *complement closure* of M is $\mathsf{cc}(M) \stackrel{\text{def}}{=} M \cup \overline{M}$. Two tuples $\mathbf{y}, \mathbf{y}' \in \mathsf{Var}^k$ are *M-distinct* if $y_i \not\approx_M y_i'$, for some $i \in [1, k]$. Given a minterm M that is E-complete for $\mathsf{var}(M)$, its *points-to closure* is $\mathsf{pc}(M) \stackrel{\text{def}}{=} \bot$ if there exist literals $x \hookrightarrow \mathbf{y}, x' \hookrightarrow \mathbf{y}' \in M$ such that $x \approx_M x'$ and $\mathbf{y}, \mathbf{y}'$ are M-distinct, and $\mathsf{pc}(M) \stackrel{\text{def}}{=} M$, otherwise. Intuitively, $\mathsf{pc}(M)$ is $\bot$ iff M contradicts the fact that the heap is a partial function[3]. The *domain closure* of M is $\mathsf{dc}(M) \overset{\text{def}}{=} \bot$ if either $\min_M = n_1$ and $\max_M = n_2$ for some $n_1, n_2 \in \mathbb{Z}$ such that $n_1 \geq n_2$, or $\min_M = |U| - n_1$ and $\max_M = |U| - n_2$, where $n_2 \geq n_1$; and otherwise:

$$\mathsf{dc}(M) \overset{\text{def}}{=} M \cup \left\{ |U| \geq \left\lceil \sqrt[k]{\max_{x \in \mathsf{av}(M)} (\delta_x(M) + 1)} \right\rceil \right\}$$
$$\cup \left\{ |U| \geq n_1 + n_2 + 1 \mid \min_M = n_1, \max_M = |U| - n_2, n_1, n_2 \in \mathbb{N} \right\}$$
$$\cup \left\{ |U| < n_1 + n_2 \mid \min_M = |U| - n_1, \max_M = n_2, n_1, n_2 \in \mathbb{N} \right\}$$

where $\delta_x(M)$ is the number of pairwise M-distinct tuples $\mathbf{y}$ for which there exists $\neg x' \hookrightarrow \mathbf{y} \in M$ such that $x \approx_M x'$. Intuitively, $\mathsf{dc}(M)$ asserts that $\min_M < \max_M$ and that the domain contains enough elements to allocate all cells. Essentially, given a structure $(\mathfrak{U}, \mathfrak{s}, \mathfrak{h})$, if $\mathfrak{h}(x)$ is known to be defined and distinct from n pairwise distinct vectors of locations $\mathbf{v}_1, \ldots, \mathbf{v}_n$, then necessarily at least $n + 1$ vectors must exist. Since there are $\|\mathfrak{U}\|^k$ vectors of length k, we must have $\|\mathfrak{U}\|^k \geq n + 1$, hence $\|\mathfrak{U}\| \geq \sqrt[k]{n+1}$. For instance, if $M = \{\neg x \hookrightarrow y_i, \mathsf{alloc}(x), y_i \not\approx y_j \mid i, j \in [1, n], i \neq j\}$, then it is clear that M is unsatisfiable if there are less than n locations, since x cannot be allocated in this case.

Definition 5. *A minterm M is* footprint-consistent[4] *if for all $x, x' \in \mathsf{Var}$ and $\mathbf{y}, \mathbf{y}' \in \mathsf{Var}^k$, such that $x \approx_M x'$ and $y_i \approx_M y_i'$ for all $i \in [1, k]$, we have (1) if $\mathsf{alloc}(x) \in M$ then $\neg\mathsf{alloc}(x') \notin M$, and (2) if $x \hookrightarrow \mathbf{y} \in M$ then $\neg\mathsf{alloc}(x'), \neg x' \hookrightarrow \mathbf{y}' \notin M$.*

We are now ready to define a boolean combination of test formulæ that is equivalent to $M_1 * M_2$, where M_1 and M_2 are minterms satisfying a number of additional conditions. Let $\mathsf{npto}(M_1, M_2) \overset{\text{def}}{=} (M_1 \cap M_2) \cap \{\neg x \hookrightarrow \mathbf{y} \mid x \notin \mathsf{av}(M_1 \cup M_2), \mathbf{y} \in \mathsf{Var}^k\}$ be the set of negative points-to literals common to M_1 and M_2, involving left-hand side variables not allocated in either M_1 or M_2.

Lemma 3. *Let M_1, M_2 be two footprint-consistent minterms that are and E-complete for $\mathsf{var}(M_1 \cup M_2)$, with $\mathsf{cc}(M_1^p) = \mathsf{cc}(M_2^p)$. Then $M_1 * M_2 \equiv \mathsf{elim}_*(M_1, M_2)$, where*

$$\mathsf{elim}_*(M_1, M_2) \overset{\text{def}}{=} M_1^e \wedge M_2^e \wedge \mathsf{dc}(M_1)^u \wedge \mathsf{dc}(M_2)^u \wedge \tag{2}$$

$$\bigwedge_{x \in \mathsf{av}(M_1),\ y \in \mathsf{av}(M_2)} \neg x \approx y \wedge \mathsf{fp}_a(M_1) \wedge \mathsf{fp}_a(M_2) \wedge \tag{3}$$

$$\mathsf{nalloc}(\mathsf{nv}(M_1) \cap \mathsf{nv}(M_2)) \wedge \mathsf{npto}(M_1, M_2) \wedge \tag{4}$$

$$|h| \geq \min_{M_1} + \min_{M_2} \ \wedge \ |h| < \max_{M_1} + \max_{M_2} - 1 \tag{5}$$

$$\wedge \ \eta_{12} \wedge \eta_{21} \tag{6}$$

and $\eta_{ij} \overset{\text{def}}{=} \bigwedge_{Y \subseteq \mathsf{nv}(M_j) \setminus \mathsf{av}(M_i)} \mathsf{alloc}(Y) \rightarrow \left(\begin{array}{c} |h| \geq \#_a(M_i) + |Y|_{M_i} + \min_{M_j} \\ \wedge\ \#_a(M_i) + |Y|_{M_i} < \max_{M_i} \end{array} \right).$

---

[3] Note that we do not assert the equality $\mathbf{y} \approx \mathbf{y}'$, instead we only check that it is not falsified. This is sufficient for our purpose because in the following we always assume that the considered minterms are E-complete.

[4] Footprint-consistency is a necessary, yet not sufficient, condition for satisfiability of minterms. For example, the minterm $M = \{x \hookrightarrow y, x' \hookrightarrow y', \neg y \approx y', |h| < 2\}$ is at the same time footprint-consistent and unsatisfiable.

Intuitively, if M_1 and M_2 hold separately, then all heap-independent literals from $M_1 \cup M_2$ must be satisfied (2), the variables allocated in M_1 and M_2 must be pairwise distinct and their footprints, relative to the allocated variables, jointly asserted (3). Moreover, unallocated variables on both sides must not be allocated and common negative points-to literals must be asserted (4). Since the heap satisfying $\mathsf{elim}_*(M_1, M_2)$ is the disjoint union of the heaps for M_1 and M_2, its bounds are the sum of the bounds on both sides (5) and, moreover, the variables that M_2 never allocates $[\mathsf{nv}(M_2)]$ may occur allocated in the heap of M_1 and viceversa, thus the constraints η_{12} and η_{21}, respectively (6).

Next, we show a similar result for the separating implication. For technical convenience, we translate the septraction $M_1 \multimap M_2$, instead of $M_1 \mathrel{-\!\!*} M_2$, as an equivalent boolean combination of test formulæ. This is without loss of generality, because $M_1 \mathrel{-\!\!*} M_2 \equiv \neg(M_1 \multimap \neg M_2)$. Unlike with the case of the separating conjunction (Lemma 3), here the definition of the boolean combination of test formulæ depends on whether the universe is finite or infinite.

If the complement of some literal $\ell \in \mathsf{fp}_a(M_1)$ belongs to M_2 then no extension by a heap that satisfies ℓ may satisfy $\bar{\ell}$. Therefore, as an additional simplifying assumption, we suppose that $\mathsf{fp}_a(M_1) \cap \overline{M_2} = \emptyset$, so that $M_1 \multimap M_2$ is not trivially unsatisfiable. We write $\phi \equiv^{fin} \psi$ $[\phi \equiv^{inf} \psi]$ if ϕ has the same truth value as ψ in all finite [infinite] structures.

Lemma 4. *Let M_1 and M_2 be footprint-consistent minterms that are E-complete for $\mathsf{var}(M_1 \cup M_2)$, such that: M_1 is A-complete for $\mathsf{var}(M_1 \cup M_2)$, $M_2^a \cup M_2^p \subseteq \mathsf{cc}(M_1^a \cup M_1^p)$ and $\mathsf{fp}_a(M_1) \cap \overline{M_2} = \emptyset$.*

Then, $M_1 \multimap M_2 \equiv^{fin} \mathsf{elim}_{\multimap}^{fin}(M_1, M_2)$ and $M_1 \multimap M_2 \equiv^{inf} \mathsf{elim}_{\multimap}^{inf}(M_1, M_2)$, where:

$$\mathsf{elim}_{\multimap}^{\dagger}(M_1, M_2) \stackrel{\text{def}}{=} \mathsf{pc}(M_1)^e \wedge M_2^e \wedge \mathsf{dc}(M_1)^u \wedge \mathsf{dc}(M_2)^u \wedge \tag{7}$$

$$\mathsf{nalloc}(\mathsf{av}(M_1)) \wedge \mathsf{fp}_{\mathsf{nv}(M_1)}(M_2) \wedge \tag{8}$$

$$|h| \geq \min_{M_2} - \max_{M_1} + 1 \wedge |h| < \max_{M_2} - \min_{M_1} \tag{9}$$

$$\wedge \, \lambda^{\dagger} \tag{10}$$

with

$$\lambda^{fin} \stackrel{\text{def}}{=} \bigwedge_{Y \subseteq \mathsf{var}(M_1 \cup M_2)} \mathsf{nalloc}(Y) \;\rightarrow\; \left(\begin{array}{l} |h| < |U| - \min_{M_1} - \#_n(Y, M_1) + 1 \\ \wedge \; |U| \geq \min_{M_2} + \#_n(Y, M_1) \end{array} \right),$$

$$\lambda^{inf} \stackrel{\text{def}}{=} \top.$$

A heap satisfies $M_1 \multimap M_2$ iff it has an extension, by a disjoint heap satisfying M_1, that satisfies M_2. Thus, $\mathsf{elim}_{\multimap}^{\dagger}(M_1, M_2)$ must entail the heap-independent literals of both M_1 and M_2 (7). Next, no variable allocated by M_1 must be allocated by $\mathsf{elim}_{\multimap}^{\dagger}(M_1, M_2)$, otherwise no extension by a heap satisfying M_1 is possible and, moreover, the footprint of M_2 relative to the unallocated variables of M_1 must be asserted (8). The heap's cardinality constraints depend on the bounds of M_1 and M_2 (9) and, if Y is a set of variables not allocated in the heap, these variables can be allocated in the extension (10). Actually, this is where the finite universe assumption first comes into play. If the universe is infinite, then there are enough locations outside the heap to be assigned to Y. However, if the universe is finite, then it is necessary to ensure that there are at least $\#_n(Y, M_1)$ free locations to be assigned to Y (10).

4.2   Translating Quantifier-Free SL^k into Minterms

We prove next that each quantifier-free SL^k formula is equivalent to a finite disjunction of minterms:

Lemma 5. *Given a quantifier-free SL^k formula ϕ, there exist two sets of minterms $\mu^{fin}(\phi)$ and $\mu^{inf}(\phi)$ such that the following equivalences hold: (1) $\phi \equiv^{fin} \bigvee_{M \in \mu^{fin}(\phi)} M$, and (2) $\phi \equiv^{inf} \bigvee_{M \in \mu^{inf}(\phi)} M$.*

The formal definition of $\mu^{fin}(\phi)$ and $\mu^{inf}(\phi)$ is given in [8] and omitted for the sake of conciseness and readability. Intuitively, these sets are defined by induction on the structure of the formula. For base cases, the following equivalences are used:

$$x \mapsto \mathbf{y} \equiv x \hookrightarrow \mathbf{y} \wedge |h| \approx 1 \qquad \mathsf{emp} \equiv |h| \approx 0 \qquad x \approx y \equiv x \approx y \wedge |h| \geq 0 \wedge |h| < \infty$$

For formulæ $\neg\psi_1$ or $\psi_1 \wedge \psi_2$, the transformation is first applied recursively on ψ_1 and ψ_2, then the obtained formula is transformed into dnf. For formulæ $\psi_1 * \psi_2$ or $\psi_1 \multimap \psi_2$, the transformation is applied on ψ_1 and ψ_2, then the following equivalences are used to shift $*$ and $\multimap$ innermost in the formula:

$$\begin{array}{ll}
(\phi_1 \vee \phi_2) * \phi \equiv (\phi_1 * \phi) \vee (\phi_2 * \phi) & (\phi_1 \vee \phi_2) \multimap \phi \equiv (\phi_1 \multimap \phi) \vee (\phi_2 \multimap \phi) \\
\phi * (\phi_1 \vee \phi_2) \equiv (\phi * \phi_1) \vee (\phi * \phi_2) & \phi \multimap (\phi_1 \vee \phi_2) \equiv (\phi \multimap \phi_1) \vee (\phi \multimap \phi_2)
\end{array}$$

Afterwards, the operands of $*$ and $\multimap$ are minterms, and the result is obtained using the equivalences in Lemmas 3 and 4, respectively (up to a transformation into dnf). The only difficulty is that these lemmas impose some additional conditions on the minterms (e.g., being E-complete, or A-complete). However, the conditions are easy to enforce by case splitting, as illustrated by the following example:

Example 1. Consider the formula $x \mapsto x \multimap y \mapsto y$. It is easy to check that $\mu^\dagger(x \mapsto x) = \{M_1\}$, for $\dagger \in \{fin, inf\}$, where $M_1 = x \hookrightarrow x \wedge |h| \geq 1 \wedge |h| < 2$ and $\mu^\dagger(y \mapsto y) = \{M_2\}$, where $M_2 = y \hookrightarrow y \wedge |h| \geq 1 \wedge |h| < 2$. To apply Lemma 4, we need to ensure that M_1 and M_2 are E-complete, which may be done by adding either $x \approx y$ or $x \not\approx y$ to each minterm. We also have to ensure that M_1 is A-complete, thus for $z \in \{x, y\}$, we add either $\mathsf{alloc}(z)$ or $\neg\mathsf{alloc}(z)$ to M_1. Finally, we must have $M_2^a \cup M_2^p \subseteq \mathsf{cc}(M_1^a \cup M_1^p)$, thus we add either $y \hookrightarrow y$ or $\neg y \hookrightarrow y$ to M_1. After removing redundancies, we get (among others) the minterms: $M_1' = x \hookrightarrow x \wedge |h| \geq 1 \wedge |h| < 2 \wedge x \approx y$ and $M_2' = y \hookrightarrow y \wedge |h| \geq 1 \wedge |h| < 2 \wedge x \approx y$. Afterwards we compute $\mathsf{elim}_\multimap^{fin}(M_1', M_2') = x \approx y \wedge \neg\mathsf{alloc}(x) \wedge |h| \geq 0 \wedge |h| < 1$.   ∎

As explained in Sect. 3.1, boolean combinations of minterms can only be transformed into sat-equivalent $\mathsf{BSR(FO)}$ formulæ if there is no positive occurrence of test formulæ $|h| \geq |U| - n$ or $\mathsf{alloc}(x)$ (see the conditions in Lemmas 1 (2) and 2). Consequently, we relate the polarity of these formulæ in some minterm $M \in \mu^{fin}(\phi) \cup \mu^{inf}(\phi)$ with that of a separating implication within ϕ. The analysis depends on whether the universe is finite or infinite.

Lemma 6. *For any quantifier-free* SL^k *formula* ϕ, *the following properties hold:*

1. *For all* $M \in \mu^{inf}(\phi)$, *we have* $M \cap \{|h| \geq |U| - n, |h| < |U| - n \mid n \in \mathbb{N}\} = \emptyset$.
2. *If* $|h| \geq |U| - n \in M$ $[|h| < |U| - n \in M]$ *for some minterm* $M \in \mu^{fin}(\phi)$, *then a formula* $\psi_1 \mathbin{-\!\!*} \psi_2$ *occurs at a positive [negative] polarity in* ϕ.
3. *If* $\mathsf{alloc}(x) \in M$ $[\neg\mathsf{alloc}(x) \in M]$ *for some minterm* $M \in \mu^{inf}(\phi)$, *then a formula* $\psi_1 \mathbin{-\!\!*} \psi_2$, *such that* $x \in \mathsf{var}(\psi_1) \cup \mathsf{var}(\psi_2)$, *occurs at a positive [negative] polarity in* ϕ.
4. *If* $M \cap \{\mathsf{alloc}(x), \neg\mathsf{alloc}(x) \mid x \in \mathsf{Var}\} \neq \emptyset$ *for some minterm* $M \in \mu^{fin}(\phi)$, *then a formula* $\psi_1 \mathbin{-\!\!*} \psi_2$, *such that* $x \in \mathsf{var}(\psi_1) \cup \mathsf{var}(\psi_2)$, *occurs in* ϕ *at some polarity* $p \in \{-1, 1\}$. *Moreover,* $\mathsf{alloc}(x)$ *occurs at a polarity* $-p$, *only if* $\mathsf{alloc}(x)$ *is in the scope of a* λ^{fin} *subformula (10) of a formula* $\mathsf{elim}^{fin}_{\mathbin{-\!\!*}}(M_1, M_2)$ *used to compute* $\bigvee_{M \in \mu^{fin}(\phi)} M$.

Given a quantifier-free SL^k formula ϕ, the number of minterms occurring in $\mu^{fin}(\phi)$ $[\mu^{inf}(\phi)]$ is exponential in the size of ϕ, in the worst case. Therefore, an optimal decision procedure cannot generate and store these sets explicitly, but rather must enumerate minterms lazily. We show that (i) the size of the minterms in $\mu^{fin}(\phi) \cup \mu^{inf}(\phi)$ is bounded by a polynomial in the size of ϕ, and that (ii) the problem *"given a minterm* M, *does* M *occur in* $\mu^{fin}(\phi)$ *[resp. in* $\mu^{inf}(\phi)$]?" is in PSPACE. To this aim, we define a measure on a quantifier-free formula ϕ, which bounds the size of the minterms in the sets $\mu^{fin}(\phi)$ and $\mu^{inf}(\phi)$, inductively on the structure of the formulæ:

$$\mathcal{M}(x \approx y) \stackrel{\text{def}}{=} 0 \qquad\qquad\qquad \mathcal{M}(\bot) \stackrel{\text{def}}{=} 0$$
$$\mathcal{M}(\mathsf{emp}) \stackrel{\text{def}}{=} 1 \qquad\qquad\qquad \mathcal{M}(x \mapsto \mathbf{y}) \stackrel{\text{def}}{=} 2$$
$$\mathcal{M}(\neg\phi_1) \stackrel{\text{def}}{=} \mathcal{M}(\phi_1) \qquad\qquad \mathcal{M}(\phi_1 \wedge \phi_2) \stackrel{\text{def}}{=} \max(\mathcal{M}(\phi_1), \mathcal{M}(\phi_2))$$
$$\mathcal{M}(\phi_1 * \phi_2) \stackrel{\text{def}}{=} \sum_{i=1}^{2}(\mathcal{M}(\phi_i) + \|\mathsf{var}(\phi_i)\|) \quad \mathcal{M}(\phi_1 \mathbin{-\!\!*} \phi_2) \stackrel{\text{def}}{=} \sum_{i=1}^{2}(\mathcal{M}(\phi_i) + \|\mathsf{var}(\phi_i)\|)$$

Definition 6. *A minterm* M *is* $\mathcal{M}$-*bounded by a formula* ϕ, *if for each literal* $\ell \in M$, *the following hold: (i)* $\mathcal{M}(\ell) \leq \mathcal{M}(\phi)$ *if* $\ell \in \{|h| \geq \min_{M_i}, |h| < \max_{M_i}\}$ *(ii)* $\mathcal{M}(\ell) \leq 2\mathcal{M}(\phi) + 1$, *if* $\ell \in \{|U| \geq n, |U| < n \mid n \in \mathbb{N}\}$.

The following lemma provides the desired result:

Lemma 7. *Given a quantifier-free* SL^k *formula* ϕ, *each minterm* $M \in \mu^{fin}(\phi) \cup \mu^{inf}(\phi)$ *is* $\mathcal{M}$-*bounded by* ϕ.

The proof goes by a careful analysis of the test formulæ introduced in Lemmas 3 and 4 or created by minterm transformations (see [8] for details). Since $\mathcal{M}(\phi)$ is polynomially bounded by $\mathsf{size}(\phi)$, this entails that it is possible to check whether $M \in \mu^{fin}(\phi)$ [resp. $\mu^{inf}(\phi)$] using space bounded also by a polynomial in $\mathsf{size}(\phi)$.

Lemma 8. *Given a minterm* M *and an* SL^k *formula* ϕ, *the problems of checking whether* $M \in \mu^{fin}(\phi)$ *and* $M \in \mu^{inf}(\phi)$ *are in* PSPACE.

Remark 1. Observe that the formulæ $\mathsf{elim}_*(M_1, M_2)$ and $\mathsf{elim}_{\multimap}^{fin}(M_1, M_2)$ in Lemmas 3 and 4 are of exponential size, because Y ranges over sets of variables. However these formulæ do not need to be constructed explicitly. To check that $M \in \mu^{fin}(\phi)$ or $M \in \mu^{inf}(\phi)$, we only have to guess such sets Y. See [8] for details.

5 Bernays-Schönfinkel-Ramsey SL^k

This section gives the results concerning decidability of the (in)finite satisfiability problems within the $\mathsf{BSR}(\mathsf{SL}^k)$ fragment. $\mathsf{BSR}(\mathsf{SL}^k)$ is the set of sentences $\forall y_1 \ldots \forall y_m \,.\, \phi$, where ϕ is a quantifier-free SL^k formula, with $\mathrm{var}(\phi) = \{x_1, \ldots, x_n, y_1, \ldots, y_m\}$, where the existentially quantified variables $x_1, \ldots, x_n$ are left free. First, we show that, contrary to $\mathsf{BSR}(\mathsf{FO})$, the satisfiability of $\mathsf{BSR}(\mathsf{SL}^k)$ is undecidable for $k \geq 2$. Second, we carve two nontrivial fragments of $\mathsf{BSR}(\mathsf{SL}^k)$, for which the infinite and finite satisfiability problems are both PSPACE-complete. These fragments are defined based on restrictions of (i) polarities of the occurrences of the separating implication, and (ii) occurrences of universally quantified variables in the scope of separating implications. These results draw a rather precise chart of decidability within the $\mathsf{BSR}(\mathsf{SL}^k)$ fragment. For $k = 1$, the satisfiability problem of $\mathsf{BSR}(\mathsf{SL}^1)$ is in PSPACE [7] (it is undecidable for arbitrary SL^1 formulæ [2] and decidable but nonelementary for *prenex* formulæ [7]).

5.1 Undecidability of $\mathsf{BSR}(\mathsf{SL}^k)$

Theorem 1. *The finite and infinite satisfiability problems are both undecidable for* $\mathsf{BSR}(\mathsf{SL}^k)$.

We provide a brief sketch of the proof, see [8] for details. We consider the finite satisfiability problem of the $[\forall, (0), (2)]_=$ fragment of FO, which consists of sentences of the form $\forall x \,.\, \phi(x)$, where ϕ is a quantifier-free boolean combination of atomic propositions $t_1 \approx t_2$, and t_1, t_2 are terms built using two function symbols f and g, of arity one, the variable x and constant c. It is known (see e.g. [1, Theorem 4.1.8]) that finite satisfiability is undecidable for $[\forall, (0), (2)]_=$. We reduce this problem to $\mathsf{BSR}(\mathsf{SL}^k)$ satisfiability. The idea is to encode the value of f and g into the heap, in such a way that every element x points to $(f(x), g(x))$. Given a sentence $\varphi = \forall x \,.\, \phi(x)$ in $[\forall, (0), (2)]_=$, we proceed by first *flattening* each term in ϕ consisting of nested applications of f and g. The result is an equivalent sentence $\varphi_{flat} = \forall x_1 \ldots \forall x_n \,.\, \phi_{flat}$, in which the only terms are x_i, c, $f(x_i)$, $g(x_i)$, $f(c)$ and $g(c)$, for $i \in [1, n]$. For example, the formula $\forall x \,.\, f(g(x)) \approx c$ is flattened into $\forall x_1 \forall x_2 \,.\, g(x_1) \not\approx x_2 \vee f(x_2) \approx c$. We define the following $\mathsf{BSR}(\mathsf{SL}^2)$ sentences $\varphi_{\mathsf{sl}}^\dagger$, for $\dagger \in \{fin, inf\}$:

$$\alpha^\dagger \wedge x_c \hookrightarrow (y_c, z_c) \wedge \forall x_1 \ldots \forall x_n \forall y_1 \ldots \forall y_n \forall z_1 \ldots \forall z_n \,.\, \bigwedge_{i=1}^{n} (x_i \hookrightarrow (y_i, z_i) \to \phi_{\mathsf{sl}}) \quad (11)$$

with $\alpha^{fin} \stackrel{\text{def}}{=} \forall x \,.\, \mathsf{alloc}(x)$ or $\alpha^{fin} \stackrel{\text{def}}{=} |h| \geq |U| - 0$, $\alpha^{inf} \stackrel{\text{def}}{=} \forall x \forall y \forall z \,.\, x \hookrightarrow (y, z) \to \mathsf{alloc}(y) \wedge \mathsf{alloc}(z)$ and ϕ_{sl} is obtained from ϕ_{flat} by replacing each occurrence of c by x_c, each term $f(c)$ $[g(c)]$ by y_c $[z_c]$ and each term $f(x_i)$ $[g(x_i)]$ by y_i $[z_i]$. Intuitively, α^{fin} asserts that the heap is a total function, and α^{inf} states that every referenced cell is allocated[5]. It is easy to check that φ and φ_{sl} are equisatisfiable. The undecidability result still holds for finite satisfiability if a single occurrence of $-\!\!*$ is allowed, in a (ground) formula $|h| \geq |U| - 0$ (see the definition of α^{fin} above).

5.2   Two Decidable Fragments of BSR(SL^k)

The reductions (11) use either positive occurences of $\mathsf{alloc}(x)$, where x is universally quantified, or test formulæ $|h| \geq |U| - n$. We obtain decidable subsets of BSR(SL^k) by eliminating the positive occurrences of both (i) $\mathsf{alloc}(x)$, with x universally quantified, and (ii) $|h| \geq |U| - n$, from $\mu^{\dagger}(\phi)$, where $\dagger \in \{fin, inf\}$ and $\forall y_1 \ldots \forall y_m \, . \, \phi$ is any BSR(SL^k) formula. Note that $\mu^{inf}(\phi)$ contains no formulæ of the form $|h| \geq |U| - n$, which explains why slightly less restrictive conditions are needed for infinite structures.

Definition 7. *Given an integer $k \geq 1$, we define:*

1. BSR^{inf}(SL^k) *as the set of sentences* $\forall y_1 \ldots \forall y_m \, . \, \phi$ *such that for all $i \in [1, m]$ and all formulæ $\psi_1 -\!\!* \psi_2$ occurring at polarity 1 in ϕ, we have $y_i \notin \mathsf{var}(\psi_1) \cup \mathsf{var}(\psi_2)$,*
2. BSR^{fin}(SL^k) *as the set of sentences* $\forall y_1 \ldots \forall y_m \, . \, \phi$ *such that no formula $\psi_1 -\!\!* \psi_2$ occurs at polarity 1 in ϕ.*

Note that BSR^{fin}(SL^k) $\subsetneq$ BSR^{inf}(SL^k) $\subsetneq$ BSR(SL^k), for any $k \geq 1$.

Remark 2. Because the polarity of the antecedent of a $-\!\!*$ is neutral, Definition 7 imposes no constraint on the occurrences of separating implications at the *left* of a $-\!\!*$[6].

The decidability result of this paper is stated below:

Theorem 2. *For any integer $k \geq 1$ not depending on the input, the infinite satisfiability problem for BSR^{inf}(SL^k) and the finite satisfiability problem for BSR^{fin}(SL^k) are both PSPACE-complete.*

We provide a brief sketch of the proof (all details are available in [8]). In both cases, PSPACE-hardness is an immediate consequence of the fact that the quantifier-free fragment of SL^k, without the separating implication, but with the separating conjunction and negation, is PSPACE-hard [4]. For PSPACE-membership, consider a formula φ in BSR^{inf}(SL^k), and its equivalent disjunction of minterms φ' (of exponential size). Lemma 8 gives us an upper bound on the size of test

---

[5] Note that the two definitions of α^{fin} are equivalent. The formula α^{fin} is unsatisfiable on infinite universes, which explains why the definitions of α^{fin} and α^{inf} differ.

[6] The idea is that if a formula $\mathsf{alloc}(x)$ or $|h| \geq |U| - n$ occurs in the antecedent of a $-\!\!*$, then it will be eliminated by the transformation in Lemma 4. In contrast, such test formulæ will not be eliminated if they occur in the subsequent of a $-\!\!*$.

formulæ in φ', hence on the number of constant symbols occurring in $\tau(\varphi')$. This, in turns, gives a bound on the cardinality of the model of $\tau(\varphi')$. We may thus guess such an interpretation, and check that it is indeed a model of $\tau(\varphi')$ by enumerating all the minterms in φ' (this is feasible in polynomial space thanks to Lemma 8) and translating them on-the-fly into first-order formulæ. The only subtle point is that the model obtained in this way is finite, whereas our aim is to test that the obtained formula has a *infinite* model. This difficulty can be overcome by adding an axiom ensuring that the domain contains more *unallocated* elements than the total number of constant symbols and variables in the formula. This is sufficient to prove that the obtained model – although finite – can be extended into an infinite model, obtained by creating infinitely many copies of these elements.

The proof for $\mathsf{BSR}^{fin}(\mathsf{SL}^k)$ is similar, but far more involved. The problem is that, if the universe is finite, then $\mathsf{alloc}(x)$ test formulæ may occur at a positive polarity, even if every $\phi_1 \mathbin{-\!\!*} \phi_2$ subformula occurs at a negative polarity, due to the positive occurrences of $\mathsf{alloc}(x)$ within λ^{fin} (10) in the definition of $\mathsf{elim}^{fin}_{-\circ}(M_1, M_2)$. As previously discussed, positive occurrences of $\mathsf{alloc}(x)$ hinder the translation into $\mathsf{BSR}(\mathsf{FO})$, because of the existential quantifiers that may occur in the scope of a universal quantifier. The solution is to distinguish a class of finite structures $(\mathfrak{U}, \mathfrak{s}, \mathfrak{h})$, the so-called α-*controlled structures*, for some $\alpha \in \mathbb{N}$, for which there are locations $\ell_1, \ldots, \ell_\alpha$, such that every location $\ell \in \mathfrak{U}$ is either ℓ_i or points to a tuple from the set $\{\ell_1, \ldots, \ell_\alpha, \ell\}$. For such structures, the formulæ $\mathsf{alloc}(x)$ can be eliminated in a straightforward way because they are equivalent to $\bigwedge_{i=1}^{\alpha}(x \approx \ell_i \rightarrow \mathsf{alloc}(\ell_i))$. If the structure is not α-controlled, then we can show that there exist sufficiently many unallocated cells, so that all the cardinality constraints of the form $|h| \leq |U| - n$ or $|U| \geq n$ are always satisfied. This ensures that the truth value of the positive occurrences of $\mathsf{alloc}(x)$ are irrelevant, because they only occur in formulæ λ^{fin} that are always true if all test formulæ $|h| \leq |U| - n$ or $|U| \geq n$ are true (see the definition of λ^{fin} in Lemma 4).

6 Conclusions and Future Work

We have studied the decidability problem for SL formulæ with quantifier prefix in the language $\exists^*\forall^*$, denoted as $\mathsf{BSR}(\mathsf{SL}^k)$. Although the fragment was found to be undecidable, we identified two non-trivial subfragments for which the infinite and finite satisfiability are **PSPACE**-complete. These fragments are defined by restricting the use of universally quantified variables within the scope of separating implications at positive polarity. The universal quantifiers and separating conjunctions are useful to express local constraints on the shape of the data-structure, whereas the separating implications allow one to express dynamic transformations of these data-structures. As a consequence, separating implications usually occur negatively in the formulæ tested for satisfiability, and the decidable classes found in this work are of great practical interest. Future work involves formalizing and implementing an invariant checking algorithm based on the above ideas, and using the techniques for proving decidability (namely the translation of quantifier-free $SL(k)$ formulæ into boolean combinations of test formulæ) to solve other logical problems, such as frame inference, abduction and possibly interpolation.

Acknowledgments. The authors wish to acknowledge the contributions of Stéphane Demri and Étienne Lozes to the insightful discussions during the early stages of this work.

References

1. Börger, E., Grädel, E., Gurevich, Y.: The Classical Decision Problem. Perspectives in Mathematical Logic. Springer, Heidelberg (1997)
2. Brochenin, R., Demri, S., Lozes, E.: On the almighty wand. Inf. Comput. **211**, 106–137 (2012)
3. Calcagno, C., Gardner, P., Hague, M.: From separation logic to first-order logic. In: Sassone, V. (ed.) FoSSaCS 2005. LNCS, vol. 3441, pp. 395–409. Springer, Berlin, Heidelberg (2005). https://doi.org/10.1007/978-3-540-31982-5_25
4. Calcagno, C., Yang, H., O'Hearn, P.W.: Computability and complexity results for a spatial assertion language for data structures. In: Hariharan, R., Vinay, V., Mukund, M. (eds.) FSTTCS 2001. LNCS, vol. 2245, pp. 108–119. Springer, Berlin, Heidelberg (2001). https://doi.org/10.1007/3-540-45294-X_10
5. Demri, S., Deters, M.: Expressive completeness of separation logic with two variables and no separating conjunction. In: Henzinger, T.A., Miller, D. (eds.), Joint Meeting of the Twenty-Third EACSL Annual Conference on Computer Science Logic (CSL) and the Twenty-Ninth Annual ACM/IEEE Symposium on Logic in Computer Science (LICS), CSL-LICS 2014, Vienna, Austria, 14–18 July 2014, pp. 37:1–37:10. ACM (2014)
6. Demri, S., Galmiche, D., Larchey-Wendling, D., Méry, D.: Separation logic with one quantified variable. Theory Comput. Syst. **61**(2), 371–461 (2017)
7. Echenim, M., Iosif, R., Peltier, N.: The complexity of prenex separation logic with one selector. CoRR, abs/1804.03556 (2018)
8. Echenim, M., Iosif, R., Peltier, N.: On the expressive completeness of Bernays-Schoenfinkel-Ramsey separation logic. ArXiv e-prints (2018)
9. Iosif, R., Rogalewicz, A., Simacek, J.: The tree width of separation logic with recursive definitions. In: Bonacina, M.P. (ed.) CADE 2013. LNCS (LNAI), vol. 7898, pp. 21–38. Springer, Heidelberg (2013). https://doi.org/10.1007/978-3-642-38574-2_2
10. Ishtiaq, S.S., O'Hearn, P.W.: BI as an assertion language for mutable data structures. ACM SIGPLAN Not. **36**, 14–26 (2001)
11. Lozes, É.: Expressivité des logiques spatiales. Thèse de doctorat, Laboratoire de l'Informatique du Parallélisme, ENS Lyon, France, November 2004
12. Ramsey, F.P.: On a problem of formal logic. In: Classic Papers in Combinatorics, pp. 1–24 (1987)
13. Reynolds, A., Iosif, R., Serban, C.: Reasoning in the Bernays-Schönfinkel-Ramsey fragment of separation logic. In: Bouajjani, A., Monniaux, D. (eds.) VMCAI 2017. LNCS, vol. 10145, pp. 462–482. Springer, Cham (2017). https://doi.org/10.1007/978-3-319-52234-0_25
14. Reynolds, J.C.: Separation logic: a logic for shared mutable data structures. In: Proceedings of the 17th Annual IEEE Symposium on Logic in Computer Science, LICS 2002, pp. 55–74. IEEE Computer Society (2002)

Towards a Structural Proof Theory of Probabilistic μ-Calculi

Christophe Lucas[1]($\boxtimes$) and Matteo Mio[2]($\boxtimes$)

[1] ENS–Lyon, Lyon, France
christophe.lucas@ens-lyon.fr
[2] CNRS and ENS–Lyon, Lyon, France
matteo.mio@ens-lyon.fr

Abstract. We present a structural proof system, based on the machinery of hypersequent calculi, for a simple probabilistic modal logic underlying very expressive probabilistic μ-calculi. We prove the soundness and completeness of the proof system with respect to an equational axiomatisation and the fundamental cut-elimination theorem.

1 Introduction

Modal and temporal logics are formalisms designed to express properties of mathematical structures representing the behaviour of computing systems, such as, e.g., Kripke frames, trees and labeled transition systems. A fundamental problem regarding such logics is the *equivalence problem*: given two formulas ϕ and ψ, establish whether ϕ and ψ are semantically equivalent. For many temporal logics, including the basic modal logic K (see, e.g., [BdRV02]) and its many extensions such as the *modal μ-calculus* [Koz83], the equivalence problem is decidable and can be answered automatically. This is, of course, a very desirable fact. However, a fully automatic approach is not always viable due to the high complexity of the algorithms involved. An alternative and complementary approach is to use *human-aided* proof systems for constructing *formal proofs* of the desired equalities. As a concrete example, the well-known equational axioms of Boolean algebras together with two axioms for the $\Diamond$ modality:

$$\Diamond \bot = \bot \qquad \Diamond(x \vee y) = \Diamond(x) \vee \Diamond(y)$$

can be used to construct formal proofs of all valid equalities between formulas of modal logic using the familiar deductive rules of *equational logic* (see Definition 3). The simplicity of equational logic is a great feature of this kind of system but sometimes comes at a cost because even seemingly trivial equalities often require significant human ingenuity to be proved.[1] The problem lies in

---

[1] Example: the law of idempotence $x \vee x = x$ can be derived from the standard axioms of Boolean algebras (i.e., complemented distributive lattices) as: $x \vee x = (x \vee x) \wedge \top = (x \vee x) \wedge (x \vee \neg x) = x \vee (x \wedge \neg x) = x \vee \bot = x$.

the *transitivity rule* ($a = b$ & $b = c \Rightarrow a = c$) which requires to guess, among infinitely many possibilities, an interpolant formula b to prove the equality $a = c$.

The field of *structural proof theory* (see [Bus98]), originated with the seminal work of Gentzen on his *sequent calculus* proof system LK for classical propositional (first-order) logic [Gen34], investigates proof systems which, roughly speaking, require less human ingenuity. The key technical result regarding the sequent calculus, the *cut-elimination theorem*, implies that when searching for a proof of a statement, only certain formulas need to be considered: the so-called *sub-formula property*. This simplifies significantly, in practice, the *proof search* endeavour. The original system LK of Gentzen has been extensively investigated and generalised and, for example, it can be extended with rules for the ◊ modality and becomes a convenient proof system for modal logic [Wan96]. Furthermore, it is possible to extend it with rules for dealing with (co)inductive definitions and it becomes a proof system for the modal μ-calculus (see, e.g., [Stu07]). Research on the structural proof theory of the modal μ-calculus is an active area of research (see, e.g., recent [Dou17]).

Probabilistic Logics and the Riesz Modal Logic. Probabilistic logics are temporal logics specifically designed to express properties of mathematical structures (e.g., Markov chains and Markov decision processes) representing the behaviour of computing systems using probabilistic features such as random bit generation. Unlike the non-probabilistic case, the equivalence problem for most expressive probabilistic logics (e.g., *pCTL* [LS82, HJ94], see also [BK08, BBLM17]) is not known to be decidable. Hence, human-aided proof systems are currently the only viable approach to establish equalities of formulas of expressive probabilistic logics. To the best of our knowledge, however, all the proof systems proposed in the literature (see, e.g., [DFHM16] for the logic pCTL, [BGZB09, Hsu17] for pRHL and [Koz85] for pPDL) are not entirely satisfactory because they include rules, such as the transitivity rule discussed above, violating the sub-formula property.

Another line of work on probabilistic logics has focused on *probabilistic μ-calculi* ([MM07, HK97, DGJP00, dA03, MS17, Mio11, Mio12a, Mio14]). These logical formalisms are, similarly to Kozen's modal μ-calculus, obtained by extending a base *real-valued* modal logic with (co)inductively defined operators. Recently, in [MFM17], a base real-valued modal logic called *Riesz modal logic* ($\mathcal{R}$) has been defined and a sound and complete equational axiomatisation has been obtained (see Definition 2). Importantly, the logic $\mathcal{R}$ extended with (co)inductively defined operators is sufficiently expressive to interpret most other probabilistic logics, including pCTL [Mio12b, Mio18, MS13a]. Hence, the Riesz modal logic appears to be a convenient base for developing the theory of probabilistic μ-calculi and, more generally, probabilistic logics.

Contributions of This Work. This work is a first step towards the development of the structural proof theory of probabilistic μ-calculi. We introduce a *hypersequent calculus* called MGA (read *modal GA*) for a version of the Riesz modal logic (the *scalar-free fragment*, see Sect. 2 for details) and by proving the cut-elimination theorem. Formally we prove:

Theorem 1. *The hypersequent calculus MGA is sound and complete with respect to the equational axioms of Fig. 1 and the CUT rule is eliminable.*

The machinery of hypersequent calculi has been introduced by Avron in [Avr87] and, independently, by Pottinger in [Pot83]. Our calculus extends the hypersequent calculus GA of Metcalfe, Olivetti and Gabbay [MOG05] (see also the book [MOG09] and the related [CM03] and [DMS18]) which is a sound and complete structural proof system for the equational theory of lattice-ordered abelian groups (axioms (1) in Fig. 1, see [Vul67] for an overview). The main contributions of this work are:

1. The careful extension of the system GA of [MOG05] with appropriate proof rules for the modality ($\lozenge$) and the proof of soundness and completeness.
2. The non-trivial adaptation of the proof-technique used in [MOG09, §5.2] to prove the cut-elimination theorem for GA.
3. The formalisation using the theorem prover Agda of our key technical results: Theorems 4 and 9. The code is freely available at [Agd].

In particular, the last point above guarantees the correctness of the proofs of all our novel technical results which, as it is often the case in proof theory, involve complex and long induction arguments. Given the availability of formalised proofs, in this work we focus on illustrating the main ideas behind our arguments rather than spelling out all technical details.

Organisation of the Paper. In Sect. 2 we provide the necessary definitions about the Riesz modal logic from [MFM17, Mio18] and about the hypersequent calculus GA of [MOG05, MOG09]. In Sect. 3 we present our hypersequent calculus MGA and state the main theorems. In Sect. 4 we sketch the main ideas behind our proof of cut-elimination. Lastly, in Sect. 5 we discuss some directions for future work.

2   Technical Background

2.1   The Riesz Modal Logic and Its Scalar-free Fragment

The Riesz modal logic $\mathcal{R}$ introduced in [MFM17] is a probabilistic logic for expressing properties of discrete or continuous Markov chains. We refer to [MFM17] for a detailed introduction. Here we just restrict ourselves to the purely *syntactical* aspects of this logic: its syntax and its axiomatisation.

Definition 1 (Syntax). *The set of formulas of the Riesz modal logic is generated by the following grammar:* $\phi, \psi ::= x \mid 0 \mid 1 \mid \phi + \psi \mid r\phi \mid \phi \sqcup \psi \mid \phi \sqcap \psi \mid \lozenge\phi$ *where* r, *called a* scalar, *ranges over the set* $\mathbb{R}$ *of real numbers. We just write* $-\phi$ *in place of* $(-1)\phi$.

A main result of [MFM17] is that two formulas ϕ and ψ are semantically equivalent if and only if the identity $\phi = \psi$ holds in all *modal Riesz spaces*.

Definition 2. *A* modal Riesz space *is an algebraic structure R over the signature $\Sigma = \{0, 1, +, r, \sqcup, \sqcap, \Diamond\}_{r \in \mathbb{R}}$ such that the following set $\mathcal{R}$ of axioms hold:*

1. *$\{R, 0, +, r, \sqcup, \sqcap\}_{r \in \mathbb{R}}$ is a Riesz space (see, e.g., [LZ71]), i.e.,*
   - *$(R, 0, +, r)_{r \in \mathbb{R}}$ is an $\mathbb{R}$-vector space,*
   - *$(R, \sqcup, \sqcap)$ is a lattice,*
   - *the lattice order $(x \le y \Leftrightarrow x \sqcap y = x)$ is compatible with addition, i.e.:*
     (a) $x \le y$ implies $x + z \le y + z$ (i.e., $(x \sqcap y) + z = ((x \sqcap y) + z) \sqcap (y + z)$),
     (b) $x \ge 0$ implies $rx \ge 0$ (i.e., $0 = 0 \sqcap r(x \sqcup 0)$) for every $r \in \mathbb{R}_{\ge 0}$,
2. *$0 \le 1$ (i.e., $0 = 0 \sqcap 1$),*
3. *the $\Diamond$ operation is linear, positive and 1-decreasing, i.e.:*
   - *$\Diamond(x + y) = \Diamond(x) + \Diamond(y)$ and $\Diamond(rx) = r\Diamond(x)$,*
   - *if $x \ge 0$ then $\Diamond(x) \ge 0$ (i.e., $0 = 0 \sqcap \Diamond(x \sqcup 0)$),*
   - *$\Diamond(1) \le 1$ (i.e., $\Diamond 1 = \Diamond 1 \sqcap 1$).*

Note that the definition of modal Riesz spaces is purely equational: all axioms of Riesz spaces (1) can be expressed equationally and so can the axioms (2) and (3). This means, by Birkoff completeness theorem, that two formulas are semantically equivalent if and only if the identity $\phi = \psi$ can be derived using the familiar deductive rules of equational logic, written as $\mathcal{R} \vdash \phi = \psi$.

Definition 3 (Deductive Rules of Equational Logic). *Rules for deriving identities from a set $\mathcal{A}$ of equational axioms:*

$$\frac{(t_1 = t_2) \in \mathcal{A}}{\mathcal{A} \vdash t_1 = t_2} Ax \qquad \frac{}{\mathcal{A} \vdash t = t} refl \qquad \frac{\mathcal{A} \vdash t_2 = t_1}{\mathcal{A} \vdash t_1 = t_2} sym \qquad \frac{\mathcal{A} \vdash t_1 = t_2}{\mathcal{A} \vdash C[t_1] = C[t_2]} ctxt$$

$$\frac{\mathcal{A} \vdash t_1 = t_2 \quad \mathcal{A} \vdash t_2 = t_3}{\mathcal{A} \vdash t_1 = t_3} trans \qquad \frac{\mathcal{A} \vdash f(\boldsymbol{s}, x, \boldsymbol{u}) = g(\boldsymbol{w}, x, \boldsymbol{z})}{\mathcal{A} \vdash f(\boldsymbol{s}, t, \boldsymbol{u}) = g(\boldsymbol{w}, t, \boldsymbol{z})} subst$$

where $C[\cdot]$ is a context and f, g are function symbols of the fixed signature.

In what follows we denote with $\mathcal{R} \vdash \phi \le \psi$ the judgment $\mathcal{R} \vdash \phi = \phi \sqcap \psi$. The following elementary facts from the theory of Riesz spaces (see, e.g., [LZ71, §2.12]) will be useful.

Proposition 1. *The following assertions hold:*

- *$\mathcal{R} \vdash \phi = \psi$ iff $\mathcal{R} \vdash \phi - \psi = 0$,*
- *$\mathcal{R} \vdash \phi = \psi$ iff $(\mathcal{R} \vdash \phi \le \psi$ and $\mathcal{R} \vdash \psi \le \phi)$.*
- *$\mathcal{R} \vdash r(x \sqcup y) = rx \sqcup ry$, $\mathcal{R} \vdash r(x \sqcap y) = rx \sqcap ry$.*

The first point says that an equality $\phi = \psi$ can always be expressed as an identity with 0. The second point says that we can express equalities with inequalities and *vice versa*. The third point, together will the other axioms, implies that scalar multiplication distributes over all other operations $\{+, \sqcup, \sqcap, \Diamond\}$.

For most practical purposes (when expressing properties of probabilistic models) the scalars in the Riesz modal logic can be restricted to be rational numbers.

Definition 4 (Rational and Scalar-free formulas). *A formula ϕ is* rational *if all its scalars are rational numbers. Similarly, ϕ is* scalar-free *if its scalars are all equal to (-1). Equivalently, the set of scalar-free formulas is generated by the following grammar: $A, B ::= x \mid 0 \mid 1 \mid A + B \mid -A \mid A \sqcup B \mid A \sqcap B \mid \Diamond(A)$.*

Note how we have switched to the letters A and B to range over scalar-free formulas to highlight this distinction.

Proposition 2. *Let ϕ be a rational formula. Then there exists a scalar-free formula A such that $\mathcal{R} \vdash \phi = 0$ iff $\mathcal{R} \vdash A = 0$.*

Proof. Let $\{r_i\}_{i \in I}$ be the list of rational scalars in ϕ, with $r_i = \frac{n_i}{m_i}$ and let $d = \prod_i m_i$ be the product of all denominators. Since scalar multiplication distributes with all operations it is easy to show that $\mathcal{R} \vdash d\phi = \psi$, for a formula ψ whose scalars are all integers. We can then obtain A from ψ by inductively replacing any sub-formula of ψ the form nB with $(B + B + \cdots + B)$ (n times) if n is positive, with $-(B + B + \cdots + B)$ if n is negative and with 0 if $n = 0$.   □

For this reason in this work we restrict attention to scalar-free formulas and we consider the restricted set of axioms $\mathbb{T}$ of Fig. 1. The axioms of Riesz spaces, when scalar multiplication is omitted, reduce to the axioms of *lattice ordered abelian groups* (see, e.g., [Vul67]). The axiom $0 \leq 1$ is unaltered and the axioms for the $\Diamond$ modality are naturally adapted. For these reasons we refer to these axioms as of those of *lattice-ordered modal abelian groups*.

---

1. **Axioms of Lattice–ordered abelian groups:**
   - Abelian Group: $x + (y + z) = (x + y) + z$, $x + y = y + x$, $x + 0 = x$, $x - x = 0$.
   - Lattice axioms: (associativity) $x \sqcup (y \sqcup z) = (x \sqcup y) \sqcup z$, $x \sqcap (y \sqcap z) = (x \sqcap y) \sqcap z$, (commutativity) $z \sqcup y = y \sqcup z$, $z \sqcap y = y \sqcap z$, (absorption) $z \sqcup (z \sqcap y) = z$, $z \sqcap (z \sqcup y) = z$, (idempotency) $x \sqcup x = x$, $x \sqcap x = x$.
   - Compatibility: $(x \sqcap y) + z = ((x \sqcap y) + z) \sqcap (y + z)$
2. **Axioms for the unit:** $0 = 0 \sqcap 1$,
3. **Modal axioms:**
   - $\Diamond(x + y) = \Diamond(x) + \Diamond(y)$, $\Diamond(-x) = -\Diamond(x)$ and $\Diamond(0) = 0$,
   - $0 = 0 \sqcap \Diamond(x \sqcup 0)$,
   - $\Diamond 1 = \Diamond 1 \sqcap 1$.

Fig. 1. Set of axioms $\mathbb{T}$ of lattice-ordered modal Abelian groups.

Remark 1. Note that from the previous discussion it does not follow directly that $\mathcal{R} \vdash A = B$ implies $\mathbb{T} \vdash A = B$. We indeed conjecture that $\mathcal{R}$ is a conservative extension of $\mathbb{T}$ but we have not proved this fact so far. In any case, this is not required for results of this work.

The main contribution of this work is the design of a sound and complete hypersequent calculus for the theory $\mathbb{T}$ and the proof of cut-elimination.

2.2 The Hypersequent Calculus GA

Our starting point is the hypersequent calculus GA of [MOG05, MOG09] for the theory of lattice-ordered abelian groups (set of axioms (1) in Fig. 1).

Definition 5 (Formulas, Sequents and hypersequents). *A formula A is a term built from a set of variables (ranged over by x, y, z) over the signature $\{0, +, -, \sqcap, \sqcup\}$. A sequent S is a pair of two (possibly empty) multisets of formulas $\Gamma = A_0, \dots, A_n$ and $\Delta = B_0, \dots, B_m$, denoted as $\Gamma \vdash \Delta$. A hypersequent G is a nonempty multiset $S_1, \dots, S_n$ of sequents, denoted as $S_1 | \dots | S_n$.*

Following [MOG05, MOG09], with some abuse of notation, we denote with S both the sequent and the hypersequent consisting of only the sequent S. The system GA is a deductive system for deriving hypersequents consisting of the rules of Fig. 2. The system GA without the CUT rule is denoted by GA^*.

Another convention we adopt from [MOG05, MOG09] is to write $d \vDash_{GA} G$ to express the fact that d is a valid GA-derivation of the hypersequent G. We write $\vDash_{GA} G$ to express the existence of a GA-derivation d such that $d \vDash_{GA} G$. Similarly, we write $d \vDash_{GA^*} G$ and $\vDash_{GA^*} G$ when referring to the subsystem GA^*.

Axioms:

$$\dfrac{}{\vdash \Delta} \, \Delta\text{-ax} \qquad \dfrac{}{A \vdash A} \, \text{ID-ax}$$

Structural rules:

$$\dfrac{G}{G | \Gamma \vdash \Delta} \, \text{Weakening (W)} \qquad \dfrac{G | \Gamma \vdash \Delta | \Gamma \vdash \Delta}{G | \Gamma \vdash \Delta} \, \text{Contraction (C)}$$

$$\dfrac{G | \Gamma_1, \Gamma_2 \vdash \Delta_1, \Delta_2}{G | \Gamma_1 \vdash \Delta_1 | \Gamma_2 \vdash \Delta_2} \, \text{Split (S)} \qquad \dfrac{G | \Gamma_1 \vdash \Delta_1 \quad G | \Gamma_2 \vdash \Delta_2}{G | \Gamma_1, \Gamma_2 \vdash \Delta_1, \Delta_2} \, \text{Mix (M)}$$

Logical rules:

$$\dfrac{G | \Gamma \vdash \Delta}{G | \Gamma, 0 \vdash \Delta} \, 0_L \qquad \dfrac{G | \Gamma \vdash \Delta}{G | \Gamma \vdash \Delta, 0} \, 0_R$$

$$\dfrac{G | \Gamma, A, B \vdash \Delta}{G | \Gamma, A + B \vdash \Delta} \, +_L \qquad \dfrac{G | \Gamma \vdash \Delta, A, B}{G | \Gamma \vdash \Delta, A + B} \, +_R$$

$$\dfrac{G | \Gamma \vdash \Delta, A}{G | \Gamma, -A \vdash \Delta} \, -_L \qquad \dfrac{G | \Gamma, A \vdash \Delta}{G | \Gamma \vdash \Delta, -A} \, -_R$$

$$\dfrac{G | \Gamma, A \vdash \Delta \quad G | \Gamma, B \vdash \Delta}{G | \Gamma, A \sqcup B \vdash \Delta} \, \sqcup_L \qquad \dfrac{G | \Gamma \vdash \Delta, A | \Gamma \vdash \Delta, B}{G | \Gamma \vdash \Delta, A \sqcup B} \, \sqcup_R$$

$$\dfrac{G | \Gamma, A \vdash \Delta | \Gamma, B \vdash \Delta}{G | \Gamma, A \sqcap B \vdash \Delta} \, \sqcap_L \qquad \dfrac{G | \Gamma \vdash \Delta, A \quad G | \Gamma \vdash \Delta, B}{G | \Gamma \vdash \Delta, A \sqcap B} \, \sqcap_R$$

CUT rule:

$$\dfrac{G | \Gamma_1 \vdash \Delta_1, A \quad G | \Gamma_2, A \vdash \Delta_2}{G | \Gamma_1, \Gamma_2 \vdash \Delta_1, \Delta_2} \, Cut$$

Fig. 2. Inference rules of the hypersequent system GA of [MOG05].

Multisets of formulas, sequents and hypersequents are interpreted as a single formula as follows:

Definition 6 (Interpretation). *A multiset of formulas* $\Gamma = \phi_1, \ldots, \phi_n$ *is interpreted as the formula* $[\![\Gamma]\!] = \phi_1 + \phi_1 + \cdots + \phi_n$ *if* $n \geq 1$ *and as* $[\![\Gamma]\!] = 0$ *if* $\Gamma = \emptyset$. *A sequent* $S = \Gamma \vdash \Delta$ *is interpreted as the formula* $[\![S]\!] = [\![\Delta]\!] - [\![\Gamma]\!]$. *Finally, a hypersequent* $G = S_0 \mid \cdots \mid S_n$ *is interpreted as the formula* $[\![G]\!] = [\![S_0]\!] \sqcup \cdots \sqcup [\![S_n]\!]$.

Example 1. Consider the hypersequent $G = \big(0 \sqcup x, y \vdash y\big) \mid \big(-y \vdash \big)$ consisting of two sequents. Then $[\![G]\!] = \big(y - ((0 \sqcup x) + y)\big) \sqcup \big(0 - (-y)\big)$.

The soundness and completeness of the hypersequent system GA with respect to the theory of lattice-ordered abelian groups (axioms (1) of Fig. 1, written as $\mathbb{T}_{(1)}$) is expressed by the following theorem.

Theorem 2 ([MOG05]). *For all formulas A and hypersequents G:*

 Soundness: if $\vDash_{GA} G$ *then* $\mathbb{T}_{(1)} \vdash [\![G]\!] \geq 0$.
 Completeness: if $\mathbb{T}_{(1)} \vdash A \geq 0$ *then* $\vDash_{GA} (\vdash A)$

Proof. The proofs presented in [MOG05] exploit the following well-known fact (see, e.g., [Vul67]): the equality $A = B$ holds in all lattice-ordered abelian groups if and only if it holds in $(\mathbb{R}, 0, +, -, \max, \min)$ under any interpretation of the variables as real numbers. In other words, $\mathbb{R}$ generates the variety of lattice-ordered abelian groups. $\square$

The main result of [MOG05] regarding GA is that the CUT rule is eliminable.

Theorem 3 (Cut-elimination [MOG05]**).** *Any GA-derivation of a hypersequent G can be effectively transformed into a GA^*-derivation of G.*

3   The Hypersequent System MGA

In this section we introduce our hypersequent calculus system MGA, a modal extension of the GA system of [MOG05]. The system MGA deals with formulas over the signature of modal lattice-ordered abelian groups (see Fig. 1) thus including the constant 1 and the unary modality $\Diamond$.

Definition 7 (Formulas of MGA). *A formula A is a term built from a set of variables (ranged over by x, y, z) over the signature $\{0, 1, +, -, \sqcap, \sqcup, \Diamond\}$.*

The definitions of sequents and hypersequents are given exactly as for the system GA in Definition 5 of Sect. 2.2. Similarly, multisets of formulas, sequents and hypersequents are interpreted as formulas exactly as already specified in Definition 6 of Sect. 2.2 for the system GA. Before presenting the deduction rules of MGA, it is useful to introduce the following abbreviations.

- For $n \in \mathbb{N}_{\geq 0}$, we denote with nF the multiset of formulas $F, F, \ldots, F$.
  So for example we write $2A, 1B \vdash 0C, D$ to denote the sequent $A, A, B \vdash D$.
- Given a multiset of formulas $\Gamma = F_0, \ldots, F_k$ and $n \in \mathbb{N}_{\geq 0}$ we denote with $n\Gamma$ the multiset of formulas $nF_0, \ldots, nF_k$. If $\Gamma = \emptyset$ then also $n\Gamma = \emptyset$.
- Given a multiset of formulas $\Gamma = F_0, \ldots, F_n$ we denote with $\Diamond \Gamma$ the multiset of formulas $\Diamond F_0, \ldots, \Diamond F_n$. Consistently, if $\Gamma = \emptyset$ then also $\Diamond \Gamma = \emptyset$.

The rules of the system MGA consist of all rules of GA (see Fig. 2) together with the additional rules of Fig. 3.

Axiom for 1:	Rule for $\Diamond$:
$\dfrac{}{\vdash 1}$ 1-ax	$\dfrac{\Gamma \vdash \Delta, n1}{\Diamond \Gamma \vdash \Diamond \Delta, n1}$ $\Diamond$-rule

Fig. 3. Additional inference rules of the hypersequent system MGA

The axiom (1-ax) for the constant 1 is straightforward and it simply expresses the axiom $0 \leq 1$ from Fig. 1 (i.e., $\mathbb{T} \vdash [\![\vdash 1]\!] \geq 0$).

The rule ($\Diamond$-rule) for the modality is more subtle as it imposes strong constraints on the shape of its premise and conclusion. First, both the conclusion and the premise are required to be hypersequents consisting of exactly one sequent. Furthermore, in the conclusion, all formulas, except those of the form 1 on the right side, need to be of the form $\Diamond C$ for some C.

The following is an illustrative example of derivation in the system MGA:

$$
\dfrac{
\dfrac{
\dfrac{
\dfrac{
\dfrac{
\dfrac{
\dfrac{\dfrac{}{1 \vdash 1} \text{ ID-ax} \quad \dfrac{}{A \vdash A} \text{ ID-ax}}{A, 1 \vdash 1, A} \text{ M}
}{A, 1, -(A) \vdash 1} -_L
}{A, 1 - A \vdash 1} +_L
}{A, A \vdash 1 \mid A, 1 - A \vdash 1} \text{ W}
}{A, A \sqcap (1-A) \vdash 1} \sqcap_L
}{A, A \sqcap (1-A) \vdash 1 \mid 1 - A, A \sqcap (1-A) \vdash 1} \text{ W}
}{A \sqcap (1-A), A \sqcap (1-A) \vdash 1} \sqcap_L
}{
\dfrac{\Diamond((A \sqcap (1-A))), \Diamond((A \sqcap (1-A))) \vdash 1}{\Diamond((A \sqcap (1-A))) + \Diamond((A \sqcap (1-A))) \vdash 1} +_L
} \Diamond\text{-rule}
$$

Our first theorem regarding MGA states its soundness and completeness with respect to the theory of modal lattice-ordered abelian groups (see Fig. 1). The proof of [MOG05] of Theorem 2 cannot be directly adapted here because, unlike the case for lattice-ordered abelian groups and $\mathbb{R}$, we are not aware of any simple modal lattice-order abelian group which generates the whole variety.

Theorem 4. *For all formulas A and hypersequents G:*

Soundness: if $\models_{MGA} G$ then $\mathbb{T} \vdash [\![G]\!] \geq 0$.

Completeness: if $\mathbb{T} \vdash A \geq 0$ then $\models_{MGA} (\vdash A)$.

Proof. Soundness is proven by translating every MGA derivation d of G to a derivation in equational logic π of $[\![G]\!] \geq 0$. This is done by induction on the complexity of d. The difficult cases correspond to when d ends by applications of either the S-rule, the M-rule or the $\sqcup_L$ rule. The formalised proof is implemented in the agda file `Syntax/Agda/MGA-Cut/Soundness.agda` in [Agd] and the type of the function is: soundness : $(G$: HSeq$) \to$ (MGA $G) \to$ botAG $\leq$S $[\![G]\!]$.

Conversely, completeness is proven by translating every equational logic derivation π of $A = B$ to the MGA derivations d_1 and d_2 of the (hyper)sequents $A \vdash B$ and $B \vdash A$ respectively. The proof goes by induction on π. First, MGA derivations are obtained for all axioms of Fig. 1. For example, for the axiom $\Diamond(x+y) = \Diamond(x) + \Diamond(y)$ we can derive the (hyper)sequent $\Diamond(x+y) \vdash \Diamond(x) + \Diamond(y)$ as showed below (left-side). Translating applications of the rules *refl* and *sym* is simple. Translating applications of the *trans* rules is immediate using the *CUT* rule of MGA. To translate applications of the *ctxt* rule, it is sufficient to prove (by induction) a simple context-lemma that states that if $A \vdash B$ is MGA derivable then also $C[A] \vdash C[B]$ is MGA derivable. Similarly, to translate applications of the *subst* rule, it is sufficient to prove (by induction) a simple substitution-lemma stating that if G is MGA derivable then $G[A/x]$ is also derivable, where $G[A/x]$ is the hypersequent where every occurrence of x is replaced by A.

Note that $\mathbb{T} \vdash A \geq 0$ means that $\mathbb{T} \vdash 0 = 0 \sqcap A$. By the translation method outlined above, the (hyper)sequent $0 \vdash 0 \sqcap A$ is MGA derivable. We can then get a MGA derivation of $\vdash A$ as follows (right-side):

$$
\begin{array}{c}
\dfrac{\dfrac{}{x \vdash x}\text{ ID-ax} \quad \dfrac{}{y \vdash y}\text{ ID-ax}}{\dfrac{\dfrac{x, y \vdash x, y}{x + y \vdash x, y}+_L}{\dfrac{\Diamond(x+y) \vdash \Diamond(x), \Diamond(y)}{\Diamond(x+y) \vdash \Diamond(x) + \Diamond(y)}+_R}\Diamond}\text{ M}
\end{array}
\qquad
\begin{array}{c}
\dfrac{\dfrac{\dfrac{}{A \vdash A}\text{ ID-ax}}{\dfrac{0 \vdash A \mid A \vdash A}{0 \sqcap A \vdash A}\sqcap_L}\text{ W} \quad \dfrac{0 \vdash 0 \sqcap A \quad \dfrac{\dfrac{}{\vdash}\Delta\text{-ax}}{\vdash 0}0_R}{\dfrac{\vdash 0 \sqcap A}{\vdash A}\text{cut}}\text{cut}}{\vdash A}
\end{array}
$$

The file `Syntax/Agda/MGA-Cut/Completeness.agda` in [Agd] contains the formalised proof and the type of the function is: completeness : $(A$: Term$) \to$ botAG $\leq$S $A \to$ MGA (head $([\,],[\,] :: A))$. □

Remark 2. The following natural looking variant of the ($\Diamond$-rule), allowing hypersequents with more than one component, is unsound:

$$
\dfrac{G \mid \Gamma \vdash \Delta, n1}{G \mid \Diamond\Gamma \vdash \Diamond\Delta, n1}
$$

Our main theorem regarding the system MGA is the cut-elimination theorem. We denote with MGA* the system without the CUT rule.

Theorem 5 (Cut-elimination). *Any MGA-derivation of a hypersequent G can be effectively transformed into a MGA*-derivation of G.*

Theorems 4 and 5 imply the statement of Theorem 1 in the Introduction.

4   Overview of the Proof of the Cut-Elimination Theorem

In this section we illustrate the structure of our proof of the cut-elimination theorem. We first explain the main ideas behind the proof of cut-elimination for GA of [MOG09, §5.2]. We then explain why these idea are not directly applicable to the system MGA. Lastly, we discuss our key technical contribution which makes it possible to adapt the proof method of [MOG09, §5.2] to prove the cut-elimination theorem for the MGA system.

4.1   The CAN-Elimination Theorem for the System GA

A key idea of [MOG09, §5.2] is to replace the CUT rule with an easier to handle rule called *cancellation* (CAN) rule. The CAN rule can derive the CUT rule in the basic cut-free system GA* as follows (right-side):

$$\dfrac{G|\Gamma, A \vdash A, \Delta}{G|\Gamma \vdash \Delta}\ \text{CAN} \qquad\qquad \left| \qquad \dfrac{\dfrac{\dfrac{d_1}{G|\Gamma_1, A \vdash \Delta_1}\quad \dfrac{d_2}{G|\Gamma_2 \vdash A, \Delta_2}}{G|\Gamma_1, \Gamma_2, A \vdash A, \Delta_1, \Delta_2}\ \text{M}}{G|\Gamma_1, \Gamma_2 \vdash \Delta_1, \Delta_2}\ \text{CAN} \right.$$

The cut-elimination theorem is obtained in [MOG09, §5.2] by proving a CAN-elimination theorem expressed as: if $\vDash_{\text{GA*}} G|\Gamma, A \vdash A, \Delta$ then $\vDash_{\text{GA*}} G|\Gamma \vdash \Delta$.

The CAN-elimination theorem for the system GA is proved in three steps:

Step A: proving the invertibility of all the logical rules ([MOG09, Lemma 5.18]). The invertibility states that if the conclusion of a logical rule (for instance, $G|\Gamma, A + B \vdash \Delta$ for the $+_L$ rule) is derivable without the CAN-rule, then all the premises (in this case $G|\Gamma, A, B \vdash \Delta$) are derivable too without the CAN-rule.

Step B: proving the atomic CAN-elimination theorem ([MOG09, Lemma 5.17]). This theorem deals with the special case of A being a variable and states that if $d \vDash_{\text{GA*}} G|\Gamma, x \vdash x, \Delta$ then $\vDash_{\text{GA*}} G|\Gamma \vdash \Delta$. This theorem is proven by induction on d and is mostly straightforward: the only difficult case is when d finishes with an application of the M-rule. A separate technical result ([MOG09, Lemma 5.16]) is used to take care of this difficult case.

Step C: proving the CAN-elimination theorem ([MOG09, Theorem 5.19]). The CAN-elimination theorem states that if $\vDash_{\text{GA*}} G|\Gamma, A \vdash A, \Delta$ then $\vDash_{\text{GA*}} G|\Gamma \vdash \Delta$. This proof is by induction on A:

- If A is a variable, we can conclude with the atomic CAN-elimination theorem.
- Otherwise we use the invertibility of the logical rules and we can conclude with the induction hypothesis. For instance, if $A = B + C$, then by invertibility of the $+_L$ and $+_R$ rules we have a GA*-derivation of $\vDash_{\text{GA*}} G|\Gamma, B, C \vdash \Delta, B, C$ and, from it, we can obtain a GA*-derivation of $G|\Gamma \vdash \Delta$ by using twice the induction hypothesis, first on B then on C.

4.2   Issues in Adapting the Proof for the System MGA

The proofs of [MOG09] can be adapted to the context of MGA without much
difficulty to perform the first two steps:

Theorem 6 (Invertibility of the logical rules). *All logical rules (including
the $\Diamond$-rule) are invertible in the system MGA^*.*

Proof. The same proof technique used in [MOG09] works. The main idea is, in
order to deal easily with the (S) and the (C) rules, to prove a slightly stronger
statement about the invertibility of more general rules. For instance, the generalisation of the rule $+_L$ is:

$$\frac{[\Gamma_i, n_i A, n_i B \vdash \Delta_i]_{i=1}^k}{[\Gamma_i, n_i(A+B) \vdash \Delta_i]_{i=1}^n} \qquad\qquad \square$$

Theorem 7 (Atomic CAN-elimination theorem). *If $\vDash_{MGA^*} \Gamma, x \vdash x, \Delta$
then $\vDash_{MGA^*} \Gamma \vdash \Delta$.*

The complication comes from the third and last Step C. We want to prove
that if $\vDash_{MGA^*} G|\Gamma, A \vdash A, \Delta$ then $\vDash_{MGA^*} G|\Gamma \vdash \Delta$. An ordinary proof by
induction on A could get stuck when $A = \Diamond B$. For instance, if the hypersequent
is $x, \Diamond B \vdash \Diamond B, x$, the invertibility of the $\Diamond$-rule can not be used because of the
syntactic constraints the $\Diamond$-rule imposes on its conclusion. Indeed the invertibility
of the $\Diamond$-rule states that if $\vDash_{MGA^*} \Diamond\Gamma \vdash \Diamond\Delta$ then $\vDash_{MGA^*} \Gamma \vdash \Delta$, but $x, \Diamond A \vdash
\Diamond A, x$ is not of this form because it contains the variable x.

For this reason, we deal with the case $A = \Diamond B$ in a different way, using
an induction argument on the derivation of $G|\Gamma, A \vdash A, \Delta$. In this argument,
however, the M-rule is hard to deal with (as already remarked it is a main source
of complications also on the proof of atomic CAN-elimination of [MOG09, §5.2]).

Our main technical result is that the M-rule can be eliminated from a simple
variant of the system MGA called MGA-SR (which stands MGA with *scalar
rules*). The system MGA-SR is obtained by modifying MGA as follows:

- The logical left-rules and right-rules for the connectives $\{0, -, +, \sqcup, \sqcap\}$ are
  generalised to deal with scalar coefficients (syntactic sugaring introduced in
  Sect. 3). For instance, the rules $+_L$ and $\sqcup_L$ become:

$$\frac{G \mid \Gamma, nA, nB \vdash \Delta}{G \mid \Gamma, n(A+B) \vdash \Delta} +_L \qquad \frac{G|\Gamma, nA \vdash \Delta \quad G|\Gamma, nB \vdash \Delta}{G|\Gamma, n(A \sqcup B) \vdash \Delta} \sqcup_L$$

- The axioms ID-ax and 1-ax are replaced by the rules

$$\frac{G|\Gamma \vdash \Delta}{G|\Gamma, nA \vdash nA, \Delta} \text{ ID-rule} \qquad \frac{G \mid \Gamma \vdash \Delta}{G \mid \Gamma \vdash \Delta, n1} \text{ 1-rule}$$

- All structural rules (C, W, S, M), the $\Diamond$-rule and the CAN rule remain exactly
  as in MGA (see Fig. 2).

It is possible to verify that MGR and MGR-SR are equivalent, i.e., they can derive exactly the same hypersequents (Theorem 8 below). The first modification (scalar rules) is technically motivated because it simplifies several proofs: in fact scalar rules are also implicitly considered in several of the proofs of [MOG09] for the system GA. The second modification (ID-rule and 1-rule) is essential. Indeed in the system MGA (and also in GA) the (hyper)sequent $x, y \vdash x, y$ is not derivable without applying the M-rule. Hence M-elimination in MGA is impossible. On the other hand the (hyper)sequent $x, y \vdash x, y$ is easily derivable in MGA-SR without requiring applications of the M rule

$$\frac{\dfrac{\overline{\vdash} \; \Delta\text{-ax}}{y \vdash y} \; \text{ID-rule}}{x, y \vdash x, y} \; \text{ID-rule}$$

and, as we will prove (Theorem 12), it is indeed possible to eliminate all applications of the M-rule from MGA-SR.

As outlined above, the presence of the M-rule was the main source of complications in adapting Step C. Once the equivalence between MGA-SR and MGA-SR without the M-rule is established, most complications disappear and the CAN-elimination proof can be obtained by performing Steps A–B–C for the system MGA-SR.

4.3   The System MGA-SR and the M-Elimination Theorem

In this subsection we introduce the system MGA-SR (MGA with *scalar rules*) for which we will prove the M-elimination theorem.

Definition 8 (MGA-SR). *The inference rules of MGA-SR are the rules of MGA modified as discussed previously. We denote by MGA-SR*, MGA-SR† and MGA-SR†* the systems without the CUT rule, the M-rule and both the CUT and M-rules, respectively.*

Theorem 8. *The two systems MGA and MGA-SR are equivalent:* $\vDash_{MGA} G$ *if and only if* $\vDash_{MGA-SR} G$.
   The two systems MGA* and MGA-SR* are equivalent: $\vDash_{MGA^*} G$ *if and only if* $\vDash_{MGA-SR^*} G$.

Proof. Translating MGA proofs to MGA-SR proofs is straightforward. All rules of MGA are specific instances of the scalar rules of MGA-SR (taking the scalar $n = 1$) and the the axioms 1-Axiom and ID-axioms are easily derivable in MGA-SR (without the need of the CAN rule) by using the id-rule and 1-rule (again, using the scalar $n = 1$). Translating MGA-SR to MGA is also mostly straightforward. Some care is needed to translate instances of the scalar-rules $\sqcup_L$, and $\sqcap_R$ from MGA-SR to MGA. This can be done by induction on the scalar n using the fact that the two premises $G|\Gamma, nA, B \vdash \Delta$ and $G|\Gamma, nB, A \vdash \Delta$ are derivable from $G|\Gamma, (n+1)A \vdash \Delta$ and $G|\Gamma, (n+1)B \vdash \Delta$. We remark that this derivation may require the usage of the M rule.   □

We now state our main technical contribution: the M-elimination theorem for the system MGA-SR.

Theorem 9 (M-elimination). *If* $d_1 \vDash_{MGA\text{-}SR^\dagger} G_1 \mid \Gamma \vdash \Delta$ *and* $d_2 \vDash_{MGA\text{-}SR^\dagger} G_2 \mid \Sigma \vdash \Pi$ *then* $\vDash_{MGA\text{-}SR^\dagger} G_1 \mid G_2 \mid \Gamma, \Sigma \vdash \Delta, \Pi$.

If $d_1 \vDash_{MGA\text{-}SR^{\dagger*}} G_1 \mid \Gamma \vdash \Delta$ *and* $d_2 \vDash_{MGA\text{-}SR^{\dagger*}} G_2 \mid \Sigma \vdash \Pi$ *then* $\vDash_{MGA\text{-}SR^{\dagger*}} G_1 \mid G_2 \mid \Gamma, \Sigma \vdash \Delta, \Pi$.

We now give a sketch of our proof argument. A formalised proof in Agda is available in [Agd] and is contained in the files `Syntax/MGA-SR/M-Elim.agda` and `Syntax/MGA-SR-CAN/M-Elim-CAN.agda`.

The general idea is to combine the derivations d_1 and d_2 in a *sequential way*. We first consider the case when no applications of the $\Diamond$-rule appear in d_1 nor d_2. First the proof d_1 is transformed into a pre-proof (i.e., where the derivation is left incomplete at some leaves) d_1' of $G_1 \mid G_2 \mid \Gamma, \Sigma \vdash \Delta, \Pi$. The pre-proof d_1' is structurally identically to d_1 and it essentially just ignores the G_2, Σ and Π components of the hypersequent. While the leaves of d_1 are all of the form $(\vdash)$ because Δ-ax is the only axiom of MGA-SR, the leaves of the pre-proof d_1' are of the form $G_2 \mid n\Sigma \vdash n\Pi$ (the ignored part carried out until the end, which can get multiplied by applications of the C and S rules). We can now proceed with the second step and provide derivations for these leaves using (easily modified versions of) the proof d_2.

When occurrences of the $\Diamond$-rule appear in d_1 or d_2 the argument requires more care. Indeed an application of the $\Diamond$-rule on d_1 acting on some hypersequent (necessarily) of the form:

$$\Diamond \Gamma_1 \vdash \Diamond \Delta_1, k1$$

cannot turned into an application of $\Diamond$-rule on:

$$G_2 \mid \Sigma, \Diamond \Gamma_1 \vdash \Diamond \Delta_1, k_1, \Pi$$

because this hypersequent violates the structural constraints of the $\Diamond$-rule. For this reason, we stop the construction of d_1' at these points and, as a results, the leaves of the pre-proof d_1' are generally of the form: $G_2 \mid n\Sigma, \Diamond \Gamma_1 \vdash \Diamond \Delta_1, k1, n\Pi$, for some Γ_1, Δ_1 and scalars n, k.

The idea now is, following the same kind of procedure, to modify the proof d_2 and turn it to a pre-proof d_2' of $G_2 \mid n\Sigma, \Diamond \Gamma_1 \vdash \Diamond \Delta_1, k1, n\Pi$. Crucially, the previous issue disappears. Indeed proof steps in d_2 acting on hypersequents of the form:

$$\Diamond \Sigma_1 \vdash \Diamond \Pi_1, m1$$

using the $\Diamond$-rule, can be turned into valid $\Diamond$-rule steps for the extended hypersequent:

$$\Diamond \Sigma_1, \Diamond \Gamma_1 \vdash \Diamond \Delta_1, k1, \Diamond \Pi_1, m_1 1$$

because the shape of the sequent is compatible with the constraint of the $\Diamond$ rule. Note that the hypersequent resulting from the application of the $\Diamond$-rule is $\Sigma_1, \Gamma_1 \vdash \Gamma_1, k_1 1, \Pi_1, m_1 1$ and has a lower modal-depth than the starting one. Hence an inductive argument on modal-complexity can be arranged to recursively reduce the general M-elimination procedure to the simpler case where d_1 and d_2 do not have occurrences of the $\Diamond$-rule (Fig. 4).

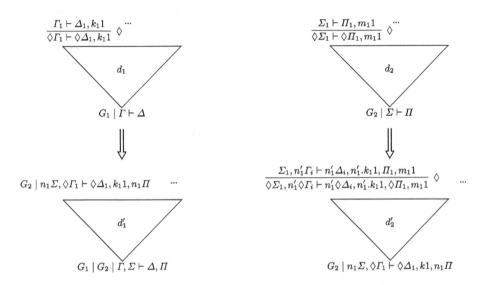

Fig. 4. Sequentially composing d_1 and d_2 in the M-elimination proof.

The following is a direct consequence Theorems 8 and 9.

Corollary 1. *The two systems MGA and MGA-SR† are equivalent:* $\vDash_{MGA} G$ *if and only if* $\vDash_{MGA-SR^\dagger} G$.
The two systems MGA* and MGA-SR$^{\dagger *}$ are equivalent: $\vDash_{MGA^*} G$ *if and only if* $\vDash_{MGA-SR^{\dagger *}} G$.

4.4 Cut-Elimination Theorem for the System MGA

We have already remarked that the cut-elimination theorem for the system MGA follows from the CAN-elimination theorem. By Corollary 1, the CAN-elimination theorem for the system MGA-SR† implies the CAN-elimination for MGA. Since there is no M-rule in MGA-SR†, the proof of CAN-elimination can follow the three Steps A–B–C outlined in Subsect. 4.1. As for Step A, we need to prove the invertibility of the logical rules in the system MGA-SR$^{\dagger *}$.

Theorem 10 (Invertibility of the logical rules). *The logical rules of the system MGA-SR$^{\dagger *}$,* $\{0_L, 0_R, +_L, +_R, \sqcup_L, \sqcup_R, \sqcap_L, \sqcup_R\}$, *are invertible.*

Remark 3. We note that, just as in [MOG09, §5.2], it is in fact possible and indeed technically useful to prove the invertibility of generalised scalar rules dealing with scalar rules, as in the proof of Theorem 6.

As for Step B we prove the atomic CAN-elimination theorem. Following the previous remark, we prove the following stronger version of the statement.

Theorem 11 (Atomic CAN-elimination). *If* $\vDash_{MGA\text{-}SR^{\dagger *}}$ $[\Gamma_i, k_i x \vdash k_i x,$ $\Delta_i]_{i=1}^{n}$ *then* $\vDash_{MGA\text{-}SR^{\dagger *}} [\Gamma_i \vdash \Delta_i]_{i=1}^{n}$.

Since we removed the M-rule, there are no significant difficulties in the induction arguments, and the proof is quite straightforward.

We also need a technical lemma regarding the constant formula 1 which is provable by a simple induction on the length of derivations.

Lemma 1. *If* $\vDash_{MGA\text{-}SR^{\dagger *}} [\Gamma_i, n_i 1 \vdash n_i 1, \Delta_i]_{i=1}^{n}$ *then* $\vdash_{MGA\text{-}SR^{\dagger *}} [\Gamma_i \vdash \Delta_i]_{i=1}^{n}$.

We can now prove the CAN-elimination theorem for MGA-SR†. This, together with Corollary 1 implies the cut-elimination (Theorem 5) for MGA.

Theorem 12 (CAN-elimination). *If* $d \vDash_{MGA\text{-}SR^{\dagger *}} G \mid \Gamma, A \vdash A, \Delta$ *then* $\vDash_{MGA\text{-}SR^{\dagger *}} G \mid \Gamma \vdash \Delta$.

Proof. Again, it is convenient to prove the stronger statement: If $d \vDash_{MGA\text{-}SR^{\dagger *}}$ $[\Gamma_i, k_i A \vdash, k_i A, \Delta_i]_{i=1}^{n}$ then $\vDash_{MGA\text{-}SR^{\dagger *}} [\Gamma_i \vdash \Delta_i]_{i=1}^{n}$. This is done by induction on the (lexicographical) complexity of the pair (A, d):

- If A is a variable, we can conclude with Theorem 11.
- If $A = 1$, we can conclude with Lemma 1.
- If $A = \Diamond B$, we look at d.
  - If d finished with the $\Diamond$-rule, then the end hypersequent is necessarily of the form: $[\Gamma_i, k_i A \vdash, k_i A, \Delta_i]_{i=1}^{n} = \Diamond \Gamma_1, n_1 \Diamond B \vdash n_1 \Diamond B, \Diamond \Delta_1, k1$, and is derived from the hypersequent $\vDash_{MGA\text{-}SR^{\dagger *}} \Gamma_1, n_1 B \vdash n_1 B, \Delta_1, k1$. By induction hypotheses (B has smaller complexity than A), we have that $\vDash_{MGA\text{-}SR^{\dagger *}} \Gamma_1 \vdash \Delta_1, k1$. Hence we can derive $\vDash_{MGA\text{-}SR^{\dagger *}} \Diamond \Gamma_1 \vdash \Diamond \Delta_1, k1$ by application of the $\Diamond$-rule.
  - Otherwise, the hypersequent is derived by application of some other rule (not active on $A = \Diamond B$) from some premises. In this case, we simply apply the inductive hypothesis on the premises (the formula A is unchanged but the complexity of the premise derivation has decreased) and use the same rule to construct a derivation of the desired hypersequent.
- Otherwise, using the same argument of [MOG09, §5.2] discussed in Sect. 4.1, we make progress in the inductive proof (reducing the complexity of A) by using the invertibility of the logical rules (Theorem 10). $\quad\square$

5 Conclusions and Future Work

We have presented a structural proof system called MGA for the scalar-free fragment of the Riesz modal logic. A natural direction of research is to extend the system MGA to deal with the full Riesz modal logic, thus handling arbitrary scalars $r \in \mathbb{R}$. The (integer-)scalar rules of the system MGA-SR could be naturally generalised to handle real-scalars but it is not clear, at the present moment, if the resulting system would satisfy a reasonable formulation of the sub-formula property. Another interesting topic of research is to consider extensions of MGA for fixed-point extensions of the Riesz modal logic (e.g., [MS17, Mio18]). In this direction, the machinery of *cyclic proofs* (see, e.g., [Stu07, MS13b, BS11, Dou17]) appears to be particularly promising.

References

1. Repository containing the proofs formalised in Agda. https://github.com/clu-cas26e4/M-elimination
2. Avron, A.: A constructive analysis of RM. J. Symbolic Logic **52**(4), 939–951 (1987)
3. Bacci, G., Bacci, G., Larsen, K.G., Mardare, R.: On the metric-based approximate minimization of Markov chains. In: Proceedings of 44th ICALP. LIPIcs, vol. 80, pp. 104:1–104:14. Schloss Dagstuhl - Leibniz-Zentrum fuer Informatik (2017)
4. Blackburn, P., de Rijke, M., Venema, Y.: Modal Logic. Cambridge Tracts in Theoretical Computer Science. Cambridge University Press, Cambridge (2002)
5. Barthe, G., Gr´egoire, B., Zanella-Beguelin, S.: Formal certification of code-based cryptographic proofs. In: Proceedings of POPL, pp. 90–101 (2009) Baier, C., Katoen, J.P.: Principles of Model Checking. The MIT Press, Cambridge (2008)
6. Brotherston, J., Simpson, A.: Sequent calculi for induction and infinite descent. J. Log. Comput. **21**(6), 1177–1216 (2011)
7. Buss, S.R.: An introduction to proof theory. In: Handbook of Proof Theory, pp. 1–78. Elsevier (1998)
8. Ciabattoni, A., Metcalfe, G.: Bounded Łukasiewicz logics. In: Cialdea Mayer, M., Pirri, F. (eds.) TABLEAUX 2003. LNCS (LNAI), vol. 2796, pp. 32–47. Springer, Heidelberg (2003). https://doi.org/10.1007/978-3- 540-45206-5_6
9. Alfaro, L.: Quantitative verification and control via the μ-calculus. In: Amadio, R., Lugiez, D. (eds.) CONCUR 2003. LNCS, vol. 2761, pp. 103–127. Springer, Heidelberg (2003). https://doi.org/10.1007/978-3-540- 45187-7_7
10. Dimitrova, R., Ferrer Fioriti, L.M., Hermanns, H., Majumdar, R.: Prob-abilistic CTL* the deductive way. In: Chechik, M., Raskin, J.-F. (eds.) TACAS 2016. LNCS, vol. 9636, pp. 280–296. Springer, Heidelberg (2016). https://doi.org/10.1007/978-3-662-49674-9_16
11. Desharnais, J., Gupta, V., Jagadeesan, R., Panangaden, P.: Approximating labelled Markov processes. In: Proceedings of LICS (2000)
12. Diaconescu, D., Metcalfe, G., Schn¨uriger, L.: A real-valued modal logic. Log. Methods Comput. Sci. **14**(1), 1–27 (2018)
13. Doumane, A.: On the infinitary proof theory of logics with fixed points. Ph.D. thesis, University Paris Diderot (2017)
14. Gentzen, G.: Untersuchungen ¨uber das logische schließen. Math. Z. 39, 405–431 (1934)
15. Hansson, H., Jonsson, B.: A logic for reasoning about time and reliability. Form. Asp. Comput. **6**, 512–535 (1994)
16. Huth, M., Kwiatkowska, M.: Quantitative analysis and model checking. In: Proceedings of LICS (1997)
17. Hsu, J.: Probabilistic couplings for probabilistic reasoning. Ph.D. thesis, University of Pennsylvania (2017)
18. Kozen, D.: Results on the propositional μ-calculus. Theor. Comput. Sci. **27**, 333–354 (1983)
19. Kozen, D.: A probabilistic PDL. J. Comput. Syst. Sci. **30**(2), 162–178 (1985)
20. Lehmann, D., Shelah, S.: Reasoning with time and chance. Inf. Control **53**(3), 165–1983 (1982)

21. Luxemburg, W.A.J., Zaanen, A.C.: Riesz Spaces. North-Holland Mathe-matical Library, vol. 1. Elsevier, Amsterdam (1971)
22. Mio, M., Furber, R., Mardare, R.: Riesz modal logic for Markov processes. In: 32nd ACM/IEEE Symposium on Logic in Computer Science (LICS), pp. 1–12. IEEE (2017). https://doi.org/10.1109/LICS.2017.8005091
23. Mio, M.: Probabilistic modal μ-calculus with independent product. In: Hofmann, M. (ed.) FoSSaCS 2011. LNCS, vol. 6604, pp. 290–304. Springer, Heidelberg (2011). https://doi.org/10.1007/978-3-642-19805-2_20
24. Mio, M.: On the equivalence of denotational and game semantics for the probabilistic μ-calculus. Log. Methods Comput. Sci. 8(2) (2012). https://lmcs.episciences. org/787, https://doi.org/10.2168/LMCS-8(2:7)2012
25. Mio, M.: Probabilistic modal μ-calculus with independent product. Log. Methods Comput. Sci. 8(4) (2012). https://lmcs.episciences.org/789, https://doi. org/10.2168/LMCS-8(4:18)2012
26. Mio, M.: Upper-expectation bisimilarity and Łukasiewicz μ-calculus. In: Muscholl, A. (ed.) FoSSaCS 2014. LNCS, vol. 8412, pp. 335–350. Springer, Heidelberg (2014). https://doi.org/10.1007/978-3-642-54830-7_22
27. Mio, M.: Riesz modal logic with threshold operators. In: 33rd ACM/IEEE Symposium on Logic in Computer Science (LICS), pp. 710–719. ACM (2018). https:// doi.org/10.1145/3209108.3209118
28. McIver, A., Morgan, C.: Results on the quantitative μ-calculus qMμ. ACM Trans. Comput. Log. 8(1) (2007). https://dl.acm.org/citation.cfm?doid=1182613.1182616
29. Metcalfe, G., Olivetti, N., Gabbay, D.M.: Sequent and hypersequent calculi for Abelian and Łukasiewicz logics. ACM Trans. Comput. Log. 6(3), 578–613 (2005)
30. Metcalfe, G., Olivetti, N., Gabbay, D.M.: Proof Theory for Fuzzy Logics. Applied Logic Series, vol. 36. Springer, Dordrecht (2009). https://doi.org/ 10.1007/978-1-4020-9409-5
31. Mio, M., Simpson, A.: Łukasiewicz μ-calculus. In: Proceedings Workshop on Fixed Points in Computer Science, FICS. EPTCS, vol. 126, pp. 87–104 (2013). https://doi.org/10.4204/EPTCS.126.7
32. Mio, M., Simpson, A.: A proof system for compositional verification of probabilistic concurrent processes. In: Pfenning, F. (ed.) FoSSaCS 2013. LNCS, vol. 7794, pp. 161–176. Springer, Heidelberg (2013). https://doi. org/10.1007/978-3-642-37075-5_11
33. Mio, M., Simpson, A.: Łukasiewicz μ-calculus. Fundam. Informaticae 150(3–4), 317–346 (2017). https://doi.org/10.3233/FI-2017-1472
34. Pottinger, G.: Uniform, cut-free formulations of T, S4 and S5 (abstract). J. Symbolic Logic 48(3), 898–910 (1983)
35. Studer, T.: On the proof theory of the modal μ-calculus. Stud. Logica. 89(3), 343–363 (2007)
36. Vulikh, B.Z.: Introduction to the Theory of Partially Ordered Spaces. Wolters-Noordhoff Scientific Publications LTD., Groningen (1967)
37. Wansing, H. (ed.): Proof Theory of Modal Logic. Applied Logic Series, vol. 2. Springer, Dordrecht (1996). https://doi.org/10.1007/978-94-017-2798-3

3

Causal Inference by String Diagram Surgery

Bart Jacobs[1], Aleks Kissinger[1], and Fabio Zanasi[2(✉)]

[1] Radboud University, Nijmegen, The Netherlands
[2] University College London, London, UK
f.zanasi@ucl.ac.uk

Abstract. Extracting causal relationships from observed correlations is a growing area in probabilistic reasoning, originating with the seminal work of Pearl and others from the early 1990s. This paper develops a new, categorically oriented view based on a clear distinction between syntax (string diagrams) and semantics (stochastic matrices), connected via interpretations as structure-preserving functors.

A key notion in the identification of causal effects is that of an intervention, whereby a variable is forcefully set to a particular value independent of any prior dependencies. We represent the effect of such an intervention as an endofunctor which performs 'string diagram surgery' within the syntactic category of string diagrams. This diagram surgery in turn yields a new, interventional distribution via the interpretation functor. While in general there is no way to compute interventional distributions purely from observed data, we show that this is possible in certain special cases using a calculational tool called comb disintegration.

We showcase this technique on a well-known example, predicting the causal effect of smoking on cancer in the presence of a confounding common cause. We then conclude by showing that this technique provides simple sufficient conditions for computing interventions which apply to a wide variety of situations considered in the causal inference literature.

Keywords: Causality · String diagrams · Probabilistic reasoning

1 Introduction

An important conceptual tool for distinguishing correlation from causation is the possibility of *intervention*. For example, a randomised drug trial attempts to destroy any confounding 'common cause' explanation for correlations between drug use and recovery by randomly assigning a patient to the control or treatment group, independent of any background factors. In an ideal setting, the observed correlations of such a trial will reflect genuine causal influence. Unfortunately, it is not always possible (or ethical) to ascertain causal effects by means of actual interventions. For instance, one is unlikely to get approval to run a clinical trial on whether smoking causes cancer by randomly assigning 50% of the patients to smoke, and waiting a bit to see who gets cancer. However, in certain situations it is possible to predict the effect of such a hypothetical intervention from purely observational data.

In this paper, we will focus on the problem of *causal identifiability*. For this problem, we are given observational data as a joint distribution on a set of variables and we are furthermore provided with a *causal structure* associated with those variables. This structure, which typically takes the form of a directed acyclic graph or some variation thereof, tells us which variables can in principle have a causal influence on others. The problem then becomes whether we can measure how strong those causal influences are, by means of computing an *interventional* distribution. That is, can we ascertain what would have happened if a (hypothetical) intervention had occurred?

Over the past 3 decades, a great deal of work has been done in identifying necessary and sufficient conditions for causal identifiability in various special cases, starting with very specific notions such as the *back-door* and *front-door* criteria [20] and progressing to more general necessary and sufficient conditions for causal identifiability based on the **do**-calculus [11], or combinatoric concepts such as confounded components in semi-Makovian models [25, 26].

This style of causal reasoning relies crucially on a delicate interplay between syntax and semantics, which is often not made explicit in the literature. The syntactic object of interest is the causal structure (e.g. a causal graph), which captures something about our understanding of the world, and the mechanisms which gave rise to some observed phenomena. The semantic object of interest is the data: joint and conditional probability distributions on some variables. Fixing a causal structure entails certain constraints on which probability distributions can arise, hence it is natural to see distributions satisfying those constraints as models of the syntax.

In this paper, we make this interplay precise using functorial semantics in the spirit of Lawvere [17], and develop basic syntactic and semantic tools for causal reasoning in this setting. We take as our starting point a functorial presentation of Bayesian networks similar to the one appearing in [7]. The syntactic role is played by string diagrams, which give an intuitive way to represent morphisms of a monoidal category as boxes plugged together by wires. Given a directed acyclic graph (dag) G, we can form a free category Syn_G whose arrows are (formal) string diagrams which represent the causal structure syntactically. Structure-preserving functors from Syn_G to Stoch, the category of stochastic matrices, then correspond exactly to Bayesian networks based on the dag G.

Within this framework, we develop the notion of intervention as an operation of 'string diagram surgery'. Intuitively, this cuts a string diagram at a certain variable, severing its link to the past. Formally, this is represented as an endofunctor on the syntactic category $\mathsf{cut}_X \colon \mathsf{Syn}_G \to \mathsf{Syn}_G$, which propagates through a model $\mathcal{F} \colon \mathsf{Syn}_G \to \mathsf{Stoch}$ to send observational probabilities $\mathcal{F}(\omega)$ to interventional probabilities $\mathcal{F}(\mathsf{cut}_X(\omega))$.

The cut_X endofunctor gives us a diagrammatic means of computing interventional distributions given complete knowledge of $\mathcal{F}$. However, more interestingly, we can sometimes compute interventionals given only partial knowledge of $\mathcal{F}$, namely some observational data. We show that this can also be done via a technique we call *comb disintegration*, which is a string diagrammatic version of a technique called *c-factorisation* introduced by Tian and Pearl [26]. Our approach generalises disintegration, a calculational tool whereby a joint state on two variables is factored into a single-variable state and a channel, representing the marginal and conditional parts of the distribution, respectively. Disintegration has recently been formulated categorically in [5] and using string diagrams in [4]. We take the latter as a starting point, but instead consider a factorisation of a three-variable state into a channel and a *comb*. The latter is a special kind of map which allows inputs and outputs to be interleaved. They were originally studied in the context of quantum communication protocols, seen as games [8], but have recently been used extensively in the study of causally-ordered quantum [3,21] and generalised [15] processes. While originally imagined for quantum processes, the categorical formulation given in [15] makes sense in both the classical case (**Stoch**) and the quantum. Much like Tian and Pearl's technique, comb factorisation allows one to characterise when the confounding parts of a causal structure are suitably isolated from each other, then exploit that isolation to perform the concrete calculation of interventional distributions.

However, unlike in the traditional formulation, the syntactic and semantic aspects of causal identifiability within our framework exactly mirror one-another. Namely, we can give conditions for causal identifiability in terms of factorisation a morphism in Syn_G, whereas the actual concrete computation of the interventional distribution involves factorisation of its interpretation in **Stoch**. Thanks to the functorial semantics, the former immediately implies the latter.

To introduce the framework, we make use of a running example taken from Pearl's book [20]: identifying the causal effect of smoking on cancer with the help of an auxiliary variable (the presence of tar in the lungs). After providing some preliminaries on stochastic matrices and the functorial presentation of Bayesian networks in Sects. 2 and 3, we introduce the smoking example in Sect. 4. In Sect. 5 we formalise the notion of intervention as string diagram surgery, and in Sect. 6 we introduce the combs and prove our main calculational result: the existence and uniqueness of comb factorisations. In Sect. 7, we show how to apply this theorem in computing the interventional distribution in the smoking example, and in 8, we show how this theorem can be applied in a more general case which captures (and slightly generalises) the conditions given in [26]. In Sect. 9, we conclude and describe several avenues of future work.

2   Stochastic Matrices and Conditional Probabilities

Symmetric monoidal categories (SMCs) give a very general setting for studying processes which can be composed in sequence (via the usual categorical composition $\circ$) and in parallel (via the monoidal composition $\otimes$). Throughout this paper, we will use *string diagram* notation [24] for depicting composition of morphisms in an SMC. In this notation, morphisms are depicted as boxes with labelled input and output wires, composition ∘ as 'plugging' boxes together, and the monoidal product ⊗ as placing boxes side-by-side. Identity morphisms are depicted simply as a wire and the unit I of ⊗ as the empty diagram. The 'symmetric' part of the structure consists of symmetry morphisms, which enable us to permute inputs and outputs arbitrarily. We depict these as wire-crossings: ✕. Morphisms whose domain is I are called *states*, and they will play a special role throughout this paper.

A monoidal category of prime interest in this paper is Stoch, whose objects are finite sets and morphisms $\boldsymbol{f} : A \to B$ are $|B| \times |A|$ dimensional stochastic matrices. That is, they are matrices of positive numbers (including 0) whose columns each sum to 1:

$$\boldsymbol{f} = \{\boldsymbol{f}_i^j \in \mathbb{R}^+ \mid i \in A, j \in B\} \quad \text{with} \quad \sum_j \boldsymbol{f}_i^j = 1, \text{ for all } i.$$

Note we adopt the physicists convention of writing row indices as superscripts and column indices as subscripts. Stochastic matrices are of interest for probabilistic reasoning, because they exactly capture the data of a conditional probability distribution. That is, if we take $A := \{1, \ldots, m\}$ and $B := \{1, \ldots, n\}$, conditional probabilities naturally arrange themselves into a stochastic matrix:

$$\boldsymbol{f}_i^j := P(B = j | A = i) \quad \rightsquigarrow \quad \boldsymbol{f} = \begin{pmatrix} P(B=1|A=1) & \cdots & P(B=1|A=m) \\ \vdots & \ddots & \vdots \\ P(B=n|A=1) & \cdots & P(B=n|A=m) \end{pmatrix}$$

States, i.e. stochastic matrices from a trivial input $I := \{*\}$, are (non-conditional) probability distributions, represented as column vectors. There is only one stochastic matrix with trivial output: the row vector consisting only of 1's. The latter, with notation ⑂ as on the right, will play a special role in this paper (see (1) below).

Composition of stochastic matrices is matrix multiplication. In terms of conditional probabilities, that is multiplication followed by marginalization over the shared variable: $\sum_B P(C|B)P(B|A)$. Identities are thus given by identity matrices, which we will often express in terms of the Kronecker delta function δ_i^j.

The monoidal product ⊗ in Stoch is the cartesian product on objects, and Kronecker product of matrices: $(\boldsymbol{f} \otimes \boldsymbol{g})_{(i,j)}^{(k,l)} := \boldsymbol{f}_i^k \boldsymbol{g}_j^l$. We will typically omit parentheses and commas in the indices, writing e.g. $\boldsymbol{h}_{ij}^{kl}$ instead of $\boldsymbol{h}_{(i,j)}^{(k,l)}$ for an arbitrary matrix entry of $\boldsymbol{h} : A \otimes B \to C \otimes D$. In terms of conditional probabilities, the Kronecker product corresponds to taking product distributions. That is, if $\boldsymbol{f}$ represents the conditional probabilities $P(B|A)$ and $\boldsymbol{g}$ the probabilities $P(D|C)$, then $\boldsymbol{f} \otimes \boldsymbol{g}$ represents $P(B|A)P(D|C)$. Stoch also comes with a natural choice of 'swap' matrices $\sigma : A \otimes B \to B \otimes A$ given by $\sigma_{ij}^{kl} := \delta_i^l \delta_j^k$, making it into a symmetric monoidal category. Every object A in Stoch has three other pieces of structure which will play a key role in our formulation of Bayesian networks and interventions: the *copy* map, the *discarding* map, and the *uniform state*:

$$\left(\curlyvee\right)_i^{jk} := \delta_i^j \delta_i^k \qquad \left(\varphi\right)_i := 1 \qquad \left(\blacktriangledown\right)^i := \frac{1}{|A|} \qquad (1)$$

Abstractly, this provides **Stoch** with the structure of a *CDU category*.

Definition 2.1. *A CDU category (for **copy**, **discard**, **uniform**) is a symmetric monoidal category* $(\mathsf{C}, \otimes, I)$ *where each object A has a copy map* $\curlyvee : A \to A \otimes A$, *a discarding map* $\dagger : A \to I$, *and a uniform state* $\downarrow : I \to A$ *satisfying the following equations:*

$$
\curlyvee\curlyvee = \curlyvee\curlyvee \qquad \curlyvee = | \qquad \mathord{\times} = \curlyvee \qquad \dot{\downarrow} = \square \tag{2}
$$

CDU functors are symmetric monoidal functors between CDU categories preserving copy maps, discard maps and uniform states.

We assume that the CDU structure on I is trivial and the CDU structure on $A \otimes B$ is constructed in the obvious way from the structure on A and B. We also use the first equation in (2) to justify writing 'copy' maps with arbitrarily many output wires: $\curlyvee$.

Similar to [2], we can form the free CDU category $\mathsf{FreeCDU}(X, \Sigma)$ over a pair (X, Σ) of a generating set of objects X and a generating set Σ of typed morphisms $f \colon u \to w$, with $u, w \in X^\star$ as follows. The category $\mathsf{FreeCDU}(X, \Sigma)$ has $X^\star$ as set of objects, and morphisms the string diagrams constructed from the elements of Σ and maps $\curlyvee \colon x \to x \otimes x$, $\dagger \colon x \to I$ and $\downarrow \colon I \to x$ for each $x \in X$, taken modulo the equations (2).

Lemma 2.2. **Stoch** *is a CDU category, with CDU structure defined as in* (1).

An important feature of **Stoch** is that $I = \{\star\}$ is the final object, with $\dagger \colon B \to I$ the map provided by the universal property, for any set B. This yields Eq. (3) on the right, for any $f \colon A \to B$, justifying the name "discarding map" for $\dagger$.

$$
\begin{array}{c} \dot{B} \\ \boxed{f} \\ |A \end{array} = \begin{array}{c} \dot{} \\ |B \end{array} \tag{3}
$$

We conclude by recording another significant feature of **Stoch**: *disintegration* [4,5]. In probability theory, this is the mechanism of factoring a joint probability distribution $P(AB)$ as a product of the first marginal $P(A)$ and a conditional distribution $P(B|A)$. We recall from [4] the string diagrammatic rendition of this process. We say that a morphism $f \colon X \to Y$ in **Stoch** has *full support* if, as a stochastic matrix, it has no zero entries. When f is a state, it is a standard result that full support ensures uniqueness of disintegrations of f.

Proposition 2.3 (Disintegration). *For any state $\omega \colon I \to A \otimes B$ with full support, there exists unique morphisms $a \colon I \to A$, $b \colon A \to B$ such that:*

$$
\begin{array}{c} |A \ |B \\ \boxed{\omega} \end{array} = \begin{array}{c} |A \quad |B \\ \quad \boxed{b} \\ \curlyvee \\ \boxed{a} \end{array} \tag{4}
$$

Note that Eq. (3) and the CDU rules immediately imply that the unique $a\colon I \to$ A in Proposition 2.3 is the marginal of ω onto A: $\boxed{\begin{smallmatrix} A & B \\ & \omega \end{smallmatrix}}$.

3   Bayesian Networks as String Diagrams

Bayesian networks are a widely-used tool in probabilistic reasoning. They give a succinct representation of conditional (in)dependences between variables as a directed acyclic graph. Traditionally, a Bayesian network on a set of variables $A, B, C, \ldots$ is defined as a directed acyclic graph (dag) G, an assignment of sets to each of the nodes $V_G := \{A, B, C, \ldots\}$ of G and a joint probability distribution over those variables which factorises as $P(V_G) = \prod_{A \in V_G} P(A \mid \mathrm{Pa}(A))$ where $\mathrm{Pa}(A)$ is the set of parents of A in G. Any joint distribution that factorises this way is said to satisfy the *global Markov property* with respect to the dag G. Alternatively, a Bayesian network can be seen as a dag equipped with a set of conditional probabilities $\{P(A \mid \mathrm{Pa}(A)) \mid A \in V_G\}$ which can be combined to form the joint state. Thanks to disintegration, these two perspectives are equivalent.

Much like in the case of disintegration in the previous section, Bayesian networks have a neat categorical description as string diagrams in the category Stoch [7,13,14]. For example, here is a Bayesian network in its traditional depiction as a dag with an associated joint distribution over its vertices, and as a string diagram in Stoch:

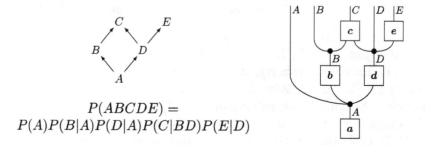

$$P(ABCDE) =$$
$$P(A)P(B|A)P(D|A)P(C|BD)P(E|D)$$

In the string diagram above, the stochastic matrix $a\colon I \to A$ contains the probabilities $P(A)$, $b\colon B \to A$ contains the conditional probabilities $P(B|A)$, $c\colon B \otimes D \to C$ contains $P(C|BD)$, and so on. The entire diagram is then equal to a state $\omega\colon I \to A \otimes B \otimes C \otimes D \otimes E$ which represents $P(ABCDE)$.

Note the dag and the diagram above look similar in structure. The main difference is the use of copy maps to make each variable (even those that are not leaves of the dag, A, B and D) an output of the overall diagram. This corresponds to a variable being *observed*. We can also consider Bayesian networks with *latent* variables, which do not appear in the joint distribution due to marginalisation. Continuing the example above, making A into a latent variable yields the following depiction as a string diagram:

$$P(BCDE) =$$
$$\sum_A P(A)P(B|A)P(D|A)P(C|BD)P(E|D)$$

In general, a Bayesian network (with possible latent variables), is a string diagram in Stoch that (1) only has outputs and (2) consists only of copy maps and boxes which each have exactly one output.

By 'a string diagram in Stoch', we mean not only the stochastic matrix itself, but also its decomposition into components. We can formalise exactly what we mean by taking a perspective on Bayesian networks which draws inspiration from Lawvere's functorial semantics of algebraic theories [16]. In this perspective, which elaborates on [7, Ch. 4], we maintain a conceptual distinction between the purely syntactic object (the diagram) and its probabilistic interpretation.

Starting from a dag $G = (V_G, E_G)$, we construct a free CDU category Syn_G which provides the syntax of causal structures labelled by G. The objects of Syn_G are generated by the vertices of G, whereas the morphisms are generated by the following signature:

$$\Sigma_G = \left\{ \begin{array}{c} \fbox{a} \\ \end{array} \;\middle|\; A \in V_G \text{ with parents } B_1, \ldots, B_k \in V_G \right\}$$

Then $\mathsf{Syn}_G := \mathsf{FreeCDU}(V_G, \Sigma_G)$.[1] The following result establishes that models (à la Lawvere) of Syn_G coincide with G-based Bayesian networks.

Proposition 3.1. *There is a 1-1 correspondence between Bayesian networks based on the dag G and CDU functors of type $\mathsf{Syn}_G \to \mathsf{Stoch}$.*

We refer to [12] for a proof. This proposition justifies the following definition of a category BN_G of G-based Bayesian networks: objects are CDU functors $\mathsf{Syn}_G \to \mathsf{Stoch}$ and arrows are monoidal natural transformations between them.

4   Towards Causal Inference: The Smoking Scenario

We will motivate our approach to causal inference via a classic example, inspired by the one given in the Pearl's book [20]. Imagine a dispute between a scientist and a tobacco company. The scientist claims that smoking causes cancer. As a source of evidence, the scientist cites a joint probability distribution ω over variables S for smoking and C for cancer, which disintegrates as in (5) below,

---

[1] Note that E_G is implicitly used in the construction of Syn_G: the edges of G determine the parents of a vertex, and hence the input types of the symbols in Σ_G.

with matrix $c = \left(\begin{smallmatrix} 0.9 & 0.7 \\ 0.1 & 0.3 \end{smallmatrix}\right)$. Inspecting this $c : S \to C$, the scientist notes that the probability of getting cancer for smokers (0.3) is three times as high as for non-smokers (0.1). Hence, the scientist claims that smoking has a significant causal effect on cancer.

An important thing to stress here is that the scientist draws this conclusion using not only the observational data ω but also from an assumed *causal structure* which gave rise to that data, as captured in the diagram in Eq. (5). That is, rather than treating diagram (5) simply as a calculation on the observational data, it can also be treated as an assumption about the actual, physical mechanism that gave rise to that data. Namely, this diagram encompasses the assumption that there is some prior propensity for people to smoke captured by $s : I \to S$, which is both observed and fed into some other process $c : S \to C$ whereby an individuals choice to smoke determines whether or not they get cancer.

The tobacco company, in turn, says that the scientists' assumptions about the provenance of this data are too strong. While they concede that *in principle* it is possible for smoking to have some influence on cancer, the scientist should allow for the possibility that there is some latent common cause (e.g. genetic conditions, stressful work environment, etc.) which leads people both to smoke and get cancer. Hence, says the tobacco company, a 'more honest' causal structure to ascribe to the data ω is (6). This structure then allows for either party to be correct. If the scientist is right, the output of $c : S \otimes H \to C$ depends mostly on its first input, i.e. the causal path from smoking to cancer. If the tabacco company is right, then c depends very little on its first input, and the correlation between S and C can be explained almost entirely from the hidden common cause.

So, who is right after all? Just from the observed distribution ω, it is impossible to tell. So, the scientist proposes a clinical trial, in which patients are randomly required to smoke or not to smoke. We can model this situation by replacing s in (6) with a process that ignores its inputs and outputs the uniform state. Graphically, this looks like 'cutting' the link s between H and S:

This captures the fact that variable S is now randomised and no longer dependent on any background factors. This new distribution ω' represents the data the scientist would have obtained had they run the trial. That is, it gives the results of an *intervention* at s. If this ω' *still* shows a strong correlation between smoking and cancer, one can conclude that smoking indeed causes cancer even when we assume the weaker causal structure (6).

Unsurprisingly, the scientist fails to get ethical approval to run the trial, and hence has only the observational data ω to work with. Given that the scientist only knows ω (and not c and h), there is no way to compute ω' in this case. However, a key insight of statistical causal inference is that sometimes it *is* possible to compute interventional distributions from observational ones. Continuing the smoking example, suppose the scientist proposes the following revision to the causal structure: they posit a structure (8) that includes a third observed variable (the presence of T of tar in the lungs), which completely mediates the causal effect of smoking on cancer.

As with our simpler structure, the diagram (8) contains some assumptions about the provenance of the data ω. In particular, by omitting wires, we are asserting there is no *direct* causal link between certain variables. The absence of an H-labelled input to t says there is no direct causal link from H to T (only mediated by S), and the absence of an S-labelled input wire into c captures that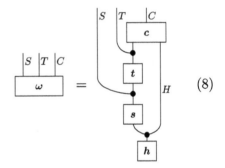

$$(8)$$

there is no direct causal link from S to C (only mediated by T). In the traditional approach to causal inference, such relationships are typically captured by a graph-theoretic property called *d-separation* on the dag associated with the causal structure.

We can again imagine intervening at S by replacing $s : H \to S$ by $\downarrow \circ \, \uparrow$. Again, this 'cutting' of the diagram will result in a new interventional distribution ω'. However, unike before, it *is* possible to compute this distribution from the observational distribution ω.

However, in order to do that, we first need to develop the appropriate categorical framework. In Sect. 5, we will model 'cutting' as a functor. In 6, we will introduce a generalisation of disintegration, which we call *comb disintegration*. These tools will enable us to compute ω' for ω, in Sect. 7.

5 Interventional Distributions as Diagram Surgery

The goal of this section is to define the 'cut' operation in (7) as an endofunctor on the category of Bayesian networks. First, we observe that such an operation exclusively concerns the string diagram part of a Bayesian network: following the functorial semantics given in Sect. 3, it is thus appropriate to define cut as an endofunctor on Syn_G, for a given dag G.

Definition 5.1. *For a fixed node $A \in V_G$ in a graph G, let $\mathrm{cut}_A \colon \mathsf{Syn}_G \to \mathsf{Syn}_G$ be the CDU functor freely obtained by the following action on the generators (V_G, Σ_G) of Syn_G:*

- *For each object $B \in V_G$, $\mathrm{cut}_A(B) = B$.*

- $\mathrm{cut}_A\left(\begin{smallmatrix} A \\ \boxed{a} \\ B_1 \cdots B_k \end{smallmatrix}\right) = \begin{smallmatrix} A \\ \blacktriangledown \\ B_1 \cdots B_k \end{smallmatrix}$ *and* $\mathrm{cut}_A\left(\begin{smallmatrix} B \\ \boxed{b} \\ C_i \cdots C_j \end{smallmatrix}\right) = \begin{smallmatrix} B \\ \boxed{b} \\ C_i \cdots C_j \end{smallmatrix}$ *for any other* $\begin{smallmatrix} B \\ \boxed{b} \\ C_i \cdots C_j \end{smallmatrix} \in \Sigma_G$.

Intuitively, cut_A applied to a string diagram f of Syn_G removes from f each occurrence of a box with output wire of type A.

Proposition 3.1 allows us to "transport" the cutting operation over to Bayesian networks. Given any Bayesian network based on G, let $\mathcal{F} \colon \mathsf{Syn}_G \to \mathsf{Stoch}$ be the corresponding CDU functor given by Proposition 3.1. Then, we can define its A-cutting as the Bayesian network identified by the CDU functor $\mathcal{F} \circ \mathrm{cut}_A$. This yields an (idempotent) endofunctor $\mathsf{Cut}_A \colon \mathsf{BN}_G \to \mathsf{BN}_G$.

6   The Comb Factorisation

Thanks to the developments of Sect. 5, we can understand the transition from left to right in (7) as the application of the functor Cut_S applied to the 'Smoking' node S. The next step is being able to actually compute the individual Stoch-morphisms appearing in (8), to give an answer to the causality question.

In order to do that, we want to work in a setting where $t \colon S \to T$ can be isolated and 'extracted' from (8). What is left behind is a stochastic matrix with a 'hole' where t has been extracted. To define 'morphisms with holes', it is convenient to pass from SMCs to compact closed categories (see e.g. [24]). Stoch is not itself compact closed, but it embeds into $\mathsf{Mat}(\mathbb{R}^+)$, whose morphisms are *all* matrices over positive numbers. $\mathsf{Mat}(\mathbb{R}^+)$ has a (self-dual) compact closed structure; that means, for any set A there is a 'cap' $\cap \colon A \otimes A \to I$ and a 'cup' $\cup \colon I \to A \otimes A$, which satisfy the 'yanking' equations on the right. As matrices, caps and cups are defined by $\cap_{ij} = \cup^{ij} = \delta_i^j$. Intuitively, they amount to 'bent' identity wires. Another aspect of $\mathsf{Mat}(\mathbb{R}^+)$ that is useful to recall is the following handy characterisation of the subcategory Stoch.

Lemma 6.1. *A morphism $f \colon A \to B$ in $\mathsf{Mat}(\mathbb{R}^+)$ is a stochastic matrix (thus a morphism of Stoch) if and only if (3) holds.*

A suitable notion of 'stochastic map with a hole' is provided by a *comb*. These structures originate in the study of certain kinds of quantum channels [3].

Definition 6.2. *A 2-comb in Stoch is a morphism $f \colon A_1 \otimes A_2 \to B_1 \otimes B_2$ satisfying, for some other morphism $f' \colon A_1 \to B_1$,*

$$\begin{array}{c} B_1 \quad B_2 \\ \boxed{f} \\ A_1 \quad A_2 \end{array} = \begin{array}{c} B_1 \\ \boxed{f'} \; \bullet \\ A_1 \quad A_2 \end{array} \tag{9}$$

This definition extends inductively to n-*combs*, where we require that discarding the rightmost output yields $\boldsymbol{f}' \otimes\, \mathord{\uparrow}\!\!\!\bullet$, for some $(n-1)$-comb $\boldsymbol{f}'$. However, for our purposes, restricting to 2-combs will suffice.

The intuition behind condition (9) is that the contribution from input A_2 is only visible via output B_2. Thus, if we discard B_2 we may as well discard A_2. In other words, the input/output pair A_2, B_2 happen 'after' the pair A_1, B_1. Hence, it is typical to depict 2-combs in the shape of a (hair) comb, with 2 'teeth', as in (10) below:

$$ (10) $$

$$ (11) $$

While combs themselves live in Stoch, $\mathsf{Mat}(\mathbb{R}^+)$ accommodates a second-order reading of the transition $\rightsquigarrow$ in (10): we can treat $\boldsymbol{f}$ as a map which expects as input a map $\boldsymbol{g} \colon B_1 \to A_2$ and produces as output a map of type $A_1 \to B_2$. Plugging $\boldsymbol{g} \colon B_1 \to A_2$ into the 2-comb can be formally defined in $\mathsf{Mat}(\mathbb{R}^+)$ by composing $\boldsymbol{f}$ and $\boldsymbol{g}$ in the usual way, then feeding the output of $\boldsymbol{g}$ into the second input of $\boldsymbol{f}$, using caps and cups, as in (11).

Importantly, for generic $\boldsymbol{f}$ and $\boldsymbol{g}$ of Stoch, there is no guarantee that forming the composite (11) in $\mathsf{Mat}(\mathbb{R}^+)$ yields a valid Stoch-morphism, i.e. a morphism satisfying the finality Eq. (3). However, if $\boldsymbol{f}$ is a 2-comb and $\boldsymbol{g}$ is a Stoch-morphism, Eq. (9) enables a discarding map plugged into the output B_2 in (11) to 'fall through' the right side of $\boldsymbol{f}$, which guarantees that the composed map satisfies the finality equation for discarding. See [12, § ??] for the explicit diagram calculation.

With the concept of 2-combs in hand, we can state our factorisation result.

Theorem 6.3. *For any state* $\boldsymbol{\omega} \colon I \to A \otimes B \otimes C$ *of* Stoch *with full support, there exists a unique 2-comb* $\boldsymbol{f} : B \to A \otimes C$ *and stochastic matrix* $\boldsymbol{g} \colon A \to B$ *such that, in* $\mathsf{Mat}(\mathbb{R}^+)$:

$$ (12) $$

Proof. The construction of $\boldsymbol{f}$ and $\boldsymbol{g}$ mimics the one of c-factors in [26], using string diagrams and (diagrammatic) disintegration. We first use $\boldsymbol{\omega}$ to construct maps $\boldsymbol{a} : I \to A, \boldsymbol{b} : A \to B, \boldsymbol{c} : A \otimes B \to C$, then construct $\boldsymbol{f}$ using $\boldsymbol{a}$ and $\boldsymbol{c}$ and construct $\boldsymbol{g}$ using $\boldsymbol{b}$. For the full proof, including uniqueness, see [12]. □

Note that Theorem 6.3 generalises the normal disintegration property given in Proposition 2.3. The latter is recovered by taking $A := I$ (or $C := I$) above.

7   Returning to the Smoking Scenario

We now return to the smoking scenario of Sect. 4. There, we concluded
by claiming that the introduction of
an intermediate variable T to the
observational distribution $\omega : I \to$
$S \otimes T \otimes C$ would enable us to calculate
the interventional distribution. That
is, we can calculate $\omega' = \mathcal{F}(\mathsf{cut}_S(\omega))$
from $\omega := \mathcal{F}(\omega)$. Thanks to Theorem
6.3, we are now able to perform that
calculation. We first observe that our
assumed causal structure for ω fits
the form of Theorem 6.3, where g is
t and f is a 2-comb containing everything else, as in the diagram on the
side.

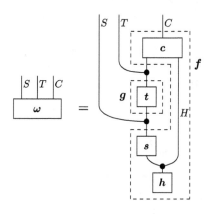

Hence, f and g are computable from ω. If we plug them back together as in
(12), we will get ω back. However, if we insert a 'cut' between f and g:

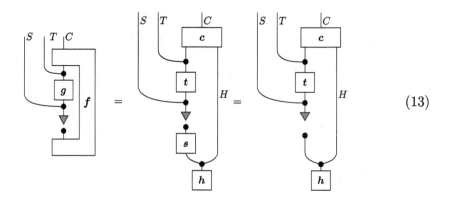

$$(13)$$

we obtain $\omega' = \mathcal{F}(\mathsf{cut}_S(\omega))$.

We now consider a concrete example. Fix interpretations $S = T = C = \{0,1\}$
and let $\omega : I \to S \otimes T \otimes C$ be the stochastic matrix:

$$\omega := \begin{pmatrix} 0.5 \\ 0.1 \\ 0.01 \\ 0.02 \\ 0.1 \\ 0.05 \\ 0.02 \\ 0.2 \end{pmatrix} \begin{matrix} \leftarrow P(S=0, T=0, C=0) \\ \leftarrow P(S=0, T=0, C=1) \\ \leftarrow P(S=0, T=1, C=0) \\ \leftarrow P(S=0, T=1, C=1) \\ \leftarrow P(S=1, T=0, C=0) \\ \leftarrow P(S=1, T=0, C=1) \\ \leftarrow P(S=1, T=1, C=0) \\ \leftarrow P(S=1, T=1, C=1) \end{matrix}$$

Now, disintegrating ω:

gives $c \approx \begin{pmatrix} 0.81 & 0.32 \\ 0.19 & 0.68 \end{pmatrix}$

The bottom-left element of c is $P(C = 1 | S = 0)$, whereas the bottom-right is $P(C = 1 | S = 1)$, so this suggests that patients are ≈ 3.5 times as likely to get cancer if they smoke (68% vs. 19%). However, comb-disintegrating ω using Theorem 6.3 gives $g: S \to T$ and a comb $f: T \to S \otimes C$ with the following stochastic matrices:

$$f \approx \begin{pmatrix} 0.53 & 0.21 \\ 0.11 & 0.42 \\ 0.25 & 0.03 \\ 0.12 & 0.34 \end{pmatrix} \qquad g \approx \begin{pmatrix} 0.95 & 0.41 \\ 0.05 & 0.59 \end{pmatrix}$$

Recomposing these with a 'cut' in between, as in the left-hand side of (13), gives the interventional distribution $\omega' \approx (0.38, 0.11, 0.01, 0.02, 0.16, 0.05, 0.07, 0.22)$. Disintegrating:

gives $c' \approx \begin{pmatrix} 0.75 & 0.46 \\ 0.25 & 0.54 \end{pmatrix}.$

From the interventional distribution, we conclude that, in a (hypothotetical) clinical trial, patients are about twice as likely to get cancer if they smoke (54% vs. 25%). So, since $54 < 68$, there was *some* confounding influence between S and C in our observational data, but after removing it via comb disintegration, we see there is still a significant causal link between smoking and cancer.

Note this conclusion depends totally on the particular observational data that we picked. For a different interpretation of ω in Stoch, one might conclude that there is *no* causal connection, or even that smoking *decreases* the chance of getting cancer. Interestingly, all three cases can arise even when a naïve analysis of the data shows a strong direct correlation between S and C. To see and/or experiment with these cases, we have provided the Python code[2] used to perform these calculations. See also [19] for a pedagocical overview of this example (using traditional Bayesian network language) with some sample calculations.

8   The General Case for a Single Intervention

While we applied the comb decomposition to a particular example, this technique applies essentially unmodified to many examples where we intervene at a single variable (called X below) within an arbitrary causal structure.

---

[2] https://gist.github.com/akissinger/aeec1751792a208253bda491ead587b6.

Theorem 8.1. *Let G be a dag with a fixed node X that has corresponding generator $x\colon Y_1 \otimes \ldots \otimes Y_n \to X$ in Syn_G. Then, suppose ω is a morphism in Syn_G of the following form:*

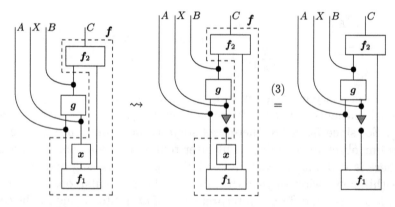

$$\tag{14}$$

for some morphisms f_1, f_2 and g in Syn_G not containing x as a subdiagram. Then the interventional distribution $\boldsymbol{\omega}' := \mathcal{F}(\mathsf{cut}_x(\omega))$ is computable from the observational distribution $\boldsymbol{\omega} = \mathcal{F}(\omega)$.

Proof. The proof is very close to the example in the previous section. Interpreting ω into Stoch, we get a diagram of stochastic maps, which we can comb-disintegrate, then recompose with $\downarrow \circ \uparrow$ to produce the interventional distribution:

The RHS above is then $\mathcal{F}(\mathsf{cut}_x(\omega))$.   □

This is general enough to cover several well-known sufficient conditions from the causality literature, including single-variable versions of the so-called *front-door* and *back-door* criteria, as well as the sufficient condition based on confounding paths given by Pearl and Tian [26]. As the latter subsumes the other two, we will say a few words about the relationship between the Pearl/Tian condition and Theorem 8.1. In [26], the authors focus on *semi-Markovian* models, where the only latent variables have exactly two observed children and no parents. Suppose we write $A \leftrightarrow B$ if two observed variables are connected by a latent common cause, then one can characterise *confounding paths* as the transitive closure of $\leftrightarrow$. They go on to show that the interventional distribution corresponding cutting X is computable whenever there are no confounding paths connecting X to one of its children.

We can compare this to the form of expression ω in Eq. (14). First, note this factorisation implies that all boxes which take X as an input must occur as sub-diagrams of g. Hence, any 'confounding path' connecting X to its children would yield at least one (un-copied) wire from f_1 to g, hence it cannot be factored as (14). Conversely, if there are no confounding paths from X to its children, then we can we can place the boxes involved in any other confounding path either entirely inside of g or entirely outside of g and obtain factorisation (14). Hence, restricting to semi-Markovian models, the no- confounding-path condition from [26] is equivalent to ours. However, Theorem 8.1 is slightly more general: its formulation doesn't rely on the causal structure ω being semi-Markovian.

9 Conclusion and Future Work

This paper takes a fresh, systematic look at the problem of causal identifiability. By clearly distinguishing syntax (string diagram surgery and identification of comb shapes) and semantics (comb-disintegration of joint states) we obtain a clear methodology for computing interventional distributions, and hence causal effects, from observational data.

A natural next step is moving beyond single-variable interventions to the general case, i.e. situations where we allow interventions on multiple variables which may have some arbitrary causal relationships connecting them. This would mean extending the comb factorisation Theorem 6.3 from a 2-comb and a channel to arbitrary n-combs. This seems to be straightforward, via an inductive extension of the proof of Theorem 6.3. A more substantial direction of future work will be the strengthening of Theorem 8.1 from sufficient conditions for causal identifiability to a full characterisation. Indeed, the related condition based on confounding paths from [26] is a necessary and sufficient condition for computing the interventional distribution on a single variable. Hence, it will be interesting to formalise this necessity proof (and more general versions, e.g. [10]) within our framework and investigate, for example, the extent to which it holds beyond the semi-Markovian case.

While we focus exclusively on the case of taking models in Stoch in this paper, the techniques we gave are posed at an abstract level in terms of composition and factorisation. Hence, we are optimistic about their prospects to generalise to other probabilistic (e.g. infinite discrete and continuous variables) and quantum settings. In the latter case, this could provide insights into the emerging field of *quantum causal structures* [6,9,18,22,23], which attempts in part to replay some of the results coming from statistical causal reasoning, but where quantum processes play a role analogous to stochastic ones. A key difficulty in applying our framework to a category of quantum processes, rather than Stoch, is the unavailability of 'copy' morphisms due to the quantum no-cloning theorem [27]. However, a recent proposal for the formulation of 'quantum common causes' [1] suggests a (partially-defined) analogue to the role played by 'copy' in our formulation constructed via multiplication of certain commuting Choi matrices. Hence, it may yet be possible to import results from classical causal reasoning into the quantum case just by changing the category of models.

Acknowledgements. FZ acknowledges support from EPSRC grant EP/R020604/1. AK would like to thank Tom Claassen for useful discussions on causal identification criteria.

References

1. Allen, J.-M.A., Barrett, J., Horsman, D.C., Lee, C.M., Spekkens, R.W.: Quantum common causes and quantum causal models. Phys. Rev. X **7**, 031021 (2017)
2. Bonchi, F., Sobociński, P., Zanasi, F.: Deconstructing Lawvere with distributive laws. J. Log. Algebr. Meth. Program. **95**, 128–146 (2018)
3. Chiribella, G., D'Ariano, G.M., Perinotti, P.: Quantum circuit architecture. Phys. Rev. Lett. **101**, 060401 (2008)
4. Cho, K., Jacobs, B.: Disintegration and Bayesian inversion, both abstractly and concretely (2017). arxiv.org/abs/1709.00322
5. Clerc, F., Danos, V., Dahlqvist, F., Garnier, I.: Pointless learning. In: Esparza, J., Murawski, A.S. (eds.) FoSSaCS 2017. LNCS, vol. 10203, pp. 355–369. Springer, Heidelberg (2017). https://doi.org/10.1007/978-3-662-54458-7_21
6. Costa, F., Shrapnel, S.: Quantum causal modelling. New J. Phys. **18**(6), 063032 (2016)
7. Fong, B.: Causal theories: a categorical perspective on Bayesian networks. Master's thesis, University of Oxford (2012). arxiv.org/abs/1301.6201
8. Gutoski, G., Watrous, J.: Toward a general theory of quantum games. In: Proceedings of the Thirty-Ninth Annual ACM Symposium on Theory of Computing, pp. 565–574. ACM (2007)
9. Henson, J., Lal, R., Pusey, M.F.: Theory-independent limits on correlations from generalized Bayesian networks. New J. Phys. **16**(11), 113043 (2014)
10. Huang, Y., Valtorta, M.: On the completeness of an identifiability algorithm for semi-Markovian models. Ann. Math. Artif. Intell. **54**(4), 363–408 (2008)
11. Huang, Y., Valtorta, M.: Pearl's calculus of intervention is complete. CoRR, abs/1206.6831 (2012)
12. Jacobs, B., Kissinger, A., Zanasi, F.: Causal inference by string diagram surgery. CoRR, abs/1811.08338 (2018)
13. Jacobs, B., Zanasi, F.: A predicate/state transformer semantics for Bayesian learning. Electr. Notes Theor. Comput. Sci. **325**, 185–200 (2016)
14. Jacobs, B., Zanasi, F.: The logical essentials of Bayesian reasoning. CoRR, abs/1804.01193 (2018)
15. Kissinger, A., Uijlen, S.: A categorical semantics for causal structure. In: 32nd Annual ACM/IEEE Symposium on Logic in Computer Science, LICS 2017, Reykjavik, Iceland, 20–23 June 2017, pp. 1–12 (2017)
16. Lawvere, F.W.: Ordinal sums and equational doctrines. In: Eckmann, B. (ed.) Seminar on Triples and Categorical Homology Theory. LNM, vol. 80, pp. 141–155. Springer, Heidelberg (1969). https://doi.org/10.1007/BFb0083085
17. Lawvere, F.W.: Functorial semantics of algebraic theories. Proc. Natl. Acad. Sci. U.S.A. **50**(5), 869 (1963)
18. Leifer, M.S., Spekkens, R.W.: Towards a formulation of quantum theory as a causally neutral theory of Bayesian inference. Phys. Rev. A **88**, 052130 (2013)
19. Nielsen, M.: If correlation doesn't imply causation, then what does? http://www.michaelnielsen.org/ddi/if-correlation-doesnt-imply-causation-then-what-does. Accessed 15 Nov 2018

20. Pearl, J.: Causality: Models, Reasoning and Inference. Cambridge University Press, Cambridge (2000)
21. Perinotti, P.: Causal structures and the classification of higher order quantum computations (2016)
22. Pienaar, J., Brukner, Č.: A graph-separation theorem for quantum causal models. New J. Phys. **17**(7), 073020 (2015)
23. Ried, K., Agnew, M., Vermeyden, L., Janzing, D., Spekkens, R.W., Resch, K.J.: A quantum advantage for inferring causal structure. Nat. Phys. **11**, 1745–2473 (2015)
24. Selinger, P.: A survey of graphical languages for monoidal categories. In: Coecke, B. (ed.) New Structures for Physics. LNP, vol. 813. Springer, Heidelberg (2011)
25. Shpitser, I., Pearl, J.: Identification of joint interventional distributions in recursive semi-Markovian causal models. In: Proceedings of the National Conference on Artificial Intelligence, vol. 21, p. 1219. AAAI Press/MIT Press, Menlo Park/Cambridge (1999/2006)
26. Tian, J., Pearl, J.: A general identification condition for causal effects. In: Proceedings of the Eighteenth National Conference on Artificial Intelligence and Fourteenth Conference on Innovative Applications of Artificial Intelligence, 28 July–1 August 2002, Edmonton, Alberta, Canada, pp. 567–573 (2002)
27. Wootters, W.K., Zurek, W.H.: A single quantum cannot be cloned. Nature **299**(5886), 802–803 (1982)

4

Universal Graphs and Good for Games Automata: New Tools for Infinite Duration Games

Thomas Colcombet[1]([⊠]) and Nathanaël Fijalkow[2]

[1] CNRS, IRIF, Université Paris-Diderot, Paris, France
thomas.colcombet@irif.fr
[2] CNRS, LaBRI, Université de Bordeaux, Bordeaux, France

Abstract. In this paper, we give a self contained presentation of a recent breakthrough in the theory of infinite duration games: the existence of a quasipolynomial time algorithm for solving parity games. We introduce for this purpose two new notions: good for small games automata and universal graphs.

The first object, good for small games automata, induces a generic algorithm for solving games by reduction to safety games. We show that it is in a strong sense equivalent to the second object, universal graphs, which is a combinatorial notion easier to reason with. Our equivalence result is very generic in that it holds for all existential memoryless winning conditions, not only for parity conditions.

1 Introduction

In this abstract, we are interested in the complexity of deciding the winner of finite turn-based perfect-information antagonistic two-player games. So typically, we are interested in parity games, or mean-payoff games, or Rabin games, etc...

In particular we revisit the recent advances showing that deciding the winner of parity games can be done in quasipolynomial time. Whether parity games can be solved in polynomial time is the main open question in this research area, and an efficient algorithm would have far-reaching consequences in verification, synthesis, logic, and optimisation. From a complexity-theoretic point of view, this is an intriguing puzzle: the decision problem is in **NP** and in **coNP**, implying that it is very unlikely to be **NP**-complete (otherwise **NP** = **coNP**). Yet no polynomial time algorithm has yet been constructed. For decades the best algorithms were exponential or mildly subexponential, most of them of the form $n^{O(d)}$, where n is the number of vertices and d the number of priorities (we refer to Section 2 for the role of these parameters).

Recently, Calude, Jain, Khoussainov, Li, and Stephan [CJK+17] constructed a quasipolynomial time algorithm for solving parity games, of complexity

$n^{O(\log d)}$. Two subsequent algorithms with similar complexity were constructed by Jurdziński and Lazić [JL17], and by Lehtinen [Leh18].

Our aim in this paper is to understand these results through the prism of good for small games automata, which are used to construct generic reductions to solving safety games. A good for small games automaton can be understood as an approximation of the original winning condition which is correct for small games. The size of good for small games automata being critical in the complexity of these algorithms, we aim at understanding this parameter better.

A concrete instanciation of good for small games automata is the notion of separating automata, which was introduced by Bojańczyk and Czerwiński [BC18] to reformulate the first quasipolynomial time algorithm of [CJK+17]. Later Czerwiński, Daviaud, Fijalkow, Jurdziński, Lazić, and Parys [CDF+19] showed that the other two quasipolynomial time algorithms also can be understood as the construction of separating automata, and proved a quasipolynomial lower bound on the size of separating automata.

In this paper, we establish in particular Theorem 9 which states an equivalence between the size of good for small games automata, non-deterministic of separating automata, of deterministic separating automata and of universal graphs. This statement is generic in the sense that it holds for any winning condition which is memoryless for the existential player, hence in particular for parity conditions. At a technical level, the key notion that we introduce to show this equivalence is the combinatorial concept of universal graphs.

Our second contribution, Theorem 10, holds for the parity condition only, and is a new equivalence between universal trees and universal graphs. In particular we use a technique of saturation of graphs which simplifies greatly the arguments. The two theorems together give an alternative simpler proof of the result in [CDF+19].

Let us mention that the equivalence results have been very recently used to construct algorithms for mean-payoff games, leading to improvements over the best known algorithm [FGO18].

Structure of the paper In Section 2 we introduce the classical notions of games, automata, and good for games automata. In Section 3, we introduce the notion of good for small games automata, and show that in the context of memoryless for the existential player winning conditions these automata can be characterised in different ways, using in particular universal graphs (Theorem 9). In Section 4, we study more precisely the case of parity conditions.

2   Games and automata

We describe in this subsection classical material: arenas, games, strategies, automata and good for games automata. Section 2.1 introduces games, Section 2.2 the concept of memoryless strategy, and Section 2.3 the class of automata we use. Finally, Section 2.4 explains how automata can be used for solving games, and in particular defines the notion of automata that are good for games.

2.1 Games

We will consider several forms of graphs, which are all directed labelled graph with a root vertex. Let us fix the terminology now. Given a set X, an X-graph $H = (V, E, \mathrm{root}_H)$ has a set of vertices V, a set of X-labelled edges $E \subseteq V \times X \times V$, and a root vertex root_H. We write $x \xrightarrow{u}_H y$ if there exists a path from vertex x to vertex y labelled by the word $u \in X^*$. We write $x \xrightarrow{u}_H \infty$ if there exists an infinite path starting in vertex x labelled by the word $u \in X^\omega$. The graph is trimmed if all vertices are reachable from the root and have out-degree at least one. Note that as soon as a graph contains some infinite path starting from the root, it can be made trimmed by removing the bad vertices. A morphism of X-graphs from G to H is a map α from vertices of G to vertices of H, that sends the root of G to the root of H, and sends each edge of G to an edge of H, i.e., for all $a \in X$, $p \xrightarrow{a}_G q$ implies $\alpha(p) \xrightarrow{a}_H \alpha(q)$. A weak morphism of X-graphs is like a morphism but we lift the property that the root of G is sent to the root of H and instead require that if $\mathrm{root} \xrightarrow{a}_G x$ then $\mathrm{root} \xrightarrow{a}_H \alpha(x)$.

Definition 1. *Let C be a set (of colors). A C-arena A is a C-graph in which vertices are split into $V = V_E \uplus V_A$. The vertices are called positions. The positions in V_E are the positions owned by the existential player, and the ones in V_A are owned by the universal player. The root is the initial position. The edges are called moves. Infinite paths starting in the initial position are called plays. Finite paths starting in the initial position are called partial plays. The dual of an arena is obtained by swapping V_A and V_E, i.e., exchanging the ownership of the positions.*

A $\mathbb{W}$-game $\mathcal{G} = (A, \mathbb{W})$ consists of a C-arena A together with a set $\mathbb{W} \subseteq C^\omega$ called the winning condition.

For simplicity, we assume in this paper the following epsilon property[1]: there is a special color $\varepsilon \in C$ such that for all words $u, v \in C^\omega$, if u and v are equal after removing all the ε-letters, then $u \in \mathbb{W}$ if and only if $v \in \mathbb{W}$.

The dual of a game is obtained by dualising the arena, and complementing the winning condition.

If one compares with usual games – for instance checkers – then the arena represents the set of possible board configurations of the game (typically, the configuration of the board plus a bit telling whose turn to play it is). The configuration is an existential position if it is the first player's turn to play, otherwise it is a universal position. There is an edge from u to v if it is a valid move for the player to go from configuration u to configuration v. The interest of having

---

[1] This assumption is satisfied in an obvious way for all winning conditions seen in this paper. It could be avoided, but at the technical price of considering slightly different forms of games: games in which the moves are positive boolean combinations of pairs of colors and positions. Such 'move relations' form a joint generalisation of existential positions (which can be understood as logical disjunction) and universal position (which can be understood as logical conjunction).

colors and winning conditions may not appear clearly in this context, but the intent would be, for example, to tell who is the winner if the play is infinite.

Informally, the game is played as follows by two players: the existential player and the universal player[2]. At the beginning, a token is placed at the initial position of the game. Then the game proceeds in rounds. At each round, if the token is on an existential position then it is the existential player's turn to play, otherwise it is the universal player's turn. This player chooses an outgoing move from the position, and the token is pushed along this move. This interaction continues forever, inducing a play (defined as an infinite path in the arena) labelled by an infinite sequence of colors. If this infinite sequence belongs to the winning condition $\mathbb{W}$, then the existential player wins the play, otherwise, the universal player wins the play. It may happen that a player has to play but there is no move available from the current position: in this case the player immediately loses.

Classical winning conditions Before describing more precisely the semantics of games, let us recall what are the classical winning conditions considered in this context.

Definition 2. *We define the following classical winning conditions:*

safety condition *The safety condition is* Safety $= \{0\}^\omega$ *over the unique color 0. Expressed differently, all plays are winning. Note that the color 0 fulfills the requirement of the epsilon property.*

Muller condition *Given a finite set of colors C, a Muller condition is a Boolean combination of winning conditions of the form "the color c appears infinitely often". In general, no color fulfills the requirement of the epsilon property, but it is always possible to add an extra fresh color ε. The resulting condition satisfies the epsilon property.*

Rabin condition *Given a number p, we define the Rabin condition* Rabin$_p \subseteq \{\{1,2,3\}^p\}^\omega$ *by $u \in$ Rabin$_p$ if there exists some $i \in 1,\ldots,p$ such that when projected on this component, 2 appears infinitely often in u, and 3 finitely often. Note that the constant vector $\mathbf{1}$ fulfills the epsilon property. The Rabin condition is a special case of Muller conditions.*

parity condition *Given a interval of integers $C = [i,j]$ (called priorities), a word $u = c_1 c_2 c_3 \cdots \in C^\omega$ belongs to* Parity$_C$ *if the largest color appearing infinitely often in u is even.*

Büchi condition *The Büchi condition* Buchi *is a parity condition over the restricted interval $[1,2]$ of priorities. A word belongs to* Buchi *if it contains infinitely many occurrences of 2.*

coBüchi condition *The coBüchi condition* coBuchi *is a parity condition over the restricted interval $[0,1]$ of priorities. A word belongs to* coBuchi *if it it has only finitely many occurrences of 1's.*

---

[2] In the literature, the players have many other names: 'Eve' and 'Adam', 'Eloise' and 'Abelard', 'Exist' and 'Forall', '0' and '1', or in specific contexts: 'Even' and 'Odd', 'Automaton' and 'Pathfinder', 'Duplicator' and 'Spoiler', ...

mean-payoff condition *Given a finite set $C \subseteq \mathbb{R}$, a word $u = c_1 c_2 c_3 \cdots \in C^\omega$ belongs to* meanpayoff$_C$ *if*

$$\liminf_{n \to \infty} \frac{c_1 + c_2 + \cdots + c_n}{n} \geqslant 0 \; .$$

There are many variants of this definition (such as replacing $\liminf$ *with* $\limsup$*), that all turn out to be equivalent on finite arenas.*

Strategies We describe now formally what it means to win a game. Let us take the point of view of the existential player. A strategy for the existential player is an object that describes how to play in every situation of the game that could be reached. It is a winning strategy if whenever these choices are respected during a play, the existential player wins this play. There are several ways one can define the notion of a strategy. Here we choose to describe a strategy as the set of partial plays that may be produced when it is used.

Definition 3. *A strategy s for the existential player s_E is a set of partial plays of the game that has the following properties:*

- *s_E is prefix-closed and non-empty,*
- *for all partial plays $\pi \in s_\mathrm{E}$ ending in some $v \in V_\mathrm{E}$, there exists exactly one partial play of length $|\pi| + 1$ in s_E that prolongs π,*
- *for all partial plays $\pi \in s_\mathrm{E}$ ending in some $v \in V_\mathrm{A}$, then all partial plays that prolong π of length $|\pi| + 1$ belong to s_E.*

A play is compatible with the strategy s_E if all its finite prefixes belong to s. A play is winning if it belongs to the winning condition $\mathbb{W}$. A game is won by the existential player if there exists a strategy for the existential player such that all plays compatible with it are won by the existential player. Such a strategy is called a winning strategy.

Symmetrically, a (winning) strategy for the universal player is a (winning) strategy for the existential player in the dual game. A game is won by the universal player if there exists a strategy for the universal player such that all infinite plays compatible with it are won by the universal player.

The idea behind this definition is that at any moment in the game, when following a strategy, a sequence of moves has already been played, yielding a partial play in the arena. The above definition guarantees that: 1. if a partial play belongs to the strategy, it is indeed reachable by a succession of moves that stay in the strategy, 2. if, while following the strategy, a partial play ends in a vertex owned by the existential player, there exists exactly one move that can be followed by the strategy at that moment, and 3. if, while following the strategy, a partial play ends in a vertex owned by the universal player, the strategy is able to face all possible choices of the opponent.

Remark 1. It is not possible that in a strategy defined in this way one reaches an existential position that would have no successor: indeed, 2. would not hold.

Remark 2. There are different ways to define a strategy in the literature. One is as a strategy tree: indeed one can see s_E as a set of nodes equipped with prefix ordering as the ancestor relation. Another way is to define a strategy as a partial map from paths to moves. All these definitions are equivalent. The literature also considers randomized strategies (in which the next move is chosen following a probability distribution): this is essential when the games are *concurrent* or *with partial information*, but not in the situation we consider in this paper.

Lemma 1 (at most one player wins). *It is not possible that both the existential player and the universal player win the same game.*

Of course, keeping the intuition of games in mind, one would expect also that one of the player wins. However, this is not necessarily the case. A game is called determined if either the existential or the universal player wins the game. The fact that a game is determined is referred to as its determinacy. A winning condition $\mathbb{W}$ is determined if all $\mathbb{W}$-games are determined. It happens that not all games are determined.

Theorem 1. *There exist winning conditions that are not determined (and it requires the axiom of choice to prove it).*

However, there are some situations in which games are determined. This is the case of finite duration games, of safety games, and more generally:

Theorem 2 (Martin's theorem of Borel determinacy [Mar75]). *Games with Borel winning conditions are determined.*

Defining the notion of Borel sets is beyond the scope of this paper. It suffices to know that this notion is sufficiently powerful for capturing a lot of natural winning conditions, and in particular all winning conditions in this paper are Borel; and thus determined.

2.2 Memory of strategies

A key insight in understanding a winning condition is to study the amount of memory required by winning strategies. To define the notion of memoryless strategies, we use an equivalent point of view on strategies, using strategy graphs.

Definition 4. *Given a C-arena A, an existential player strategy graph S_E, γ in A is a trimmed C-graph S_E together with a graph morphism γ from S_E to A such that for all vertices x in S_E,*

– *if $\gamma(x)$ is an existential position, then there exists exactly one edge of the form (x, c, y) in S_E,*
– *if $\gamma(x)$ is a universal position, then β induces a surjection between the edges originating from x in S_E and the moves originating from $\beta(x)$, i.e., for all moves of the form $(\beta(x), c, v)$, there exists an edge of the form (x, c, y) in S_E such that $\beta(y) = v$.*

The existential player strategy graph S_E, γ *is memoryless if* γ *is injective. In general the memory of the strategy is the maximal cardinality of* $\gamma^{-1}(v)$ *for* v *ranging over all positions in the arena. For* $\mathcal{G}$ *a* $\mathbb{W}$*-game with* $\mathbb{W} \subseteq C^\omega$*, an existential player strategy graph* S_E *is winning if the labels of all its paths issued from the root belong to* $\mathbb{W}$.

The (winning) universal player strategy graphs are defined as the (winning) existential player strategy graphs in the dual game.

The winning condition $\mathbb{W}$ *is memoryless for the existential player if, whenever the existential player wins in a* $\mathbb{W}$*-game, there is a memoryless winning existential player strategy graph. It is memoryless for the existential player over finite arenas if this holds for finite* $\mathbb{W}$*-games only. The dual notion is the one of memoryless for the universal player winning condition.*

Of course, as far as existence is concerned the two notions of strategy coincide:

Lemma 2. *There exists a winning existential player strategy graph if and only if there exists a winning strategy for the existential player.*

Proof. A strategy for the existential player s_E can be seen as a C-graph (in fact a tree) S_E of vertices s_E, of root ε, and with edges of the form $(\pi, a, \pi a)$ for all $\pi a \in s_E$. If the strategy s_E is winning, then the strategy graph S_E is also winning. Conversely, given an existential player strategy graph S_E, the set s_E of its paths starting from the root is itself a strategy for the existential player. Again, the winning property is preserved.   □

We list a number of important results stating that some winning conditions do not require memory.

Theorem 3 ([EJ91]). *The parity condition is memoryless for the existential player and for the universal player.*

Theorem 4 ([EM79, GKK88]). *The mean-payoff condition is memoryless for the existential player over finite arenas as well as for the universal player.*

Theorem 5 ([GH82]). *The Rabin condition is memoryless for the existential player, but not in general for the universal player.*

Theorem 6 ([McN93]). *Muller conditions are finite-memory for both players.*

Theorem 7 ([CFH14]). *Topologically closed conditions for which the residuals are totally ordered by inclusion are memoryless for the existential player.*

2.3   Automata

Definition 5 (automata over infinite words).   *Let* $\mathbb{W} \subseteq C^\omega$. *A (nondeterministic)* $\mathbb{W}$*-automaton* $\mathcal{A}$ *over the alphabet* A *is a* $(C \times A)$*-graph. The convention is to call states its vertices, and transitions its edges. The root vertex is called the initial state. The set* $\mathbb{W}$ *is called the accepting condition (whereas it* *is the winning condition for games). The automaton $\mathcal{A}_p$ is obtained from $\mathcal{A}$ by setting the state p to be initial.*

A run of the automaton $\mathcal{A}$ over $u \in A^\omega$ is an infinite path in $\mathcal{A}$ that starts in the initial state and projects on its A-component to u. A run is accepting if it projects on its C-component to a word $v \in \mathbb{W}$. The language accepted by $\mathcal{A}$ is the set $\mathcal{L}(\mathcal{A})$ of infinite words $u \in A^\omega$ such that there exists an accepting run of $\mathcal{A}$ on u.

An automaton is deterministic (resp. complete) if for all states p and all letters $a \in A$, there exists at most one (resp. at least one) transition of the form $(p, (a, c), q)$. If the winning condition is parity, this is a parity automaton. If the winning condition is safety, this is a safety automaton, and we do not mention the C-component since there is only one color. I.e., the transitions form a subset of $Q \times A \times Q$, and the notion coincides with the one of a A-graph. For this reason, we may refer to the language $\mathcal{L}(H)$ accepted by an A-graph H: this is the set of labelling words of infinite paths starting in the root vertex of H.

Note that here we use non-deterministic automata for simplicity. However, the notions developed in this paper can be adapted to alternating automata.

The notion of ω-regularity. It is not the purpose of this paper to describe the rich theory of automata over infinite words. It suffices to say that a robust concept of ω-regular language emerges. These are the languages that are equivalently defined by means of Büchi automata, parity automata, Rabin automata, Muller automata, deterministic parity automata, deterministic Rabin automata, deterministic Muller automata, as well as many other formalisms (regular expressions, monadic second-order logic, ω-semigroup, alternating automata, ...). However, safety automata and deterministic Büchi automata define a subclass of ω-regular languages.

Note that the mean-payoff condition does not fall in this category, and automata defined with this condition do not recognize ω-regular languages in general.

2.4   Automata for solving games

There is a long tradition of using automata for solving games. The general principle is to use automata as reductions, i.e. starting from a $\mathbb{V}$-game $\mathcal{G}$ and a $\mathbb{W}$-automaton $\mathcal{A}$ that accepts the language $\mathbb{V}$, we construct a $\mathbb{W}$-game $\mathcal{G} \times \mathcal{A}$ called the product game that combines the two, and which is expected to have the same winner: this means that to solve the $\mathbb{V}$-game $\mathcal{G}$, it is enough to solve the $\mathbb{W}$-game $\mathcal{G} \times \mathcal{A}$. We shall see below that, unfortunately, this expected property does not always hold (Remark 4). The automata that guarantee the correction of the construction are called good for games, originally introduced by Henzinger and Piterman [HP06].

We begin our description by making precise the notion of product game. Informally, the new game requires the players to play like in the original game, and after each step, the existential player is required to provide a transition in the automaton that carries the same label.

Definition 6. *Let $\mathcal{D}$ be an arena over colors C, with positions P and moves M. Let also $\mathcal{A}$ be a $\mathbb{W}$-automaton over the alphabet C with states Q and transitions Δ. We construct the product arena $\mathcal{D} \times \mathcal{A}$ as follows:*

- *The set of positions in the product game is $(P \uplus M) \times Q$.*
- *The initial position is $(\text{init}_{\mathcal{D}}, \text{init}_{\mathcal{A}})$, in which $\text{init}_{\mathcal{D}}$ is the initial position of $\mathcal{G}$, and $\text{init}_{\mathcal{A}}$ is the initial state of $\mathcal{A}$.*
- *The positions of the form $(x, p) \in P \times Q$ are called game positions and are owned by the owner of x in $\mathcal{G}$. There is a move, called a game move, of the form $((x, p), \varepsilon, ((x, c, y), p))$ for all moves $(x, c, y) \in M$.*
- *The positions of the form $((x, c, y), p) \in M \times Q$ are called automaton positions and are owned by the existential player. There is a move, called an automaton move, of the form $(((x, c, y), p), d, (y, q))$ for all transitions of the form $(p, (c, d), q)$ in $\mathcal{A}$.*

Note that every game move $((x, p), \varepsilon, ((x, c, y), p))$ of $\mathcal{G} \times \mathcal{A}$ can be transformed into a move (x, c, y) of $\mathcal{G}$, called its game projection. Similarly every automaton move $(((x, c, y), p), d, (y, q))$ can be turned into a transition $(p, (c, d), q)$ of the automaton $\mathcal{A}$ called its automaton projection. Hence, every play π of the product game can be projected into the pair of a play π' in $\mathcal{G}$ of label u (called the game projection), and an infinite run ρ of the automaton over u (called the automaton projection). The product game is the game over the product arena, using the winning condition of the automaton.

Lemma 3 (folklore[3]). *Let $\mathcal{G}$ be a $\mathbb{V}$-game, and $\mathcal{A}$ be a $\mathbb{W}$-automaton that accepts a language $L \subseteq \mathbb{V}$, then if the existential player wins $\mathcal{G} \times Q_{\mathcal{A}}$, she wins $\mathcal{G}$.*

Proof. Assume that the existential player wins the game $\mathcal{G} \times \mathcal{A}$ using a strategy s_{E}. This strategy can be turned into a strategy for the existential player s'_{E} in $\mathcal{G}$ by performing a game projection. It is routine to check that this is a valid strategy.

Let us show that this strategy s'_{E} is $\mathbb{V}$-winning, and hence conclude that the existential player wins the game $\mathcal{G}$. Indeed, let π' be a play compatible with s'_{E}, say labelled by u. This play π' has been obtained by game projection of a play π compatible with s_{E} in $\mathcal{G} \times \mathcal{A}$. The automaton projection ρ of π is a run of $\mathcal{A}$ over u, and is accepting since s_{E} is a winning strategy. Hence, u is accepted by $\mathcal{A}$ and as a consequence belongs to $\mathbb{V}$. We have proved that s_{E} is winning. $\square$

Corollary 1. *Let $\mathcal{G}$ be a $\mathbb{V}$-game, and $\mathcal{A}$ be a deterministic $\mathbb{W}$-automaton that accepts the language $\mathbb{V}$, then the games $\mathcal{G}$ and $\mathcal{G} \times \mathcal{A}$ have the same winner.*

Proof. We assume without loss of generality that $\mathcal{A}$ is deterministic and complete (note that this may require to slightly change the accepting condition, for instance in the case of safety). The results then follows from the application of Lemma 3 to the game $\mathcal{G}$ and its dual. $\square$

---

[3] This technique of reduction is in fact more general, since the automaton may not be a safety automaton. Its use can be traced back, for instance, to the work of Büchi and Landweber [BL69].

The consequence of the above lemma is that when we know how to solve W-games, and we have a deterministic W-automaton $\mathcal{A}$ for a language $\mathbb{V}$, then we can decide the winner of $\mathbb{V}$-games by performing the product of the game with the automaton, and deciding the winner of the resulting game. Good for games automata are automata that need not be deterministic, but for which this kind of arguments still works.

Definition 7 (good for games automata [HP06]). *Let $\mathbb{V}$ be a language, and $\mathcal{A}$ be a W-automaton. Then $\mathcal{A}$ is good for $\mathbb{V}$-games if for all $\mathbb{V}$-games $\mathcal{G}$, $\mathcal{G}$ and $\mathcal{G} \times \mathcal{A}$ have the same winner.*

Note that Lemma 1 says that deterministic automata are good for games automata.

Remark 3. It may seem strange, a priori, not to require in the definition that $\mathcal{L}(\mathcal{A}) = \mathbb{V}$. In fact, it holds anyway: if an automaton is good for $\mathbb{V}$-games, then it accepts the language $\mathbb{V}$. Indeed, let us assume that there exists a word $u \in \mathcal{L}(\mathcal{A}) \setminus \mathbb{V}$, then one can construct a game that has exactly one play, labelled u. This game is won by the universal player since $u \notin \mathbb{V}$, but the existential player wins $\mathcal{G} \times \mathcal{A}$. A contradiction. The same argument works if there is a word in $\mathbb{V} \setminus \mathcal{L}(\mathcal{A})$.

Examples of good for games automata can be found in [BKS17], together with a structural analysis of the extent to which they are non-deterministic.

Remark 4. We construct an automaton which is not good for games. The alphabet is $\{a, b\}$. The automaton $\mathcal{A}$ is a Büchi automaton: it has an initial state from which goes two ϵ-transitions: the first transition guesses that the word contains infinitely many a's, and the second transition guesses that the word contains infinitely many b's. Note that any infinite word contains either infinitely many a's or infinitely many b's, so the language $\mathbb{V}$ recognised by this automaton is the set of all words. However, this automaton requires a choice to be made at the very first step about which of the two alternatives hold. This makes it not good for games: indeed, consider a game $\mathcal{G}$ where the universal player picks any infinite word, letter by letter, and the winning condition is $\mathbb{V}$. It has only one position owned by the universal player. The existential player wins $\mathcal{G}$ because all plays are winning. However, the existential player loses $\mathcal{G} \times \mathcal{A}$, because in this game she has to declare at the first step whether there will be infinitely many a's or infinitely many b's, which the universal player can later contradict.

Let us conclude this part with Lemma 4, stating the possibility to compose good for games automata. We need before hand to defined the composition of automata.

Given $A \times B$-graph $\mathcal{A}$, and $B \times C$-graph $\mathcal{B}$, the composed graph $\mathcal{B} \circ \mathcal{A}$ has as states the product of the sets of states, as initial state the ordered pair of the initial states, and there is a transition $((p, q), (a, c), (p', q'))$ if there is a transition $(p, (a, b), p')$ in $\mathcal{A}$ and a transition $(q, (b, c), q')$. If $\mathcal{A}$ is in fact an automaton that uses the accepting condition $\mathbb{V}$, and $\mathcal{B}$ an automaton that uses the accepting condition $\mathbb{W}$, then the composed automaton $\mathcal{B} \circ \mathcal{A}$ uses has as underlying graph the composed graphs, and as accepting condition $\mathbb{W}$.

Lemma 4 (composition of good for games automata). *Let $\mathcal{A}$ be a good for games $\mathbb{W}$-automaton for the language $\mathbb{V}$, and $\mathcal{B}$ be good for games $\mathbb{V}$-automaton for the language L, then the composed automaton $\mathcal{A} \circ \mathcal{B}$ is a good for games $\mathbb{W}$-automaton for the language L.*

3   Efficiently solving games

From now on, graphs, games and automata are assumed to be finite.

We now present more recent material. We put forward the notion of good for n-games automata (good for small games) as a common explanation for the several recent algorithms for solving parity games 'efficiently'. After describing this notion in Section 3.1, we shall give more insight about it in the context of winning conditions that are memoryless for the existential player in Section 3.2

Much more can be said for parity games and good for small games safety automata: this will be the subject of Section 4.

3.1   Good for small games automata

We introduce the concept of (strongly) good for n-games automata (good for small games). The use of these automata is the same as for good for games automata, except that they are cannot be composed with any game, but only with small ones. In other words, a good for $(\mathbb{W}, n)$-game automaton yields a reduction for solving $\mathbb{W}$-games with at most n positions (Lemma 6). We shall see in Section 3.2 that as soon as the underlying winning condition is memoryless for the existential player, there are several characterisations for the smallest strongly good for n-games automata. It is good to keep in mind the definition of good for games automata (Definition 7) when reading the following one.

Definition 8. *Let $\mathbb{V}$ be a language, and $\mathcal{A}$ be a $\mathbb{W}$-automaton. Then $\mathcal{A}$ is good for $(\mathbb{V}, n)$-games if for all $\mathbb{V}$-games $\mathcal{G}$ with at most n positions, $\mathcal{G}$ and $\mathcal{G} \times \mathcal{A}$ have the same winner (we also write good for small games when there is no need for $\mathbb{V}$ and n to be explicit).*

It is strongly good for $(\mathbb{V}, n)$-games if it is good for $(\mathbb{V}, n)$-games and the language accepted by $\mathcal{A}$ is contained in $\mathbb{V}$.

Example 1 (automata that are good for small games). We have naturally the following chain of implications:

$$\text{good for games} \implies \text{strongly good for } n\text{-games} \implies \text{good for } n\text{-games}$$

The first implication is from Remark 3, and the second is by definition. Thus the first examples of automata that are strongly good for small games are the automata that are good for games.

Example 2. We consider the case of the coBüchi condition: recall that the set of colors is $\{0,1\}$ and the winning plays are the ones such that there ultimately contain only 0's. It can be shown that if the existential player wins in a coBüchi game with has at most n positions, then she also wins for the winning condition $L = (0^*(\varepsilon + 1))^n 0^\omega$, i.e., the words in which there is at most n occurrences of 1 (indeed, a winning memoryless strategy for the condition coBuchi cannot contain a 1 in a cycle, and hence cannot contain more than n occurrences of 1 in the same play; thus the same strategy is also winning in the same game with the new winning condition L). As a consequence, a deterministic safety automaton that accepts the language $L \subseteq$ coBuchi (the minimal one has $n + 1$ states) is good for (coBuchi, n)-games.

Mimicking Lemma 4 which states the closure under composition of good for games automata, we obtain the following variant for good for small games automata:

Lemma 5 (composition of good for small games automata). *Let $\mathcal{B}$ be a good for n-games $\mathbb{V}$-automaton for the language L with k states, and $\mathcal{A}$ be a good for kn-games $\mathbb{W}$-automaton for the language $\mathbb{V}$, then the composed automaton $\mathcal{A} \circ \mathcal{B}$ is a good for n-games $\mathbb{W}$-automaton for the language L.*

We also directly get an algorithm from such reductions.

Lemma 6. *Assume that there exists an algorithm for solving $\mathbb{W}$-games of size m in time $f(m)$. Let $\mathcal{G}$ be a $\mathbb{V}$-game with at most n positions and $\mathcal{A}$ be a good for $(\mathbb{V}, n)$-games $\mathbb{W}$-automaton of size k, there exists an algorithm for solving $\mathcal{G}$ of complexity $f(kn)$.*

Proof. Construct the game $\mathcal{G} \times \mathcal{A}$, and solve it.   □

The third quasipolynomial time algorithm for solving parity games due to Lehtinen [Leh18] can be phrased using good for small games automata (note that it is not originally described in this form).

Theorem 8 ([Leh18, BL19]). *Given positive integers n, d, there exists a parity automaton with $n^{(\log d + O(1))}$ states and $1 + \lfloor \log n \rfloor$ priorities which is strongly good for n-games.*

Theorem 8 combined with Lemma 6 yields a quasipolynomial time algorithm for solving parity games. Indeed, consider a parity game $\mathcal{G}$ with n positions and d priorities. Let $\mathcal{A}$ be the good for n-games automaton constructed by Theorem 8. The game $\mathcal{G} \times \mathcal{A}$ is a parity game equivalent to $\mathcal{G}$, which has $m = n^{(\log d + O(1))}$ states and $d' = 1 + \lfloor \log n \rfloor$ priorities. Solving this parity game with a simple algorithm (of complexity $O(m^{d'})$) yields an algorithm of quasipolynomial complexity:

$$O(m^{d'}) = O(n^{(\log d + O(1))d'}) = n^{O(\log(d) \log(n))}.$$

3.2   The case of memoryless winning conditions

In this section we fix a winning condition $\mathbb{W}$ which is memoryless for the existential player, and we establish several results characterising the smallest strongly good for small games automata in this case.

Our prime application is the case of parity conditions, that will be studied specifically in Section 4, but this part also applies to conditions such as mean-payoff or Rabin.

The goal is to establish the following theorem (the necessary definitions are introduced during the proof).

Theorem 9. *Let $\mathbb{W}$ be a winning condition which is memoryless for the existential player, then the following quantities coincide for all positive integers n:*

1. *the least number of states of a strongly $(\mathbb{W}, n)$-separating deterministic safety automaton,*
2. *the least number of states of a strongly good for $(\mathbb{W}, n)$-games safety automaton,*
3. *the least number of states of a strongly $(\mathbb{W}, n)$-separating safety automaton,*
4. *the least number of vertices of a $(\mathbb{W}, n)$-universal graph.*

The idea of separating automata[4] was introduced by Bojańczyk and Czerwiński [BC18] to reformulate the first quasipolynomial time algorithm [CJK+17]. Czerwiński, Daviaud, Fijalkow, Jurdziński, Lazić, and Parys [CDF+19] showed that the other two quasipolynomial time algorithms [JL17, Leh18] also can be understood as the construction of separating automata.

The proof of Theorem 9 spans over Sections 3.2 and 3.3. It it a consequence of Lemmas 7, 8, 11, and 12. We begin our proof of Theorem 9 by describing the notion of strongly separating automata.

Definition 9. *An automaton $\mathcal{A}$ is strongly $(\mathbb{W}, n)$-separating if*

$$\mathbb{W}|_n \subseteq \mathcal{L}(\mathcal{A}) \subseteq \mathbb{W} \ ,$$

in which $\mathbb{W}|_n$ is the union of all the languages accepted by safety automata with n states that accept sublanguages of $\mathbb{W}$.[5]

Lemma 7. *In the statement of Theorem 9, (1) $\implies$ (2) $\implies$ (3).*

Proof. Assume (1), i.e., there exists a strongly $(\mathbb{W}, n)$-separating deterministic safety automaton $\mathcal{A}$, then $\mathcal{L}(\mathcal{A}) \subseteq \mathbb{W}$. Let $\mathcal{G}$ be a $\mathbb{W}$-game with at most n positions. By Lemma 3, if the existential player wins $\mathcal{G} \times \mathcal{A}$, she wins the

---

[4] The definition used in [BC18] is not strictly equivalent to the one we use here: a separating automaton in [BC18] is a strongly separating automaton in our sense, but not conversely.

[5] Note that there is a natural, more symetric, notion of $(\mathbb{W}, n)$-separating automata in which the requested inclusions are $\mathbb{W}|_n \subseteq \mathcal{L}(\mathcal{A}) \subseteq \left(\mathbb{W}^{\complement} \big|_n \right)^{\complement}$. However, nothing is known about this notion.

game $\mathcal{G}$. Conversely, assume that the existential player wins $\mathcal{G}$, then, by assumption she has a winning memoryless strategy graph $S_E, \gamma \colon S_E \to \mathcal{G}$, i.e., $\mathcal{L}(S_E) \subseteq \mathbb{W}$ and γ is injective. By injectivity of γ, S_E has at most n vertices and hence $\mathcal{L}(S_E) \subseteq \mathbb{W}|_n \subseteq \mathcal{L}(\mathcal{A})$. As a consequence, for every (partial) play π compatible with S_E, there exists a (partial) run of $\mathcal{A}$ over the labels of π (call this property $\star$). We construct a new strategy for the existential player in $\mathcal{G} \times \mathcal{A}$ as follows: When the token is in a game position, the existential player plays as in S_E; When the token is in an automaton position, the existential player plays the only available move (indeed, the move exists by property $\star$, and is unique by the determinism assumption). Since this is a safety game, the new strategy is winning. Hence the existential player wins $\mathcal{G} \times \mathcal{A}$, proving that $\mathcal{A}$ is good for $(\mathbb{W}, n)$-games. Item 2 is established.

Assume now (2), i.e., that $\mathcal{A}$ is some strongly good for $(\mathbb{W}, n)$-games automaton. Then by definition $\mathcal{L}(\mathcal{A}) \subseteq \mathbb{W}$. Now consider some word u in $\mathbb{W}|_n$. By definition, there exists some safety automaton $\mathcal{B}$ with at most n states such that $u \in \mathcal{L}(\mathcal{B}) \subseteq \mathbb{W}$. This automaton can be seen as a $\mathbb{W}$-game $\mathcal{G}$ in which all positions are owned by the universal player. Since $\mathcal{L}(\mathcal{B}) \subseteq \mathbb{W}$, the existential player wins the game $\mathcal{G}$. Since furthermore $\mathcal{A}$ is good for $(\mathbb{W}, n)$-games, the existential player has a winning strategy S_E in $\mathcal{G} \times \mathcal{A}$. Assume now that the universal player is playing the letters of u in the game $\mathcal{G} \times \mathcal{A}$, then the winning strategy S_E constructs an accepting run of $\mathcal{A}$ on u. Thus $u \in \mathcal{L}(\mathcal{A})$, and Item 3 is established. $\qquad\square$

We continue our proof of Theorem 9 by introducing the notion of $(\mathbb{W}, n)$-universal graph.

Definition 10. *Given a winning condition $\mathbb{W} \subseteq C^\omega$ and a positive integer n, a C-graph U is $(\mathbb{W}, n)$-universal[6] if*

- $\mathcal{L}(U) \subseteq \mathbb{W}$, and
- *for all C-graphs H such that $\mathcal{L}(U) \subseteq \mathbb{W}$ and with at most n vertices, there is a weak graph morphism from H to U.*

We are now ready to prove one more implication of Theorem 9.

Lemma 8. *In the statement of Theorem 9, (4) $\implies$ (1)*

Proof. Assume that there is a $(\mathbb{W}, n)$-universal graph U. We show that U seen as an safety automaton is strongly good for $(\mathbb{W}, n)$-games. One part is straightforward: $\mathcal{L}(U) \subseteq \mathbb{W}$ is by assumption. For the other part, consider a $\mathbb{W}$-game $\mathcal{G}$ with at most n positions. Assume that the existential player wins $\mathcal{G}$, this means that there exists a winning memoryless strategy for the existential player $S_E, \gamma \colon S_E \to \mathcal{G}$ in $\mathcal{G}$. We then construct a strategy for the existential player S'_E that maintains the property that the only game positions in $\mathcal{G} \times U$ that are met in S'_E are of the form $(x, \gamma(x))$. This is done as follows: when a game position is encountered, the existential player plays like the strategy S_E, and when an automaton position is encountered, the existential player plays in order to follow γ. This is possible since γ is a weak graph morphism. $\qquad\square$

---

[6] Note that this is not the notion of (even weak) universality in categorical terms since U is not in general itself of size n.

3.3   Maximal graphs

In order to continue our proof of Theorem 9, more insight is needed: we have to understand what are the $\mathbb{W}$-maximal graphs. This is what we do now.

Definition 11. *A C-graph H is $\mathbb{W}$-maximal if $\mathcal{L}(H) \subseteq \mathbb{W}$ and if it is not possible to add a single edge to it without breaking this property, i.e., without producing an infinite path from the root vertex that does not belong to $\mathbb{W}$.*

Lemma 9. *For a winning condition $\mathbb{W} \subseteq C$ which is memoryless for the existential player, and H a $\mathbb{W}$-maximal graph, then the ε-edges in H form a transitive and total relation.*

Proof. Transitivity arises from the epsilon property of winning conditions (Definition 1): Consider three vertices x, y and z such that $\alpha = (x, \varepsilon, y)$ and $\beta = (y, \varepsilon, z)$ are edges of H. Let us add a new edge $\delta = (x, \varepsilon, y)$ yielding a new graph H'. Let us consider now any infinite path π in H' starting in the root (this path may contain finitely of infinitely many occurrences of δ, but not almost only δ's since $x \neq y$). Let π' be obtained from π by replacing each occurrence of δ by the sequence $\alpha\beta$. The resulting path π' belongs H, and thus its labelling belongs to $\mathbb{W}$. But since the labelings of π and π' agree after removing all the occurrences of ε, the epsilon property guarantees that the labelling of π belongs to $\mathbb{W}$. Since this holds for all choices of π, we obtain $\mathcal{L}(H') \subseteq \mathbb{W}$. Hence, by maximality, $\delta \in H$, which means that the ε-edges form a transitive relation.

Let us prove the totality. Let x and y be distinct vertices of H. We have to show that either $x \xrightarrow{\varepsilon} y$ or $y \xrightarrow{\varepsilon} x$. We can turn H into a game $\mathcal{G}$ as follows:

- all the vertices of H become positions that are owned by the universal player and we add a new position z owned by the existential player;
- all the edges of H that end in x or y become moves of $\mathcal{G}$ that now end in z,
- all the other edges of H become moves of $\mathcal{G}$ without change,
- and there are two new moves in $\mathcal{G}$, (z, ε, x) and (z, ε, y).

We claim first that the game $\mathcal{G}$ is won by the existential player. Let us construct a strategy s_E in $\mathcal{G}$ as follows. The only moment the existential player has a choice to make is when the play reaches the position z. This has to happen after a move of the form (t, a, z). This move originates either from an edge of the form (t, a, x), or from an edge of the form (t, a, y). In the first case the strategy s_E chooses the move (z, ε, x), and in the second case the move (z, ε, y). Let us consider a play π compatible with s_E, and let π' be obtained from π by replacing each occurrence of $(t, a, z)(z, \varepsilon, x)$ with (t, a, x) and each occurrence of $(t, a, z)(z, \varepsilon, y)$ with (t, a, y). The resulting π' is a path in H and hence its labeling belongs to $\mathbb{W}$. Since the labelings of π and π' are equivalent up to ε-letters, by the epsilon property, the labeling of π also belongs to $\mathbb{W}$. Hence the strategy s_E witnesses the victory of the existential player in $\mathcal{G}$. The claim is proved.

By assumption on W, this means that there exists a winning memory-less strategy for the existential player S_E in $\mathcal{G}$. In this strategy, either the existential player always chooses (z, ε, x), or she always chooses (z, ε, y). Up to symmetry, we can assume the first case. Let now H' be the graph H to which a new edge $\delta = (y, \varepsilon, x)$ has been added. We aim that $\mathcal{L}(H') \subseteq W$. Let π be an infinite path in H' starting from the root vertex. In this path, each occurrences of δ are preceded by an edge of the form (t, a, y). Thus, let π' be obtained from π by replacing each occurrence of a sequence of the form $(t, a, y)\delta$ by (t, a, y). The resulting path is a play compatible with S_E. Hence the labeling of π' belongs to W, and as a consequence, by the epsilon property, this is also the case for π. Since this holds for all choices of π, we obtain that $\mathcal{L}(H') \subseteq W$. Hence, by W-maximality assumption, (y, ε, x) is an edge of H.

Overall, the ε-edges form a total transitive relation. $\square$

Let $\leqslant_\varepsilon$ be the least relation closed under reflexivity and that extends the ε-edge relation.

Lemma 10. *For a winning condition W which is memoryless for the existential player, and H a W-maximal graph, then the following properties hold:*

- *The relation $\leqslant_\varepsilon$ is a total preorder.*
- *$x' \leqslant_\varepsilon x \xrightarrow{a}_H y \leqslant_\varepsilon y'$ implies $x' \xrightarrow{a}_H y'$, for all vertices x', x, y, y' and colors a.*
- *For all vertices p, q, $\mathcal{L}(H_p) \subseteq \mathcal{L}(H_q)$ if and only $q \leqslant_\varepsilon p$.*
- *for all vertices p, q and colors a, $a\mathcal{L}(H_q) \subseteq \mathcal{L}(H_p)$ if and only if $p \xrightarrow{a}_H q$.*

Proof. The first part is obvious from Lemma 9. For the second part, it is sufficient to prove that $x \xrightarrow{a} y \xrightarrow{\varepsilon} z$ implies $x \xrightarrow{a} y$ and that $x \xrightarrow{\varepsilon} y \xrightarrow{a} z$ implies $x \xrightarrow{a} y$. Both cases are are similar to the proof of transitivity in Lemma 9[7].

The two next items are almost the same. The difficult direction is to assume the language inclusion, and deduce the existence of an edge (left to right). Let us assume for an instant that H would be a finite word automaton, with all its states accepting. Then it is an obvious induction to show that if $a\mathcal{L}(H_q) \subseteq \mathcal{L}(H_p)$ (as languages of finite words), it is safe to add an ε-transitions from q to p without changing the language. The two above items are then obtained by limit passing (this is possible because the safety condition is topologically closed). $\square$

We are now ready to provide the missing proofs for Theorem 9: from (3) to (4), and from (3) to (1). Both implications arise from Lemma 9.

Lemma 11. *In the statement of Theorem 9, (3) $\implies$ (4).*

---

[7] This arises in fact from a more general simple phenomenon: if the sequence ab is 'indistinguishable in any context' from c (meaning that if one substitutes simultaneously infinitely many occurrences of ab with occurrences of c one does not change the membership to W), then $x \xrightarrow{a} y \xrightarrow{b} z$ implies $x \xrightarrow{c} z$.

Proof. Let us start from a strongly $(\mathbb{W}, n)$-separating safety automaton $\mathcal{A}$. Without loss of generality, we can assume it is $\mathbb{W}$-maximal. We claim that it is $(\mathbb{W}, n)$-universal.

Let us define first for all languages $K \subseteq C^\omega$, its closure

$$\overline{K} = \bigcap_{\mathcal{L}(\mathcal{A}_s) \supseteq K} \mathcal{L}(\mathcal{A}_s)$$

(in case of an empty intersection, we assume C^ω). This is a closure operator: $K \subseteq K'$ implies $\overline{K} \subseteq \overline{K'}$, $K \subseteq \overline{K}$, and $\overline{\overline{K}} = \overline{K}$. Futhermore, $a\overline{K} \subseteq \overline{aK}$, for all letters $a \in C$. Let now H be a trimmed graph with at most n vertices such that $\mathcal{L}(H) \subseteq \mathbb{W}$. We have $\mathcal{L}(H) \subseteq \mathbb{W}|_n$ by definition of $\mathbb{W}|_n$.

We claim that for each vertex x of H, there is a state $\alpha(x)$ of $\mathcal{A}$ such that

$$\mathcal{L}(\mathcal{A}_{\alpha(x)}) = \overline{\mathcal{L}(Hx)} .$$

Indeed, note first that, since H is trimmed, there exists some word u such that $\mathrm{root}_H \xrightarrow{u} x$. Hence, using the fact that $\mathcal{A}$ is strongly $(\mathbb{W}, n)$-separating, we get that for all $v \in \mathcal{L}(Hx)$, $uv \in \mathcal{L}(H) \subseteq \mathbb{W}|_n \subseteq \mathcal{L}(\mathcal{A})$. Let $\beta(v)$ be the state assumed after reading u by a run of $\mathcal{A}$ accepting uv. It is such that $v \in \mathcal{L}(\mathcal{A}_{\beta(v)})$. Since $\mathcal{A}$ is finite and its states are totally ordered under inclusion of residuals (Lemma 10), this means that there exists a state $\alpha(x)$ (namely the maximum over all the $\beta(w)$ for $w \in \mathcal{L}(Hx)$) such that $\mathcal{L}(\mathcal{A}_{\alpha(x)}) = \overline{\mathcal{L}(Hx)}$.

Let us show that α is a weak graph morphism[8] from H to $\mathcal{A}$. Consider some edge (x, a, y) of H. We have $a\mathcal{L}(Hy) \subseteq \mathcal{L}(Hx)$. Hence

$$a\mathcal{L}(\mathcal{A}_{\alpha(y)}) = a\overline{\mathcal{L}(Hy)} \subseteq \overline{a\mathcal{L}(Hy)} \subseteq \overline{\mathcal{L}(Hx)} = \mathcal{L}(\mathcal{A}_{\alpha(x)}) ,$$

which implies by Lemma 10 that $\alpha(x) \xrightarrow{a}_{\mathcal{A}} \alpha(y)$. Let now $\mathrm{root}_H \xrightarrow{a}_H x$ be some edge. By hypothesis, we have

$$a\mathcal{L}(Hx) \subseteq \mathcal{L}(H) \subseteq \mathbb{W}|_n \subseteq \mathcal{L}(\mathcal{A}) .$$

Thus $\mathcal{L}(\mathcal{A}_{\alpha(x)}) = \overline{a\mathcal{L}(Hx)} \subseteq \overline{\mathcal{L}(\mathcal{A})} = \mathcal{L}(\mathcal{A}_{\mathrm{root}_{\mathcal{A}}})$. We obtain $\mathrm{root}_{\mathcal{A}} \xrightarrow{a}_{\mathcal{A}} \alpha(x)$ by Lemma 10. Hence, α is a weak graph morphism.

Since this holds for all choices of H, we have proved that $\mathcal{A}$ is a $(\mathbb{W}, n)$-universal graph. $\qquad\qquad\square$

Lemma 12. *In the statement of Theorem 9, (3) $\implies$ (1).*

Proof. Let us start from a strongly $(\mathbb{W}, n)$-separating safety automaton $\mathcal{A}$. Without loss of generality, we can assume it is maximal. Thus Lemma 10 holds.

---

[8] Note that in general that α is not a (non-weak) graph morphism, even for conditions like parity. Even more, such a graph morphism does not exist in general.

We now construct a deterministic safety automaton $\mathcal{D}$.

- the states of $\mathcal{D}$ are the same as the states of $\mathcal{A}$,
- the initial state of $\mathcal{D}$ is the initial state of $\mathcal{A}$,
- given a state $p \in \Delta_{\mathcal{D}}$ and a letter a, a transition of the form (p, a, q) exists if and only if there is some transition of the form (p, a, r) in $\mathcal{A}$, and q is chosen to be the least state r with this property.

We have to show that this deterministic safety automaton is strongly $(\mathbb{W}, n)$-separating. Note first that by definition $\mathcal{D}$ is obtained from $\mathcal{A}$ by removing transitions. Hence $\mathcal{L}(\mathcal{D}) \subseteq \mathcal{L}(\mathcal{A}) \subseteq \mathbb{W}$. Consider now some $u \in \mathbb{W}|_n$. By assumption, $u \in \mathcal{L}(\mathcal{A})$. Let $\rho = (p_0, u_1, p_1)(p_1, u_2, p_2) \cdots$ be the corresponding accepting run of $\mathcal{A}$. We construct by induction a (the) run of $\mathcal{D}$ $(q_0, u_1, q_1)(q_1, u_2, q_2) \cdots$ in such a way that $q_i \leqslant_{\varepsilon} p_i$. For the initial state, $p_0 = q_0$. Assume the run up to $q_i \leqslant_{\varepsilon} p_i$ has been constructed. By Lemma 10, (q_i, u_{i+1}, p_{i+1}) is a transition of $\mathcal{A}$. Hence the least r such that (q_i, u_{i+1}, r) is a transition of $\mathcal{A}$ does exist, and is $\leqslant_{\varepsilon} p_{i+1}$. Let us call it q_{i+1}; we indeed have that (q_i, u_{i+1}, q_{i+1}) is a transition of $\mathcal{D}$. Hence, u is accepted by $\mathcal{D}$. Thus $\mathbb{W}|_n \subseteq \mathcal{L}(\mathcal{D})$.

Overall $\mathcal{D}$ is a strongly $(\mathbb{W}, n)$-separating deterministic safety automaton that has at most as many states as $\mathcal{A}$. $\square$

4 The case of parity conditions

We have seen above some general results on the notion of universal graphs, separating automata, and automata that are good for small games. In particular, we have seen Theorem 9 showing the equivalence of these objects for memoryless for the existential player winning conditions.

We are paying now a closer attention to the particular case of the parity condition. The technical developments that follow give an alternative proof of the equivalence results proved in [CDF+19] between strongly separating automata and universal trees.

4.1 Parity and cycles

We begin with a first classical lemma, which reduces the questions of satisfying a parity condition to checking the parity of cycles.

In a directed graph labelled by priorities, an even cycle is a cycle (all cycles are directed) such that the maximal priority occurring in it is even. Otherwise, it is an odd cycle. As usual, an elementary cycle is a cycle that does not meet twice the same vertex.

Lemma 13. *For a $[i, j]$-graph H that has all its vertices reachable from the root, the following properties are equivalent:*

- $\mathcal{L}(H) \subseteq \text{Parity}_{[i,j]}$,
- *having all its cycles even,*
- *having all its elementary cycles even.*

Proof. Clearly, since all vertices are reachable, $\mathcal{L}(H) \subseteq \mathbb{W}$ implies that all the cycles are even. Also, if all cycles are even, then all elementary cycles also are. Finally assume that all the elementary cycles are even. Then we can consider H as a game, in which every positions is owned by the universal player. Assume that some infinite path from the root would not satisfy $\text{Parity}_{[i,j]}$, then this path would be a winning strategy for the universal player in this game. Since $\text{Parity}_{[i,j]}$ is a winning condition memoryless for the universal player, this means that the universal player has a winning memoryless strategy. But this winning memoryless strategy is nothing but a lasso, and thus contains an elementary cycle of maximal odd priority.   □

4.2   The shape and size of universal graphs for parity games

We continue with a fixed d, and we consider parity conditions using priorities in $[0, 2d]$. More precisely, we relate the size of universal graphs for the parity condition with priorities $[0, 2d]$ to universal d-trees as defined now:

Definition 12. *A d-tree t is a balanced, unranked, ordered tree of height d (the root does not count: all branches contain exactly $d+1$ nodes). The order between nodes of same level is denoted $\leqslant_t$. Given a leaf x, and $i = 0 \ldots i$, we denote $\text{anc}_i^t(t)$ the ancestor at depth i of x (0 is the root, d is x).*

The d-tree t is n-universal if for all d-trees s with at most n nodes, there is a d-tree embedding of s into t, in which a d-tree embedding is an injective mapping from nodes of s to nodes of t that preserves the height of nodes, the ancestor relation, and the order of nodes. Said differently, s is obtained from t by pruning some subtrees (while keeping the structure of a d-tree).

Definition 13.   *Given a d-tree t, $\text{Graph}(t)$ is a $[0, 2d]$-graph with the following characteristics:*

- *the vertices are the leaves of t,*
- *for $0 \leqslant i \leqslant d$, $x \xrightarrow{2(d-i)}_{\text{Graph}(t)} y$ if $\text{anc}_i^t(x) \leqslant_t \text{anc}_i^t(y)$,*
- *for $0 < i \leqslant d$, $x \xrightarrow{2(d-i)+1}_{\text{Graph}(t)} y$ if $\text{anc}_i^t(x) < \text{anc}_i^t(y)$.*

Lemma 14.   *For all d-trees t, $\mathcal{L}(\text{Graph}(t)) \subseteq \text{Parity}_{[0,2d]}$.*

Proof. Using Lemma 13, it is sufficient to prove that all cycle in $\text{Graph}(t)$ are even. Thus, let us consider a cycle ρ. Assume that the highest priority occurring in α is $2(d-i)+1$. Note then that for all edges $\alpha = (x, k, y)$ occurring in ρ:

- $\text{anc}_i^t(x) \leqslant_t \text{anc}_i^t(y)$ since $k \leqslant i+1$,
- if $k = 2(d-i)+1$, $\text{anc}_i^t(x) < \text{anc}_i^t(y)$.

As a consequence, the first and last vertex of α cannot have the same ancestor at level i, and thus are different.   □

Below, we develop sufficient results for establishing:

Theorem 10 ([CF18]). *For all positive integers d, n, the two following quantities are equal:*

- *the smallest number of leaves of an n-universal d-tree, and*
- *the smallest number of vertices of a $(\mathtt{Parity}_{[0,2d]}, n)$-universal graph.*

Proof. We shall see below (Definition 14) a construction $\mathtt{Tree}$ that maps all $\mathtt{Parity}_{[0,2d]}$-maximal graphs G to a d-tree $\mathtt{Tree}(G)$ of smaller or same size. Corollary 4 establishes that this construction is in some sense the converse of $\mathtt{Tree}$ (in fact they form an adjunction). and that this correspondence preserves the notions of universality. This proves the above result: Given a n-universal d-tree t, then, by Corollary 4, $\mathtt{Graph}(t)$ is a $(\mathtt{Parity}_{[0,2d]}, n)$-universal graph that has as many vertices as leaves of graphs. Conversely, consider a $(\mathtt{Parity}_{[0,2d]}, n)$-universal graph G. One can add to it edges until it becomes a $\mathtt{Parity}_{[0,2d]}$-maximal graph G' with as many vertices. Then, by Corollary 4, $\mathtt{Tree}(G')$ is an n-universal d-tree that has as much or less leaves than vertices of G'. $\qquad\square$

Example 3. The complete d-tree t of degree n (that has n^d leaves) is n-universal. The $[0, 2d]$-graph $\mathtt{Graph}(t)$ obtained in this way is used in the small progress measure algorithm [Jur00].

However, there exists n-universal d-trees that are much smaller than in the above example. The next theorem provides an upper and a lower bound.

Theorem 11 ([Fij18, CDF+19]). *Given positive integers n, d,*

- *there exists an n-universal d-tree with*

$$n \cdot \binom{\lceil \log(n) \rceil + d - 1}{\lceil \log(n) \rceil}$$

leaves.
- *all n-universal d-trees have at least*

$$\binom{\lfloor \log(n) \rfloor + d - 1}{\lfloor \log(n) \rfloor}$$

leaves.

Corollary 2. *The complexity of solving $\mathtt{Parity}_{[0,d]}$-games with at most n-vertices is*

$$O\left(mn \log(n) \log(d) \cdot \binom{\lceil \log(n) \rceil + d/2 - 1}{\lceil \log(n) \rceil} \right).$$

and no algorithm based on good for small safety games can be faster than quasipolynomial time.

Maximal universal graphs for the parity condition We shall now analyse in detail the shape of $\mathtt{Parity}_{[0,2d]}$-maximal graphs. This analysis culminates with the precise description of such graphs in Lemma 19, that essentially establishes a bijection with graphs of the form $\mathtt{Graph}(t)$ (Corollary 4).

Let us note that, since the parity condition is memoryless for the existential player, using Lemma 10, and the fact that the parity condition is unchanged by modifying finite prefixes, we can always assume that the root vertex is the minimal one for the $\leqslant_\varepsilon$ ordering. Thus, from now, we do not have to pay attention to the root, in particular in weak graph morphisms. Thus, from now, we just mention the term morphism for weak graph morphisms.

Let us recall preference ordering $\sqsubseteq$ between the non-negative integers is defined as follows:

$$\cdots \sqsubseteq 2d+1 \sqsubseteq 2d-1 \sqsubseteq \cdots \sqsubseteq 3 \sqsubseteq 1 \sqsubseteq 0 \sqsubseteq 2 \sqsubseteq \cdots \sqsubseteq 2d-2 \sqsubseteq 2d \sqsubseteq \cdots$$

Fact 1. *Let $k \sqsubseteq \ell$ and u, v sequences of priorities. If the maximal priority occurring in ukv is even, then the maximal priority occurring in $u\ell v$ is also even.*

Lemma 15. *Let G be a $\mathtt{Parity}_{[0,2d]}$-maximal graph and $k \sqsubseteq \ell$ be priorities in $[0,2d]$. For all vertices x, y of G, $x \xrightarrow{k}_G y$ implies $x \xrightarrow{\ell}_G y$.*

Proof. Let us add (x, ℓ, y) to G. Let $u(x, \ell, y)v$ be some elementary cycle of the new graph involving the new edge (x, ℓ, y). By Lemma 13, $u(x, k, y)v$ is an even cycle in the original graph. Hence, by Fact 1, $u(x, \ell, y)v$ is also an even cycle. Thus, by Lemma 13, G with the newly added edge also satisfies $\mathcal{L}(G) \subseteq \mathtt{Parity}_{[0,2d]}$. Using the maximality assumption for G, we obtain that (x, ℓ, y) was already present in G. $\qquad\square$

Lemma 16. *Let G be a $\mathtt{Parity}_{[0,2d]}$-maximal graph. For all vertices x, y, z of G, if $x \xrightarrow{k}_G y$ and $y \xrightarrow{\ell}_G z$, then $y \xrightarrow{\max(k,\ell)}_G z$.*

Proof. Let us add $(x, \max(k, \ell), z)$ to G. Let $u(x, \max(k, \ell), z)v$ be an elementary cycle in the new graph. By Lemma 13, $u(x, k, y)(y, \ell, z)v$, being a cycle of G, has to be even. Since, furthermore, the maximal priority that occurs in $u(x, k, y)(y, \ell, z)v$ is the same as the maximal one in $u(x, \max(k, \ell), z)v$, the cycle $u(x, \max(k, \ell), z)v$ is also even. Using the maximality assumption of G, we obtain that $(x, \max(k, \ell), z)$ was already present in G. $\qquad\square$

Lemma 17. *Let G be a $\mathtt{Parity}_{[0,2d]}$-maximal graph, and x, y be vertices, then $x \xrightarrow{0}_G x$, and $x \xrightarrow{2d}_G y$.*

Proof. For $x \xrightarrow{0}_G x$, it is sufficient to notice that adding the edge $(x, 0, x)$, if it was not present, simply creates one new elementary cycle to G, namely $(x, 0, x)$. Since it is an even cycle, by Lemma 13, the new graph also satisfies $\mathcal{L}(G) \subseteq \mathtt{Parity}_{[0,2d]}$. Hence, by maximality assumption, the edge was already present in G before.

Consider the graph G with an extra edge $(x, 2d, y)$ added. Consider now an elementary cycle that contains $(x, 2d, y)$, i.e., of the form $u(x, 2d, y)v$. Its maximal priority is $2d$, and thus even. Hence by Lemma 13 and maximality assumption, the edge was already present in G. □

Lemma 18. *Let G be a $\mathtt{Parity}_{[0,2d]}$-maximal graph and $k = 0, 2, \ldots, 2d - 2$. For all vertices x, y, $x \xrightarrow{k+1}_G y$ holds if and only if $y \xrightarrow{k}_G x$ does not hold.*

Proof. Assume first that $y \xrightarrow{k+1}_G x$ and $x \xrightarrow{k}_G y$ both holds. Then $y \xrightarrow{k+1}_G x \xrightarrow{k}_G y$ is an odd cycle contradicting Lemma 13.

Conversely, assume that adding the edge $x \xrightarrow{k+1}_G y$ would break the property $\mathcal{L}(G) \subseteq \mathtt{Parity}_{[0,2d]}$. This means that there is an elementary cycle of the form $u(x, k+1, y)v$ which is odd. Let ℓ be the maximal priority in vu. If $\ell \geqslant k+1$, then ℓ is odd, and thus $\ell \sqsubseteq k$, and we obtain $y \xrightarrow{k}_G x$ by Lemma 15. Otherwise, $\ell \leqslant k$, and again $\ell \sqsubseteq k$. Once more $y \xrightarrow{k}_G x$ holds by Lemma 15. □

Lemma 19. *A $[0, 2d]$-graph G is a $\mathtt{Parity}_{[0,2d]}$-maximal graph if and only if all the following properties hold:*

1. $\xrightarrow{k}_G$ *is a total preorder for all $k = 0, 2, \ldots, 2d$,*
2. $\xrightarrow{k}_G \subseteq \xrightarrow{k+2}_G$ *for all $k = 0, 2, \ldots, 2d - 2$,*
3. $\xrightarrow{2d}_G$ *is the total equivalence relation,*
4. $\xrightarrow{k+1}_G = (\xleftarrow{k}_G)^{\complement}$ *for all $k = 0, 2, \ldots, 2d - 2$.*[9]

Proof. First direction. Assume first that G is a $\mathtt{Parity}_{[0,2d]}$-maximal graph.

(1) Let $k = 0, 2, \ldots, 2d$; $\xrightarrow{k}_G$ is transitive by Lemma 16. Furthermore, by Lemma 17, $x \xrightarrow{0}_G x$ for all vertices x, and thus by Lemma 15, since $0 \sqsubseteq k$, $x \xrightarrow{k}_G x$. Hence $\xrightarrow{k}_G$ is also reflexive and hence a preorder. Consider now another vertex y. By Lemma 18, either $x \xrightarrow{k}_G y$ or $y \xrightarrow{k+1}_G x$. But by Lemma 15, $y \xrightarrow{k+1}_G x$ implies $y \xrightarrow{k}_G x$. Hence either $x \xrightarrow{k}_G y$ or $y \xrightarrow{k}_G k$. Thus $\xrightarrow{k}_G$ is a total preorder.

(2) For $k = 0, 2, \ldots, 2d - 2$, since $k \sqsubseteq k + 2$, by Lemma 15, $\xrightarrow{k}_G \subseteq \xrightarrow{k+2}_G$.

(3) $\xrightarrow{2d}_G$ is the maximal relation by Lemma 15.

(4) For $k = 0, 2, \ldots, 2d - 2$ and x, y, we know that $y \xrightarrow{k}_G x$ holds if and only if $x \xrightarrow{k+1}_G y$ does not. This shows $\xrightarrow{k+1}_G = (\xleftarrow{k}_G)^{\complement}$.

Second direction. Assume now that G satisfies the conditions (1)-(4). Let us first show that $\mathcal{L}(G) \subseteq \mathtt{Parity}_{[0,2d]}$. For the sake of contradiction, consider an elementary cycle that would be odd. It can be written as $u(x, k, y)v$ with a

---

[9] Note that this also means, since $\xrightarrow{k}_G$ is a total preorder, that $\xrightarrow{k+1}_G = \xrightarrow{k}_G \setminus \xleftarrow{k}_G$.

maximal odd priority k. Note first that $\xrightarrow{\ell} \subseteq \xrightarrow{k-1}$ for all $\ell \leqslant k$: indeed, by (2), this is true if ℓ is even, and by (1) and (4), $\xrightarrow{j} \subseteq \xrightarrow{j-1}$ for all j odd. Also $\xrightarrow{k}_G$ is the strict version of the preorder $\xrightarrow{k-1}_G$. Hence, the path $u(x,k,y)v$ has to strictly advance with respect to the preorder $\xrightarrow{k-1}_G$: it cannot be a cycle.

Assume now that an edge (x,k,y) is not present in G. If k is even, since (x,k,y) is not present, by (4) this means that $(y,k+1,x)$ is present. Hence, adding the edge (x,k,y) would create the odd cycle $(x,k,y)(y,k+1,x)$. If k is odd, since (x,k,y) is not present, by (4) this means that $(y,k-1,x)$ is present. Hence, adding the edge (x,k,y) would create the odd cycle $(x,k,y)(y,k-1,x)$. Hence G is $\texttt{Parity}_{[0,2d]}$-maximal.   □

Corollary 3. *Given a morphism α from a $\texttt{Parity}_{[0,2d]}$-maximal graph H to a $\texttt{Parity}_{[0,2d]}$-maximal graph G, then $x \xrightarrow{k}_H y$ if and only if $\alpha(x) \xrightarrow{k}_G \alpha(y)$, for all vertices x,y of H and integers k in $[0,2d]$. Furthermore, if α is surjective, then every map β from G to H, such that $\alpha \circ \beta$ is the identity on G is an injective morphism.*

Proof. First part. From left to right, this is the definition of a morphism. The other direction is by (4) of Lemma 19: if $\alpha(x) \xrightarrow{k}_G \alpha(y)$ and k is odd, then $\alpha(x) \xrightarrow{k-1}_G \alpha(y)$ does not hold by (4), thus $x \xrightarrow{k-1}_H y$ does not hold by morphism, thus $x \xrightarrow{k}_H y$ holds by (4) again. The case of k even is similar (using $k+1$ this time).

For the second part, since $\alpha \circ \beta$ is the identity, β has to be injective. It is a morphism by the first part.   □

The next definition, allowing to go from graphs to trees is shown meaningful by Lemma 19:

Definition 14. *Let G be a $\texttt{Parity}_{[0,2d]}$-maximal graph. The d-tree $\texttt{Tree}(G)$ is constructed as follows:*

- *the nodes of level $i = 0, \ldots, d$ are the pairs (i, C) for C ranging over the equivalence classes of $\xrightarrow{2(d-i)}_G \cap \xleftarrow{2(d-i)}_G$,*
- *a node (i, C) is an ancestor of (j, D) if $i \leqslant j$ and $D \subseteq C$,*
- *$(i, C) \leqslant_{\texttt{Tree}(G)} (i, D)$ if $x \xrightarrow{2(d-i)}_G x'$ for all $x \in C$ and $x' \in C'$.*

We shall see that $\texttt{Graph}$ and $\texttt{Tree}$ are almost the inverse one of the other. This is already transparent in the following lemma, which is just a reformulation of the definitions.

Lemma 20. *Let q be the quotient map from vertices of G to leaves of $\texttt{Tree}(G)$ that maps each vertex to its $(\xrightarrow{0}_G \cap \xleftarrow{0}_G)$-equivalence class. It has the following property for all vertices x, y of G:*

$$x \xrightarrow{2(d-i)}_G y \quad \text{if and only if} \quad \text{anc}_i^{\text{Tree}(G)}(q(x)) \leqslant_{\text{Tree}(G)} \text{anc}_i^{\text{Tree}(G)}(q(y)) \,,$$

$$\text{and} \quad x \xrightarrow{2(d-i)+1}_G y \quad \text{if and only if} \quad \text{anc}_i^{\text{Tree}(G)}(q(x)) < [\text{Tree}(G)]\text{anc}_i^{\text{Tree}(G)}(q(y)) \,.$$

The identity maps the vertices of Graph(t) *to the leaves of* t, *and has the property that for all vertices* x, y:

$$x \xrightarrow{2(d-i)}_{\text{Graph}(t)} y \quad \text{if and only if} \quad \text{anc}_i^t(x) \leqslant_t \text{anc}_i^t(y) \,,$$

$$\text{and} \quad x \xrightarrow{2(d-i)+1}_{\text{Graph}(t)} y \quad \text{if and only if} \quad \text{anc}_i^t(x) < \text{anc}_i^t(y) \,.$$

Corollary 4. [10] *For all* Parity$_{[0,2d]}$*-maximal graphs* G, H, *all* d*-trees* t, *and all positive integers* n,

- Graph(Tree(G)) *is a quotient and an induced subgraph of* G,
- Tree(Graph(t)) *is isomorphic to* t,
- *there is a morphism from* H *to* Graph(t) *if and only if there is a tree embedding from* Tree(H) *to* t,
- Tree(G) *is* n*-universal if and only if* G *is* (Parity$_{[0,2d]}, n$)*-universal,*
- Graph(t) *is* (Parity$_{[0,2d]}, n$)*-universal if and only if* t *is* n*-universal.*

Proof. Let q be the quotient from Lemma 20. It can be seen as a surjective map from vertices of Graph(Tree(G)) to G. By Lemma 20 it is a morphism. By Corollary 3, Graph(Tree(G)) is also an induced subgraph of G.

The leaves of Tree(Graph(t)) are the singletons consisting of leaves of t. Hence, there is a bijective map from leaves of Tree(Graph(t)) to leaves of t that sends $\{\ell\}$ to ℓ. By Lemma 20, this is a morphism, and by Corollary 3 an isomorphism.

For the third item, assume first that there is a morphism from H to Graph(t). By the first point, there is an injective morphism from Graph(Tree(H)) to H. By composition, we obtain a morphism from Graph(Tree(H)) to Graph(t). By Lemma 20, it is also a tree embedding from Tree(H) to t. Conversely, assume that there exists an embedding from Tree(H) to t. It can be raised by Lemma 20 to a morphism from Graph(Tree(H)) to Graph(t). By the first point, there is a morphism from H to Graph(Tree(H)). By composition, we get a morphism from H to Graph(t).

The two last items are obvious from the one just before. $\square$

Acknowledgements. We thank Pierre Ohlmann for many interesting discussions, and Marcin Jurdziński for his comments on an earlier draft of this paper.

---

[10] The careful reader will recognize Tree and Graph as left and right adjoints.

References

1. Boja´nczyk, M., Czerwi´nski, W.: An automata toolbox, February 2018. https://www.mimuw.edu.pl/~bojan/papers/toolbox-reduced-feb6.pdf

2. Boker, U., Kupferman, O., Skrzypczak, M.: How deterministic are good-for-games automata? In: FSTTCS, pp. 18:1–18:14 (2017)

3. B¨uchi, J.R., Landweber, L.H.: Definability in the monadic second-order theory of successor. J. Symbolic Logic **34**(2), 166–170 (1969)

4. Boker, U., Lehtinen, K.: Register games. Logical Methods Comput. Sci.(Submitted, 2019)

5. Czerwi´nski, W., Daviaud, L., Fijalkow, N., Jurdzi´nski, M., Lazi´c, R., Parys, P.: Universal trees grow inside separating automata: quasi-polynomial lower bounds for parity games. In: SODA, pp. 2333–2349 (2019)

6. Colcombet, T., Fijalkow, N.: Parity games and universal graphs. CoRR, abs/1810.05106 (2018)

7. Colcombet, T., Fijalkow, N., Horn, F.: Playing safe. In: FSTTCS, pp. 379–390 (2014)

8. Calude, C.S., Jain, S., Khoussainov, B., Li, W., Stephan, F.: Deciding parity games in quasipolynomial time. In: STOC, pp. 252–263 (2017)

9. Emerson, E.A., Jutla, C.S.: Tree automata, mu-calculus and determinacy (extended abstract). In: FOCS, pp. 368–377 (1991)

10. Ehrenfeucht, A., Mycielski, J.: Positional strategies for mean payoff games. Int. J. Game Theory **109**(8), 109–113 (1979)

11. Fijalkow, N., Gawrychowski, P., Ohlmann, P.: The complexity of mean payoff games using universal graphs. CoRR, abs/1812.07072 (2018) Fijalkow, N.: An optimal value iteration algorithm for parity games. CoRR, abs/1801.09618 (2018)

12. Gurevich, Y., Harrington, L.: Trees, automata, and games. In: STOC, pp. 60–65 (1982)

13. Gurvich, V.A., Karzanov, A.V., Khachiyan, L.G.: Cyclic games and an algorithm to find minimax cycle means in directed graphs. USSR Comput. Math. Math. Phys. **28**, 85–91 (1988)

14. Henzinger, T.A., Piterman, N.: Solving games without determinization. In:´Esik, Z. (ed.) CSL 2006. LNCS, vol. 4207, pp. 395–410. Springer, Heidelberg (2006). https://doi.org/10.1007/11874683_26

15. Jurdzi´nski, M., Lazi´c, R.: Succinct progress measures for solving parity games. In: LICS, pp. 1–9 (2017)

16. Jurdzi´nski, M.: Small progress measures for solving parity games. In: Reichel, H., Tison, S. (eds.) STACS 2000. LNCS, vol. 1770, pp. 290–301. Springer, Heidelberg (2000). https://doi.org/10.1007/3-540-46541-3 24 Lehtinen, K.: A modal-µ perspective on solving parity games in quasi-polynomial time. In: LICS, pp. 639–648 (2018)

17. Martin, D.A.: Borel determinacy. Ann. Math. **102**(2), 363–371 (1975) McNaughton, R.: Infinite games played on finite graphs. Ann. Pure Appl. Logic **65**(2), 149–184 (1993)

5

The Impatient May Use Limited Optimism to Minimize Regret

Michaël Cadilhac[1], Guillermo A. Pérez[2(✉)], and Marie van den Bogaard[3]

[1] University of Oxford, Oxford, UK
`michael@cadilhac.name`
[2] University of Antwerp, Antwerp, Belgium
`guillermoalberto.perez@uantwerpen.be`
[3] Université libre de Bruxelles, Brussels, Belgium
`marie.van.den.bogaard@ulb.ac.be`

Abstract. Discounted-sum games provide a formal model for the study of reinforcement learning, where the agent is enticed to get rewards early since later rewards are discounted. When the agent interacts with the environment, she may realize that, with hindsight, she could have increased her reward by playing differently: this difference in outcomes constitutes her *regret value*. The agent may thus elect to follow a *regret-minimal* strategy. In this paper, it is shown that (1) there always exist regret-minimal strategies that are admissible—a strategy being inadmissible if there is another strategy that always performs better; (2) computing the minimum possible regret or checking that a strategy is regret-minimal can be done in $\mathsf{coNP}^{\mathsf{NP}}$, disregarding the computational cost of numerical analysis (otherwise, this bound becomes PSpace).

Keywords: Admissibility · Discounted-sum games · Regret minimization

1 Introduction

A pervasive model used to study the strategies of an agent in an unknown environment is *two-player infinite horizon games played on finite weighted graphs*. Therein, the set of vertices of a graph is split between two players, Adam and Eve, playing the roles of the environment and the agent, respectively. The play starts in a given vertex, and each player decides where to go next when the play reaches one of their vertices. Questions asked about these games are usually of the form: *Does there exist a strategy of Eve such that. . . ?* For such a question to be well-formed, one should provide:

1. A valuation function: given an infinite play, what is Eve's reward?
2. Assumptions about the environment: is Adam trying to help or hinder Eve?

The valuation function can be Boolean, in which case one says that Eve *wins* or *loses* (one very classical example has Eve winning if the maximum value appearing infinitely often along the edges is even). In this setting, it is often assumed that Adam is adversarial, and the question then becomes: *Can Eve always win?* (The names of the players stem from this view: *is there* a strategy of ∃ve that *always* beats ∀dam?) The literature on that subject spans more than 35 years, with newly found applications to this day (see [4] for comprehensive lecture notes, and [7] for an example of recent use in the analysis of attacks in cryptocurrencies).

The valuation function can also aggregate the numerical values along the edges into a reward value. We focus in this paper on *discounted sum*: if w is the weight of the edge taken at the n-th step, Eve's reward grows by $\lambda^n \cdot w$, where $\lambda \in (0, 1)$ is a prescribed discount factor. Discounting future rewards is a classical notion used in economics [18], Markov decision processes [9,16], systems theory [1], and is at the heart of Q-learning, a reinforcement learning technique widely used in machine learning [19]. In this setting, we consider three attitudes towards the environment:

- The adversarial environment hypothesis translates to Adam trying to minimize Eve's reward, and the question becomes: *Can Eve always achieve a reward of x?* This problem is in NP ∩ coNP [20] and showing a P upper-bound would constitute a major breakthrough (namely, it would imply the same for so-called parity games [15]). A strategy of Eve that maximizes her rewards against an adversarial environment is called *worst-case optimal*. Conversely, a strategy that maximizes her rewards assuming a *collaborative* environment is called *best-case optimal*.
- Assuming that the environment is adversarial is drastic, if not pessimistic. Eve could rather be interested in settling for a strategy σ which is not *consistently* bad: if another strategy σ' gives a better reward in one environment, there should be another environment for which σ is better than σ'. Such strategies, called *admissible* [5], can be seen as an *a priori* rational choice.
- Finally, Eve could put no assumption on the environment, but regret not having done so. Formally, the *regret value* of Eve's strategy is defined as the maximal difference, for all environments, between the best value Eve *could* have obtained and the value she actually obtained. Eve can thus be interested in following a strategy that achieves the minimal regret value, aptly called a *regret-minimal* strategy [10]. This constitutes an *a posteriori* rational choice [12]. Regret-minimal strategies were explored in several contexts, with applications including competitive online algorithm synthesis [3,11] and robot-motion planning [13,14].

In this paper, we single out a class of strategies for Eve that first follow a best-case optimal strategy, then switch to a worst-case optimal strategy after some precise time; we call these strategies *optipess*. Our main contributions are then:

1. Optipess strategies are not only regret-minimal (a fact established in [13]) but also admissible—note that there are regret-minimal strategies that are not admissible and *vice versa*. On the way, we show that for any strategy of

Eve there is an admissible strategy that performs at least as well; this is a peculiarity of discounted-sum games.

2. The regret value of a given time-switching strategy can be computed with an NP algorithm (disregarding the cost of numerical analysis). The main technical hurdle is showing that exponentially long paths can be represented succinctly, a result of independent interest.

3. The question *Can Eve's regret be bounded by x?* is decidable in $\mathsf{NP^{coNP}}$ (again disregarding the cost of numerical analysis, PSpace otherwise), improving on the implicit NExp algorithm of [13]. The algorithm consists in guessing a time-switching strategy and computing its regret value; since optipess strategies are time-switching strategies that are regret-minimal, the algorithm will eventually find the minimal regret value of the input game.

Structure of the Paper. Notations and definitions are introduced in Sect. 2. The study of admissibility appears in Sect. 3, and is independent from the complexity analysis of regret. The main algorithm devised in this paper (point 2 above) is presented in Theorem 5, Sect. 6; it relies on technical lemmas that are the focus of Sects. 4 and 5. We encourage the reader to go through the statements of the lemma sections, then through the proof of Theorem 5, to get a good sense of the role each lemma plays.

In more details, in Sect. 4 we provide a crucial lemma that allows to represent long paths succinctly, and in Sect. 5, we argue that the important values of a game (regret, best-case, worst-case) have short witnesses. In Sect. 6, we use these lemmas to devise our algorithms.

2   Preliminaries

We assume familiarity with basic graph and complexity theory. Some more specific definitions and known results are recalled here.

Game, Play, History. A *(discounted-sum) game* $\mathcal{G}$ is a tuple $(V, v_0, V_\exists, E, w, \lambda)$ where V is a finite set of vertices, v_0 is the starting vertex, $V_\exists \subseteq V$ is the subset of vertices that belong to Eve, $E \subseteq V \times V$ is a set of directed edges, $w \colon E \to \mathbb{Z}$ is an (edge-)weight function, and $0 < \lambda < 1$ is a rational *discount factor*. The vertices in $V \setminus V_\exists$ are said to belong to Adam. Since we consider games played for an infinite number of turns, we will always assume that every vertex has at least one outgoing edge.

A *play* is an infinite path $v_1 v_2 \cdots \in V^\omega$ in the digraph (V, E). A *history* $h = v_1 \cdots v_n$ is a finite path. The *length of* h, written $|h|$, is the number of *edges* it contains: $|h| \overset{\text{def}}{=} n - 1$. The set **Hist** consists of all histories that start in v_0 and end in a vertex from $V_\exists$.

Strategies. A *strategy of Eve* in $\mathcal{G}$ is a function σ that maps histories ending in some vertex $v \in V_\exists$ to a neighbouring vertex v' (i.e., $(v, v') \in E$). The strategy

σ is *positional* if for all histories h, h' ending in the same vertex, $\sigma(h) = \sigma(h')$. *Strategies of Adam* are defined similarly.

A history $h = v_1 \cdots v_n$ is said to be *consistent with a strategy* σ of Eve if for all $i \geq 2$ such that $v_i \in V_\exists$, we have that $\sigma(v_1 \cdots v_{i-1}) = v_i$. Consistency with strategies of Adam is defined similarly. We write $\mathbf{Hist}(\sigma)$ for the set of histories in $\mathbf{Hist}$ that are consistent with σ. A play is consistent with a strategy (of either player) if all its prefixes are consistent with it.

Given a vertex v and both Adam and Eve's strategies, τ and σ respectively, there is a unique play starting in v that is consistent with both, called the *outcome* of τ and σ on v. This play is denoted $\mathbf{out}^v(\sigma, \tau)$.

For a strategy σ of Eve and a history $h \in \mathbf{Hist}(\sigma)$, we let σ_h be the strategy of Eve that assumes h has already been played. Formally, $\sigma_h(h') = \sigma(h \cdot h')$ for any history h' (we will use this notation only on histories h' that start with the ending vertex of h).

Values. The *value of a history* $h = v_1 \cdots v_n$ is the discounted sum of the weights on the edges:

$$\mathbf{Val}(h) \overset{\text{def}}{=} \sum_{i=0}^{|h|-1} \lambda^i w(v_i, v_{i+1}) \ .$$

The *value of a play* is simply the limit of the values of its prefixes.

The *antagonistic value* of a strategy σ of Eve with history $h = v_1 \cdots v_n$ is the value Eve achieves when Adam tries to hinder her, after h:

$$\mathbf{aVal}^h(\sigma) \overset{\text{def}}{=} \mathbf{Val}(h) + \lambda^{|h|} \cdot \inf_\tau \mathbf{Val}(\mathbf{out}^{v_n}(\sigma_h, \tau)) \ ,$$

where τ ranges over all strategies of Adam. The *collaborative value* $\mathbf{cVal}^h(\sigma)$ is defined in a similar way, by substituting "sup" for "inf." We write $\mathbf{aVal}^h$ (resp. $\mathbf{cVal}^h$) for the best antagonistic (resp. collaborative) value achievable by Eve with any strategy.

Types of Strategies. A strategy σ of Eve is *strongly worst-case optimal* (SWO) if for every history h we have $\mathbf{aVal}^h(\sigma) = \mathbf{aVal}^h$; it is *strongly best-case optimal* (SBO) if for every history h we have $\mathbf{cVal}^h(\sigma) = \mathbf{cVal}^h$.

We single out a class of SWO strategies that perform well if Adam turns out to be helping. A SWO strategy σ of Eve is *strongly best worst-case optimal* (SBWO) if for every history h we have $\mathbf{cVal}^h(\sigma) = \mathbf{acVal}^h$, where:

$$\mathbf{acVal}^h \overset{\text{def}}{=} \sup\{\mathbf{cVal}^h(\sigma') \mid \sigma' \text{ is a SWO strategy of Eve}\} \ .$$

In the context of discounted-sum games, strategies that are positional and strongly optimal always exist. Furthermore, the set of all such strategies can be characterized by local conditions.

Lemma 1 (Follows from [20, Theorem 5.1]). *There exist positional SWO, SBO, and SBWO strategies in every game. For any positional strategy σ of Eve:*

- $(\forall v \in V)\,[\mathbf{aVal}^v(\sigma) = \mathbf{aVal}^v]$ *iff σ is SWO;*
- $(\forall v \in V)\,[\mathbf{cVal}^v(\sigma) = \mathbf{cVal}^v]$ *iff σ is SBO;*
- $(\forall v \in V)\,[\mathbf{aVal}^v(\sigma) = \mathbf{aVal}^v \wedge \mathbf{cVal}^v(\sigma) = \mathbf{acVal}^v]$ *iff σ is SBWO.*

Regret. The *regret* of a strategy σ of Eve is the maximal difference between the value obtained by using σ and the value obtained by using an alternative strategy:

$$\mathbf{Reg}\,(\sigma) \overset{\text{def}}{=} \sup_{\tau} \left(\left(\sup_{\sigma'} \mathbf{Val}(\mathbf{out}^{v_0}(\sigma',\tau)) \right) - \mathbf{Val}(\mathbf{out}^{v_0}(\sigma,\tau)) \right) \,,$$

where τ and σ' range over all strategies of Adam and Eve, respectively. The *(minimal) regret of $\mathcal{G}$* is then $\mathbf{Reg} \overset{\text{def}}{=} \inf_{\sigma} \mathbf{Reg}\,(\sigma)$.

Regret can also be characterized by considering the point in history when Eve should have done things differently. Formally, for any vertices u and v let $\mathbf{cVal}^u_{\neg v}$ be the maximal $\mathbf{cVal}^u(\sigma)$ for strategies σ verifying $\sigma(u) \neq v$. Then:

Lemma 2 ([13, Lemma 13]). *For all strategies σ of Eve:*

$$\mathbf{Reg}\,(\sigma) = \sup \left\{ \lambda^n \left(\mathbf{cVal}^{v_n}_{\neg\sigma(h)} - \mathbf{aVal}^{v_n}(\sigma_h) \right) \,\middle|\, h = v_0 \cdots v_n \in \mathbf{Hist}(\sigma) \right\} \,.$$

Switching and Optipess Strategies. Given strategies σ_1, σ_2 of Eve and a *threshold function* $t \colon V_\exists \to \mathbb{N} \cup \{\infty\}$, we define the *switching strategy* $\sigma_1 \overset{t}{\to} \sigma_2$ for any history $h = v_1 \cdots v_n$ ending in $V_\exists$ as:

$$\sigma_1 \overset{t}{\to} \sigma_2(h) = \begin{cases} \sigma_2(h) & \text{if } (\exists i)[i \geq t(v_i)], \\ \sigma_1(h) & \text{otherwise.} \end{cases}$$

We refer to histories for which the first condition above holds as *switched histories*, to all others as *unswitched histories*. The strategy $\sigma = \sigma_1 \overset{t}{\to} \sigma_2$ is said to be *bipositional* if both σ_1 and σ_2 are positional. Note that in that case, for all histories h, if h is switched then $\sigma_h = \sigma_2$, and otherwise σ_h is the same as σ but with $t(v)$ changed to $\max\{0, t(v) - |h|\}$ for all $v \in V_\exists$. In particular, if $|h|$ is greater than $\max\{t(v) < \infty\}$, then σ_h is nearly positional: it switches to σ_2 as soon as it sees a vertex with $t(v) \neq \infty$.

A strategy σ is *perfectly optimistic-then-pessimistic* (optipess, for short) if there are positional SBO and SBWO strategies σ^{sbo} and σ^{sbwo} such that $\sigma = \sigma^{\text{sbo}} \overset{t}{\to} \sigma^{\text{sbwo}}$ where $t(v) = \inf \left\{ i \in \mathbb{N} \,\middle|\, \lambda^i \left(\mathbf{cVal}^v - \mathbf{aVal}^v \right) \leq \mathbf{Reg} \right\}$.

Theorem 1 ([13]). *For all optipess strategies σ of Eve, $\mathbf{Reg}\,(\sigma) = \mathbf{Reg}$.*

Conventions. *As we have done so far, we will assume throughout the paper that a game $\mathcal{G}$ is fixed—with the notable exception of the results on complexity, in which we assume that the game is given with all numbers in binary. Regarding strategies, we assume that bipositional strategies are given as two positional strategies and a threshold function encoded as a table with binary-encoded entries.*

Example 1. Consider the following game, where round vertices are owned by Eve, and square ones by Adam. The double edges represent Eve's positional strategy σ:

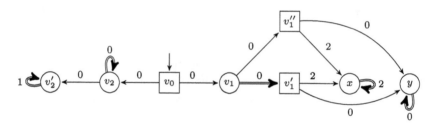

Eve's strategy has a regret value of $2\lambda^2/(1-\lambda)$. This is realized when Adam plays from v_0 to v_1, from v_1'' to x, and from v_1' to y. Against that strategy, Eve ensures a discounted-sum value of 0 by playing according to σ while regretting not having played to v_1'' to obtain $2\lambda^2/(1-\lambda)$. ∎

3   Admissible Strategies and Regret

There is no reason for Eve to choose a strategy that is consistently worse than another one. This classical idea is formalized using the notions of *strategy domination* and *admissible strategies*. In this section, which is independent from the rest of the paper, we study the relation between admissible and regret-minimal strategies. Let us start by formally introducing the relevant notions:

Definition 1. *Let σ_1, σ_2 be two strategies of Eve. We say that σ_1 is weakly dominated by σ_2 if $\mathbf{Val}(\mathbf{out}^{v_0}(\sigma_1, \tau)) \leq \mathbf{Val}(\mathbf{out}^{v_0}(\sigma_2, \tau))$ for every strategy τ of Adam. We say that σ_1 is dominated by σ_2 if σ_1 is weakly dominated by σ_2 but not conversely. A strategy σ of Eve is admissible if it is not dominated by any other strategy.*

In other words, admissible strategies are maximal elements for the weak-domination pre-order.

Example 2. Consider the following game, where the strategy σ of Eve is shown by the double edges:

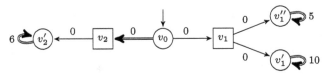

This strategy guarantees a discounted-sum value of $6\lambda^2(1-\lambda)$ against any strategy of Adam. Furthermore, it is worst-case optimal since playing to v_1 instead of v_2 would allow Adam the opportunity to ensure a strictly smaller value by playing to v_1''. The latter also implies that σ is admissible. Interestingly, playing to v_1 is also an admissible behavior of Eve since, against a strategy of Adam that plays from v_1 to v_1', it obtains $10\lambda^2(1-\lambda) > 6\lambda^2(1-\lambda)$. ∎

The two examples above can be used to argue that the sets of strategies that are regret minimal and admissible, respectively, are in fact incomparable.

Proposition 1. *There are regret-optimal strategies that are not admissible and admissible strategies that have suboptimal regret.*

Proof (Sketch). Consider once more the game depicted in Example 1 and recall that the strategy σ of Eve corresponding to the double edges has minimal regret. This strategy is *not* admissible: it is dominated by the alternative strategy σ' of Eve that behaves like σ from v_1 but plays to v_2' from v_2. Indeed, if Adam plays to v_1 from v_0 then the outcomes of σ and σ' are the same. However, if Adam plays to v_2 then the value of the outcome of σ is 0 while the value of the outcome of σ' is strictly greater than 0.

Similarly, the strategy σ depicted by double edges in the game from Example 2 is admissible but *not* regret-minimizing. In fact, her strategy σ' that consists in playing v_1 from v_0 has a smaller regret. □

In the rest of this section, we show that (1) any strategy is weakly dominated by an admissible strategy; (2) being dominated entails more regret; (3) optipess strategies are both regret-minimal and admissible. We will need the following:

Lemma 3 ([6]). *A strategy σ of Eve is admissible if and only if for every history $h \in \mathbf{Hist}(\sigma)$ the following holds: either $\mathbf{cVal}^h(\sigma) > \mathbf{aVal}^h$ or $\mathbf{aVal}^h(\sigma) = \mathbf{cVal}^h(\sigma) = \mathbf{aVal}^h = \mathbf{acVal}^h$.*

The above characterization of admissible strategies in so-called *well-formed games* was proved in [6, Theorem 11]. Lemma 3 follows from the fact that discounted-sum games are well-formed.

3.1 Any Strategy Is Weakly Dominated by an Admissible Strategy

We show that discounted-sum games have the distinctive property that every strategy is weakly dominated by an admissible strategy. This is in stark contrast with most cases where admissibility has been studied previously [6].

Theorem 2. *Any strategy of Eve is weakly dominated by an admissible strategy.*

Proof (Sketch). The main idea is to construct, based on σ, a strategy σ' that will switch to a SBWO strategy as soon as σ does not satisfy the characterization of Lemma 3. The first part of the argument consists in showing that σ is indeed weakly dominated by σ'. This is easily done by comparing, against each strategy τ of Adam, the values of σ and σ'. The second part consists in verifying that σ' is indeed admissible. This is done by checking that each history h consistent with σ' satisfies the characterization of Lemma 3, that is $\mathbf{cVal}^h(\sigma') > \mathbf{aVal}^h$ or $\mathbf{aVal}^h(\sigma') = \mathbf{cVal}^h(\sigma') = \mathbf{aVal}^h = \mathbf{acVal}^h$. $\square$

3.2   Being Dominated Is Regretful

Theorem 3. *For all strategies σ, σ' of Eve such that σ is weakly dominated by σ', it holds that $\mathbf{Reg}\,(\sigma') \leq \mathbf{Reg}\,(\sigma)$.*

Proof. Let σ, σ' be such that σ is weakly dominated by σ'. This means that for every strategy τ of Adam, we have that $\mathbf{Val}(\pi) \leq \mathbf{Val}(\pi')$ where $\pi = \mathbf{out}^{v_0}(\sigma, \tau)$ and $\pi' = \mathbf{out}^{v_0}(\sigma', \tau)$. Consequently: we obtain

$$\left(\sup_{\sigma''} \mathbf{Val}(\mathbf{out}^{v_0}(\sigma'', \tau))\right) - \mathbf{Val}(\pi') \leq \left(\sup_{\sigma''} \mathbf{Val}(\mathbf{out}^{v_0}(\sigma'', \tau))\right) - \mathbf{Val}(\pi) \ .$$

As this holds for any τ, we can conclude that $\sup_\tau \sup_{\sigma''}(\mathbf{Val}(\mathbf{out}^{v_0}(\sigma'', \tau)) - \mathbf{Val}(\mathbf{out}^{v_0}(\sigma', \tau))) \leq \sup_\tau \sup_{\sigma''}(\mathbf{Val}(\mathbf{out}^{v_0}(\sigma'', \tau)) - \mathbf{Val}(\mathbf{out}^{v_0}(\sigma, \tau)))$, that is $\mathbf{Reg}\,(\sigma') \leq \mathbf{Reg}\,(\sigma)$. $\square$

It follows from Proposition 1, however, that the converse of the theorem is false.

3.3   Optipess Strategies Are both Regret-Minimal and Admissible

Recall that there are admissible strategies that are not regret-minimal and *vice versa* (Proposition 1). However, as a direct consequence of Theorems 2 and 3, there always exist regret-minimal admissible strategies. It turns out that optipess strategies, which are regret-minimal (Theorem 1), are also admissible:

Theorem 4. *All optipess strategies of Eve are admissible.*

Proof. Let $\sigma = \sigma^{\mathrm{sbo}} \xrightarrow{t} \sigma^{\mathrm{sbwo}}$ be an optipess strategy; we show it is admissible. To this end, let $h = v_0 \dots v_n \in \mathbf{Hist}(\sigma)$; we show that one of the properties of Lemma 3 holds. There are two cases:

   (h is switched.)   In that case, $\sigma_h = \sigma^{\mathrm{sbwo}}$. Since σ^{sbwo} is an SBWO strategy, $\mathbf{cVal}^h(\sigma^{\mathrm{sbwo}}) = \mathbf{acVal}^h$. Now if $\mathbf{acVal}^h > \mathbf{aVal}^h$, then:

$$\mathbf{cVal}^h(\sigma) = \mathbf{cVal}^h(\sigma^{\mathrm{sbwo}}) = \mathbf{acVal}^h > \mathbf{aVal}^h \ ,$$

and σ satisfies the first property of Lemma 3. Otherwise $\mathbf{acVal}^h = \mathbf{aVal}^h$ and the second property holds: we have that $\mathbf{cVal}^h(\sigma) = \mathbf{acVal}^h$, and as σ^{sbwo} is an SWO and $\mathbf{aVal}^h(\sigma) = \mathbf{aVal}^h(\sigma^{\mathrm{sbwo}})$, we also have that $\mathbf{aVal}^h(\sigma) = \mathbf{aVal}^h$.

(h is unswitched.) We show that $\mathbf{cVal}^h(\sigma) > \mathbf{aVal}^h$. Since h is unswitched, we have in particular that:

$$\mathbf{Reg}(\sigma) = \mathbf{Reg} < \lambda^n \left(\mathbf{cVal}^{v_n} - \mathbf{aVal}^{v_n} \right) . \tag{1}$$

Furthermore:

$$\lambda^n \left(\mathbf{cVal}^{v_n} - \mathbf{aVal}^{v_n} \right) = \left(\mathbf{Val}(h) + \lambda^n \mathbf{cVal}^{v_n} \right) - \left(\mathbf{Val}(h) + \lambda^n \mathbf{aVal}^{v_n} \right)$$
$$= \mathbf{cVal}^h - \mathbf{aVal}^h ,$$

and combining the previous equation with Eq. 1, we obtain:

$$\mathbf{cVal}^h - \mathbf{Reg}(\sigma) > \mathbf{aVal}^h .$$

To conclude, we show that $\mathbf{Reg}(\sigma) \geq \mathbf{cVal}^h - \mathbf{cVal}^h(\sigma)$. Consider a strategy τ of Adam such that h is consistent with both σ^{sbo} and τ and satisfying $\mathbf{Val}(\mathbf{out}^{v_0}(\sigma^{\mathrm{sbo}}, \tau)) = \mathbf{cVal}^h$. (That such a τ exists is intuitively clear since σ has been following the SBO strategy σ^{sbo} along h.) It holds immediately that $\mathbf{cVal}^h(\sigma) \geq \mathbf{Val}(\mathbf{out}^{v_0}(\sigma, \tau))$. Now by definition of the regret:

$$\mathbf{Reg}(\sigma) \geq \mathbf{Val}(\mathbf{out}^{v_0}(\sigma^{\mathrm{sbo}}, \tau)) - \mathbf{Val}(\mathbf{out}^{v_0}(\sigma, \tau))$$
$$\geq \mathbf{cVal}^h - \mathbf{cVal}^h(\sigma) . \qquad \square$$

4 Minimal Values Are Witnessed by a Single Iterated Cycle

We start our technical work towards a better algorithm to compute the regret value of a game. Here, we show that there are succinctly presentable histories that witness small values in the game. Our intention is to later use this result to apply a modified version of Lemma 2 to bipositional strategies to argue there are small witnesses of a strategy having too much regret.

More specifically, we show that for any history h, there is another history h' of the same length that has smaller value and such that $h' = \alpha \cdot \beta^k \cdot \gamma$ where $|\alpha\beta\gamma|$ is small. This will allow us to find the smallest possible value among exponentially long histories by guessing α, β, γ, and k, which will all be small. This property holds for a wealth of different valuation functions, hinting at possible further applications. For discounted-sum games, the following suffices to prove the desired property holds.

Lemma 4. *For any history $h = \alpha \cdot \beta \cdot \gamma$ with α and γ same-length cycles:*

$$\min\{\mathbf{Val}(\alpha^2 \cdot \beta), \mathbf{Val}(\beta \cdot \gamma^2)\} \leq \mathbf{Val}(h) .$$

Within the proof of the key lemma of this section, and later on when we use it (Lemma 9), we will rely on the following notion of cycle decomposition:

Definition 2. *A simple-cycle decomposition (SCD) is a pair consisting of paths and iterated simple cycles. Formally, an SCD is a pair $D = \langle (\alpha_i)_{i=0}^n, (\beta_j, k_j)_{j=1}^n \rangle$, where each α_i is a path, each β_j is a simple cycle, and each k_j is a positive integer. We write $D(j) = \beta_j^{k_j} \cdot \alpha_j$ and $D(\star) = \alpha_0 \cdot D(1)D(2) \cdots D(n)$.*

By carefully iterating Lemma 4, we have:

Lemma 5. *For any history h there exists an history $h' = \alpha \cdot \beta^k \cdot \gamma$ with:*

- *h and h' have the same starting and ending vertices, and the same length;*
- *$\mathbf{Val}(h') \leq \mathbf{Val}(h)$;*
- *$|\alpha\beta\gamma| \leq 4|V|^3$ and β is a simple cycle.*

Proof. In this proof, we focus on SCDs for which each path α_i is simple; we call them ßCDs. We define a wellfounded partial order on ßCDs. Let $D = \langle (\alpha_i)_{i=0}^n, (\beta_j, k_j)_{j=1}^n \rangle$ and $D' = \langle (\alpha_i')_{i=0}^{n'}, (\beta_j', k_j')_{j=1}^{n'} \rangle$ be two ßCDs; we write $D' < D$ iff all the following holds:

- $D(\star)$ and $D'(\star)$ have the same starting and ending vertices, the same length, and satisfy $\mathbf{Val}(D'(\star)) \leq \mathbf{Val}(D(\star))$ and $n' \leq n$;
- Either $n' < n$, or $|\alpha_0' \cdots \alpha_{n'}'| < |\alpha_0 \cdots \alpha_n|$, or $|\{k_i' \geq |V|\}| < |\{k_i \geq |V|\}|$.

That this order has no infinite descending chain is clear. We show two claims:

1. Any ßCD with n greater than $|V|$ has a smaller ßCD;
2. Any ßCD with two $k_j, k_{j'} > |V|$ has a smaller ßCD.

Together they imply that for a smallest ßCD D, $D(\star)$ is of the required form. Indeed let j be the unique value for which $k_j > |V|$, then the statement of the Lemma is satisfied by letting $\alpha = \alpha_0 \cdot D(1) \cdots D(j-1)$, $\beta = \beta_j$, $k = k_j$, and $\gamma = \alpha_j \cdot D(j+1) \cdots D(n)$.

Claim 1. Suppose D has $n > |V|$. Since all cycles are simple, there are two cycles $\beta_j, \beta_{j'}$, $j < j'$, of same length. We can apply Lemma 4 on the path $\beta_j \cdot (\alpha_j D(j+1) \cdots D(j'-1)) \cdot \beta_{j'}$, and remove one of the two cycles while duplicating the other; we thus obtain a similar path of smaller value. This can be done repeatedly until we obtain a path with only one of the two cycles, say $\beta_{j'}$, the other case being similar. Substituting this path in $D(\star)$ results in:

$$\alpha_0 \cdot D(1) \cdots D(j) \cdot \left(\alpha_j \cdot D(j+1) \cdots D(j'-1) \cdot \beta_{j'}^{k_j+k_{j'}} \right) \cdot \alpha_{j'} \cdot D(j'+1) \cdots D(n) \ .$$

This gives rise to a smaller ßCD as follows. If $\alpha_{j-1}\alpha_j$ is still a simple path, then the above history is expressible as an ßCD with a smaller number of cycles. Otherwise, we rewrite $\alpha_{j-1}\alpha_j = \alpha_{j-1}'\beta_j'\alpha_j'$ where α_{j-1}' and α_j' are simple paths and β_j' is a simple cycle; since $|\alpha_{j-1}'\alpha_j'| < |\alpha_{j-1}\alpha_j|$, the resulting ßCD is smaller.

Claim 2. Suppose D has two $k_j, k_{j'} > |V|$, $j < j'$. Since each cycle in the ßCD is simple, k_j and $k_{j'}$ are greater than both $|\beta_j|$ and $|\beta_{j'}|$; let us write $k_j = b|\beta_{j'}| + r$ with $0 \leq r < |\beta_{j'}|$, and similarly, $k_{j'} = b'|\beta_j| + r'$. We have:

$$D(j) \cdots D(j') = \beta_j^r \cdot \left((\beta_{j'}^{|\beta_{j'}|})^b \cdot \alpha_j \cdot D(j+1) \cdots D(j'-1) \cdot (\beta_{j'}^{|\beta_j|})^{b'} \right) \cdot \beta_{j'}^{r'} \cdot \alpha_{j'} \ .$$

Noting that $\beta_{j'}^{|\beta_j|}$ and $\beta_j^{|\beta_{j'}|}$ are cycles of the same length, we can transfer all the occurrences of one to the other, as in Claim 1. Similarly, if two simple paths get merged and give rise to a cycle, a smaller ßCD can be constructed; if not, then there are now at most $r < |V|$ occurrences of $\beta_{j'}$ (or conversely, r' of β_j), again resulting in a smaller ßCD.   □

5   Short Witnesses for Regret, Antagonistic, and Collaborative Values

We continue our technical work towards our algorithm for computing the regret value. In this section, the overarching theme is that of *short witnesses*. We show that (1) the regret value of a strategy is witnessed by histories of bounded length; (2) the collaborative value of a game is witnessed by a simple path and an iterated cycle; (3) the antagonistic value of a strategy is witnessed by an SCD and an iterated cycle.

5.1   Regret Is Witnessed by Histories of Bounded Length

Lemma 6. *Let $\sigma = \sigma_1 \xrightarrow{t} \sigma_2$ be an arbitrary bipositional switching strategy of Eve and let $C = 2|V| + \max\{t(v) < \infty\}$. We have that:*

$$\mathbf{Reg}\,(\sigma) = \max \left\{ \lambda^n \left(\mathbf{cVal}_{\neg\sigma(h)}^{v_n} - \mathbf{aVal}^{v_n}(\sigma_h) \right) \,\Big|\right.$$
$$\left. h = v_0 \ldots v_n \in \mathbf{Hist}(\sigma), n \leq C \right\} \ .$$

Proof. Consider a history h of length greater than C, and write $h = h_1 \cdot h_2$ with $|h_1| = \max\{t(v) < \infty\}$. Let $h_2 = p \cdot p'$ where p is the maximal prefix of h_2 such that $h_1 \cdot p$ is unswitched—we set $p = \epsilon$ if h is switched. Note that one of p or p' is longer than $|V|$—say p, the other case being similar. This implies that there is a cycle in p, i.e., $p = \alpha \cdot \beta \cdot \gamma$ with β a cycle. Let $h' = h_1 \cdot \alpha \cdot \gamma \cdot p'$; this history has the same starting and ending vertex as h. Moreover, since $|h_1|$ is larger than any value of the threshold function, $\sigma_h = \sigma_{h'}$. Lastly, h' is still in $\mathbf{Hist}(\sigma)$, since the removed cycle did not play a role in switching strategy. This shows:

$$\mathbf{cVal}_{\neg\sigma(h)}^{v_n} - \mathbf{aVal}^{v_n}(\sigma_h) = \mathbf{cVal}_{\neg\sigma(h')}^{v_n} - \mathbf{aVal}^{v_n}(\sigma_{h'}) \ .$$

Since the length of h is greater than the length of h', the discounted value for h' will be greater than that of h, resulting in a higher regret value. There is thus no need to consider histories of size greater than C.   □

It may seem from this lemma and the fact that $t(v)$ may be very large that we will need to guess histories of important length. However, since we will be considering bipositional switching strategies, we will only be interested in guessing *some* properties of the histories that are not hard to verify:

Lemma 7. *The following problem is decidable in* NP:

> **Given:** A game, a bipositional switching strategy σ,
>
> a number n in binary, a Boolean b, and two vertices v, v'
>
> **Question:** Is there a $h \in \mathbf{Hist}(\sigma)$ of length n, switched if b,
>
> ending in v, with $\sigma(h) = v'$?

Proof. This is done by guessing multiple flows within the graph (V, E). Here, we call *flow* a valuation of the edges E by integers, that describes the number of times a path crosses each edge. Given a vector in $\mathbb{N}^E$, it is not hard to check whether there is a path that it represents, and to extract the initial and final vertices of that path [17].

We first order the different thresholds from the strategy $\sigma = \sigma_1 \xrightarrow{t} \sigma_2$: let $V_\exists = \{v_1, v_2, \ldots, v_k\}$ with $t(v_i) \leq t(v_{i+1})$ for all i. We analyze the structure of histories consistent with σ. Let $h \in \mathbf{Hist}(\sigma)$, and write $h = h' \cdot h''$ where h' is the maximal unswitched prefix of h. Naturally, h' is consistent with σ_1 and h'' is consistent with σ_2. Then $h' = h_0 h_1 \cdots h_i$, for some $i < |V_\exists|$, with:

- $|h_0| = t(v_1)$ and for all $1 \leq j < i$, $|h_j| = t(v_{j+1}) - t(v_j)$;
- For all $0 \leq j \leq i$, h_j does not contain a vertex v_k with $k \leq j$.

To confirm the existence of a history with the given parameters, it is thus sufficient to guess the value $i \leq |V_\exists|$, and to guess i connected flows (rather than paths) with the above properties that are consistent with σ_1. Finally, we guess a flow for h'' consistent with σ_2 if we need a switched history, and verify that it is starting at a switching vertex. The flows must sum to $n + 1$, with the last vertex being v', and the previous v. $\square$

5.2 Short Witnesses for the Collaborative and Antagonistic Values

Lemma 8. *There is a set P of pairs (α, β) with α a simple path and β a simple cycle such that:*

- $\mathbf{cVal}^{v_0} = \max\{\mathbf{Val}(\alpha \cdot \beta^\omega) \mid (\alpha, \beta) \in P\}$ *and*
- *membership in P is decidable in polynomial time w.r.t. the game.*

Proof. We argue that the set P of all pairs (α, β) with α a simple path, β a simple cycle, and such that $\alpha \cdot \beta$ is a path, gives us the result.

The first part of the claim is a consequence of Lemma 1: Consider positional SBO strategies τ and σ of Adam and Eve, respectively. Since they are positional, the path $\mathbf{out}^{v_0}(\sigma, \tau)$ is of the form $\alpha \cdot \beta^\omega$, as required, and its value is $\mathbf{cVal}^{v_0}$. We can thus let P be the set of all pairs obtained from such SBO strategies.

Moreover, it can be easily checked that for all pairs (α, β) such that $\alpha \cdot \beta$ is a path in the game there exists a pair of strategies with outcome $\alpha \cdot \beta^\omega$. (Note that verifying whether $\alpha \cdot \beta$ is a path can indeed be done in polynomial time given α and β.) Finally, the value $\mathbf{Val}(\alpha \cdot \beta^\omega)$ will, by definition, be at most $\mathbf{cVal}^{v_0}$. $\square$

Lemma 9. *Let σ be a bipositional switching strategy of Eve. There is a set K of pairs (D, β) with D an SCD and β a simple cycle such that:*

- $\mathbf{aVal}^{v_0}(\sigma) = \min\{\mathbf{Val}(D(\star) \cdot \beta^\omega) \mid (D, \beta) \in K\}$ *and*
- *the size of each pair is polynomially bounded, and membership in K is decidable in polynomial time w.r.t. σ and the game.*

Proof. We will prove that the set K of all pairs (D, β) with D an SCD of polynomial length (which will be specified below), β a simple cycle, and such that $D(\star) \cdot \beta$ is a path, satisfies our claims.

Let $C = \max\{t(v) < \infty\}$, and consider a play π consistent with σ that achieves the value $\mathbf{aVal}^{v_0}(\sigma)$. Write $\pi = h \cdot \pi'$ with $|h| = C$, and let v be the final vertex of h. Naturally:

$$\mathbf{aVal}^{v_0}(\sigma) = \mathbf{Val}(\pi) = \mathbf{Val}(h) + \lambda^{|h|}\mathbf{Val}(\pi') \ .$$

We first show how to replace π' by some $\alpha \cdot \beta^\omega$, with α a simple path and β a simple cycle. First, since π witnesses $\mathbf{aVal}^{v_0}(\sigma)$, we have that $\mathbf{Val}(\pi') = \mathbf{aVal}^v(\sigma_h)$. Now σ_h is positional, because $|h| \geq C$.[1] It is known that there are optimal positional antagonistic strategies τ for Adam, that is, that satisfy $\mathbf{aVal}^v(\sigma_h) = \mathbf{out}^v(\sigma_h, \tau)$. As in the proof of Lemma 8, this implies that $\mathbf{aVal}^v(\sigma_h) = \mathbf{Val}(\alpha \cdot \beta^\omega) = \mathbf{Val}(\pi')$ for some α and β; additionally, any (α, β) that are consistent with σ_h and a potential strategy for Adam will give rise to a larger value.

We now argue that $\mathbf{Val}(h)$ is witnessed by an SCD of polynomial size. This bears similarity to the proof of Lemma 7. Specifically, we will reuse the fact that histories consistent with σ can be split into histories played "between thresholds."

Let us write $\sigma = \sigma_1 \xrightarrow{t} \sigma_2$. Again, we let $V_\exists = \{v_1, v_2, \ldots, v_k\}$ with $t(v_i) \leq t(v_{i+1})$ for all i and write $h = h' \cdot h''$ where h' is the maximal unswitched prefix of h. We note that h' is consistent with σ_1 and h'' is consistent with σ_2. Then $h' = h_0 h_1 \cdots h_i$, for some $i < |V_\exists|$, with:

- $|h_0| = t(v_1)$ and for all $1 \leq j < i$, $|h_j| = t(v_{j+1}) - t(v_j)$;
- For all $0 \leq j \leq i$, h_j does not contain a vertex v_k with $k \leq j$.

We now diverge from the proof of Lemma 7. We apply Lemma 5 on each h_j in the game where the strategy σ_1 is hardcoded (that is, we first remove every edge $(u, v) \in V_\exists \times V$ that does not satisfy $\sigma_1(u) = v$). We obtain a history $h'_0 h'_1 \cdots h'_i$ that is still in $\mathbf{Hist}(\sigma)$, thanks to the previous splitting of h. We also apply Lemma 5 to h', this time in the game where σ_2 is hardcoded, obtaining h''. Since each h'_j and h'' are expressed as $\alpha \cdot \beta^k \cdot \gamma$, there is an SCD D with no more

---

[1] Technically, σ_h is positional in the game that records whether the switch was made.

than $|V_\exists|$ elements that satisfies $\mathbf{Val}(D(\star)) \leq \mathbf{Val}(h)$—naturally, since $\mathbf{Val}(h)$ is minimal and $D(\star) \in \mathbf{Hist}(\sigma)$, this means that the two values are equal. Note that it is not hard, given an SCD D, to check whether $D(\star) \in \mathbf{Hist}(\sigma)$, and that SCDs that are not valued $\mathbf{Val}(h)$ have a larger value. $\square$

6 The Complexity of Regret

We are finally equipped to present our algorithms. To account for the cost of numerical analysis, we rely on the problem PosSLP [2]. This problem consists in determining whether an arithmetic circuit with addition, subtraction, and multiplication gates, together with input values, evaluates to a positive integer. PosSLP is known to be decidable in the so-called counting hierarchy, itself contained in the set of problems decidable using polynomial space.

Theorem 5. *The following problem is decidable in* $\mathsf{NP}^{\mathsf{PosSLP}}$:

> **Given:**   *A game, a bipositional switching strategy σ,*
>
> *a value $r \in \mathbb{Q}$ in binary*
>
> **Question:** *Is $\mathbf{Reg}(\sigma) > r$?*

Proof. Let us write $\sigma = \sigma_1 \xrightarrow{t} \sigma_2$. Lemma 6 indicates that $\mathbf{Reg}(\sigma) > r$ holds if there is a history h of some length $n \leq C = 2|V| + \max\{t(v) < \infty\}$, ending in some v_n such that:

$$\lambda^n \left(\mathbf{cVal}^{v_n}_{\neg\sigma(h)} - \mathbf{aVal}^{v_n}(\sigma_h) \right) > r \ . \tag{2}$$

Note that since σ is bipositional, we do not need to know everything about h. Indeed, the following properties suffice: its length n, final vertex v_n, $v' = \sigma(h)$, and whether it is switched. Rather than guessing h, we can thus rely on Lemma 7 to get the required information. We start by simulating the NP machine that this lemma provides, and verify that n, v_n, and v are consistent with a potential history.

Let us now concentrate on the collaborative value that we need to evaluate in Eq. 2. To compute $\mathbf{cVal}$, we rely on Lemma 8, which we apply in the game where v_n is set initial, and its successor forced not to be v. We guess a pair $(\alpha_c, \beta_c) \in P$; we thus have $\mathbf{Val}(\alpha_c \cdot \beta_c^\omega) \leq \mathbf{cVal}^{v_n}_{\neg\sigma(h)}$, with at least one guessed pair (α_c, β_c) reaching that latter value.

Let us now focus on computing $\mathbf{aVal}^{v_n}(\sigma_h)$. Since σ is a bipositional switching strategy, σ_h is simply σ where $t(v)$ is changed to $\max\{0, t(v) - n\}$. Lemma 9 can thus be used to compute our value. To do so, we guess a pair $(D, \beta_a) \in K$; we thus have $\mathbf{Val}(D(\star) \cdot \beta_a^\omega) \geq \mathbf{aVal}^{v_n}(\sigma_h)$, and at least one pair (D, β_a) reaches that latter value.

Our guesses satisfy:

$$\mathbf{cVal}^{v_n}_{\neg\sigma(h)} - \mathbf{aVal}^{v_n}(\sigma_h) \geq \mathbf{Val}(\alpha_c \cdot \beta_c^\omega) - \mathbf{Val}(D(\star) \cdot \beta_a^\omega) \ ,$$

and there is a choice of our guessed paths and SCD that gives exactly the left-hand side. Comparing the left-hand side with r can be done using an oracle to PosSLP, concluding the proof.   □

Theorem 6. *The following problem is decidable in* $\mathsf{coNP}^{\mathsf{NP}^{\mathsf{PosSLP}}}$:

> **Given:**   *A game, a value* $r \in \mathbb{Q}$ *in binary*
> **Question:** *Is* $\mathbf{Reg} > r$?

Proof. To decide the problem at hand, we ought to check that *every* strategy has a regret value greater than r. However, optipess strategies being regret-minimal, we need only check this for a class of strategies that contains optipess strategies: bipositional switching strategies form one such class.

What is left to show is that optipess strategies can be encoded in *polynomial space*. Naturally, the two positional strategies contained in an optipess strategy can be encoded succinctly. We thus only need to show that, with t as in the definition of optipess strategies (page 5), $t(v)$ is at most exponential for every $v \in V_\exists$ with $t(v) \in \mathbb{N}$. This is shown in the long version of this paper.   □

Theorem 7. *The following problem is decidable in* $\mathsf{coNP}^{\mathsf{NP}^{\mathsf{PosSLP}}}$:

> **Given:**   *A game, a bipositional switching strategy* σ
> **Question:** *Is* σ *regret optimal?*

Proof. A consequence of the proof of Theorem 5 and the existence of optipess strategies is that the value $\mathbf{Reg}$ of a game can be computed by a polynomial size arithmetic circuit. Moreover, our reliance on PosSLP allows the input r in Theorem 5 to be represented as an arithmetic circuit without impacting the complexity. We can thus verify that for all bipositional switching strategies σ' (with sufficiently large threshold functions) and all possible polynomial size arithmetic circuits, $\mathbf{Reg}(\sigma) > r$ implies that $\mathbf{Reg}(\sigma') > r$. The latter holds if and only if σ is regret optimal since, as we have argued in the proof of Theorem 6, such strategies σ' include optipess strategies and thus regret-minimal strategies.   □

7   Conclusion

We studied *regret*, a notion of interest for an agent that does not want to assume that the environment she plays in is simply adversarial. We showed that there are strategies that both minimize regret, and are not consistently worse than any other strategies. The problem of computing the minimum regret value of a game was then explored, and a better algorithm was provided for it.

The exact complexity of this problem remains however open. The only known lower bound, a straightforward adaptation of [14, Lemma 3] for discounted-sum games, shows that it is at least as hard as solving parity games [15].

Our upper bound could be significantly improved if we could efficiently solve the following problem:

PosRatBase

> **Given:** $(a_i)_{i=1}^n \in \mathbb{Z}^n$, $(b_i)_{i=1}^n \in \mathbb{N}^n$, and $r \in \mathbb{Q}$ all in binary,
>
> **Question:** Is $\sum_{i=1}^n a_i \cdot r^{b_i} > 0$?

This can be seen as the problem of comparing succinctly represented numbers in a rational base. The PosSLP oracle in Theorem 5 can be replaced by an oracle for this seemingly simpler arithmetic problem. The variant of PosRatBase in which r is an integer was shown to be in P by Cucker, Koiran, and Smale [8], and they mention that the complexity is open for rational values. To the best of our knowledge, the exact complexity of PosRatBase is open even for $n = 3$.

Acknowledgements. We thank Raphaël Berthon and Ismaël Jecker for helpful conversations on the length of maximal (and minimal) histories in discounted-sum games, James Worrell and Joël Ouaknine for pointers on the complexity of comparing succinctly represented integers, and George Kenison for his writing help.

References

1. de Alfaro, L., Henzinger, T.A., Majumdar, R.: Discounting the future in systems theory. In: Baeten, J.C.M., Lenstra, J.K., Parrow, J., Woeginger, G.J. (eds.) ICALP 2003. LNCS, vol. 2719, pp. 1022–1037. Springer, Heidelberg (2003). https://doi.org/10.1007/3-540-45061-0_79
2. Allender, E., Bürgisser, P., Kjeldgaard-Pedersen, J., Miltersen, P.B.: On the complexity of numerical analysis. SIAM J. Comput. **38**(5), 1987–2006 (2009). https://doi.org/10.1137/070697926
3. Aminof, B., Kupferman, O., Lampert, R.: Reasoning about online algorithms with weighted automata. ACM Trans. Algorithms **6**(2), 28:1–28:36 (2010). https://doi.org/10.1145/1721837.1721844
4. Apt, K.R., Grädel, E.: Lectures in Game Theory for Computer Scientists. Cambridge University Press, New York (2011)
5. Brenguier, R., et al.: Non-zero sum games for reactive synthesis. In: Dediu, A.-H., Janoušek, J., Martín-Vide, C., Truthe, B. (eds.) LATA 2016. LNCS, vol. 9618, pp. 3–23. Springer, Cham (2016). https://doi.org/10.1007/978-3-319-30000-9_1
6. Brenguier, R., Pérez, G.A., Raskin, J.F., Sankur, O.: Admissibility in quantitative graph games. In: Lal, A., Akshay, S., Saurabh, S., Sen, S. (eds.) 36th IARCS Annual Conference on Foundations of Software Technology and Theoretical Computer Science, FSTTCS 2016. LIPIcs, Chennai, India, 13–15 December 2016, vol. 65, pp. 42:1–42:14. Schloss Dagstuhl - Leibniz-Zentrum fuer Informatik (2016). https://doi.org/10.4230/LIPIcs.FSTTCS.2016.42
7. Chatterjee, K., Goharshady, A.K., Ibsen-Jensen, R., Velner, Y.: Ergodic mean-payoff games for the analysis of attacks in crypto-currencies. In: Schewe, S., Zhang, L. (eds.) 29th International Conference on Concurrency Theory, CONCUR 2018. LIPIcs, Beijing, China, 4–7 September 2018, vol. 118, pp. 11:1–11:17. Schloss Dagstuhl - Leibniz-Zentrum fuer Informatik (2018). https://doi.org/10.4230/LIPIcs.CONCUR.2018.11

8. Cucker, F., Koiran, P., Smale, S.: A polynomial time algorithm for diophantine equations in one variable. J. Symb. Comput. **27**(1), 21–29 (1999). https://doi.org/10.1006/jsco.1998.0242
9. Filar, J., Vrieze, K.: Competitive Markov Decision Processes. Springer, Heidelberg (2012). https://doi.org/10.1007/978-1-4612-4054-9
10. Filiot, E., Le Gall, T., Raskin, J.-F.: Iterated regret minimization in game graphs. In: Hliněný, P., Kučera, A. (eds.) MFCS 2010. LNCS, vol. 6281, pp. 342–354. Springer, Heidelberg (2010). https://doi.org/10.1007/978-3-642-15155-2_31
11. Filiot, E., Jecker, I., Lhote, N., Pérez, G.A., Raskin, J.F.: On delay and regret determinization of max-plus automata. In: 32nd Annual ACM/IEEE Symposium on Logic in Computer Science, LICS 2017, Reykjavik, Iceland, 20–23 June 2017, pp. 1–12. IEEE Computer Society (2017). https://doi.org/10.1109/LICS.2017.8005096
12. Halpern, J.Y., Pass, R.: Iterated regret minimization: a new solution concept. Games Econ. Behav. **74**(1), 184–207 (2012). https://doi.org/10.1016/j.geb.2011.05.012
13. Hunter, P., Pérez, G.A., Raskin, J.F.: Minimizing regret in discounted-sum games. In: Talbot, J.M., Regnier, L. (eds.) 25th EACSL Annual Conference on Computer Science Logic, CSL 2016. LIPIcs, Marseille, France, 29 August–1 September 2016, vol. 62, pp. 30:1–30:17. Schloss Dagstuhl - Leibniz-Zentrum fuer Informatik (2016). https://doi.org/10.4230/LIPIcs.CSL.2016.30
14. Hunter, P., Pérez, G.A., Raskin, J.F.: Reactive synthesis without regret. Acta Inf. **54**(1), 3–39 (2017). https://doi.org/10.1007/s00236-016-0268-z
15. Jurdzinski, M.: Deciding the winner in parity games is in UP ∩ co-UP. Inf. Process. Lett. **68**(3), 119–124 (1998). https://doi.org/10.1016/S0020-0190(98)00150-1
16. Puterman, M.L.: Markov Decision Processes. Wiley-Interscience, New York (2005)
17. Reutenauer, C.: The Mathematics of Petri Nets. Prentice-Hall Inc., Upper Saddle River (1990)
18. Shapley, L.S.: Stochastic games. Proc. Natl. Acad. Sci. **39**(10), 1095–1100 (1953)
19. Watkins, C.J.C.H., Dayan, P.: Technical note Q-learning. Mach. Learn. **8**, 279–292 (1992). https://doi.org/10.1007/BF00992698
20. Zwick, U., Paterson, M.: The complexity of mean payoff games on graphs. Theor. Comput. Sci. **158**(1&2), 343–359 (1996). https://doi.org/10.1016/0304-3975(95)00188-3

6

Kleene Algebra with Hypotheses

Amina Doumane[1,2], Denis Kuperberg[1]([✉]), Damien Pous[1], and Pierre Pradic[1,2]

[1] Univ Lyon, EnsL, UCBL, CNRS, LIP, 69342 Lyon Cedex 07, France
`denis.kuperberg@ens-lyon.fr`
[2] Warsaw University, MIMUW, Warsaw, Poland

Abstract. We study the Horn theories of Kleene algebras and star continuous Kleene algebras, from the complexity point of view. While their equational theories coincide and are PSPACE-complete, their Horn theories differ and are undecidable. We characterise the Horn theory of star continuous Kleene algebras in terms of downward closed languages and we show that when restricting the shape of allowed hypotheses, the problems lie in various levels of the arithmetical or analytical hierarchy. We also answer a question posed by Cohen about hypotheses of the form $1 = S$ where S is a sum of letters: we show that it is decidable.

Keywords: Kleene algebra · Hypotheses · Horn theory · Complexity

1 Introduction

Kleene algebras [6,10] are idempotent semirings equipped with a unary operation *star* such that x^* intuitively corresponds to the sum of all powers of x. They admit several models which are important in practice: formal languages, where L^* is the Kleene star of a language L; binary relations, where R^* is the reflexive transitive closure of a relation R; matrices over various semirings, where M^* can be used to perform flow analysis.

A fundamental result is that their equational theory is decidable, and actually PSPACE-complete. This follows from a completeness result which was proved independently by Kozen [11] and Krob [17] and Boffa [3], and the fact that checking language equivalence of two regular expressions is PSPACE-complete: given two regular expressions, we have

$$\mathsf{KA} \vdash e \leq f \quad \text{iff} \quad [e] \subseteq [f]$$

(where $\mathsf{KA} \vdash e \leq f$ denotes provability from Kleene algebra axioms, and $[e]$ is the language of a regular expression e).

Because of their interpretation in the algebra of binary relations, Kleene algebras and their extensions have been used to reason abstractly about program correctness [1,2,9,12,15]. For instance, if two programs can be abstracted into two relational expressions $(R^*; S)^*$ and $((R \cup S)^*; S)^=$, then we can deduce that these programs are equivalent by checking that the regular expression $(a^*b)^*$ and $(a+b)^*b+1$ denote the same language. This technique made it possible to automate reasoning steps in proof assistants [4,16,19].

In such a scenario, one often has to reason under assumptions. For instance, if we can abstract our programs into relational expressions $(R+S)^*$ and $S^*; R^*$, then we can deduce algebraically that the starting programs are equal if we know that $R; S = R$ (i.e., that S is a no-op when executed after R). When doing so, we move from the equational theory of Kleene algebras to their Horn theory: we want to know whether a given set of equations, the *hypotheses*, entails another equation in all Kleene algebras. Unfortunately, this theory is undecidable in general [13]. In this paper, we continue the work initiated by Cohen [5] and pursued by Kozen [13], by characterising the precise complexity of new subclasses of this general problem.

A few cases have been shown to be decidable in the literature, when we restrict the form of the hypotheses:

- when they are of the form $e = 0$ [5],
- when they are of the form $a \leq 1$ for a a letter [5],
- when they are of the form $1 = w$ or $a = w$ for a a letter and w a word, provided that those equations seen as a word rewriting system satisfy certain properties [14,18]; this includes equations like idempotency ($x = xx$) or self-invertibility ($1 = xx$).

(In the first two cases, the complexity can be shown to remain in PSPACE.) We add one positive case, which was listed as open by Cohen [5], and which is typically useful to express that a certain number of predicates cover all cases:

- when hypotheses are of the form $S = 1$ for S a sum of letters.

Conversely, Kozen also studied the precise complexity of various undecidable sub-classes of the problem [13]. For those, one has to be careful about the precise definition of Kleene algebras. Indeed, these only form a quasi-variety (their definition involves two implications), and one often consider *-*continuous* Kleene algebras [6], which additionally satisfy an infinitary implication (We define these formally in Sect. 2). While the equational theory of Kleene algebras coincides with that of *-continuous Kleene algebras, this is not the case for their Horn theories: there exist Horn sentences which are valid in all *-continuous Kleene algebras but not in all Kleene algebras.

Kozen [13] showed for instance that when hypotheses are of the form $pq = qp$ for pairs of letters (p, q), then validity of an implication in all *-continuous Kleene algebras is Π_1^0-complete, while it is only known to be EXPSPACE-hard for plain Kleene algebras. In fact, for plain Kleene algebras, the only known negative result is that the problem is undecidable for hypotheses of the form $u = v$ for

	$1 = \sum a$	$a \leq \sum b$	$a \leq \sum w$	$a \leq g$
$\mathsf{KA}_H \vdash u \leq f$	Decidable	EXPTIME − complete	Σ_1^0−complete	Σ_1^0−complete
$\mathsf{KA}_H \vdash e \leq f$	Decidable	Undecidable	Σ_1^0−complete	Σ_1^0−complete
$\mathsf{KA}_H^* \vdash u \leq f$	Decidable	EXPTIME − complete	Σ_1^0−complete	Π_1^1−complete
$\mathsf{KA}_H^* \vdash e \leq f$	Decidable	Π_1^0−complete	Π_2^0−complete	Π_1^1−complete

Fig. 1. Summary of the main results.

pairs (u, v) of words (Kleene star plays no role in this undecidability result: this is just the word problem). We show that it is already undecidable, and in fact Σ_1^0-complete when hypotheses are of the form $a \leq S$ where a is a letter and S is a sum of letters. We use a similar encoding as in [13] to relate the Horn theories of KA and KA^* to runs of Turing Machines and alternating linearly bounded automata. This allows us to show that deciding whether an inequality $w \leq f$ holds where w is a word, in presence of sum-of-letters hypotheses, is EXPTIME-complete. We also refine the Π_1^1-completeness result obtained in [13] for general hypotheses, by showing that hypotheses of the form $a \leq g$ where a is a letter already make the problem Π_1^1-complete.

The key notion we define and exploit in this paper is the following: given a set H of equations, and given a language L, write $\mathrm{cl}_H(L)$ for the smallest language containing L such that for all hypotheses $(e \leq f) \in H$ and all words u, v,

$$\text{if} \quad u[f]v \subseteq \mathrm{cl}_H(L) \quad \text{then} \quad u[e]v \subseteq \mathrm{cl}_H(L) \ .$$

This notion makes it possible to characterise the Horn theory of ∗-continuous Kleene algebras, and to approximate that of Kleene algebras: we have

$$\mathsf{KA}_H \vdash e \leq f \quad \Rightarrow \quad \mathsf{KA}_H^* \vdash e \leq f \quad \Leftrightarrow \quad [e] \subseteq \mathrm{cl}_H([f])$$

where $\mathsf{KA}_H \vdash e \leq f$ (resp. $\mathsf{KA}_H^* \vdash e \leq f$) denotes provability in Kleene algebra (resp. ∗-continuous Kleene algebra). We study downward closed languages and prove the above characterisation in Sect. 3.

The first implication can be strengthened into an equivalence in a few cases, for instance when the regular expression e and the right-hand sides of all hypotheses denote finite languages, or when hypotheses have the form $1 = S$ for S a sum of letters. We obtain decidability in those cases (Sect. 4).

Then we focus on cases where hypotheses are of the form $a \leq e$ for a a letter, and we show that most problems are already undecidable there. We do so by exploiting the characterisation in terms of downward closed languages to provide encodings of various undecidable problems on Turing machines, total Turing machines, and linearly bounded automata (Sect. 5).

We summarise our results in Fig. 1. The top of each column restricts the type of allowed hypotheses. Variables e, f stand for general expressions, u, w for words, and a, b for letters. Grayed statements are implied by non-grayed ones.

Notations. We let a, b range over the letters of a finite alphabet Σ. We let u, v, w range over the words over Σ, whose set is written Σ^*. We write ϵ for the empty word; uv for the concatenation of two words u, v; $|w|$ for the length of a word w. We write Σ^+ for the set of non-empty words. We let e, f, g range over the regular expressions over Σ, whose set is written Exp_Σ. We write $[e]$ for the language of such a an expression e: $[e] \subseteq \Sigma^*$. We sometimes implicitly regard a word as a regular expression. If X is a set, $\mathcal{P}(X)$ (resp. $\mathcal{P}_{\mathrm{fin}}(X)$) is the set of its subsets (resp. finite subsets) and $|X|$ for its cardinality.

A long version of this extended abstract is available on HAL [8], with most proofs in appendix.

2   The Systems KA and KA*

Definition 1 (KA, KA*). *A Kleene algebra is a tuple $(M, 0, 1, +, \cdot, *)$ where $(M, 0, 1, +, \cdot)$ is an idempotent semiring and the following axioms and implications, where the partial order $\leq$ is defined by $x \leq y$ if $x + y = y$, hold for all $x, y \in M$.*

$$1 + xx^* \leq x^* \qquad\qquad xy \leq y \;\Rightarrow\; x^*y \leq y$$

$$1 + x^*x \leq x^* \qquad\qquad yx \leq y \;\Rightarrow\; yx^* \leq y$$

A Kleene algebra is $*$-continuous if it satisfies the following implication:

$$(\forall i \in \mathbb{N}, \; xy^i z \leq t) \;\Rightarrow\; xy^* z \leq t$$

A hypothesis is an inequation of the form $e \leq f$, where e and f are regular expressions. If H is a set of hypotheses, and e, f are regular expressions, we write $\mathsf{KA}_H \vdash e \leq f$ (resp. $\mathsf{KA}_H^* \vdash e \leq f$) if $e \leq f$ is derivable from the axioms and implications of KA (resp. KA) as well as the hypotheses from H. We omit the subscript when H is empty.*

Note that the letters appearing in the hypotheses are constants: they are not universally quantified. In particular if $H = \{aa \leq a\}$, we may deduce $\mathsf{KA}_H \vdash a^* \leq a$ but not $\mathsf{KA}_H \vdash b^* \leq b$.

Languages over the alphabet Σ form a $*$-continuous Kleene algebra, as well as binary relations over an arbitrary set.

In absence of hypotheses, provability in KA is coincides with provability in KA* and with language inclusion:

Theorem 1 (Kozen [11]).

$$\mathsf{KA} \vdash e \leq f \quad\Leftrightarrow\quad \mathsf{KA}^* \vdash e \leq f \quad\Leftrightarrow\quad [e] \subseteq [f]$$

We will classify the theories based on the shape of hypotheses we allow; we list them below (I is a finite non-empty set):

Name of the hypothesis	Its shape		
$(1 = \sum x)$ – hypothesis	$1 = \sum_{i \in I} a_i$	where	$a_i \in \Sigma$
$(w \leq \sum w)$ – hypothesis	$v \leq \sum_{i \in I} v_i$	where	$v, v_i \in \Sigma^*$
$(x \leq \sum w)$ – hypothesis	$a \leq \sum_{i \in I} v_i$	where	$a \in \Sigma, v_i \in \Sigma^*$
$(x \leq \sum x)$ – hypothesis	$a \leq \sum_{i \in I} a_i$	where	$a, a_i \in \Sigma$
$(1 \leq \sum x)$ – hypothesis	$1 \leq \sum_{i \in I} a_i$	where	$a_i \in \Sigma$
$(x \leq 1)$ – hypothesis	$a \leq 1$	where	$a \in \Sigma$

We call *letter hypotheses* any class of hypotheses where the left-hand side is a letter (the last four ones). In the rest of the paper, we study the following problem from a complexity point of view: given a set of C-hypotheses H, where C is one of the classes listed above, and two expressions $e, f \in \mathsf{Exp}_\Sigma$, can we decide whether $\mathsf{KA}_H \vdash e \leq f$ (resp. $\mathsf{KA}_H^* \vdash e \leq f$) holds? We call it the problem of **deciding KA (resp. KA*) under C-hypotheses.**

3   Closure of Regular Languages

It is known that provability in KA and KA^* can be characterised by language inclusions (Theorem 1). In the presence of hypotheses, this is not the case anymore: we need to take the hypotheses into account in the semantics. We do so by using the following notion of *downward closure* of a language.

3.1   Definition of the Closure

Definition 2 (H-closure). *Let H be a set of hypotheses and $L \subseteq \Sigma^*$ be a language. The H-closure of L, denoted $\mathrm{cl}_H(L)$, is the smallest language K such that $L \subseteq K$ and for all hypotheses $e \leq f \in H$ and all words $u, v \in \Sigma^*$, we have*

$$u[f]v \subseteq C \qquad \Rightarrow \qquad u[e]v \subseteq K$$

Alternatively, $\mathrm{cl}_H(L)$ can be defined as the least fixed point of the function $\phi_L : \mathcal{P}(\Sigma^*) \to \mathcal{P}(\Sigma^*)$ defined by $\phi_L(X) = L \cup \psi_H(X)$, where

$$\psi_H(X) = \bigcup_{(e \leq f) \in H} \{u[e]v \mid u, v \in \Sigma^*, u[f]v \subseteq X\}.$$

Example 1. If $H = \{ab \leq ba\}$ then $\mathrm{cl}_H([b^*a^*]) = [(a+b)^*]$, while $\mathrm{cl}_H([a^*b^*]) = [a^*b^*]$.

In order to manipulate closures more conveniently, we introduce a syntactic object witnessing membership in a closure: derivation trees.

Definition 3. *Let H be a set of hypotheses and L a regular language. We define an infinitely branching proof system related to $\mathrm{cl}_H(L)$, where statements are regular expressions, and rules are the following, called respectively* axiom, extension, *and* hypothesis:

$$\frac{}{u}\ u \in L \qquad \frac{(u)_{u\in[e]}}{e} \qquad \frac{ufv}{uwv}\ w \in [e],\ e \le f \in H$$

We write $\vdash_{H,L} e$ if e is derivable in this proof system, i.e. if there is a well-founded tree using these rules, with root e and all leaves labelled by words in L. Such a tree will be called a derivation tree *for $[e] \subseteq \mathrm{cl}_H(L)$ (or $e \in \mathrm{cl}_H(L)$ if e is a word).*

Example 2. The following derivation is a derivation tree for $bababa \in \mathrm{cl}_H([b^*a^*])$, where $H = \{ab \le ba\}$.

$$\frac{\displaystyle\frac{\displaystyle\frac{\displaystyle\frac{}{bbbaaa}}{bba\mathbf{b}aa}}{bba\mathbf{ab}a}}{ba\mathbf{ba}ba}$$

Derivation trees witness membership to the closure as shown by the following proposition.

Proposition 1. $[e] \subseteq \mathrm{cl}_H(L)$ *iff* $\vdash_{H,L} e$.

(See [8, App. A] for a proof.)

3.2   Properties of the Closure Operator

We summarise in this section some useful properties of the closure. Lemma 1 shows in particular that the closure is idempotent, monotonic (both for the set of hypotheses and its language argument) and invariant by context application. Lemma 2 shows that internal closure operators can be removed in the evaluation of regular expressions. Those two lemmas are proved in [8, App. A].

Lemma 1. *Let $A, B, U, V \subseteq \Sigma^*$. We have*

1. $A \subseteq \mathrm{cl}_H(A)$
2. $\mathrm{cl}_H(\mathrm{cl}_H(A)) = \mathrm{cl}_H(A)$
3. $A \subseteq B$ *implies* $\mathrm{cl}_H(A) \subseteq \mathrm{cl}_H(B)$
4. $H \subseteq H'$ *implies* $\mathrm{cl}_H(A) \subseteq \mathrm{cl}_{H'}(A)$
5. $\mathrm{cl}_H(A) \subseteq \mathrm{cl}_H(B)$ *if and only if* $A \subseteq \mathrm{cl}_H(B)$.
6. $A \subseteq \mathrm{cl}_H(B)$ *implies* $UAV \subseteq \mathrm{cl}_H(UBV)$.

Lemma 2. *Let $A, B \subseteq \Sigma^*$, then*

1. $\mathrm{cl}_H(A + B) = \mathrm{cl}_H(\mathrm{cl}_H(A) + \mathrm{cl}_H(B))$,
2. $\mathrm{cl}_H(AB) = \mathrm{cl}_H(\mathrm{cl}_H(A)\mathrm{cl}_H(B))$,
3. $\mathrm{cl}_H(A^*) = \mathrm{cl}_H(\mathrm{cl}_H(A)^*)$

3.3 Relating Closure and Provability in KA_H and KA_H^*

We show that provability in KA^* can be characterized by closure inclusions. In KA, provability implies closure inclusions but the converse is not true in general.

Theorem 2. *Let H be a set of hypotheses and e, f be two regular expressions.*

$$\mathsf{KA}_H \vdash e \le f \quad \Rightarrow \quad \mathsf{KA}_H^* \vdash e \le f \quad \Leftrightarrow \quad [e] \subseteq \mathrm{cl}_H([f])$$

Proof. Let $\mathsf{CReg}_{H,\Sigma} = \{\mathrm{cl}_H(L) \mid L \in \mathsf{Reg}_\Sigma\}$, on which we define the following operations:

$$X \oplus Y = \mathrm{cl}_H(X + Y) \qquad X \odot Y = \mathrm{cl}_H(X \cdot Y) \qquad X^\circledast = \mathrm{cl}_H(X^*).$$

We define the *closure model* $F_{H,\Sigma} = (\mathsf{CReg}_{H,\Sigma}, \emptyset, \{\epsilon\}, \oplus, \odot, \circledast)$.

We write $\le$ for the inequality induced by $\oplus$ in $F_{H,\Sigma}$: $X \le Y$ if $X \oplus Y = Y$.

Lemma 3. $F_{H,\Sigma} = (\mathsf{CReg}_{H,\Sigma}, \emptyset, \{\epsilon\}, \oplus, \odot, \circledast)$ *is a $*$-continuous Kleene algebra. The inequality $\le$ of $F_{H,\Sigma}$ coincides with inclusion of languages.*

Proof. By Lemma 2, the function $\mathrm{cl}_H : (\mathcal{P}(\Sigma^*), +, \cdot, *) \to (\mathsf{CReg}_{H,\Sigma}, \oplus, \odot, \circledast)$ is a homomorphism. We show that $F_{H,\Sigma}$ is a $*$-continuous Kleene algebra. First, identities of $\mathsf{Lang}_\Sigma = (\mathcal{P}(\Sigma^*), +, \cdot, *)$ are propagated through the morphism cl_H, so only Horn formulas defining $*$-continuous Kleene algebras remain to be verified. It suffices to prove that $F_{H,\Sigma}$ satisfies the $*$-continuity implication, because the implication $xy \le y \to x^*y \le y$ and its dual can be deduced from it. Let $A, B, C \in F_{H,\Sigma}$ such that for all $i \in \mathbb{N}$, $A \odot B^{\textcircled{i}} \odot C \le D$, where $B^{\textcircled{i}} = B \odot \cdots \odot B$. By Lemma 2, $A \odot B^{\textcircled{i}} \odot C = \mathrm{cl}_H(AB^iC)$, so we have $\mathrm{cl}_H(AB^iC) \le D$, and in particular $AB^iC \le D$ for all i. By $*$-continuity of Lang_Σ, we obtain $AB^*C \le D$. By Lemma 1 and using $D = \mathrm{cl}_H(D)$, we obtain $\mathrm{cl}_H(AB^*C) \le D$ and finally by Lemma 2, $A \odot B^\circledast \odot C \le D$. This achieves the proof that $F_{H,\Sigma}$ is a $*$-continuous Kleene algebra.

Let $A, B \in \mathsf{CReg}_{H,\Sigma}$. We have $A \le B \Leftrightarrow A \oplus B = B \Leftrightarrow \mathrm{cl}_H(A + B) = B \Leftrightarrow A \subseteq B$. Finally, if $e \le f$ is a hypothesis from H, then we have $\mathrm{cl}_H[e] \subseteq \mathrm{cl}_H([f])$, so the hypothesis is verified in $F_{H,\Sigma}$. $\square$

The implications $\mathsf{KA}_H^{(*)} \vdash e \le f \Rightarrow [e] \subseteq \mathrm{cl}_H(f)$ follow from the fact that if an inequation $e \le f$ is derivable in KA_H (resp. KA_H^*) then it is true in every model, in particular in the model $F_{H,\Sigma}$, thus $\mathrm{cl}_H([e]) \subseteq \mathrm{cl}_H([f])$ or, equivalently. $[e] \subseteq \mathrm{cl}_H([f])$.

Let us prove that for any regular expressions e, f, if $[e] \subseteq \mathrm{cl}_H([f])$ then $\mathsf{KA}_H^* \vdash e \le f$. Let e, f be two such expressions and let T be a derivation tree for $[e] \subseteq \mathrm{cl}_H([f])$, i.e. witnessing $\vdash_{H,L} e \le f$. We show that we can transform this tree T into a proof tree in KA_H^*. The extension rule is an occurrence of [8, App. A, Lem. 12]. Finally, the hypothesis rule is also provable in KA_H^*, using the hypothesis $e \le f$ together with compatibility of $\le$ with concatenation, and completeness of KA^* for membership of $u \in [e]$. We can therefore build from the tree T a proof in KA_H^* witnessing $\mathsf{KA}_H^* \vdash e \le f$. $\square$

When we restrict the shape of the expression e to words, and hypotheses to $(w \le \sum w)$-hypotheses, we get the implication missing from Theorem 2.

Proposition 2. *Let H be a set of $(w \leq \sum w)$-hypotheses, $w \in \Sigma^*$ and $f \in \mathsf{Exp}_\Sigma$.*

$$\mathsf{KA}_H \vdash w \leq f \qquad \Leftrightarrow \qquad w \in \mathrm{cl}_H([f])$$

Proof. Let us show that $w \in \mathrm{cl}_H([f])$ implies $\mathsf{KA}_H \vdash w \leq f$. We proceed by induction on the height of a derivation tree for $w \in \mathrm{cl}_H([f])$. If this tree is just a leaf, then $w \in [f]$ and by Theorem 1 $\mathsf{KA} \vdash w \leq f$. Otherwise, this derivation starts with the following steps:

$$\frac{\dfrac{\cdots}{\left(\overline{uw_i v}\right)_i}}{\dfrac{u(\sum_i w_i)v}{uwv}} \quad w \leq \sum_i w_i \in H$$

Our inductive assumption is that $\mathsf{KA}_H \vdash uw_i v \leq f$ for all i, thus $\mathsf{KA}_H \vdash \sum_i uw_i v \leq f$. We also have $\mathsf{KA}_H \vdash w \leq (\sum_i w_i)$ hence $\mathsf{KA} \vdash w \leq f$ by distributivity. $\qquad\qquad\square$

4   Decidability of **KA** and **KA*** with $(1 = \sum x)$-Hypotheses

In this section, we answer positively the decidability problem of KA_H, where H is a set of $(1 = \sum x)$-hypotheses, posed by Cohen [5]:

Theorem 3. *If H is a set of $(1 = \sum x)$-hypotheses, then KA_H is decidable.*

To prove this theorem we show that in the case of $(1 = \sum x)$-hypotheses:

(P1) $\mathsf{KA}_H \vdash e \leq f$ if and only if $[e] \subseteq \mathrm{cl}_H([f])$.
(P2) $\mathrm{cl}_H([f])$ is regular and we can compute effectively an expression for it.

Decidability of KA_H follows immediately from (P1) and (P2), since it amounts to checking language inclusion for two regular expressions.

To show $(P1)$ and $(P2)$, it is enough to prove the following result:

Theorem 4. *Let H be a set of $(1 = \sum x)$-hypotheses and let f be a regular expression. The language $\mathrm{cl}_H([f])$ is regular and we can compute effectively an expression c such that $[c] = \mathrm{cl}_H([f])$ and $\mathsf{KA}_H \vdash c \leq f$.*

(P2) follows immediately from Theorem 4. To show (P1), it is enough to prove that $[e] \subseteq \mathrm{cl}_H([f])$ implies $\mathsf{KA}_H \vdash e \leq f$, since the other implication is always true (Theorem 2). Let e, f such that $[e] \subseteq \mathrm{cl}_H([f])$. If c is the expression given by Theorem 4, we have $\mathsf{KA}_H \vdash c \leq f$ and $[e] \subseteq [c]$ so by Theorem 1 $\mathsf{KA} \vdash e \leq c$, and this concludes the proof.

To prove Theorem 4, we first show that the closure of $(1 = \sum x)$-hypotheses can be decomposed into the closure of $(x \leq 1)$-hypotheses followed by the closure of $(1 \leq \sum x)$-hypotheses:

Proposition 3 (Decomposition result). *Let $H = \{1 = S_j \mid j \in J\}$ be a set of $(1 = \sum x)$-hypotheses.*
We set $H_{sum} = \{1 \leq S_j \mid j \in J\}$ and $H_{id} = \{a \leq 1 \mid a \in [S_j], j \in J\}$. For every language $L \subseteq \Sigma^*$, we have $\mathrm{cl}_H(L) = \mathrm{cl}_{H_{sum}}(\mathrm{cl}_{H_{id}}(L))$.

Sketch. We show that rules from H_{id} can be locally permuted with rules of H_{sum} in a derivation tree. This allows to compute a derivation tree where all rules from H_{id} occur after (i.e. closer to leaves than) rules from H_{sum}.   □

Now, we will show results similar to Theorem 4, but which apply to $(x \leq 1)$-hypotheses and $(1 \leq \sum x)$-hypotheses (Propositions 5 and 6 below). To prove Theorem 4, the idea is to decompose H into H_{id} and H_{sum} using the decomposition property Proposition 3, then applying Propositions 5 and 6 to H_{id} and H_{sum} respectively.

To show these two propositions, we make use of a result from [7]:

Definition 4. *Let $\mathcal{A} = (Q, \Delta, \iota, F)$ be an NFA, H be a set of hypotheses and $\varphi : Q \to \mathsf{Exp}_\Sigma$ a function from states to expressions. We say that φ is H-compatible with $\mathcal{A}$ if:*

- $\mathsf{KA}_H \vdash 1 \leq \varphi(q)$ *whenever* $q \in F$,
- $\mathsf{KA}_H \vdash a\varphi(r) \leq \varphi(q)$ *for all transitions* $(q, a, r) \in \Delta$.

We set $\varphi^{\mathcal{A}} = \varphi(\iota)$.

Proposition 4 ([7]). *Let $\mathcal{A}$ be a NFA, H be a set of hypothesis and φ be a function H-compatible with $\mathcal{A}$. We can construct a regular expression $f_{\mathcal{A}}$ such that:*

$$[f_{\mathcal{A}}] = [\mathcal{A}] \quad and \quad \mathsf{KA}_H \vdash f_{\mathcal{A}} \leq \varphi^{\mathcal{A}}$$

Proposition 5. *Let H be a set of $(x \leq 1)$-hypotheses and let f be a regular expression. The language $\mathrm{cl}_H([f])$ is regular and we can compute effectively an expression c such that $[c] = \mathrm{cl}_H([f])$ and $\mathsf{KA}_H \vdash c \leq f$.*

Proof. Let $K = \mathrm{cl}_H([f])$ and $\Gamma = \{a \mid (a \leq 1) \in H\}$, we show that K is regular. If $\mathcal{A}$ is a NFA for f, a NFA $\mathcal{A}_{id}$ recognizing K can be built from $\mathcal{A}$ by adding a Γ-labelled loop on every state. It is straightforward to verify that the resulting NFA recognizes K, by allowing to ignore any letter from Γ.

For every $q \in Q$, let f_q be a regular expression such that $[f_q] = [q]_{\mathcal{A}}$, where $[q]_{\mathcal{A}}$ denotes the language accepted from q in $\mathcal{A}$. Let $\varphi : Q \to \mathsf{Exp}_\Sigma$ which maps each state q of $\mathcal{A}_{id}$ (which is also a state of $\mathcal{A}$) to $\varphi(q) = f_q$. Let us show that φ is H-compatible with $\mathcal{A}$. If $q \in F$, then $1 \in [f_q]$, so by completeness of KA, we have $\mathsf{KA} \vdash 1 \leq f_q$. Let (p, a, q) be a transition of $\mathcal{A}_{id}$. Either $(p, a, q) \in \Delta$, in which case we have $a[f_q] \subseteq [f_p]$, and so by Theorem 1 $\mathsf{KA} \vdash af_q \leq f_p$. Or $p = q$ (this transition is a loop that we added). Then $\mathsf{KA}_H \vdash a \leq 1$, so $\mathsf{KA}_H \vdash af_p \leq f_p$, and this concludes the proof.

By Proposition 4, we can now construct a regular expression c which satisfies the desired properties.   □

Definition 5. *Let Γ be a set of letters. A language L is said to be Γ-closed if:*

$$\forall u, v \in \Sigma^*, \forall a \in \Gamma \quad uv \in L \quad \Rightarrow \quad uav \in L$$

If $H = \{1 \leq S_i \mid i \in I\}$ is a set of $(1 \leq \sum x)$-hypotheses, we say that a language L is H-closed if if it is Γ-closed where $\Gamma = \cup_{i \in I}[S_i]$.

Remark 1. If H is a set of $(x \leq 1)$-hypothesis, and $\Gamma = \{a \mid (a \leq 1) \in H\}$, then $\text{cl}_H(L)$ is Γ-closed for every language L.

Proposition 6. *Let H be a set of $(1 \leq \sum x)$-hypotheses and let f be a regular expression whose language is H-closed. The language $\text{cl}_H([f])$ is regular and we can compute effectively an expression c such that $[c] = \text{cl}_H([f])$ and $\text{KA}_H \vdash c \leq f$.*

Proof. We set $L = [f]$, $H = \{1 \leq S_j \mid j \in J\}$ and $\Gamma = \{a \mid a \in [S_j], j \in J\}$.

Let us show that $\text{cl}_H(L)$ is regular. The idea is to construct a set of words $L_\sharp$, where each word $u_\sharp$ is obtained from a word u of $\text{cl}_H(L)$, by adding at the position where a rule $(1 \leq S_j)$ is applied in the derivation tree for $\text{cl}_H(L) \vdash u$, a new symbol $\sharp_j$. We will show that this set satisfies the two following properties:

- $\text{cl}_H(L)$ is obtained from $L_\sharp$ by erasing the symbols $\sharp_j$.
- $L_\sharp$ is regular.

Since the operation that erases letters preserves regularity, we obtain as a corollary that $\text{cl}_H(L)$ is regular.

Let us now introduce more precisely the language $L_\sharp$ and show the properties that it satisfies. Let $\Theta_\sharp = \{\sharp_j \mid j \in J\}$ be a set of new letters and $\Sigma_\sharp = \Sigma \cup \Theta_\sharp$ be the alphabet Σ enriched with these new letters.

We define the function $exp : \Sigma_\sharp \to \mathcal{P}(\Sigma)$ that expands every letter $\sharp_j$ into the sum of the letters corresponding to its rule in H as follows:

$$
\begin{array}{ll}
exp(a) = a & \text{if } a \in \Sigma \\
exp(\sharp_j) = \{a \mid a \in [S_j]\} & \forall j \in J
\end{array}
$$

This function can naturally be extended to $exp : (\Sigma_\sharp)^* \to \mathcal{P}(\Sigma^*)$. If $L \subseteq \Sigma^*$, we define $L_\sharp \subseteq (\Sigma_\sharp)^*$ as follows:

$$
L_\sharp = exp^{-1}(\mathcal{P}(L)) = \{u \in (\Sigma_\sharp)^* \mid exp(u) \subseteq L\}
$$

We define the morphism $\pi : (\Sigma_\sharp)^* \to \Sigma^*$ that erases the letters from $\Theta_\sharp$ as follows: $\pi(a) = a$ if $a \in \Sigma$ and $\pi(\sharp_j) = \epsilon$ for all $j \in J$. Our goal is to prove that $\text{cl}_H(L) = \pi(L_\sharp)$ and that $L_\sharp$ is regular. To prove the first part, we need an alternative presentation of $L_\sharp$ as the closure of a new set of hypotheses $H_\sharp$ which we define as follows:

$$
H_\sharp = \{\sharp_j \leq S_j \mid j \in J\} \cup \{\sharp_j \leq 1 \mid j \in J\}
$$

Lemma 4. *We have $L_\sharp = \text{cl}_{H_\sharp}(L)$. In particular $L_\sharp$ is $\Theta_\sharp$-closed.*

See App. B for a detailed proof of Lemma 4.

Lemma 5. $\text{cl}_H(L) = \pi(L_\sharp)$.

Proof. If $u \in \pi(L_\sharp)$, let $v \in L_\sharp$ such that $u = \pi(v)$. By Lemma 4, there is a derivation tree T_v for $v \in \mathrm{cl}_{H_\sharp}(L)$. Erasing all occurrences of $\sharp_j$ in T_v yields a derivation tree for $u \in \mathrm{cl}_H(L)$.

Conversely, if $u \in \mathrm{cl}_H(L)$ is witnessed by some derivation tree T_u, we show by induction on T_u that there exists $v \in L_\sharp \cap \pi^{-1}(u)$. If T_u is a single leaf, we have $u \in L$, and therefore it suffices to take $v = u$.

Otherwise, the rule applied at the root of T_u partitions u into $u = wz$, and has premises $\{wbz \mid b \in [S_j]\}$ for some $j \in J$ and $w, z \in \Sigma^*$. By induction hypothesis, for all $b \in [S_j]$, there is $v_b \in L_\sharp \cap \pi^{-1}(wbz)$. Let $w = w_1 \ldots w_n$ and $z = z_1 \ldots z_m$ be the decompositions of w, z into letters of Σ. By definition of π, for all $b \in [S_j]$, v_b can be written $v_b = \alpha_{b,1} w_1 \alpha_{b,2} w_2 \ldots w_n \alpha_{b,n+1} b \alpha_{b,n+1} z_1 \alpha_{b,n+2} \ldots z_m \alpha_{b,n+m+3}$, with $\alpha_{b,0} \ldots \alpha_{b,n+m+3} \in (\Theta_\sharp)^*$. For each $k \in [0, n+m+3]$, let $\alpha_k = \Pi_{b \in [S_j]} \alpha_{b,k}$. Let $w' = \alpha_0 w_1 \alpha_1 \ldots w_n \alpha_{n+1}$ and $z' = \alpha_{n+2} z_1 \alpha_{n+3} \ldots z_m \alpha_{n+m+3}$. By Lemma 4, $L_\sharp$ is $\Theta_\sharp$-closed, so for each $b \in [S_j]$ the word $v_b' = w' b z'$ is in $L_\sharp$, since v_b' is obtained from v_b by adding letters from $\Theta_\sharp$. We can finally build $v = w' \sharp_j z'$. We have $exp(v) = \bigcup_{b \in [S_j]} exp(v_b') \subseteq L$, and $\pi(v) = \pi(w') \pi(z') = wz = u$. □

Lemma 6. $L_\sharp$ *is a regular language, computable effectively.*

Sketch. From a DFA $\mathcal{A} = (\Sigma, Q, q_0, F, \delta)$ for for L, we first build a DFA $\mathcal{A}_\wedge = (\Sigma, \mathcal{P}(Q), q_0, \mathcal{P}(F), \delta_\wedge)$, which corresponds to a powerset construction, except that accepting states are $\mathcal{P}(F)$. This means that the semantic of a state P is the conjunction of its members. We then build $\mathcal{A}_\sharp = (\Sigma, \mathcal{P}(Q), q_0, \mathcal{P}(F), \delta_\sharp)$ based on $\mathcal{A}_\wedge$, which can additionally read letters of the form $\sharp_j$, by expanding them using the powerset structure of $\mathcal{A}_\wedge$. □

Lemma 7. *We can construct a regular expression c such that $[c] = \mathrm{cl}_H(L)$ and* $\mathsf{KA}_H \vdash c \leq f$.

Proof. Let $\mathcal{A}_\sharp$ be the DFA constructed for $L_\sharp$ in the proof of Lemma 6. We will use the notations of this proof in the following.

Let $\pi(\mathcal{A}_\sharp) = (\Sigma, \mathcal{P}(Q), q_0, \mathcal{P}(F), \pi(\delta_\sharp))$ be the NFA obtained from $\mathcal{A}_\sharp$ by replacing every transition $\delta_\sharp(P, \sharp_j) = R$, where $j \in J$, by a transition $\pi(\delta_\sharp)(P, \epsilon) = R$. By Lemma 5, the automaton $\pi(\mathcal{A}_\sharp)$ recognizes the language $\mathrm{cl}_H(L)$. Let us construct a regular expression c for this automaton such that $\mathsf{KA}_H \vdash c \leq f$.

For every $P \in \mathcal{P}(Q)$, let f_P be a regular expression such that $[f_P] = [P]_{\mathcal{A}_\wedge}$.

Let $\varphi : \mathcal{P}(Q) \to \mathsf{Exp}_\Sigma$ be the function which maps each state P of $\pi(\mathcal{A}_\sharp)$ to $\varphi(P) = f_P$. Let us show that φ is H-compatible.

If $P \in \mathcal{P}(F)$, then P is a final state of $\mathcal{A}_\wedge$, so $1 \in [f_P]$, and by completeness of KA, $\mathsf{KA} \vdash 1 \leq f_P$. Let $(P, a, R) \in \pi(\Delta_\sharp)$. Either $a \in \Sigma$, so $(P, a, R) \in \Delta_\wedge$ and $a[f_R] \subseteq [f_P]$, so by Theorem 1 $\mathsf{KA} \vdash a f_R \leq f_P$. Or $a = \epsilon$ so there is $j \in J$ such that $(P, \sharp_j, R) \in \Delta_\sharp$. This means that $R = \cup_{b \in [S_j]} R_b$ where $\delta_\wedge(P, b) = R_b, \forall b \in [S_j]$. We have then that $b[f_{R_b}] \subseteq [f_P]$ for all $b \in [S_j]$. Note that for all $b \in [S_j]$, $R_b \subseteq R$, so $[f_R] \subseteq [f_{R_b}]$ and then $S_j[f_R] \subseteq [f_P]$. By Theorem 1 $\mathsf{KA} \vdash S_j f_R \leq f_P$. We have also that $\mathsf{KA}_H \vdash \sharp_j \leq S_j$, so $\mathsf{KA}_H \vdash \sharp_j f_R \leq f_P$.

By Proposition 4, we can construct the desired regular expression c. □

5 Complexity Results for Letter Hypotheses

In this section, we give a recursion-theoretic characterization of KA_H and KA_H^* where H is a set of letter hypotheses or $(w \leq \sum w)$-hypotheses. In all the section, by "deciding $\mathsf{KA}_H^{(*)}$" we mean deciding whether $\mathsf{KA}_H^{(*)} \vdash e \leq f$, given e, f, H as input.

Theses various complexity classes will be obtained by reduction from some known problems concerning Turing Machines (TM) and alternating linearly bounded automata (LBA), such as halting problem and universality.

To obtain these reductions, we build on a result which bridges TMs and LBAs on one hand and closures on the other: the set of co-reachable configurations of a TM (resp. LBA) can be seen as the closure of a well-chosen set of hypotheses.

We present this result in Sect. 5.1, and show in Sect. 5.2 how to instantiate it to get our complexity classes.

5.1 Closure and Co-reachable States of TMs and LBAs

Definition 6. *An* alternating Turing Machine *over* Σ *is a tuple* $\mathcal{M} = (Q, Q_F, \Gamma, \iota, B, \Delta)$ *consisting of a finite set of states* Q *and final states* $Q_F \subseteq Q$, *a finite set of states* Q, *a finite working alphabet* $\Gamma \supseteq \Sigma$, *an initial state* $\iota \in Q$, $B \in \Gamma$ *the blank symbol and a transition function* $\Delta : (Q \setminus Q_F) \times \Gamma \to \mathcal{P}(\mathcal{P}(\{L, R\} \times \Gamma \times Q))$. *Let* $\#_L, \#_R \notin \Gamma$ *be fresh symbols to mark the ends of the tape, and* $\Gamma_\# = \Gamma \cup \{\#_L, \#_R\}$.

A configuration *is a word* $uqav = \#_L \Gamma^* Q \Gamma^+ \#_R$, *where* $\#_L$ *and* $\#_R$ *are special symbols not in* Γ, *meaning that the head of the TM points to the letter* a. *We denote by* C *the set of configurations of* $\mathcal{M}$. *A configuration is* final *if it is of the form* $\#_L \Gamma^* Q_F \Gamma^+ \#_L$.

The execution of the TM $\mathcal{M}$ *over input* $w \in \Sigma$ *may be seen as a game-like scenario between two players* $\exists$loise *and* $\forall$belard *over a graph* $C \sqcup (C \times \mathcal{P}(\{L, R\} \times \Gamma \times Q))$, *with initial position* ιw *which proceeds as follows.*

- *over a configuration* $uqav$ *with* $a \in \Gamma$, $u, v \in \Gamma_\#^*$, $\exists$loise *picks a transition* $X \in \Delta(q, a)$ *to move to position* $(uqav, X)$
- *over a position* $(uqav, X)$ *with* $a \in \Gamma$, $u, v \in \Gamma^*$, $\forall$belard *picks a triple* $(d, c, r) \in X$ *to move in configuration*
  - $ucrB\#_R$ *if* $v = \#_R$ *and* $d = R$
  - $ucrv$ *if* $v \neq \#_R$ *and* $d = R$
  - $\#_L r B c v$ *if* $u = \#_L$ *and* $d = L$
  - $u'rbcv$ *if* $u = \#_R u'b$ *and* $d = L$

Given a subset of configurations $D \subseteq C$, *we define* $\mathrm{Attr}^{\exists\mathrm{loise}}(D)$ *the* $\exists$loise attractor *for* D *as the set of configurations from which* $\exists$loise *may force the execution to go through* D.

A deterministic *TM* $\mathcal{M}$ *is one where every* $\Delta(q, a) \subseteq \{\{(d, c, r)\}\}$ *for some* $(d, c, r) \in \{L, R\} \times \Gamma \times Q$ *In such a case, we may identify* $\mathcal{M}$ *with the underlying partial function* $[\mathcal{M}] : \Sigma^* \rightharpoonup Q_F$.

An alternating linearly bounded automaton *over the alphabet* Σ *is a tuple* $\mathcal{A} = (Q, Q_F, \Gamma, \iota, \Delta)$ *where* $(Q, Q_F, \Gamma \sqcup \{B\}, \iota, B, \Delta)$ *is a TM that does not insert* B *symbols. This means that the head can point to* $\natural_d$, *and for every* $X \in \Delta(q, \#_d)$ *and* $(d', a, r) \in X$, *we have* $d \neq d'$ *and* $a = \#_d$.

An LBA is deterministic if its underlying TM is.

Definition 7. *A set of* $(w \leq \sum w)$-*hypotheses is said to be* length-preserving *if for every* $(v \leq \sum_{i \in I} v_i) \in H$, *we have that* $|v| = |v_i|$ *for all* $i \in I$.

The following lemma generalizes a similar construction from [13].

Lemma 8. *For every TM* $\mathcal{M}$ *of working alphabet* Γ, *there exists a set of* $(w \leq \sum w)$-*hypotheses* $H_{\mathcal{M}}$ *over the alphabet* $\Theta = Q \cup \Gamma$ *such that, for any set of configurations* $D \subseteq C$ *we have that:* $\mathrm{cl}_{H_{\mathcal{A}}}(D) = \mathrm{Attr}^{\exists \text{loise}}(D)$. *Furthermore, this reduction is polytime computable, and* $H_{\mathcal{A}}$ *is length-preserving if* $\mathcal{M}$ *is an LBA.*

A configuration c is *co-reachable* if $\exists$loise has a strategy to reach a final configuration from c. Lemma 8 shows that the set of co-reachable configurations can be seen as the closure by $(w \leq \sum w)$-hypotheses. Since we are also interested in $(x \leq \sum x)$-hypotheses, we will show that $(w \leq \sum w)$ hypotheses can be transformed into letter hypotheses. Moreover, this transformation preserves the length-preserving property.

Theorem 5. *Let* Σ *be an alphabet,* H *be a set of* $(w \leq \sum w)$-*hypotheses over* Σ. *There exists an extended alphabet* $\Sigma' \supseteq \Sigma$, *a set of* $(x \leq \sum w)$-*hypotheses* H' *over* Σ' *and a regular expression* $h \in \mathsf{Exp}_{\Sigma'}$ *such that the following holds for every* $f \in \mathsf{Exp}_\Sigma$ *and* $w \in \Sigma^*$.

$$w \in \mathrm{cl}_H([f]) \qquad \text{if and only if} \qquad w \in \mathrm{cl}_{H'}([f + h])$$

Furthermore, we guarantee the following:

- (Σ', H', h) *can be computed in polynomial time from* (Σ, H).
- H' *is length-preserving whenever* H *is.*

5.2   Complexity Results

Lemma 9. *If* H *is a set of length-preserving* $(w \leq \sum w)$-*hypotheses (resp. a set of* $(x \leq \sum x)$-*hypotheses),* $w \in \Sigma^*$ *and* $f \in \mathsf{Exp}_\Sigma$, *deciding* $\mathsf{KA}_H \vdash w \leq f$ *is* EXPTIME $-$ complete.

Proof. We actually show that our problem is complete in alternating-PSPACE (APSPACE), which enables us to conclude as EXPTIME and APSPACE coincide. First, notice that by completeness of KA_H over this fragment (Proposition 2), we have $\mathsf{KA}_H \vdash w \leq f \Leftrightarrow w \in \mathrm{cl}_H([f])$. Hence, we work directly with the latter notion. It suffices to show hardness for the $(x \leq \sum x)$ case and membership for the $(w \leq \sum w)$ case.

Given an arbitrary alternating Turing Machine $\mathcal{M}$ in APSPACE there exists a polynomial $p \in \mathbb{N}[X]$ such that executions of $\mathcal{M}$ over words w are bisimilar to executions of the LBA($\mathcal{M}$) over $wB^{p(|w|)}$. Hence, by Lemma 8 and Theorem 5, the problem with $(x \leq \sum x)$-hypotheses is APSPACE-hard. Conversely, we may show that our problem with $(w \leq \sum w)$-hypotheses falls into APSPACE. On input w, the alternating algorithm first checks whether $w \in [f]$ in linear time. If it is the case, it returns "yes". Otherwise, it non-deterministically picks a factorization $w = uxv$ with $x \in \Sigma^*$ and a hypothesis $x \leq \sum_i y_i$. It then universally picks $y_i \in \Sigma^{|x|}$, and replaces x by y_i on the tape, so that the new tape content is $w' = uy_iv$. Then the algorithm loops back to its first step. In parallel, we keep track of the number of steps and halt by returning "no" as soon as we reach $|\Sigma|^{|w|}$ steps. This is correct because, if there is a derivation tree witnessing $w \in \mathrm{cl}_H([f])$, there is one where on every path, all nodes have distinct labels, so the nondeterministic player can play according to this tree, while the universal player selects a branch. □

Theorem 6. *Deciding* KA_H^* *is* Π_1^0*-complete for* $(x \leq \sum x)$*-hypotheses.*

Proof. By Lemma 9 and the fact that regular expressions are in recursive bijection with natural numbers, our set is clearly Π_1^0. To show completeness, we effectively reduce the set of universal LBAs, which is known to be Π_1^0-complete, to our set of triples. Indeed, by Lemma 8, an LBA $\mathcal{A}$ is universal if and only if $\#_L\{\iota\}\Sigma^*\#_R \subseteq \mathrm{cl}_H(C_F)$ where C_F is the set of final configurations. □

Theorem 7. *If H is a set of $(x \leq \sum w)$-hypotheses, $w \in \Sigma^*$ and $f \in \mathsf{Exp}_\Sigma$, deciding $\mathsf{KA}_H^{(*)} \vdash w \leq f$ is Σ_1^0-complete.*

Proof. As KA_H is a recursively enumerable theory, our set is Σ_1^0. By the completeness theorem (Proposition 2), we have $\mathsf{KA}_H \vdash w \leq f \Leftrightarrow \mathsf{KA}_H^* \vdash w \leq f \Leftrightarrow w \in \mathrm{cl}_H([f])$, so we may work directly with closure. In order to show completeness, we reduce the halting problem for Turing machines (on empty input) to this problem. Let $\mathcal{M}$ be a Turing machine with alphabet Σ and final state q_f, and $H_\mathcal{M}$ be the set of $(w \leq \sum w)$-hypotheses given effectively by Lemma 8. Let $f = \Sigma^* q_f \Sigma^*$, by Lemma 8 we have $\mathcal{M}$ halts on empty input if and only if $q_0 \in \mathrm{cl}_{H_\mathcal{M}}(f)$. Notice that hypotheses of H' are of the form $u \leq V$ where $u \in \Theta^3$ and $V \subseteq \Theta^3$. By Theorem 5, we can compute a set H' of $(x \leq \sum x)$-hypotheses, and an expression h on an extended alphabet such that $q_0 \in \mathrm{cl}_{H_\mathcal{M}}([f]) \Leftrightarrow q_0 \in \mathrm{cl}_{H'}([f + h])$. □

Theorem 8. *Deciding* KA_H^* *is* Π_2^0*-complete for* $(x \leq \sum w)$*-hypotheses.*

Proof. This set is Π_2^0 by Theorem 7. It is complete by reduction from the set of Turing Machines accepting all inputs, which is known to be Π_2^0. Indeed, let $\mathcal{M}$ be a Turing Machine on alphabet Σ with final state q_f, by Lemma 8, we can compute a set of $(w \leq \sum w)$-hypotheses $H_\mathcal{M}$ with finite language in second components such that $c \in \mathrm{cl}_{H_\mathcal{M}}(c')$ if and only if configuration c' is reachable from c. As before, by Theorem 5, we can compute a set of letter hypotheses H' with finite languages in second components, and a regular expression h on an extended alphabet, such that for any $\mathrm{cl}_{H'}([f + h]) \cap \Theta^* = \mathrm{cl}_H([f])$ for any $f \in \mathsf{Exp}_\Theta$. Let $C_f = \Sigma^* q_f \Sigma^*$, we obtain that $\mathcal{M}$ accepts all inputs if and only if $[q_0 \Sigma^*] \subseteq \mathrm{cl}_{H'}([C_f + h])$, which achieves the proof of Π_2^0-completeness. □

Theorem 9. *Deciding* KA_H^* *is* Π_1^1*-complete for* $(x \leq g)$*-hypotheses* $(g \in \mathsf{Exp}_\Sigma)$.

Sketch. It is shown in [13] that the problem is complete with hypotheses of the form $H = H_w \cup \{x \leq g\}$, where H_w is a set of length-preserving $(w \leq \sum w)$ hypotheses. A slight refinement of Theorem 5 allows us to reduce this problem to hypotheses of the form $x \leq g$.   □

5.3   Undecidability of KA_H for Sums of Letters

Fix an alphabet Σ, a well-behaved coding function $\lceil \cdot \rceil$ of Turing machines with final states $\{0, 1\}$ into Σ^* and a recursive pairing function $\langle \cdot, \cdot \rangle : \Sigma^* \times \Sigma^* \to \Sigma^*$. A *universal total* $F : \Sigma^* \to \{0, 1\}$ is a function such that, for every total Turing machine $\mathcal{M}$ and input $w \in \Sigma^*$ we have $F(\langle \lceil \mathcal{M} \rceil, w \rangle) = [M](w)$. In particular, F should be total and is not uniquely determined over codes of partial Turing machines. The next folklore lemma follows from an easy diagonal argument.

Lemma 10. *There is no universal total Turing machine.*

Our strategy is to show that decidability of KA_H with $(x \leq \sum x)$ hypotheses would imply the existence of a universal total TM. To do so, we need one additional lemma.

Lemma 11. *Suppose that* $\mathcal{M} = (Q, Q_F, \Gamma, \iota, B, \Delta)$ *is a total Turing machine with final states* $\{0, 1\}$ *and initial state* ι. *Let* $w \in \Sigma^*$ *be an input word for* $\mathcal{M}$.
  Then there is effectively a set of length-preserving $(w \leq \sum w)$*-hypotheses* H *and expressions* e_w, h *such that* $[\mathcal{M}](w) = 1$ *if and only if* $\mathsf{KA}_H \vdash e_w \leq h$.

Theorem 10. KA_H *is undecidable for* $(x \leq \sum x)$*-hypotheses.*

Proof. Assume that KA_H is decidable. This means that we have an algorithm $\mathcal{A}$ taking tuples (Σ, w, f, H), with H consisting only of sum-of-letters hypotheses and returning true when $\mathsf{KA}_H \vdash w \leq f$ and false otherwise. Without loss of generality, we can assume that $\mathcal{A}$ is total. By Theorem 5, we may even provide an algorithm $\mathcal{A}'$ taking as input tuples (w, f, H) where H is a set of length-preserving $(w \leq \sum w)$-hypotheses with a similar behaviour: $\mathcal{A}'$ returns true when $\mathsf{KA}_H \vdash w \leq f$ and false otherwise.

Given $\mathcal{A}'$, consider $\mathcal{M}$ defined so that $[\mathcal{M}](\lceil \mathcal{N} \rceil, w) = [\mathcal{A}'](e_w, h, H)$, where the last tuple is given by Lemma 11. We show that $\mathcal{M}$ is a total universal Turing machine. Since such a machine cannot exist by Lemma 10, this is enough to conclude. Since $\mathcal{A}'$ is total, so is $\mathcal{M}$. For total Turing Machines $\mathcal{N}$, Lemma 11 guarantees that $[\mathcal{N}](w) = 1$ if and only if $[\mathcal{A}'](e_w, h, H) = [\mathcal{M}](\lceil \mathcal{N} \rceil, w) = 1$. Since both $[\mathcal{A}']$ and $[\mathcal{M}]$ are total with codomain $\{0, 1\}$, we really have $[\mathcal{M}](\lceil \mathcal{N} \rceil, w) = [\mathcal{N}](w)$.   □

References

1. Anderson, C.J., et al.: NetKAT: semantic foundations for networks. In: Proceedings of the POPL, pp. 113–126. ACM (2014). https://doi.org/10.1145/2535838.2535862
2. Angus, A., Kozen, D.: Kleene algebra with tests and program schematology. Technical report TR2001-1844, CS Dpt., Cornell University, July 2001. http://hdl.handle.net/1813/5831
3. Boffa, M.: Une remarque sur les systèmes complets d'identités rationnelles. Informatique Théorique et Applications **24**, 419–428 (1990). http://archive.numdam.org/article/ITA19902444190.pdf
4. Braibant, T., Pous, D.: An efficient Coq tactic for deciding Kleene algebras. In: Kaufmann, M., Paulson, L.C. (eds.) ITP 2010. LNCS, vol. 6172, pp. 163–178. Springer, Heidelberg (2010). https://doi.org/10.1007/978-3-642-14052-5_13
5. Cohen, E.: Hypotheses in Kleene algebra. Technical report, Bellcore, Morristown, N.J. (1994). http://www.researchgate.net/publication/2648968_Hypotheses_in_Kleene_Algebra
6. Conway, J.H.: Regular Algebra and Finite Machines. Chapman and Hall, London (1971)
7. Das, A., Doumane, A., Pous, D.: Left-handed completeness for Kleene algebra, via cyclic proofs. In: Proceedings of the LPAR. EPiC Series in Computing, vol. 57, pp. 271–289. EasyChair (2018). https://doi.org/10.29007/hzq3
8. Doumane, A., Kuperberg, D., Pous, D., Pradic, P.: Kleene algebra with hypotheses. Full version of this extended abstract (2019). https://hal.archives-ouvertes.fr/hal-02021315
9. Hoare, C.A.R.T., Möller, B., Struth, G., Wehrman, I.: Concurrent Kleene algebra. In: Bravetti, M., Zavattaro, G. (eds.) CONCUR 2009. LNCS, vol. 5710, pp. 399–414. Springer, Heidelberg (2009). https://doi.org/10.1007/978-3-642-04081-8_27
10. Kleene, S.C.: Representation of events in nerve nets and finite automata. In: Automata Studies, pp. 3–41. Princeton University Press (1956). http://www.rand.org/pubs/research_memoranda/2008/RM704.pdf
11. Kozen, D.: A completeness theorem for Kleene algebras and the algebra of regular events. Inform. Comput. **110**(2), 366–390 (1994). https://doi.org/10.1006/inco.1994.1037
12. Kozen, D.: On Hoare logic and Kleene algebra with tests. ACM Trans. Comput. Log. **1**(1), 60–76 (2000). https://doi.org/10.1145/343369.343378
13. Kozen, D.: On the complexity of reasoning in Kleene algebra. Inform. Comput. **179**, 152–162 (2002). https://doi.org/10.1006/inco.2001.2960
14. Kozen, D., Mamouras, K.: Kleene algebra with equations. In: Esparza, J., Fraigniaud, P., Husfeldt, T., Koutsoupias, E. (eds.) ICALP 2014. LNCS, vol. 8573, pp. 280–292. Springer, Heidelberg (2014). https://doi.org/10.1007/978-3-662-43951-7_24
15. Kozen, D., Patron, M.-C.: Certification of compiler optimizations using Kleene algebra with tests. In: Lloyd, J., et al. (eds.) CL 2000. LNCS (LNAI), vol. 1861, pp. 568–582. Springer, Heidelberg (2000). https://doi.org/10.1007/3-540-44957-4_38
16. Krauss, A., Nipkow, T.: Proof pearl: regular expression equivalence and relation algebra. JAR **49**(1), 95–106 (2012). https://doi.org/10.1007/s10817-011-9223-4
17. Krob, D.: Complete systems of B-rational identities. TCS **89**(2), 207–343 (1991). https://doi.org/10.1016/0304-3975(91)90395-I

18. Mamouras, K.: Extensions of Kleene algebra for program verification. Ph.D. thesis, Cornell University, Ithaca, NY (2015). https://ecommons.cornell.edu/handle/1813/40960
19. Pous, D.: Kleene algebra with tests and Coq tools for while programs. In: Blazy, S., Paulin-Mohring, C., Pichardie, D. (eds.) ITP 2013. LNCS, vol. 7998, pp. 180–196. Springer, Heidelberg (2013). https://doi.org/10.1007/978-3-642-39634-2_15

7

Deciding Equivalence of Separated Non-nested Attribute Systems in Polynomial Time

Helmut Seidl[1], Raphaela Palenta[1]([✉]), and Sebastian Maneth[2]

[1] Fakultät für Informatik, TU München, Munich, Germany
{seidl,palenta}@in.tum.de
[2] FB3 - Informatik, Universität Bremen, Bremen, Germany
maneth@uni-bremen.de

Abstract. In 1982, Courcelle and Franchi-Zannettacci showed that the equivalence problem of separated non-nested attribute systems can be reduced to the equivalence problem of total deterministic separated basic macro tree transducers. They also gave a procedure for deciding equivalence of transducer in the latter class. Here, we reconsider this equivalence problem. We present a new alternative decision procedure and prove that it runs in polynomial time. We also consider extensions of this result to partial transducers and to the case where parameters of transducers accumulate strings instead of trees.

1 Introduction

Attribute grammars are a well-established formalism for realizing computations on syntax trees [20,21], and implementations are available for various programming languages, see, e.g. [12,28,29]. A fundamental question for any such specification formalism is whether two specifications are semantically equivalent. As a particular case, attribute grammars have been considered which compute uninterpreted trees. Such devices that translate input trees (viz. the parse trees of a context-free grammar) into output trees, have also been studied under the name "attributed tree transducer" [14] (see also [15]). In 1982, Courcelle and Franchi-Zannettacci showed that the equivalence problem for (strongly noncircular) attribute systems reduces to the equivalence problem for primitive recursive schemes with parameters [3]; the latter model is also known under the name *macro tree transducer* [9]. Whether or not equivalence of attributed tree transducers (ATTs) or of (deterministic) macro tree transducers (MTTs) is decidable remain two intriguing (and very difficult) open problems.

For several subclasses of ATTs it has been proven that equivalence is decidable. The most general and very recent result that covers almost all other known ones about deterministic tree transducers is that "deterministic top-down tree-to-string transducers" have decidable equivalence [27]. Notice that the complexity of this problem remains unknown (the decidability is proved via two semi-decision procedures). The only result concerning deterministic tree transducers that we are aware of and that is *not* covered by this general result, is the one by Courcelle and Franchi-Zannettacci about decidability of equivalence of "separated non-nested" ATTs (which they reduce to the same problem for "separated non-nested" MTTs). However, in their paper no statement is given concerning the complexity of the problem. In this paper we close this gap and study the complexity of deciding equivalence of separated non-nested MTTs. To do so we propose a new approach that we feel is simpler and easier to understand than the one of [3]. Using our approach we can prove that the problem can be solved in polynomial time.

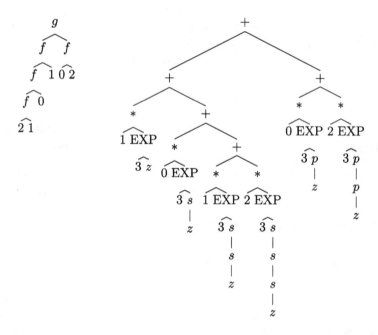

Fig. 1. Input tree for 2101.01 (in ternary) and corresponding output tree of M_{tern}.

In a separated non-nested attribute system, distinct sets of operators are used for the construction of inherited and synthesized attributes, respectively, and inherited attributes may depend on inherited attributes only. Courcelle and Franchi-Zannettacci's algorithm first translates separated non-nested attribute grammars into separated total deterministic non-nested macro tree transducers. In the sequel we will use the more established term *basic* macro-tree transducers instead of non-nested MTTs. Here, a macro tree transducer is called *separated* if the alphabets used for the construction of parameter values and outside of parameter positions are disjoint. And the MTT is *basic* if there is no nesting of state calls, i.e., there are no state calls inside of parameter positions. Let us consider an example. We want to translate ternary numbers into expressions over +, *, EXP, plus the constants 0, 1, and 2. Additionally, operators s, p, and z are used to represent integers in unary. The ternary numbers are parsed into particular binary trees; e.g., the left of Fig. 1 shows the binary tree for the

$$q_0(g(x_1, x_2)) \quad \rightarrow \quad +(q(x_1, z), q'(x_2, p(z)))$$
$$q(f(x_1, x_2), y) \quad \rightarrow \quad +(r(x_2, y), q(x_1, s(y)))$$
$$q'(f(x_1, x_2), y) \quad \rightarrow \quad +(r(x_1, y), q'(x_2, p(y)))$$
$$\phi(i, y) \quad \rightarrow \quad *(i, \mathrm{EXP}(3, y)) \quad \text{for } i \in \{0, 1, 2\}, \phi \in \{q, q', r\}$$

Fig. 2. Rules of the transducer M_tern.

number 2101.02. This tree is translated by our MTT into the tree in the right of Fig. 1 (which indeed evaluates to $64.\overline{2}$ in decimal). The rules of our transducer M_tern are shown in Fig. 2. The example is similar to the one used by Knuth [20] in order to introduce attribute grammars. The transducer is indeed basic and separated: the operators p, s, and z are only used in parameter positions.

Our polynomial time decision procedure works in two phases: first, the transducer is converted into an "earliest" normal form. In this form, output symbols that are not produced within parameter positions are produced as early as possible. In particular it means that the root output symbols of the right-hand sides of rules for one state must differ. For instance, our transducer M_tern is *not* earliest, because all three r-rules produce the same output root symbol $(*)$. Intuitively, this symbol should be produced earlier, e.g., at the place when the state r is called. The earliest form is a common technique used for normal forms and equivalence testing of different kinds of tree transducers [8,13,22]. We show that equivalent states of a transducer in this earliest form produce their state-output exactly in the same way. This means especially that the output of parameters is produced in the same places. It is therefore left to check, in the second phase, that also these parameter outputs are equivalent. To this end, we build an equivalence relation on states of earliest transducers that combines the two equivalence tests described before. Technically speaking, the equivalence relation is tested by constructing sets of Herbrand equalities. From these equalities, a fixed point algorithm can, after polynomially many iterations, produce a stable set of equalities.

The proofs of Lemmata 1 and 2 can be found in the appendix of an extended version at http://arxiv.org/abs/1902.03858.

2　Separated Basic Macro Tree Transducers

Let Σ be a ranked alphabet, i.e., every symbol of the finite set Σ has associated with it a fixed rank $k \in \mathbb{N}$. Generally, we assume that the input alphabet Σ is *non-trivial*, i.e., Σ has cardinality at least 2, and contains at least one symbol of rank 0 and at least one symbol of rank > 0. The set T_Σ is the set of all (finite, ordered, rooted) trees over the alphabet Σ. We denote a tree as a string over Σ and parenthesis and commas, i.e., $f(a, f(a, b))$ is a tree over Σ, where f is of rank 2 and a, b are of rank zero. We use Dewey dotted decimal notation to refer to a node of a tree: The root node is denoted ε, and for a node u, its i-th child is denoted $u.i$. For instance, in the tree $f(a, f(a, b))$ the b-node is at position 2.2. A *pattern* (or k-pattern) (over Δ) is a tree $p \in T_{\Delta \cup \{\top\}}$ over a ranked alphabet Δ and a disjoint symbol $\top$ (with exactly k occurrences of the symbol $\top$). The occurrences of the dedicated symbol $\top$ serve as place holders for other patterns. Assume that p is a k-pattern and that $p_1, \ldots, p_k$ are patterns; then $p[p_1, \ldots, p_k]$ denotes the pattern obtained from p by replacing, for $i = 1, \ldots, k$, the i-th occurrence (from left-to-right) of $\top$ by the pattern p_i.

A *macro tree transducer* (*MTT*) M is a tuple $(Q, \Sigma, \Delta, \delta)$ where Q is a ranked alphabet of states, Σ and Δ are the ranked input and output alphabets, respectively, and δ is a finite set of rules of the form:

$$q(f(x_1, \ldots, x_k), y_1, \ldots, y_l) \to T \tag{1}$$

where $q \in Q$ is a state of rank $l + 1$, $l \geq 0$, $f \in \Sigma$ is an input symbol of rank $k \geq 0$, $x_1, \ldots, x_k$ and $y_1, \ldots, y_l$ are the formal input and output parameters, respectively, and T is a tree built up according to the following grammar:

$$T ::= a(T_1, \ldots, T_m) \mid q'(x_i, T_1, \ldots, T_n) \mid y_j$$

for output symbols $a \in \Delta$ of rank $m \geq 0$ and states $q' \in Q$ of rank $n + 1$, input parameter x_i with $1 \leq i \leq k$, and output parameter y_j with $1 \leq j \leq l$. For simplicity, we assume that all states q have the same number l of parameters. Our definition of an MTT does not contain an initial state. We therefore consider an MTT always together with an axiom $A = p[q_1(x_1, \underline{T_1}), \ldots, q_m(x_1, \underline{T_m})]$ where $\underline{T_1}, \ldots, \underline{T_m} \in \mathcal{T}_\Delta^l$ are vectors of output trees (of length l each). Sometimes we only use an MTT M without explicitly mentioning an axiom A, then some A is assumed implicitly. Intuitively, the state q of an MTT corresponds to a function in a functional language which is defined through pattern matching over its first argument, and which constructs tree output using tree top-concatenation only; the second to $(l+1)$-th arguments of state q are its accumulating output parameters. The output produced by a state for a given input tree is determined by the right-hand side T of a rule of the transducer which matches the root symbol f of the current input tree. This right-hand side is built up from accumulating output parameters and calls to states for subtrees of the input and applications of output symbols from Δ. In general MTTs are nondeterministic and only partially defined. Here, however, we concentrate on total deterministic transducers. The MTT M is *deterministic*, if for every $(q, f) \in Q \times \Sigma$ there is at most one rule of the form (1). The MTT M is *total*, if for every $(q, f) \in Q \times \Sigma$ there is at least one rule of the form (1). For total deterministic transducers, the semantics of a state $q \in Q$ with the rule $q(f(x_1, \ldots, x_k), y_1, \ldots, y_l) \to T$ can be considered as a function

$$[\![q]\!] : \mathcal{T}_\Sigma \times \mathcal{T}_\Delta^l \to \mathcal{T}_\Delta$$

which inductively is defined by:

$$[\![q]\!](f(t_1, \ldots, t_k), \underline{S}) = [\![T]\!](t_1, \ldots, t_k)\,\underline{S}$$
$$\text{where}$$
$$[\![a(T_1, \ldots, T_m)]\!]\,\underline{t}\,\underline{S} = a([\![T_1]\!]\,\underline{t}\,\underline{S}, \ldots, [\![T_m]\!]\,\underline{t}\,\underline{S})$$

$$\llbracket y_j \rrbracket \, \underline{t} \, \underline{S} = S_j$$
$$\llbracket q'(x_i, T_1, \ldots, T_l) \rrbracket \, \underline{t} \, \underline{S} = \llbracket q' \rrbracket (t_i, \llbracket T_1 \rrbracket \, \underline{t} \, \underline{S}, \ldots, \llbracket T_l \rrbracket \, \underline{t} \, \underline{S})$$

where $\underline{S} = (S_1, \ldots, S_l) \in \mathcal{T}_\Delta^l$ is a vector of output trees. The semantics of a pair (M, A) with MTT M and axiom $A = p[q_1(x_1, \underline{T_1}), \ldots, q_m(x_1, \underline{T_m})]$ is defined by $\llbracket (M, A) \rrbracket (t) = p[\llbracket q_1 \rrbracket (t, \underline{T_1}), \ldots, \llbracket q_m \rrbracket (t, \underline{T_m})]$. Two pairs (M_1, A_1), (M_2, A_2) consisting of MTTs M_1, M_2 and corresponding axioms A_1, A_2 are *equivalent*, $(M_1, A_1) \equiv (M_2, A_2)$, iff for all input trees $t \in \mathcal{T}_\Sigma$, and parameter values $\underline{T} \in \mathcal{T}_{\Delta_{in}}^l$, $\llbracket (M_1, A_1) \rrbracket (t, \underline{T}) = \llbracket (M_2, A_2) \rrbracket (t, \underline{T})$.

The MTT M is *basic*, if each argument tree T_j of a subtree $q'(x_i, T_1, \ldots, T_n)$ of right-hand sides T of rules (1) may not contain further occurrences of states, i.e., is in $\mathcal{T}_{\Delta \cup Y}$. The MTT M is *separated basic*, if M is basic, and Δ is the disjoint union of ranked alphabets Δ_{out} and Δ_{in} so that the argument trees T_j of subtrees $q'(x_i, T_1, \ldots, T_n)$ are in $\mathcal{T}_{\Delta_{in} \cup Y}$, while the output symbols a outside of such subtrees are from Δ_{out}. The same must hold for the axiom. Thus, letters directly produced by a state call are in Δ_{out} while letters produced in the parameters are in Δ_{in}. The MTT M_{tern} from the Introduction is separated basic with $\Delta_{out} = \{0, 1, 2, 3, *, +, \text{EXP}\}$ and $\Delta_{in} = \{p, s, z\}$.

As separated basic MTTs are in the focus of our interests, we make the grammar for their right-hand side trees T explicit:

$$T ::= a(T_1, \ldots, T_m) \mid y_j \mid q'(x_i, T_1', \ldots, T_n')$$
$$T' ::= b(T_1', \ldots, T_{m'}') \mid y_j$$

where $a \in \Delta_{out}$, $q' \in Q$, $b \in \Delta_{in}$ of ranks $m, n + 1$ and m', respectively, and p is an n-pattern over Δ. For separated basic MTTs only axioms $A = p[q_1(x_1, \underline{T_1}), \ldots, q_m(x_1, \underline{T_m})]$ with $T_1, \ldots, T_m \in \mathcal{T}_{\Delta_{in}}^l$ are considered.

Note that equivalence of nondeterministic transducers is undecidable (even already for very small subclasses of transductions [18]). Therefore, we assume for the rest of the paper that all MTTs are deterministic and separated basic. We will also assume that all MTTs are total, with the exception of Sect. 5 where we also consider partial MTTs.

Example 1. We reconsider the example from the Introduction and adjust it to our formal definition. The transducer was given without an axiom (but with a tacitly assumed "start state" q_0). Let us now remove the state q_0 and add the axiom $A = q(x_1, z)$. The new q rule for g is:

$$q(g(x_1, x_2), y) \rightarrow +(q(x_1, y), q'(x_2, p(y))).$$

To make the transducer total, we add for state q' the rule

$$q'(g(x_1, x_2), y) \rightarrow +(*(0, \text{EXP}(3, y)), *(0, \text{EXP}(3, y))).$$

For state r we add rules $q(\alpha(x_1, x_2), y) \rightarrow *(0, \text{EXP}(3, y))$ with $\alpha = f, g$. The MTT is separated basic with $\Delta_{out} = \{0, 1, 2, 3, *, +, \text{EXP}\}$ and $\Delta_{in} = \{p, s, z\}$. $\square$

We restricted ourselves to *total* separated basic MTTs. However, we would like to be able to decide equivalence for *partial* transducers as well. For this reason we define now top-down tree automata, and will then decide equivalence of MTTs relative to some given DTA D. A *deterministic top-down tree automaton* (*DTA*) D is a tuple $(B, \Sigma, b_0, \delta_D)$ where B is a finite set of states, Σ is a ranked alphabet of input symbols, $b_0 \in B$ is the initial state, and δ_D is the partial transition function with rules of the form $b(f(x_1, \ldots, x_k)) \rightarrow (b_1(x_1), \ldots, b_k(x_k))$, where $b, b_1, \ldots, b_k \in B$ and $f \in \Sigma$ of rank k. W.l.o.g. we always assume that all states b of a DTA are productive, i.e., $\mathsf{dom}(b) \neq \emptyset$. If we consider a MTT M relative to a DTA D we implicitly assume a mapping $\pi : Q \rightarrow B$, that maps each state of M to a state of D, then we consider for q only input trees in $\mathsf{dom}(\pi(q))$.

3 Top-Down Normalization of Transducers

In this section we show that each total deterministic basic separated MTT can be put into an "earliest" normal form relative to a fixed DTA D. Intuitively, state output (in Δ_{out}) is produced as early as possible for a transducer in the normal form. It can then be shown that two equivalent transducers in normal form produce their state output in exactly the same way.

Recall the definition of patterns as trees over $\mathcal{T}_{\Delta \cup \{\top\}}$. Substitution of $\top$-symbols by other patterns induces a partial ordering $\sqsubseteq$ over patterns by $p \sqsubseteq p'$ if and only if $p = p'[p_1, \ldots, p_m]$ for some patterns $p_1, \ldots, p_m$. W.r.t. this ordering, $\top$ is the *largest* element, while all patterns without occurrences of $\top$ are minimal. By adding an artificial *least* element $\bot$, the resulting partial ordering is in fact a *complete lattice*. Let us denote this complete lattice by $\mathcal{P}_\Delta$.

Let $\Delta = \Delta_{in} \cup \Delta_{out}$. For $T \in \mathcal{T}_{\Delta \cup Y}$, we define the Δ_{out}-*prefix* as the pattern $p \in \mathcal{T}_{\Delta_{out} \cup \{\top\}}$ as follows. Assume that $T = a(T_1, \ldots, T_m)$.

- If $a \in \Delta_{out}$, then $p = a(p_1, \ldots, p_m)$ where for $j = 1, \ldots, m$, p_j is the Δ_{out}-prefix of T_j.
- If $a \in \Delta_{in} \cup Y$, then $p = \top$.

By this definition, each tree $t \in \mathcal{T}_{\Delta \cup Y}$ can be uniquely decomposed into a Δ_{out}-prefix p and subtrees $t_1, \ldots, t_m$ whose root symbols all are contained in $\Delta_{in} \cup Y$ such that $t = p[t_1, \ldots, t_m]$.

Let M be a total separated basic MTT M, D be a given DTA. We define the Δ_{out}-prefix of a state q of M relative to D as the minimal pattern $p \in \mathcal{T}_{\Delta_{out} \cup \{\top\}}$ so that each tree $[\![q]\!](t, \underline{T})$, $t \in \mathsf{dom}(\pi(q))$, $\underline{T} \in \mathcal{T}_\Delta^l$, is of the form $p[T_1, \ldots, T_m]$ for some sequence of subtrees $T_1, \ldots, T_m \in \mathcal{T}_\Delta$. Let us denote this unique pattern p by $\mathsf{pref}_o(q)$. If $q(f, y_1, \ldots, y_l) \rightarrow T$ is a rule of a separated basic MTT and there is an input tree $f(t_1, \ldots, t_k) \in \mathsf{dom}(\pi(q))$ then $|\mathsf{pref}_o(q)| \leq |T|$.

Lemma 1. *Let M be a total separated basic MTT and D a given DTA. Let $t \in \mathsf{dom}(\pi(q))$ be a smallest input tree of a state q of M. The Δ_{out}-prefix of every state q of M relative to D can be computed in time $\mathcal{O}(|t| \cdot |M|)$.*

The proof is similar to the one of [8, Theorem 8] for top-down tree transducers. This construction can be carried over as, for the computation of Δ_{out}-prefixes, the precise contents of the output parameters y_j can be ignored.

Example 2. We compute the Δ_{out}-prefix of the MTT M from Example 1. We consider M relative to the trivial DTA D that consists only of one state b with $dom(b) = \mathcal{T}_\Sigma$. We therefore omit D in our example. We get the following system of in-equations: from the rules of state r we obtain $Y_r \sqsubseteq *(i, \mathrm{EXP}(3, \top))$ with $i \in \{0, 1, 2\}$. From the rules of state q we obtain $Y_q \sqsubseteq +(Y_q, Y_{q'})$, $Y_q \sqsubseteq +(Y_r, Y_q)$ and $Y_q \sqsubseteq *(i, \mathrm{EXP}(3, \top))$ with $i \in \{0, 1, 2\}$. From the rules of state q' we obtain $Y_{q'} \sqsubseteq +(*(0, \mathrm{EXP}(3, \top)), *(0, \mathrm{EXP}(3, \top)))$, $Y_{q'} \sqsubseteq +(Y_r, Y_{q'})$ and $Y_{q'} \sqsubseteq *(i, \mathrm{EXP}(3, \top))$ with $i \in \{0, 1, 2\}$. For the fixpoint iteration we initialize $Y_r^{(0)}$, $Y_q^{(0)}$, $Y_{q'}^{(0)}$ with $\bot$ each. Then $Y_r^{(1)} = *(\top, \mathrm{EXP}(3, \top)) = Y_r^{(2)}$ and $Y_q^{(1)} = \top$, $Y_{q'}^{(1)} = \top$. Thus, the fixpoint iteration ends after two rounds with the solution $\mathsf{pref}_o(q) = \top$.   □

Let M be a separated basic MTT M and D be a given DTA D. M is called D-earliest if for every state $q \in Q$ the Δ_{out}-prefix with respect to $\pi(q)$ is $\top$.

Lemma 2. *For every pair (M, A) consisting of a total separated basic MTT M and axiom A and a given DTA D, an equivalent pair (M', A') can be constructed so that M' is a total separated basic MTT that is D-earliest. Let t be an output tree of (M, A) for a smallest input tree $t' \in \mathsf{dom}(\pi(q))$ where q is the state occurring in A. Then the construction runs in time $\mathcal{O}(|t| \cdot |(M, A)|)$.*

The construction follows the same line as the one for the earliest form of top-down tree transducer, cf. [8, Theorem 11]. Note that for partial separated basic MTTs the size of the Δ_{out}-prefixes is at most exponential in the size of the transducer. However for total transducer that we consider here the Δ_{out}-prefixes are linear in the size of the transducer and can be computed in quadratic time, cf. [8].

Corollary 1. *For (M, A) consisting of a total deterministic separated basic MTT M and axiom A and the trivial DTA D accepting $\mathcal{T}_\Sigma$ an equivalent pair (M', A') can be constructed in quadratic time such that M' is an D-earliest total deterministic separated basic MTT.*

Example 3. We construct an equivalent earliest MTT M' for the transducer from Example 1. In Example 2 we already computed the Δ_{out}-prefixes of states q, q', r; $\mathsf{pref}_o(q) = \top$, $\mathsf{pref}_o(q') = \top$ and $\mathsf{pref}_o(r) = *(\top, \mathrm{EXP}(3, \top))$. As there is only one occurrence of symbol $\top$ in the Δ_{out}-prefixes of q and q' we call states $\langle q, 1 \rangle$ and $\langle q', 1 \rangle$ by q and q', respectively. Hence, a corresponding earliest transducer has axiom $A = q(x_1, z)$. The rules of q and q' for input symbol g do not change. For input symbol f we obtain

$$q(f(x_1, x_2), y) \rightarrow +(*(r(x_2, y), \mathrm{EXP}(3, y)), q(x1, s(y))) \quad \text{and}$$
$$q'(f(x_1, x_2), y) \rightarrow +(*(r(x_1, y), \mathrm{EXP}(3, y), q'(x_2, p(y))).$$

As there is only one occurrence of symbol $\top$ related to a recursive call in $\mathsf{pref}_o(r)$ we call $\langle r, 1 \rangle$ by r. For state r we obtain new rules $r(\alpha(x_1, x_2), y) \rightarrow 0$ with $\alpha \in \{f, g\}$ and $r(i, y) \rightarrow i$ with $i \in \{0, 1, 2\}$.   □

We define a family of equivalence relation by induction, $\cong_b \subseteq ((Q, T_{\Delta_{in}}^k) \cup T_{\Delta_{in}}) \times ((Q, T_{\Delta_{in}}^k) \cup T_{\Delta_{in}})$ with b a state of a given DTA is the intersection of the equivalence relations $\cong_b^{(h)}$, i.e., $X \cong_b Z$ if and only if for all $h \geq 0$, $X \cong_b^{(h)} Z$. We let $(q, \underline{T}) \cong_b^{(h+1)} (q', \underline{T'})$ if for all $f \in \mathrm{dom}(b)$ with $b(f(x_1, \ldots, x_k)) \rightarrow (b_1, \ldots, b_k)$, there is a pattern p such that $q(f(x_1, \ldots, x_k), y) \rightarrow p[t_1, \ldots, t_m]$ and $q'(f(x_1, \ldots, x_k), y') \rightarrow p[t'_1, \ldots, t'_m]$ with

- if t_i and t'_i are both recursive calls to the same subtree, i.e., $t_i = q_i(x_{j_i}, \underline{T_i})$, $t'_i = q'_i(x_{j'_i}, \underline{T'_i})$ and $j_i = j'_i$, then $(q_i, \underline{T_i})[\underline{T}/y] \cong_{b_{j_i}}^h (q'_i, \underline{T'_i})[\underline{T'}/y']$
- if t_i and t'_i are both recursive calls but on different subtrees, i.e., $t_i = q_i(x_{j_i}, \underline{T_i})$, $t'_i = q'_i(x_{j'_i}, \underline{T'_i})$ and $j_i \neq j'_i$, then $\hat{t} := [\![q_i]\!](s, \underline{T_i})[\underline{T}/y] = [\![q'_i]\!](s, \underline{T'_i})[\underline{T}/y]$ for some $s \in \Sigma^{(0)}$ and $(q_i, \underline{T_i})[\underline{T}/y] \cong_{b_{j_i}}^{(h)} \hat{t} \cong_{b_{j'_i}}^{(h)} (q'_i, \underline{T'_i})[\underline{T}/y]$
- if t_i and t'_i are both parameter calls, i.e., $t_i = y_{j_i}$ and $t'_i = y'_{j'_i}$, then $T_{j_i} = T'_{j'_i}$
- if t_i is a parameter call and t'_i a recursive call, i.e., $t_i = y_{j_i}$ and $t'_i = q'_i(x_{j'_i}, \underline{T'_i})$, then $T_{j_i} \cong_{b_{j'_i}}^{(h)} (q'_i, \underline{T'_i})[\underline{T'}/y']$
- (symmetric to the latter case) if t_i is a recursive call and t'_i a parameter call, i.e., $t_i = q_i(x_{j_i}, \underline{T_i})$ and $t'_i = y'_{j'_i}$, then $(q_i, \underline{T_i})[\underline{T}/y] \cong_{b_{j_i}}^{(h)} T'_{j'_i}$.

We let $T \cong_b^{(h+1)} (q', \underline{T'})$ if for all $f \in \mathrm{dom}(b)$ with $r(f(x_1, \ldots, x_k)) \rightarrow (b_1, \ldots, b_k)$, $q'(f(\underline{x}), y) \rightarrow t'$,

- if $t' = y_j$ then $T = T'_j$
- if $t' = q'_1(x_i, \underline{T'_1})$ then $T \cong_{b_i}^{(h)} (q'_1, \underline{T'_1})[\underline{T'}/y']$.

Intuitively, $(q, \underline{T}) \cong_b^h (q', \underline{T'})$ if for all input trees $t \in \mathrm{dom}(b)$ of height h, $[\![q]\!](t, \underline{T}) = [\![q']\!](t, \underline{T'})$. Then $(q, \underline{T}) \cong_b (q', \underline{T'})$ if for all input trees $t \in \mathrm{dom}(b)$ (independent of the height), $[\![q]\!](t, \underline{T}) = [\![q']\!](t, \underline{T'})$.

Theorem 1. *For a given DTA D with initial state b, let M, M' be D-earliest total deterministic separated basic MTTs with axioms A and A', respectively. Then (M, A) is equivalent to (M', A') relative to D, iff there is a pattern p such that $A = p[q_1(x_1, \underline{T_1}), \ldots, q_m(x_1, \underline{T_m})]$, and $A' = p[q'_1(x_1, \underline{T'_1}), \ldots, q'_m(x_1, \underline{T'_m})]$ and for $j = 1, \ldots, m$, $(q_j, \underline{T_j}) \cong_b (q'_j, \underline{T'_j})$, i.e., q_j and q'_j are equivalent on the values of output parameters $\underline{T_j}$ and $\underline{T'_j}$.*

Proof. Let Δ be the output alphabet of M and M'. Assume that $(M, A) \cong_b (M', A')$. As M and M' are earliest, the Δ_{out}-prefix of $[\![(M, A)]\!](t)$ and $[\![(M', A')]\!](t)$, for $t \in \mathrm{dom}(b)$ is the same pattern p and therefore $A = p[q_1(x_1, \underline{T_1}), \ldots, q_m(x_1, \underline{T_m})]$ and $A' = p[q'_1(x_1, \underline{T'_1}), \ldots, q'_m(x_1, \underline{T'_m})]$. To show that $(q_i, \underline{T_i}) \cong_b (q'_i, \underline{T'_i})$ let u_i be the position of the i-th $\top$-node in the pattern p. For some $t \in \mathrm{dom}(b)$ and $\underline{T} \in T_{\Delta_{in}}$ let t_i and t'_i be the subtree of $[\![(M, A)]\!](t, \underline{T})$ and $[\![(M', A')]\!](t, \underline{T})$, respectively. Then $t_i = t'_i$ and therefore $(q_i, \underline{T_i}) \cong_b (q'_i, \underline{T'_i})$.

Now, assume that the axioms $A = p[q_1(x_1, \underline{T_1}), \ldots, q_m(x_1, \underline{T_m})]$ and $A' = p[q'_1(x_1, \underline{T'_1}), \ldots, q'_m(x_1, \underline{T'_m})]$ consist of the same pattern p and for $i = 1, \ldots, m$, $(q_i, \underline{T_i}) \cong_b (q'_i, \underline{T'_i})$. Let $t \in \mathrm{dom}(b)$ be an input tree then

$$\begin{aligned}
[\![(M, A)]\!](t) &= p[[\![q_1]\!](t, \underline{T_1}), \dots, [\![q_m]\!](t, \underline{T_m})] \\
&= p[[\![q_1']\!](t, \underline{T_1'}), \dots, [\![q_m']\!](t, \underline{T_m'})] \\
&= [\![(M', A')]\!](t).
\end{aligned}$$

4 Polynomial Time

In this section we prove the main result of this paper, namely, that for each fixed DTA D, equivalence of total deterministic basic separated MTTs (relative to D) can be decided in polynomial time. This is achieved by taking as input two D-earliest such transducers, and then collecting conditions on the parameters of pairs of states of the respective transducers for their produced outputs to be equal.

Example 4. Consider a DTA D with a single state only which accepts all inputs, and states q, q' with

$$q(a, y_1, y_2) \to g(y_1) \qquad q'(a, y_1', y_2') \to g(y_2')$$

Then q and q' can only produce identical outputs for the input a (in $\mathsf{dom}(b)$) if parameter y_2' of q' contains the same output tree as parameter y_1 of q. This precondition can be formalized by the equality $y_2' \doteq y_1$. Note that in order to distinguish the output parameters of q' from those of q we have used primed copies y_i' for q'.   □

It turns out that *conjunctions* of equalities such as in Example 4 are sufficient for proving equivalence of states. For states q, q' of total separated basic MTTs M, M', respectively, that are both D-earliest for some fixed DTA D, $h \geq 0$ and some fresh variable z, we define

$$\Psi_{b,q}^{(h)}(z) = \bigwedge_{b(f\underline{x}) \to (b_1, \dots, b_k)} \bigwedge_{q(f\underline{x}, \underline{y}) \to y_j} (z \doteq y_j) \qquad \wedge$$
$$\bigwedge_{q(f\underline{x}, \underline{y}) \to \hat{q}(x_i, \underline{T})} \Psi_{b_i, \hat{q}}^{(h-1)}(z)[\underline{T}/\underline{y}] \wedge$$
$$\bigwedge_{\substack{q(f\underline{x}, \underline{y}) \to p[\dots] \\ p \neq \top}} \bot$$

where $\bot$ is the boolean value *false*. We denote the output parameters in $\Psi_{b,q}^{(h)}(z)$ by $\underline{y}$, we define $\Psi_{b,q'}'^{(h)}(z)$ in the same lines as $\Psi_{b,q}^{(h)}(z)$ but using $\underline{y}'$ for the output parameters. To substitute the output parameters with trees $\underline{T}, \underline{T}'$, we therefore use $\Psi_{b,q}^{(h)}(z)[\underline{T}/\underline{y}]$ and $\Psi_{b,q'}'^{(h)}(z)[\underline{T}'/\underline{y}']$. Assuming that q is a state of the D-earliest separated basic MTT M then $\Psi_{b,q}^{(h)}(z)$ is true for all ground parameter values $\underline{s}$ and some $T \in \mathcal{T}_{\Delta \cup Y}$ if $[\![q]\!](t, \underline{s}) = T[\underline{s}/\underline{y}]$ for all input trees $t \in \mathsf{dom}(b)$ of height at most h. Note that, since M is D-earliest, T is necessarily in $\mathcal{T}_{\Delta_{in} \cup Y}$. W.l.o.g., we assume that every state b of D is productive, i.e., $\mathsf{dom}(b) \neq \emptyset$. For each state b of D, we therefore may choose some input tree $t_b \in \mathsf{dom}(b)$ of minimal depth. We define $s_{b,q}$ to be the output of q for a minimal input tree $t_r \in \mathsf{dom}(b)$ and parameter values y—when considering formal output parameters as output symbols in Δ_{in}, i.e., $s_{b,q} = [\![q]\!](t_r, y)$.

Example 5. We consider again the trivial DTA D with only one state b that accepts all $t \in T_\Sigma$. Thus, we may choose $t_b = a$. For a state q with the following two rules $q(a, y_1, y_2) \to y_1$ and $q(f(x), y_1, y_2) \to q(x, h(y_2), b)$, we have $s_{b,q} = y_1$. Moreover, we obtain

$$\Psi_{b,q}^{(0)}(z) = z \doteq y_1$$

$$\Psi_{b,q}^{(1)}(z) = (z \doteq y_1) \wedge (z \doteq h(y_2))$$

$$\Psi_{b,q}^{(2)}(z) = (z \doteq y_1) \wedge (z \doteq h(y_2)) \wedge (z \doteq h(b))$$
$$\equiv (y_2 \doteq b) \wedge (y_1 \doteq h(b)) \wedge (z \doteq h(b))$$

$$\Psi_{b,q}^{(3)}(z) = (z \doteq y_1) \wedge (b \doteq b) \wedge (h(y_2) \doteq h(b)) \wedge (z \doteq h(b))$$
$$\equiv (y_2 \doteq b) \wedge (y_1 \doteq h(b)) \wedge (z \doteq h(b))$$

We observe that $\Psi_{b,q}^{(2)}(z) = \Psi_{b,q}^{(3)}(z)$ and therefore for every $h \geq 2$, $\Psi_{b,q}^{(h)}(z) = \Psi_{b,q}^{(3)}(z)$. □

According to our equivalence relation $\cong_b$, b state of the DTA D, we define for states q, q' of D-earliest total deterministic separated basic MTTs M, M', and $h \geq 0$, the conjunction $\Phi_{b,(q,q')}^{(h)}$ by

$$\bigwedge_{\substack{b(f\underline{x}) \to (b_1,\ldots,b_k) \\ q(f\underline{x},\underline{y}) \to p[\underline{t}] \\ q'(f\underline{x},\underline{y'}) \to p[\underline{t'}]}} \left(\bigwedge_{\substack{t_i = y_{j_i}, \\ t'_i = v'_{j'_i}}} (y_{j_i} \doteq y'_{j'_i}) \right. \wedge$$

$$\bigwedge_{\substack{t_i = y_{j_i}, \\ t'_i = q'_i(x_{j'_i}, \underline{T'})}} \Psi_{b_{j'_i}, q'_i}^{\prime(h-1)}(y_{j_i})[\underline{T'}/\underline{y'}] \wedge$$

$$\bigwedge_{\substack{t'_i = v'_{j'_i}, \\ t_i = q_i(x_{j_i}, \underline{T})}} \Psi_{b_{j_i}, q_i}^{(h-1)}(y'_{j'_i})[\underline{T}/\underline{y}] \wedge$$

$$\bigwedge_{\substack{t_i = q_i(x_{j_i}, \underline{T}), \\ t'_i = q'_i(x_{j'_i}, \underline{T'}) \\ j_i = j'_i}} \Phi_{b_{j_i}, (q_i, q'_i)}^{(h-1)}[\underline{T}/\underline{y}, \underline{T'}/\underline{y'}] \wedge$$

$$\left. \bigwedge_{\substack{t_i = q_i(x_{j_i}, \underline{T}), \\ t'_i = q'_i(x_{j'_i}, \underline{T'}) \\ j_i \neq j'_i}} (\Psi_{b_{j_i}, q_i}^{(h-1)}(s_{b,q_i})[\underline{T}/\underline{y}] \wedge \Psi_{b_{j'_i}, q'_i}^{\prime(h-1)}(s_{b,q_i}[\underline{T}/\underline{y}])[\underline{T'}/\underline{y'}]) \right) \wedge$$

$$\bigwedge_{\substack{b(f) \to (b_1,\ldots,b_k) \\ p \neq p', q(f\underline{x},\underline{y}) \to p[\underline{t}] \\ q'(f\underline{x},\underline{y}) \to p'[\underline{t'}]}} \bot$$

$\Phi_{b,(q,q')}^{(h)}$ is defined in the same lines as the equivalence relation $\cong_b^{(h)}$. $\Phi_{b,(q,q')}^{(h)}$ is true for all values of output parameters $\underline{T}, \underline{T'}$ such that $[\![q]\!](t, \underline{T}) = [\![q']\!](t, \underline{T'})$ for $t \in \mathsf{dom}(b)$ of height at most h. By induction on $h \geq 0$, we obtain:

Lemma 3. *For a given DTA D, states q, q' of D-earliest total separated basic MTTs, vectors of trees $\underline{T}, \underline{T}'$ over Δ_{in}, b a state of D. $s \in \text{dom}(b)$, and $h \geq 0$ the following two statements hold:*

$$(q, \underline{T}) \cong_b^{(h)} (q', \underline{T}') \Leftrightarrow \Phi_{b,(q,q')}^{(h)}[\underline{T}/\underline{y}, \underline{T}'/\underline{y}'] \equiv \text{true}$$

$$s \cong_b^{(h)} (q', \underline{T}') \Leftrightarrow \Psi_{b,q'}^{(h)}(t)[\underline{T}'/\underline{y}] \equiv \text{true}$$

$\square$

$\Phi_{b,(q,q')}^{(h)}$ is a conjunction of equations of the form $y_i \doteq y_j$, $y_i \doteq t$ with $t \in \Delta_{in}$. Every satisfiable conjunction of equalities is equivalent to a (possible empty) finite conjunction of equations of the form $y_i \doteq t_i$, $t_i \in T_{\Delta_{in} \cup Y}$ where the y_i are distinct and no equation is of the form $y_j \doteq y_j$. We call such conjunctions *reduced*. If we have two inequivalent reduced conjunctions ϕ_1 and ϕ_2 with $\phi_1 \Rightarrow \phi_2$ then ϕ_1 contains strictly more equations. From that follows that for every sequence $\phi_0 \Rightarrow \ldots \phi_m$ of pairwise inequivalent reduced conjunctions ϕ_j with k variables, $m \leq k + 1$ holds. This observation is crucial for the termination of the fixpoint iteration we will use to compute $\Phi_{b,(q,q')}^{(h)}$.

For $h \geq 0$ we have:

$$\Psi_{b,q}^{(h)}(z) \Rightarrow \Psi_{b,q}^{(h-1)}(z) \tag{2}$$

$$\Phi_{b,(q,q')}^{(h)} \Rightarrow \Phi_{b,(q,q')}^{(h-1)} \tag{3}$$

As we fixed the number of output parameters to the number l, for each pair (q, q') the conjunction $\Phi_{b,(q,q')}^{(h)}$ contains at most $2l$ variables y_i, y'_i. Assuming that the MTTs to which state q and q' belong have n states each, we conclude that $\Phi_{b,(q,q')}^{(n^2(2l+1))} \equiv \Phi_{b,(q,q')}^{(n^2(2l+1)+i)}$ and $\Psi_{b,q}^{(n(l+1))} \equiv \Psi_{b,q}^{(n(l+1)+i)}$ for all $i \geq 0$. Thus, we can define $\Phi_{b,(q,q')} := \Phi_{b,(q,q')}^{(n^2(2l+1))}$ and $\Psi_{b,q} := \Psi_{b,q}^{(n(l+1))}$. As $(q, \underline{T}) \cong_b (q', \underline{T}')$ iff for all $h \geq 0$, $(q, \underline{T}) \cong_b^{(h)} (q', \underline{T}')$ holds, observation (3) implies that

$$(q, \underline{T}) \cong_b (q', \underline{T}') \Leftrightarrow \Phi_{b,(q,q')}[\underline{T}/\underline{y}][\underline{T}'/\underline{y}'] \equiv \text{true}$$

Therefore, we have:

Lemma 4. *For a DTA D, states q, q' of D-earliest separated basic MTTs M, M' and states b of D, the formula $\Phi_{b,(q,q')}$ can be computed in time polynomial in the sizes of M and M'.*

Proof. We successively compute the conjunctions $\Psi_{b,q}^{(h)}(z), \Psi_{b,q'}^{(h)}(z), \Phi_{b,(q,q')}^{(h)}$, $h \geq 0$, for all states b, q, q'. As discussed before, some $h \leq n^2(2l+1)$ exists such that the conjunctions for $h+1$ are equivalent to the corresponding conjunctions for h—in which case, we terminate. It remains to prove that the conjunctions for h can be computed from the conjunctions for $h-1$ in polynomial time. For that, it is crucial that we maintain *reduced* conjunctions. Nonetheless, the *sizes* of occurring right-hand sides of equalities may be quite large. Consider for example the conjunction $x_1 \doteq a \wedge x_2 \doteq f(x_1, x_1) \wedge \ldots \wedge x_n \doteq f(x_{n-1}, x_{n-1})$. The corresponding reduced conjunction is then given by $x_1 \doteq a \wedge x_2 \doteq f(a, a) \wedge \ldots \wedge x_n \doteq f(f(f(\ldots(f(a, a))\ldots)$ where the sizes of right-hand sides grow exponentially. In order to arrive at a polynomial-size representation, we therefore rely on compact representations where isomorphic subtrees are represented only once. W.r.t. this representation, reduction of a non-reduced conjunction, implications between reduced conjunctions as well as substitution of variables in conjunctions can all be realized in polynomial time. From that, the assertion of the lemma follows.

Example 6. Let D be a DTA with the following rules $b(f(x)) \rightarrow (b)$, $b(g) \rightarrow ()$ and $b(h) \rightarrow ()$. Let q and q' be states of separated basic MTTs M, M', respectively, that are D-earliest and π, π' be the mappings from the states of D to the states of M, M' with $(b, q) \in \pi$ and $(b, q') \in \pi'$.

$$q(f(x), y_1, y_2) \rightarrow a(q(x, b(y_1, y_1), c(y_2), d))$$
$$q(g, y_1, y_2) \rightarrow y_1$$
$$q(h, y_1, y_2) \rightarrow y_2$$

$$q'(f(x), y_1', y_2') \rightarrow a(q'(x, c(y_1'), b(y_2', y_2'), d))$$
$$q'(g, y_1', y_2') \rightarrow y_2'$$
$$q'(h, y_1', y_2') \rightarrow y_1'$$

$$\Phi^{(0)}_{r,(q,q')} = (y_1 \doteq y_2') \wedge (y_2 \doteq y_1')$$
$$\Phi^{(1)}_{r,(q,q')} = (y_1 \doteq y_2') \wedge (y_2 \doteq y_1') \wedge (b(y_1, y_1) \doteq b(y_2', y_2')) \wedge (c(y_2) \doteq c(y_1'))$$
$$\equiv (y_1 \doteq y_2') \wedge (y_2 \doteq y_1') = \Phi^{(0)}_{r,(q,q')}$$

$\square$

In summary, we obtain the main theorem of our paper.

Theorem 2. *Let (M, A) and (M', A') be pairs consisting of total deterministic separated basic MTTs M, M' and corresponding axioms A, A' and D a DTA. Then the equivalence of (M, A) and (M', A') relative to D is decidable. If D accepts all input trees, equivalence can be decided in polynomial time.*

Proof. By Lemma 2 we build pairs (M_1, A_1) and (M_1', A_1') that are equivalent to (M, A) and (M', A') where M_1, M_1' are D-earliest separated basic MTTs. If D is trivial the construction is in polynomial time, cf. Corollary 1. Let the axioms be $A_1 = p[q_1(x_{i_1}, \underline{T_1}), \ldots, q_k(x_{i_k}, \underline{T_k})]$ and $A_1' = p'[q_1'(x_{i_1'}, \underline{T_1}), \ldots, q_k'(x_{i_{k'}'}, \underline{T_{k'}})]$. According to Lemma 3 (M_1, A_1) and (M_1', A_1') are equivalent iff

- $p = p'$, $k = k'$ and
- for all $j = 1, \ldots, k$, $\Phi_{b,(q_j,q_j')}[\underline{T_j}/\underline{y}, \underline{T_j}/\underline{y'}]$ is equivalent to **true**.

By Lemma 4 we can decide the second statements in time polynomial in the sizes of M_1 and M_1'.

5 Applications

In this section we show several applications of our equivalence result. First, we consider partial transductions of separated basic MTTs. To decide the equivalence of partial transductions we need to decide (a) whether the domain of two given MTTs is the same and if so, (b) whether the transductions on this domain are the same. How the second part of the decision procedure is done was shown in detail in this paper if the domain is given by a DTA. It therefore remains to discuss how this DTA can be obtained. It was shown[4, Theorem 3.1] that the domain of every top-down tree transducer T can be accepted by some DTA B_T and this automaton can be constructed from T in exponential time. This construction can easily be extended to basic MTTs. The decidability of equivalence of DTAs is well-known and can be done in polynomial time [16,17]. To obtain a total transducer we add for each pair (q, f), $q \in Q$ and $f \in \Sigma$ that has no rule a new rule $q(f(\underline{x}), \underline{y}) \to \perp$, where $\perp$ is an arbitrary symbol in Δ_{out} of rank zero.

Example 7. In Example 1 we discussed how to adjust the transducer from the introduction to our formal definition. We therefore had to introduce additional rules to obtain a total transducer. Now we still add rules for the same pairs (q, f) but only with right-hand sides $\perp$. Therefore the original domain of the transducer is given by a DTA $D = (R, \Sigma, r_0, \delta_D)$ with the rules $r_0(g(x_1, x_2)) \to (r(x_1), r(x_2))$, $r(f(x_1, x_2)) \to (r(x_1), r(x_2))$ and $r(i) \to (\ )$ for $i = 1, 2, 3$. □

Corollary 2. *The equivalence of deterministic separated basic MTTs with a partial transition function is decidable.*

Next, we show that our result can be used to decide the equivalence of total separated basic MTTs with look-ahead. A total macro tree transducer with regular look-ahead (MTT^R) is a tuple $(Q, \Sigma, \Delta, \delta, R, \delta_R)$ where R is a finite set of look-ahead states and δ_R is a total function from $R^k \to R$ for every $f \in \Sigma^{(k)}$. Additionally we have a deterministic bottom-up tree automaton $(P, \Sigma, \delta, -)$ (without final states). A rule of the MTT is of the form

$$q(f(t_1, \ldots, t_k), y_1, \ldots, y_k) \to t \qquad \langle p_1, \ldots, p_k \rangle$$

and is applicable to an input tree $f(t_1, \ldots, t_k)$ if the look-ahead automaton accepts t_i in state p_i for all $i = 1, \ldots, k$. For every $q, f, p_1, \ldots, p_k$ there is exactly one such rule. Let $N_1 = (Q_1, \Sigma_1, \Delta_1, \delta_1, R_1, \delta_{R1}), N_2 = (Q_2, \Sigma_2, \Delta_2, \delta_2, R_2, \delta_{R2})$ be two total separated basic MTTs with look-ahead. We construct total separated basic MTTs M_1, M_2 *without* look-ahead as follows. The input alphabet contains for every $f \in \Sigma$ and $r_1, \ldots, r_k \in R_1$, $r'_1, \ldots, r'_k \in R_2$ the symbols $\langle f, r_1, \ldots, r_k, r'_1, \ldots, r'_k \rangle$. For $q(f(x_1, \ldots, x_k), \underline{y}) \to p[T_1, \ldots, T_m] \langle r_1, \ldots, r_k \rangle$ and $q'(f(x_1, \ldots, x_k), \underline{y}') \to p'[T'_1, \ldots, T'_m] \langle r'_1, \ldots, r'_k \rangle$ we obtain for M_1 the rules

$$\hat{q}(\langle f(x_1, \ldots, x_k), r_1, \ldots, r_k, r'_1, \ldots, r'_k \rangle, \underline{y}) \to p[\hat{T}_1, \ldots, \hat{T}_m]$$

with $\hat{T}_i = \hat{q}_i(\langle x_{j_i}, \hat{r_1}, \ldots, \hat{r_l}, \hat{r_1'}, \ldots, \hat{r_l'} \rangle, Z_i)$ if $T_i = q_i(x_{j_i}, Z_i)$ and $q_i(x_{j_i}, \underline{y}) \rightarrow \hat{T}_i \ \langle \hat{r_1}, \ldots, \hat{r_l} \rangle$ and $q_i'(x_{j_i}, \underline{y'}) \rightarrow \hat{T}_i' \ \langle \hat{r_1'}, \ldots, \hat{r_l'} \rangle$. If $T_i = y_{j_i}$ then $\hat{T}_i = y_{j_i}$. The total separated basic $\overline{\text{MTT}}$ M_2 is constructed in the same lines. Thus, N_i, $i = 1, 2$ can be simulated by M_i, $i = 1, 2$, respectively, if the input is restricted to the regular tree language of new input trees that represent correct runs of the look-ahead automata.

Corollary 3. *The equivalence of total separated basic MTTs with regular look-ahead is decidable in polynomial time.*

Last, we consider separated basic MTTs that concatenate strings instead of trees in the parameters. We abbreviate this class of transducers by MTT^{yp}. Thus, the alphabet Δ_{in} is not longer a ranked alphabet but a unranked alphabet which elements/letters can be concatenated to words. The procedure to decide equivalence of MTT^{yp} is essentially the same as we discussed in this paper but instead of conjunctions of equations of trees over $\Delta_{in} \cup Y$ we obtain conjunctions equations of words. Equations of words is a well studied problem [23, 24, 26]. In particular, the confirmed Ehrenfeucht conjecture states that each conjunction of a set of word equations over a finite alphabet and using a finite number of variables, is equivalent to the conjunction of a finite subset of word equations [19]. Accordingly, by a similar argument as in Sect. 4, the sequences of conjunctions $\Psi_{b,q}^{(h)}(z), \Psi_{b,q'}'^{(h)}(z), \Phi_{b,(q,q')}^{(h)}, h \geq 0$, are ultimately stable. Using an encoding of words by integer matrices and applying techniques as in [19], we obtain:

Theorem 3. *The equivalence of total separated basic MTTs that concatenate words instead of trees in the parameters (Δ_{in} is unranked) is decidable.*

6 Related Work

For several subclasses of attribute systems equivalence is known to be decidable. For instance, attributed grammars without inherited attributes are equivalent to deterministic top-down tree transducers (DT) [3,5]. For this class equivalence was shown to be decidable by Esik [10]. Later, a simplified algorithm was provided in [8]. If the tree translation of an attribute grammar is of linear size increase, then equivalence is decidable, because it is decidable for deterministic macro tree transducers (DMTT) of linear size increase. This follows from the fact that the latter class coincides with the class of (deterministic) MSO definable tree translations (DMSOTT) [6] for which equivalence is decidable [7]. Figure 3 shows a Hasse diagram of classes of translations realized by certain deterministic tree transducers. The prefixes "l", "n", "sn", "b" and "sb" mean "linear size increase", "non-nested", "separated non-nested", "basic" and "separated basic", respectively. A minimal class where it is still open whether equivalence is decidable is the class of *non-nested* attribute systems (nATT) which, on the macro tree transducer side, is included in the class of *basic* deterministic macro tree transducers (bDMTT).

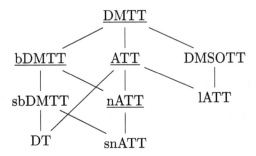

Fig. 3. Classes with and without (underlined) known decidability of equivalence

For deterministic top-down tree transducers, equivalence can be decided in EXPSPACE, and in NLOGSPACE if the transducers are total [25]. For the latter class of transducers, one can decide equivalence in polynomial time by transforming the transducer into a canonical normal form (called "earliest normal form") and then checking isomorphism of the resulting transducers [8]. In terms of hardness, we know that equivalence of deterministic top-down tree transducers is EXPTIME-hard. For linear size increase deterministic macro tree transducers the precise complexity is not known (but is at least NP-hard). More complexity results are known for other models of tree transducers such as streaming tree transducers [1], see [25] for a summary.

7 Conclusion

We have proved that the equivalence problem for separated non-nested attribute systems can be decided in polynomial time. In fact, we have shown a stronger statement, namely that in polynomial time equivalence of *separated basic total deterministic macro tree transducers* can be decided. To see that the latter is a strict superclass of the former, consider the translation that takes a binary tree as input, and outputs the same tree, but under each leaf a new monadic tree is output which represents the inverse Dewey path of that node. For instance, the tree $f(f(a,a),a)$ is translated into the tree $f(f(a(1(1(e))),a(2(1(e)))),a(2(e)))$. A macro tree transducer of the desired class can easily realize this translation using a rule of the form $q(f(x_{1,2}),y) \to f(q(x_1,1(y)),q(x_2,2(y)))$. In contrast, no attribute system can realize this translation. The reason is that for every attribute system, the number of distinct output subtrees is linearly bounded by the size of the input tree. For the given translation there is no linear such bound (it is bounded by $|s|\log(|s|)$).

The idea of "separated" to use different output alphabets, is related to the idea of transducers "with origin" [2,11]. In future work we would like to define adequate notions of origin for macro tree transducer, and prove that equivalence of such (deterministic) transducers with origin is decidable.

References

1. Alur, R., D'Antoni, L.: Streaming tree transducers. J. ACM **64**(5):31:1–31:55 (2017)
2. Bojańczyk, M.: Transducers with origin information. In: Esparza, J., Fraigniaud, P., Husfeldt, T., Koutsoupias, E. (eds.) ICALP 2014, Part II. LNCS, vol. 8573, pp. 26–37. Springer, Heidelberg (2014). https://doi.org/10.1007/978-3-662-43951-7_3
3. Courcelle, B., Franchi-Zannettacci, P.: Attribute grammars and recursive program schemes I. Theor. Comput. Sci. **17**(2), 163–191 (1982)
4. Engelfriet, J.: Top-down tree transducers with regular look-ahead. Math. Syst. Theory **10**, 289–303 (1977)
5. Engelfriet, J.: Some open questions and recent results on tree transducers and tree languages. In: Formal Language Theory, pp. 241–286. Elsevier (1980)
6. Engelfriet, J., Maneth, S.: Macro tree translations of linear size increase are MSO definable. SIAM J. Comput. **32**(4), 950–1006 (2003)
7. Engelfriet, J., Maneth, S.: The equivalence problem for deterministic MSO tree transducers is decidable. Inf. Process. Lett. **100**(5), 206–212 (2006)
8. Engelfriet, J., Maneth, S., Seidl, H.: Deciding equivalence of top-down XML transformations in polynomial time. J. Comput. Syst. Sci. **75**(5), 271–286 (2009)
9. Engelfriet, J., Vogler, H.: Macro tree transducers. J. Comput. Syst. Sci. **31**(1), 71–146 (1985)
10. Ésik, Z.: Decidability results concerning tree transducers I. Acta Cybern. **5**(1), 1–20 (1980)
11. Filiot, E., Maneth, S., Reynier, P., Talbot, J.: Decision problems of tree transducers with origin. Inf. Comput. 261(Part), 311–335 (2018)
12. Fors, N., Cedersjö, G., Hedin, G.: JavaRAG: a Java library for reference attribute grammars. In: Proceedings of the 14th International Conference on Modularity, MODULARITY 2015, pp. 55–67. ACM, New York (2015)
13. Friese, S., Seidl, H., Maneth, S.: Earliest normal form and minimization for bottom-up tree transducers. Int. J. Found. Comput. Sci. **22**(7), 1607–1623 (2011)
14. Fülöp, Z.: On attributed tree transducers. Acta Cybern. **5**(3), 261–279 (1981)
15. Fülöp, Z., Vogler, H.: Syntax-Directed Semantics - Formal Models Based on Tree Transducers. Monographs in Theoretical Computer Science. An EATCS Series. Springer, Heidelberg (1998). https://doi.org/10.1007/978-3-642-72248-6
16. Gécseg, F., Steinby, M.: Minimal ascending tree automata. Acta Cybern. **4**(1), 37–44 (1978)
17. Gécseg, F., Steinby, M.: Tree Automata. Akadéniai Kiadó, Budapest (1984)
18. Griffiths, T.V.: The unsolvability of the equivalence problem for lambda-free non-deterministic generalized machines. J. ACM **15**(3), 409–413 (1968)
19. Honkala, J.: A short solution for the HDT0L sequence equivalence problem. Theor. Comput. Sci. **244**(1–2), 267–270 (2000)
20. Knuth, D.E.: Semantics of context-free languages. Math. Syst. Theory **2**(2), 127–145 (1968)
21. Knuth, D.E.: Correction: semantics of context-free languages. Math. Syst. Theory **5**(1), 95–96 (1971)
22. Laurence, G., Lemay, A., Niehren, J., Staworko, S., Tommasi, M.: Normalization of sequential top-down tree-to-word transducers. In: Dediu, A.-H., Inenaga, S., Martín-Vide, C. (eds.) LATA 2011. LNCS, vol. 6638, pp. 354–365. Springer, Heidelberg (2011). https://doi.org/10.1007/978-3-642-21254-3_28

23. Lothaire, M.: Algebraic Combinatorics on Words. Cambridge University Press, Cambridge (2002)
24. Makanin, G.S.: The problem of solvability of equations in a free semigroup. Math. USSR-Sb. **32**(2), 129 (1977)
25. Maneth, S.: A survey on decidable equivalence problems for tree transducers. Int. J. Found. Comput. Sci. **26**(8), 1069–1100 (2015)
26. Plandowski, W.: Satisfiability of word equations with constants is in PSPACE. In: 40th Annual Symposium on Foundations of Computer Science, FOCS 1999, New York, NY, USA, 17–18 October 1999, pp. 495–500. IEEE Computer Society (1999)
27. Seidl, H., Maneth, S., Kemper, G.: Equivalence of deterministic top-down tree-to-string transducers is decidable. J. ACM **65**(4), 21:1–21:30 (2018)
28. Sloane, A.M., Kats, L.C., Visser, E.: A pure embedding of attribute grammars. Sci. Comput. Program. **78**(10), 1752–1769 (2013). Special Section on Language Descriptions Tools and Applications (LDTA 2008 and 2009) & Special Section on Software Engineering Aspects of Ubiquitous Computing and Ambient Intelligence (UCAm I 2011)
29. Van Wyk, E., Bodin, D., Gao, J., Krishnan, L.: Silver: an extensible attribute grammar system. Sci. Comput. Program. **75**(1–2), 39–54 (2010)

8

Coalgebra Learning via Duality

Simone Barlocco[1], Clemens Kupke[1][(✉)], and Jurriaan Rot[2]

[1] University of Strathclyde, Glasgow, UK
{simone.barlocco,clemens.kupke}@strath.ac.uk
[2] Radboud University, Nijmegen, Netherlands
j.rot@cs.ru.nl

Abstract. Automata learning is a popular technique for inferring minimal automata through membership and equivalence queries. In this paper, we generalise learning to the theory of coalgebras. The approach relies on the use of logical formulas as tests, based on a dual adjunction between states and logical theories. This allows us to learn, e.g., labelled transition systems, using Hennessy-Milner logic. Our main contribution is an abstract learning algorithm, together with a proof of correctness and termination.

1 Introduction

In recent years, automata learning is applied with considerable success to infer models of systems and in order to analyse and verify them. Most current approaches to active automata learning are ultimately based on the original algorithm due to Angluin [4], although numerous improvements have been made, in practical performance and in extending the techniques to different models [30].

Our aim is to move from automata to *coalgebras* [14,26], providing a generalisation of learning to a wide range of state-based systems. The key insight underlying our work is that dual adjunctions connecting coalgebras and tailor-made logical languages [12,19,21,22,26] allow us to devise a generic learning algorithm for coalgebras that is parametric in the type of system under consideration. Our approach gives rise to a fundamental distinction between *states* of the learned system and *tests*, modelled as logical formulas. This distinction is blurred in the classical DFA algorithm, where tests are also used to specify the (reachable) states. It is precisely the distinction between tests and states which allows us to move beyond classical automata, and use, for instance, Hennessy-Milner logic to learn bisimilarity quotients of labelled transition systems.

To present learning via duality we need to introduce new notions and refine existing ones. First, in the setting of coalgebraic modal logic, we introduce the new notion of *sub-formula closed* collections of formulas, generalising suffix-closed sets of words in Angluin's algorithm (Sect. 4). Second, we import the abstract notion of *base* of a functor from [8], which allows us to speak about 'successor states' (Sect. 5). In particular, the base allows us to characterise *reachability* of coalgebras in a clear and concise way. This yields a canonical procedure for computing the reachable part from a given initial state in a coalgebra, thus generalising the notion of a generated subframe from modal logic.

We then rephrase *coalgebra learning* as the problem of inferring a coalgebra which is reachable, minimal and which cannot be distinguished from the original coalgebra held by the teacher using tests. This requires suitably adapting the computation of the reachable part to incorporate tests, and only learn 'up to logical equivalence'. We formulate the notion of *closed table*, and an associated procedure to close tables. With all these notions in place, we can finally define our abstract algorithm for coalgebra learning, together with a proof of correctness and termination (Sect. 6). Overall, we consider this correctness and termination proof as the main contribution of the paper; other contributions are the computation of reachability via the base and the notion of sub-formula closedness. At a more conceptual level, our paper shows how states and tests interact in automata learning, by rephrasing it in the context of a dual adjunction connecting coalgebra (systems) and algebra (logical theories). As such, we provide a new foundation of learning state-based systems.

Related Work. The idea that tests in the learning algorithm should be formulas of a distinct logical language was proposed first in [6]. However, the work in *loc. cit.* is quite ad-hoc, confined to Boolean-valued modal logics, and did not explicitly use duality. This paper is a significant improvement: the dual adjunction framework and the definition of the base [8] enables us to present a description of Angluin's algorithm in purely categorical terms, including a proof of correctness and, crucially, termination. Our abstract notion of logic also enables us to recover *exactly* the standard DFA algorithm (where tests are words) and the algorithm for learning Mealy machines (where test are many-valued), something that is not possible in [6] where tests are modal formulas. Closely related to our work is also the line of research initiated by [15] and followed up within the CALF project [11–13] which applies ideas from category theory to automata learning. Our approach is orthogonal to CALF: the latter focuses on learning a general version of *automata*, whereas our work is geared towards learning bisimilarity quotients of state-based transition systems. While CALF lends itself to studying automata in a large variety of base categories, our work thus far is concerned with varying the type of transition structures.

2 Learning by Example

The aim of this section is twofold: (i) to remind the reader of the key elements of Angluin's L* algorithm [4] and (ii) to motivate and outline our generalisation.

In the classical L* algorithm, the learner tries to learn a regular language $\mathcal{L}$ over some alphabet A or, equivalently, a DFA $\mathcal{A}$ accepting that language. Learning proceeds by asking queries to a teacher who has access to this automaton. *Membership queries* allow the learner to test whether a given word is in the language, and *equivalence queries* to test whether the correct DFA has been learned already. The algorithm constructs so-called tables (S, E) where $S, E \subseteq A^*$ are the rows and columns of the table, respectively. The value at position (s, e) of the table is the answer to the membership query "$se \in \mathcal{L}$?".

Words play a double role: On the one hand, a word $w \in S$ represents the state which is reached when reading w at the initial state. On the other hand, the set E represents the set of membership queries that the learner is asking about the states in S. A table is *closed* if for all $w \in S$ and all $a \in A$ either $wa \in S$ or there is a state $v \in S$ such that wa is equivalent to v w.r.t. membership queries of words in E. If a table is not closed we extend S by adding words of the form wa for $w \in S$ and $a \in A$. Once it is closed, one can define a *conjecture*,[1] i.e., a DFA with states in S. The learner now asks the teacher whether the conjecture is correct. If it is, the algorithm terminates. Otherwise the teacher provides a *counterexample*: a word on which the conjecture is incorrect. The table is now extended using the counterexample. As a result, the table is not closed anymore and the algorithm continues again by closing the table.

Our version of L* introduces some key conceptual differences: tables are pairs (S, Ψ) such that S (set of rows) is a selection of states of $\mathcal{A}$ and Ψ (set of columns) is a collection of tests/formulas. Membership queries become checks of tests in Ψ at states in S and equivalence queries verify whether or not the learned structure is logically equivalent to the original one. A table (S, Ψ) is closed if for all successors x' of elements of S there exists an $x \in S$ such that x and x' are equivalent w.r.t. formulas in Ψ. The clear distinction between states and tests in our algorithm means that counterexamples are formulas that have to be added to Ψ. Crucially, the move from words to formulas allows us to use the rich theory of coalgebra and coalgebraic logic to devise a generic algorithm.

We consider two examples within our generic framework: classical DFAs, yielding essentially the L* algorithm, and labelled transition systems, which is to the best of our knowledge not covered by standard automata learning algorithms.

For the DFA case, let $L = \{u \in \{a, b\}^* \mid$ number of a's mod $3 = 0\}$ and assume that the teacher uses the following (infinite) automaton describing L:

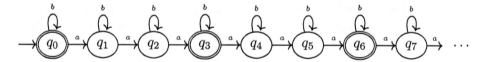

As outlined above, the learner starts to construct tables (S, Ψ) where S is a selection of states of the automaton and Ψ are formulas. For DFAs we will see (Example 1) that our formulas are just words in $\{a, b\}^*$. Our starting table is $(\{q_0\}, \emptyset)$, i.e., we select the initial state and do not check any logical properties. This table is trivially closed, as all states are equivalent w.r.t. $\emptyset$. The first conjecture is the automaton consisting of one accepting state q_0 with a- and b-loops, whose language is $\{a, b\}^*$. This is incorrect and the teacher provides, e.g., aa as counterexample. The resulting table is $(\{q_0\}, \{\varepsilon, a, aa\})$ where the

---

[1] The algorithm additionally requires *consistency*, but this is not needed if counterexamples are added to E. This idea goes back to [22].

second component was generated by closing $\{aa\}$ under suffixes. Suffix closedness features both in the original L^* algorithm and in our framework (Sect. 4). The table $(\{q_0\}, \{\varepsilon, a, aa\})$ is not closed as q_1, the a-successor of q_0, does not accept ε whereas q_0 does. Therefore we extend the table to $(\{q_0, q_1\}, \{\varepsilon, a, aa\})$. Note that, unlike in the classical setting, exploring successors of already selected states cannot be achieved by appending letters to words, but we need to *locally* employ the transition structure on the automaton $\mathcal{A}$ instead. A similar argument shows that we need to extend the table further to $(\{q_0, q_1, q_2\}, \{\varepsilon, a, aa\})$ which is closed. This leads to the (correct) conjecture depicted on the right below. The acceptance condition and transition structure has been read off from the original automaton, where the transition from q_2 to q_0 is obtained by realising that q_2's successor q_3 is represented by the equivalent state $q_0 \in S$.

A key feature of our work is that the L^* algorithm can be systematically generalised to new settings, in particular, to the learning of bisimulation quotients of transition systems. Consider the following labelled transition system (LTS). We would like to learn its minimal representation, i.e., its quotient modulo bisimulation.

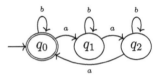

Our setting allows us to choose a suitable logical language. For LTSs, the language consists of the formulas of standard multi-modal logic (cf. Example 3). The

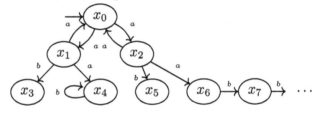

semantics is as usual where $\langle a \rangle \phi$ holds at a state if it has an a-successor that makes ϕ true.

As above, the algorithm constructs tables, starting with $(S = \{x_0\}, \Psi = \emptyset)$. The table is closed, so the first conjecture is a single state with an a-loop with no proposition letter true (note that x_0 has no b or c successor and no proposition is true at x_0). It is, however, easy for the teacher to find a counterexample. For example, the formula $\langle a \rangle \langle b \rangle \top$ is true at the root of the original LTS but false in the conjecture. We add the counterexample and all its subformulas to Ψ and obtain a new table $(\{x_0\}, \Psi')$ with $\Psi' = \{\langle a \rangle \langle b \rangle \top, \langle b \rangle \top, \top\}$. Now, the table is not closed, as x_0 has successor x_1 that satisfies $\langle b \rangle \top$ whereas x_0 does not satisfy $\langle b \rangle \top$. Therefore we add x_1 to the table to obtain $(\{x_0, x_1\}, \Psi')$. Similar arguments will lead to the closed table $(\{x_0, x_1, x_3, x_4\}, \Psi')$ which also yields the correct conjecture. Note that the state x_2 does not get added to the table as it is equivalent to x_1 and thus already represented. This demonstrates a remarkable fact: we computed the bisimulation quotient of the LTS without inspecting the (infinite) right-hand side of the LTS.

Another important example that fits smoothly into our framework is the well-known variant of Angluin's algorithm to learn Mealy machines (Example 2). Thanks to our general notion of logic, our framework allows to use an intuitive language, where a formula is simply an input word w whose truth value at a state

x is the observed output after entering w at x. This is in contrast to [6] where formulas had to be Boolean valued. Multi-valued logics fit naturally in our setting; this is expected to be useful to deal with systems with quantitative information.

3   Preliminaries

The general learning algorithm in this paper is based on the theory of *coalgebras*, which provides an abstract framework for representing state-based transition systems. In what follows we assume that the reader is familiar with basic notions of category theory and coalgebras [14, 26]. We briefly recall the notion of pointed coalgebra, modelling a coalgebra with an initial state. Let C be a category with a terminal object 1 and let $B: C \to C$ be a functor. A pointed B-coalgebra is a triple (X, γ, x_0) where $X \in C$ and $\gamma: X \to BX$ and $x_0: 1 \to X$, specifying the coalgebra structure and the point ("initial state") of the coalgebra, respectively.

Coalgebraic Modal Logic. Modal logics are used to describe properties of state-based systems, modelled here as coalgebras. The close relationship between coalgebras and their logics is described elegantly via dual adjunctions [18, 20, 21, 24].

Our basic setting consists of two categories C, D connected by functors P, Q forming a dual adjunction $P \dashv Q: C \leftrightarrows D^{\mathrm{op}}$. In other words, we have a natural bijection $C(X, Q\Delta) \cong D(\Delta, PX)$ for $X \in C, \Delta \in D$. Moreover, we assume two functors, $B: C \to C, L: D \to D$, see (1). The functor L represents the syntax of the (modalities in the) logic: assuming that L has an initial algebra

$$B \,\circlearrowright\, C \underset{Q}{\overset{P}{\rightleftarrows}} D^{\mathrm{op}} \,\circlearrowleft\, L \qquad (1)$$

$\alpha: L\Phi \to \Phi$ we think of Φ as the collection of formulas, or tests. In this logical perspective, the functor P maps an object X of C to the collection of predicates and the functor Q maps an object Δ of D to the collection $Q\Delta$ of Δ-theories.

The connection between coalgebras and their logics is specified via a natural transformation $\delta: LP \Rightarrow PB$, sometimes referred to as the one-step semantics of the logic. The δ is used to define the semantics of the logic on a B-coalgebra (X, γ) by initiality, as in (2). Furthermore, using

$$\begin{array}{ccc} L\Phi & \xrightarrow{\ L[\![-]\!]\ } LPX \xrightarrow{\ \delta_X\ } PBX \\ {\scriptstyle\alpha}\downarrow & & \downarrow{\scriptstyle P\gamma} \\ \Phi & \dashrightarrow{\ \exists![\![-]\!]\ } & PX \end{array} \qquad (2)$$

the bijective correspondence of the dual adjunction between P and Q, the map $[\![-]\!]$ corresponds to a map $th^\gamma: X \to Q\Phi$ that we will refer to as the theory map of (X, γ).

The theory map can be expressed directly via a universal property, by making use of the so-called *mate* $\delta^\flat: BQ \Rightarrow QL$ of the one-step semantics δ (cf. [18, 24]). More precisely, we have

$$\begin{array}{ccc} BX & \xrightarrow{\ B\,th^\gamma\ } BQ\Phi \xrightarrow{\ \delta^\flat_\Phi\ } QL\Phi \\ {\scriptstyle\gamma}\uparrow & & \uparrow{\scriptstyle Q\alpha} \\ X & \dashrightarrow{\ \exists!\,th^\gamma\ } & Q\Phi \end{array} \qquad (3)$$

$\delta^\flat = QL\varepsilon \circ Q\delta Q \circ \eta BQ$, where η, ε are the unit and counit of the adjunction. Then $th^\gamma: X \to Q\Phi$ is the unique morphism making (3) commute.

Example 1. Let $\mathcal{C} = \mathcal{D} = \mathsf{Set}, P = Q = 2^-$ the contravariant power set functor, $B = 2 \times -^A$ and $L = 1 + A \times -$. In this case B-coalgebras can be thought of as deterministic automata with input alphabet A (e.g., [25]). It is well-known that the initial L-algebra is $\Phi = A^*$ with structure $\alpha = [\varepsilon, \mathrm{cons}]: 1 + A \times A^* \to A^*$ where ε selects the empty word and cons maps a pair $(a, w) \in A \times A^*$ to the word $aw \in A^*$, i.e., in this example our tests are words with the intuitive meaning that a test succeeds if the word is accepted by the given automaton. For $X \in \mathcal{C}$, the X-component of the (one-step) semantics $\delta: LP \Rightarrow PB$ is defined as follows: $\delta_X(*) = \{(i, f) \in 2 \times X^A \mid i = 1\}$, and $\delta_X(a, U) = \{(i, f) \in 2 \times X^A \mid f(a) \in U\}$. It is matter of routine checking that the semantics of tests in Φ on a B-coalgebra (X, γ) is as follows: we have $[\![\varepsilon]\!] = \{x \in X \mid \pi_1(\gamma(x)) = 1\}$ and $[\![aw]\!] = \{x \in X \mid \pi_2(\gamma(x))(a) \in [\![w]\!]\}$, where π_1 and π_2 are the projection maps. The theory map th^γ sends a state to the language accepted by that state in the usual way.

Example 2. Again let $\mathcal{C} = \mathcal{D} = \mathsf{Set}$ and consider the functors $P = Q = O^-$, $B = (O \times -)^A$ and $L = A \times (1 + -)$, where A and O are fixed sets, thought of as input and output alphabet, respectively. Then B-coalgebras are Mealy machines and the initial L-algebra is given by the set A^+ of finite non-empty words over A. For $X \in \mathcal{C}$, the one-step semantics $\delta_X: A \times (1 + O^X) \to O^{BX}$ is defined by $\delta_X(a, \mathrm{inl}(*)) = \lambda f.\pi_1(f(a))$ and $\delta_X(a, \mathrm{inr}(g)) = \lambda f.g(\pi_2(f(a)))$. Concretely, formulas are words in A^+; the (O-valued) semantics of $w \in A^+$ at state x is the output $o \in O$ that is produced after processing the input w from state x.

Example 3. Let $\mathcal{C} = \mathsf{Set}$ and $\mathcal{D} = \mathsf{BA}$, where the latter denotes the category of Boolean algebras. Again $P = 2^-$, but this time 2^X is interpreted as a Boolean algebra. The functor Q maps a Boolean algebra to the collection of ultrafilters over it [7]. Furthermore $B = (\mathcal{P}-)^A$ where $\mathcal{P}$ denotes covariant power set and A a set of actions. Coalgebras for this functor correspond to labelled transition systems, where a state has a set of successors that depends on the action/input from A. The dual functor $L: \mathsf{BA} \to \mathsf{BA}$ is defined as $LY := F_{\mathsf{BA}}(\{\langle a \rangle\, y \mid a \in A, y \in Y\})/\equiv$ where $F_{\mathsf{BA}}: \mathsf{Set} \to \mathsf{BA}$ denotes the free Boolean algebra functor and where, roughly speaking, $\equiv$ is the congruence generated from the axioms $\langle a \rangle \perp \equiv \perp$ and $\langle a \rangle (y_1 \vee y_2) \equiv \langle a \rangle (y_1) \vee \langle a \rangle (y_2)$ for each $a \in A$. This is explained in more detail in [21]. The initial algebra for this functor is the so-called Lindenbaum-Tarski algebra [7] of modal formulas $(\phi ::= \perp | \phi \vee \phi | \neg \phi | \langle a \rangle \phi)$ quotiented by logical equivalence. The definition of an appropriate δ can be found in, e.g., [21]—the semantics $[\![\_]\!]$ of a formula then amounts to the standard one [7].

Different types of probabilistic transition systems also fit into the dual adjunction framework, see, e.g, [17].

Subobjects and Intersection-Preserving Functors. We denote by $\mathsf{Sub}(X)$ the collection of subobjects of an object $X \in \mathcal{C}$. Let $\leq$ be the order on subobjects $s: S \rightarrowtail X, s': S' \rightarrowtail X$ given by $s \leq s'$ iff there is $m: S \to S'$ s.t. $s = s' \circ m$. The *intersection* $\bigwedge J \rightarrowtail X$ of a family $J = \{s_i: S_i \to X\}_{i \in I}$ is defined as the greatest lower bound w.r.t. the order $\leq$. In a complete category, it can be computed by (wide) pullback. We denote the maps in the limiting cone by $x_i\colon \bigwedge J \rightarrowtail S_i$.

For a functor $B\colon \mathcal{C} \rightarrow \mathcal{D}$, we say B *preserves (wide) intersections* if it preserves these wide pullbacks, i.e., if $(B(\bigwedge J), \{Bx_i\}_{i \in I})$ is the pullback of $\{Bs_i\colon BS_i \rightarrow BX\}_{i \in I}$. By [2, Lemma 3.53] (building on [29]), *finitary* functors on Set 'almost' preserve wide intersections: for every such functor B there is a functor B' which preserves wide intersections and agrees with B on all non-empty sets. Finally, if B preserves intersections, then it preserves monos.

Minimality Notions. The algorithm that we will describe in this paper learns a minimal and reachable representation of an object. The intuitive notions of minimality and reachability are formalised as follows.

Definition 4. *We call a B-coalgebra (X, γ) minimal w.r.t. logical equivalence if the theory map $th^\gamma\colon X \rightarrow Q\Phi$ is a monomorphism.*

Definition 5. *We call a pointed B-coalgebra (X, γ, x_0) reachable if for any subobject $s\colon S \rightarrow X$ and $s_0\colon 1 \rightarrow S$ with $x_0 = s \circ s_0$: if S is a subcoalgebra of (X, γ) then s is an isomorphism.*

For expressive logics [27], behavioural equivalence coincides with logical equivalence. Hence, in that case, our algorithm learns a "well-pointed coalgebra" in the terminology of [2], i.e., a pointed coalgebra that is reachable and minimal w.r.t. behavioural equivalence. All logics appearing in this paper are expressive.

Assumption on $\mathcal{C}$ and Factorisation System. Throughout the paper we will assume that $\mathcal{C}$ is a complete and well-powered category. Well-powered means that for each $X \in \mathcal{C}$ the collection $\mathsf{Sub}(X)$ of subobjects of a given object forms a set. Our assumptions imply [10, Proposition 4.4.3] that every morphism f in $\mathcal{C}$ factors uniquely (up to isomorphism) as $f = m \circ e$ with m a mono and e a strong epi. Recall that an epimorphism $e\colon X \rightarrow Y$ is strong if for every commutative square in (4) where the bottom arrow is a monomorphism, there exists a unique diagonal morphism d such that the entire diagram commutes.

$$\begin{array}{ccc} X & \xrightarrow{e} & Y \\ {\scriptstyle h}\downarrow & \nearrow^{d} & \downarrow{\scriptstyle g} \\ U & \xrightarrow[m]{} & Z \end{array} \qquad (4)$$

4   Subformula Closed Collections of Formulas

Our learning algorithm will construct conjectures that are "partially" correct, i.e., correct with respect to a subobject of the collection of all formulas/tests. Recall this collection of all tests are formalised in our setting as the initial L-algebra $(\Phi, \alpha\colon L\Phi \rightarrow \Phi)$. To define a notion of partial correctness we need to consider subobjects of Φ to which we can restrict the theory map. This is formalised via the notion of "subformula closed" subobject of Φ.

The definition of such subobjects is based on the notion of *recursive coalgebra*. For $L: \mathcal{D} \to \mathcal{D}$ an endofunctor, a coalgebra $f: X \to LX$ is called *recursive* if for every L-algebra $g: LY \to Y$ there is a unique 'coalgebra-to-algebra' map $g^\dagger$ making (5) commute.

$$
\begin{array}{ccc}
LX & \xrightarrow{Lg^\dagger} & LY \\
{\scriptstyle f}\uparrow & & \downarrow{\scriptstyle g} \\
X & \xrightarrow{g^\dagger} & Y
\end{array}
\qquad (5)
$$

Definition 6. *A subobject $j: \Psi \to \Phi$ is called a* subformula closed collection *(of formulas) if there is a unique L-coalgebra structure $\sigma: \Psi \to L\Psi$ such that (Ψ, σ) is a recursive L-coalgebra and j is the (necessarily unique) coalgebra-to-algebra map from (Ψ, σ) to the initial algebra (Φ, α).*

Remark 7. The uniqueness of σ in Definition 6 is implied if L preserves monomorphisms. This is the case in our examples. The notion of recursive coalgebra goes back to [23, 28]. The paper [1] contains a claim that the first item of our definition of subformula closed collection is implied by the second one if L preserves preimages. In our examples both properties of (Ψ, σ) are verified directly, rather than by relying on general categorical results.

Example 8. In the setting of Example 1, where the initial L-algebra is based on the set A^* of words over the set (of inputs) A, a subset $\Psi \subseteq A^*$ is subformula-closed if it is suffix-closed, i.e., if for all $aw \in \Psi$ we have $w \in \Psi$ as well.

Example 9. In the setting that $B = (\mathcal{P}-)^A$ for some set of actions A, $\mathcal{C} = \mathsf{Set}$ and $\mathcal{D} = \mathsf{BA}$, the logic is given as a functor L on Boolean algebras as discussed in Example 3. As a subformula closed collection is an object in Ψ, we are not simply dealing with a set of formulas, but with a Boolean algebra. The connection to the standard notion of being closed under taking subformulas in modal logic [7] can be sketched as follows: given a set Δ of modal formulas that is closed under taking subformulas, we define a Boolean algebra $\Psi_\Delta \subseteq \Phi$ as the smallest Boolean subalgebra of Φ that is generated by the set $\hat{\Delta} = \{[\phi]_\Phi \mid \phi \in \Delta\}$ where for a formula ϕ we let $[\phi]_\Phi \in \Phi$ denote its equivalence class in Φ.

It is then not difficult to define a suitable $\sigma: \Psi_\Delta \to L\Psi_\Delta$. As Ψ_Δ is generated by closing $\hat{\Delta}$ under Boolean operations, any two states x_1, x_2 in a given coalgebra (X, γ) satisfy $(\forall b \in \Psi_\Delta . x_1 \in [\![b]\!] \Leftrightarrow x_2 \in [\![b]\!])$ iff $\left(\forall b \in \hat{\Delta} . x_1 \in [\![b]\!] \Leftrightarrow x_2 \in [\![b]\!]\right)$. In other words, equivalence w.r.t. Ψ_Δ coincides with equivalence w.r.t. the *set* of formulas Δ. This explains why in the concrete algorithm, we do not deal with Boolean algebras explicitly, but with subformula closed sets of formulas instead.

The key property of subformula closed collections Ψ is that we can restrict our attention to the so-called Ψ-theory map. Intuitively, subformula closedness is what allows us to define this theory map inductively.

$$
\begin{array}{ccccc}
X & \xrightarrow{\quad th^\gamma_\Psi \quad} & & & Q\Psi \\
{\scriptstyle \gamma}\downarrow & & & & \uparrow{\scriptstyle Q\sigma} \\
BX & \xrightarrow{Bth^\gamma_\Psi} & BQ\Psi & \xrightarrow{\delta^\flat_\Psi} & QL\Psi
\end{array}
\qquad (6)
$$

Lemma 10. *Let $\Psi \overset{j}{\rightarrowtail} \Phi$ be a sub-formula closed collection, with coalgebra structure $\sigma\colon \Psi \to L\Psi$. Then $th_\Psi^\gamma = Qj \circ th_\Phi^\gamma$ is the unique map making (6) commute. We call th_Ψ^γ the Ψ-theory map, and omit the Ψ if it is clear from the context.*

5   Reachability and the Base

In this section, we define the notion of *base* of an endofunctor, taken from [8]. This allows us to speak about the (direct) successors of states in a coalgebra, and about reachability, which are essential ingredients of the learning algorithm.

Definition 11. *Let $B\colon \mathcal{C} \to \mathcal{C}$ be an endofunctor. We say B has a base if for every arrow $f\colon X \to BY$ there exist $g\colon X \to BZ$ and $m\colon Z \rightarrowtail Y$ with m a monomorphism such that $f = Bm \circ g$, and for any pair $g'\colon X \to BZ', m'\colon Z' \rightarrowtail Y$ with $Bm' \circ g' = f$ and m' a monomorphism there is a unique arrow $h\colon Z \to Z'$ such that $Bh \circ g = g'$ and $m' \circ h = m$, see Diagram (7). We call (Z, g, m) the (B)-base of the morphism f.*

We sometimes refer to $m\colon Z \rightarrowtail Y$ as the base of f, omitting the g when it is irrelevant, or clear from the context. Note that the terminology 'the' base is justified, as it is easily seen to be unique up to isomorphism.

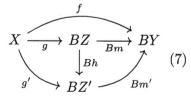

$$\tag{7}$$

For example, let $B\colon \mathsf{Set} \to \mathsf{Set}$, $BX = 2 \times X^A$. The base of a map $f\colon X \to BY$ is given by $m\colon Z \rightarrowtail Y$, where $Z = \{(\pi_2 \circ f)(x)(a) \mid x \in X, a \in A\}$, and m is the inclusion. The associated $g\colon X \to BZ$ is the corestriction of f to BZ.

For $B = (\mathcal{P}-)^A\colon \mathsf{Set} \to \mathsf{Set}$, the B-base of $f\colon X \to Y$ is given by the inclusion $m\colon Z \rightarrowtail Y$, where $Z = \{y \in Y \mid \exists x \in X, \exists a \in A \text{ s.t. } y \in f(x)(a)\}$.

Proposition 12. *Suppose $\mathcal{C}$ is complete and well-powered, and $B\colon \mathcal{C} \to \mathcal{C}$ preserves (wide) intersections. Then B has a base.*

If $\mathcal{C}$ is a locally presentable category, then it is complete and well-powered [3, Remark 1.56]. Hence, in that case, any functor $B\colon \mathcal{C} \to \mathcal{C}$ which preserves intersections has a base. The following lemma will be useful in proofs.

Lemma 13. *Let $B\colon \mathcal{C} \to \mathcal{C}$ be a functor that has a base and that preserves preimages. Let $f\colon S \to BX$ and $h\colon X \to Y$ be morphisms, let (Z, g, m) be the base of f and let $e\colon Z \to W, m'\colon W \to Y$ be the (strong epi, mono)-factorisation of $h \circ m$. Then $(W, Be \circ g, m')$ is the base of $Bh \circ f$.*

The B-base provides an elegant way to relate reachability within a coalgebra to a monotone operator on the (complete) lattice of subobjects of the carrier of the coalgebra. Moreover, we will see that the least subcoalgebra that contains a given subobject of the carrier can be obtained via a standard least fixpoint construction. Finally, we will introduce the notion of prefix closed subobject of a coalgebra, generalising the prefix closedness condition from Angluin's algorithm.

By our assumption on $\mathcal{C}$ at the end of Sect. 3, the collection of subobjects $(\mathsf{Sub}(X), \leq)$ ordered as usual (cf. Section 3) forms a complete lattice. Recall that the meet on $\mathsf{Sub}(X)$ (intersection) is defined via pullbacks. In categories with coproducts, the join $s_1 \vee s_2$ of subobjects $s_1, s_2 \in \mathsf{Sub}(X)$ is defined as the mono part of the factorisation of the map $[s_1, s_2] \colon S_1 + S_2 \to X$, i.e., $[s_1, s_2] = (s_1 \vee s_2) \circ e$ for a strong epi e. In Set, this amounts to taking the union of subsets.

For a binary join $s_1 \vee s_2$ we denote by $inl_\vee \colon S_1 \to (S_1 \vee S_2)$ and $inr_\vee \colon S_2 \to (S_1 \vee S_2)$ the embeddings that exist by $s_i \leq s_1 \vee s_2$ for $i = \{1, 2\}$. Let us now define the key operator of this section.

$$
\begin{array}{ccc}
S & \xrightarrow{\ \ s\ \ } & X \\
{\scriptstyle g}\Big\downarrow & & \Big\downarrow{\scriptstyle \gamma} \\
B\Gamma(S) & \xrightarrow{B\Gamma_\gamma^B(s)} & BX
\end{array}
\qquad (8)
$$

Definition 14. *Let B be a functor that has a base, $s \colon S \rightarrowtail X$ a subobject of some $X \in \mathcal{C}$ and let (X, γ) be a B-coalgebra. Let $(\Gamma(S), g, \Gamma_\gamma^B(s))$ be the B-base of $\gamma \circ s$, see Diagram (8). Whenever B and γ are clear from the context, we write $\Gamma(s)$ instead of $\Gamma_\gamma^B(s)$.*

Lemma 15. *Let $B \colon \mathcal{C} \to \mathcal{C}$ be a functor with a base and let (X, γ) be a B-coalgebra. The operator $\Gamma \colon \mathsf{Sub}(X) \to \mathsf{Sub}(X)$ defined by $s \mapsto \Gamma(s)$ is monotone.*

Intuitively, Γ computes for a given set of states S the set of "immediate successors", i.e., the set of states that can be reached by applying γ to an element of S. We will see that pre-fixpoints of Γ correspond to subcoalgebras. Furthermore, Γ is the key to formulate our notion of closed table in the learning algorithm.

Proposition 16. *Let $s \colon S \rightarrowtail X$ be a subobject and $(X, \gamma) \in \mathsf{Coalg}(B)$ for $X \in \mathcal{C}$ and $B \colon \mathcal{C} \to \mathcal{C}$ a functor that has a base. Then s is a subcoalgebra of (X, γ) if and only if $\Gamma(s) \leq s$. Consequently, the collection of subcoalgebras of a given B-coalgebra forms a complete lattice.*

Using this connection, reachability of a pointed coalgebra (Definition 5) can be expressed in terms of the least fixpoint lfp of an operator defined in terms of Γ.

Theorem 17. *Let $B \colon \mathcal{C} \to \mathcal{C}$ be a functor that has a base. A pointed B-coalgebra (X, γ, x_0) is reachable iff $X \cong \mathsf{lfp}(\Gamma \vee x_0)$ (isomorphic as subobjects of X, i.e., equal).*

This justifies defining the reachable part from an initial state $x_0 \colon 1 \rightarrowtail X$ as the least fixpoint of the monotone operator $\Gamma \vee x_0$. Standard means of computing the least fixpoint by iterating this operator then give us a way to compute this subcoalgebra. Further, Γ provides a way to generalise the notion of "prefixed closedness" from Anguin's L* algorithm to our categorical setting.

Definition 18. *Let $s_0, s \in \mathsf{Sub}(X)$ for some $X \in \mathcal{C}$ and let (X, γ) be a B-coalgebra. We call s s_0-prefix closed w.r.t. γ if $s = \bigvee_{i=0}^n s_i$ for some $n \geq 0$ and a collection $\{s_i \mid i = 1, \ldots, n\}$ with $s_{j+1} \leq \Gamma(\bigvee_{i=0}^j s_i)$ for all j with $0 \leq j < n$.*

6   Learning Algorithm

We define a general learning algorithm for B-coalgebras. First, we describe the setting, in general and slightly informal terms. The teacher has a pointed B-coalgebra (X, γ, s_0). Our task is to 'learn' a pointed B-coalgebra $(S, \hat{\gamma}, \hat{s}_0)$ s.t.:

- $(S, \hat{\gamma}, \hat{s}_0)$ is *correct* w.r.t. the collection Φ of all tests, i.e., the theory of (X, γ) and $(S, \hat{\gamma})$ coincide on the initial states s_0 and $\hat{s}_0$, (Definition 25);
- $(S, \hat{\gamma}, \hat{s}_0)$ is minimal w.r.t. logical equivalence;
- $(S, \hat{\gamma}, \hat{s}_0)$ is reachable.

The first point means that the learned coalgebra is 'correct', that is, it agrees with the coalgebra of the teacher on all possible tests from the initial state. For instance, in case of deterministic automata and their logic in Example 1, this just means that the language of the learned automaton is the correct one.

In the learning game, we are only provided limited access to the coalgebra $\gamma \colon X \to BX$. Concretely, the teacher gives us:

- for any subobject $S \rightarrowtail X$ and sub-formula closed subobject Ψ of Φ, the composite theory map $\ S \; \rightarrowtail \; X \xrightarrow{\ th^{\gamma}_{\Psi}\ } Q\Psi$;
- for $(S, \hat{\gamma}, \hat{s}_0)$ a pointed coalgebra, whether or not it is correct w.r.t. the collection Φ of all tests;
- in case of a negative answer to the previous question, a *counterexample*, which essentially is a subobject Ψ' of Φ representing some tests on which the learned coalgebra is wrong (defined more precisely below);
- for a given subobject S of X, the 'next states'; formally, the computation of the B-base of the composite arrow $\ S \; \rightarrowtail \; X \xrightarrow{\ \gamma\ } BX$.

The first three points correspond respectively to the standard notions of membership query ('filling in' the table with rows S and columns Ψ), equivalence query and counterexample generation. The last point, about the base, is more unusual: it does not occur in the standard algorithm, since there a canonical choice of (X, γ) is used, which allows to represent next states in a fixed manner. It is required in our setting of an arbitrary coalgebra (X, γ).

In the remainder of this section, we describe the abstract learning algorithm and its correctness. First, we describe the basic ingredients needed for the algorithm: tables, closedness, counterexamples and a procedure to close a given table (Sect. 6.1). Based on these notions, the actual algorithm is presented (Sect. 6.2), followed by proofs of correctness and termination (Sect. 6.3).

Assumption 19. *Throughout this section, we assume*

- *that we deal with coalgebras over the base category $\mathcal{C} = \mathsf{Set}$;*
- *a functor $B \colon \mathcal{C} \to \mathcal{C}$ that preserves pre-images and wide intersections;*
- *a category $\mathcal{D}$ with an initial object 0 s.t. arrows with domain 0 are monic;*
- *a functor $L \colon \mathcal{D} \to \mathcal{D}$ with an initial algebra $L\Phi \xrightarrow{\cong} \Phi$;*
- *an adjunction $P \dashv Q \colon \mathcal{C} \leftrightarrows \mathcal{D}^{\mathrm{op}}$, and a logic $\delta \colon LP \Rightarrow PB$.*

Moreover, we assume a pointed B-coalgebra (X, γ, s_0).

Remark 20. We restrict to $\mathcal{C} = \mathsf{Set}$, but see it as a key contribution to state the algorithm in categorical terms: the assumptions cover a wide class of functors on Set, which is the main direction of generalisation. Further, the categorical approach will enable future generalisations. The assumptions on the category $\mathcal{C}$ are: it is complete, well-powered and satisfies that for all (strong) epis $q\colon S \rightarrow \overline{S} \in \mathcal{C}$ and all monos $i\colon S' \rightarrow S$ such that $q \circ i$ is mono there is a morphism $q^{-1}\colon \overline{S} \rightarrow S$ such that (i) $q \circ q^{-1} = \mathsf{id}$ and $q^{-1} \circ q \circ i = i$.

6.1   Tables and Counterexamples

Definition 21. *A* table *is a pair* $(S \overset{s}{\rightarrowtail} X, \Psi \overset{i}{\rightarrowtail} \Phi)$ *consisting of a subobject s of X and a subformula-closed subobject i of Φ.*

To make the notation a bit lighter, we sometimes refer to a table by (S, Ψ), using s and i respectively to refer to the actual subobjects. The pair (S, Ψ) represents 'rows' and 'columns' respectively, in the table; the 'elements' of the table are given abstractly by the map $th_\Psi^\gamma \circ s$. In particular, if $\mathcal{C} = \mathcal{D} = \mathsf{Set}$ and $Q = 2^-$, then this is a map $S \rightarrow 2^\Psi$, assigning a Boolean value to every pair of a row (state) and a column (formula).

For the definition of closedness, we use the operator $\Gamma(S)$ from Definition 14, which characterises the successors of a subobject $S \rightarrowtail X$.

$$\begin{array}{ccc} S & \overset{s}{\rightarrowtail} X & \overset{th^\gamma}{\longrightarrow} Q\Psi \\ {\scriptstyle k}\big\uparrow & \nearrow {\scriptstyle th^\gamma} & \\ \Gamma(S) & \underset{\Gamma(s)}{\longrightarrow} X & \end{array} \qquad (9)$$

Definition 22. *A table (S, Ψ) is* closed *if there exists a map* $k\colon \Gamma(S) \rightarrow S$ *such that Diagram (9) commutes. A table (S, Ψ) is* sharp *if the composite map*

$$S \overset{s}{\longrightarrow} X \overset{th^\gamma}{\longrightarrow} Q\Psi \quad \text{is monic.}$$

Thus, a table (S, Ψ) is closed if all the successors of states (elements of $\Gamma(S)$) are already represented in S, up to equivalence w.r.t. the tests in Ψ. In other terms, the rows corresponding to successors of existing rows are already in the table. Sharpness amounts to minimality w.r.t. logical equivalence: every row has a unique value. The latter will be an invariant of the algorithm (Theorem 32).

A *conjecture* is a coalgebra on S, which is not quite a subcoalgebra of X: instead, it is a subcoalgebra 'up to equivalence w.r.t. Ψ', that is, the successors agree up to logical equivalence.

$$\begin{array}{ccc} S & \overset{s}{\rightarrowtail} X & \overset{\gamma}{\longrightarrow} BX \\ {\scriptstyle \hat\gamma}\big\downarrow & & \big\downarrow {\scriptstyle Bth^\gamma} \\ BS & \underset{Bs}{\longrightarrow} BX & \underset{Bth^\gamma}{\longrightarrow} BQ\Psi \end{array} \qquad (10)$$

Definition 23. *Let (S, Ψ) be a table. A coalgebra structure $\hat\gamma\colon S \rightarrow BS$ is called a* conjecture *(for (S, Ψ)) if Diagram (10) commutes.*

It is essential to be able to construct a conjecture from a closed table. The following, stronger result is a variation of Proposition 16.

Theorem 24. *A sharp table is closed iff there exists a conjecture for it. Moreover, if the table is sharp and B preserves monos, then this conjecture is unique.*

Our goal is to learn a pointed coalgebra which is correct w.r.t. all formulas. To this aim we ensure correctness w.r.t. an increasing sequence of subformula closed collections Ψ.

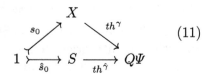

$$(11)$$

Definition 25. *Let (S, Ψ) be a table, and let $(S, \hat{\gamma}, \hat{s}_0)$ be a pointed B-coalgebra on S. We say $(S, \hat{\gamma}, \hat{s}_0)$ is correct w.r.t. Ψ if Diagram (11) commutes.*

All conjectures constructed during the learning algorithm will be correct w.r.t. the subformula closed collection Ψ of formulas under consideration.

Lemma 26. *Suppose (S, Ψ) is closed, and $\hat{\gamma}$ is a conjecture. Then $th_\Psi^\gamma \circ s = th_\Psi^{\hat{\gamma}} \colon S \to Q\Psi$. If $\hat{s}_0 \colon 1 \to S$ satisfies $s \circ \hat{s}_0 = s_0$ then $(S, \hat{\gamma}, \hat{s}_0)$ is correct w.r.t. Ψ.*

We next define the crucial notion of *counterexample* to a pointed coalgebra: a subobject Ψ' of Ψ on which it is 'incorrect'.

Definition 27. *Let (S, Ψ) be a table, and let $(S, \hat{\gamma}, \hat{s}_0)$ be a pointed B-coalgebra on S. Let Ψ' be a subformula closed subobject of Φ, such that Ψ is a subcoalgebra of Ψ'. We say Ψ' is a* counterexample *(for $(S, \hat{\gamma}, \hat{s}_0)$, extending Ψ) if $(S, \hat{\gamma}, \hat{s}_0)$ is not correct w.r.t. Ψ'.*

The following elementary lemma states that if there are no more counterexamples for a coalgebra, then it is correct w.r.t. the object Φ of all formulas.

Lemma 28. *Let (S, Ψ) be a table, and let $(S, \hat{\gamma}, \hat{s}_0)$ be a pointed B-coalgebra on S. Suppose that there are no counterexamples for $(S, \hat{\gamma}, \hat{s}_0)$ extending Ψ. Then $(S, \hat{\gamma}, \hat{s}_0)$ is correct w.r.t. Φ.*

The following describes, for a given table, how to extend it with the successors (in X) of all states in S. As we will see below, by repeatedly applying this construction, one eventually obtains a closed table.

Definition 29. *Let (S, Ψ) be a sharp table. Let $(\overline{S}, q, r)$ be the (strong epi, mono)-factorisation of the map $th^\gamma \circ (s \vee \Gamma(s))$, as in the diagram:*

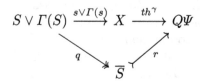

We define $\mathsf{close}(S, \Psi) := \{\overline{s} \colon \overline{S} \rightarrowtail X \mid th^\gamma \circ \overline{s} = r, s \leq \overline{s} \leq s \vee \Gamma(s)\}$. *For each $\overline{s} \in \mathsf{close}(S, \Psi)$ we have $s \leq \overline{s}$ and thus $s = \overline{s} \circ \kappa$ for some $\kappa \colon S \to \overline{S}$.*

Lemma 30. *In Definition 29, for each $\overline{s} \in \mathsf{close}(S, \Psi)$, we have $\kappa = q \circ inl_\vee$.*

We will refer to $\kappa = q \circ inl_\vee$ as the connecting map from s to $\overline{s}$.

Lemma 31. *In Definition 29, if there exists $q^{-1} \colon \overline{S} \to S \vee \Gamma(S)$ such that $q \circ q^{-1} = \mathsf{id}$ and $q^{-1} \circ q \circ inl_\vee = inl_\vee$, then $\mathsf{close}(S, \Psi)$ is non-empty.*

By our assumptions, the hypothesis of Lemma 31 is satisfied (Remark 20), hence $\mathsf{close}(S, \Psi)$ is non-empty. It is precisely (and only) at this point that we need the strong condition about existence of right inverses to epimorphisms.

6.2 The Algorithm

Having defined closedness, counterexamples and a procedure for closing a table, we are ready to define the abstract algorithm. In the algorithm, the teacher has access to a function $\mathsf{counter}((S, \hat{\gamma}, \hat{s}_0), \Psi)$, which returns the set of all counterexamples (extending Ψ) for the conjecture $(S, \hat{\gamma}, \hat{s}_0)$. If this set is empty, the coalgebra $(S, \hat{\gamma}, \hat{s}_0)$ is correct (see Lemma 28), otherwise the teacher picks one of its elements Ψ'. We also make use of $\mathsf{close}(S, \Psi)$, as given in Definition 29.

Algorithm 1. Abstract learning algorithm

1: $(S \overset{s}{\rightarrowtail} X) \leftarrow (1 \overset{s_0}{\rightarrowtail} X)$
2: $\hat{s}_0 \leftarrow \mathsf{id}_1$
3: $\Psi \leftarrow 0$
4: **while true do**
5:     **while** $(S \overset{s}{\rightarrowtail} X, \Psi)$ is not closed **do**
6:         let $(\overline{S} \overset{\overline{s}}{\rightarrowtail} X) \in \mathsf{close}(S, \Psi)$, with connecting map $\kappa \colon S \rightarrowtail \overline{S}$
7:         $(S \overset{s}{\rightarrowtail} X) \leftarrow (\overline{S} \overset{\overline{s}}{\rightarrowtail} X)$
8:         $\hat{s}_0 \leftarrow \kappa \circ \hat{s}_0$
9:     **end while**
10:     let $(S, \hat{\gamma})$ be a conjecture for (S, Ψ)
11:     **if** $\mathsf{counter}((S, \hat{\gamma}, \hat{s}_0), \Psi) = \emptyset$ **then**
12:         **return** $(S, \hat{\gamma}, \hat{s}_0)$
13:     **else**
14:         $\Psi \leftarrow \Psi'$ for some $\Psi' \in \mathsf{counter}((S, \hat{\gamma}, \hat{s}_0), \Psi)$
15:     **end if**
16: **end while**

The algorithm takes as input the coalgebra (X, γ, s_0) (which we fixed throughout this section). In every iteration of the outside loop, the table is first closed by repeatedly applying the procedure in Definition 29. Then, if the conjecture corresponding to the closed table is correct, the algorithm returns it (Line 12). Otherwise, a counterexample is chosen (Line 14), and the algorithm continues.

6.3 Correctness and Termination

Correctness is stated in Theorem 33. It relies on establishing loop invariants:

Theorem 32. *The following is an invariant of both loops in Algorithm 1 in Sect. 6.2: 1. (S, Ψ) is sharp, 2. $s \circ \hat{s}_0 = s_0$, and 3. s is s_0-prefix closed w.r.t. γ.*

Theorem 33. *If Algorithm 1 in Sect. 6.2 terminates, then it returns a pointed coalgebra $(S, \hat{\gamma}, \hat{s}_0)$ which is minimal w.r.t. logical equivalence, reachable and correct w.r.t. Φ.*

In our termination arguments, we have to make an assumption about the coalgebra which is to be learned. It does not need to be finite itself, but it should be finite up to logical equivalence—in the case of deterministic automata, for instance, this means the teacher has a (possibly infinite) automaton representing a regular language. To speak about this precisely, let Ψ be a subobject of Φ. We take a (strong epi, mono)-factorisation of the theory map, i.e.,

$$th_\Psi^\gamma = \left(X \xrightarrow{e_\Psi} |X|_\Psi \stackrel{m_\Psi}{\rightarrowtail} Q\Psi \right)$$ for some strong epi e and mono m. We call

the object $|X|_\Psi$ in the middle the Ψ-*logical quotient*. For the termination result (Theorem 37), $|X|_\Phi$ is assumed to have finitely many quotients and subobjects, which just amounts to finiteness, in **Set**.

We start with termination of the inner while loop (Corollary 36). This relies on two results: first, that once the connecting map κ is an iso, the table is closed, and second, that—under a suitable assumption on the coalgebra (X, γ)—during execution of the inner while loop, the map κ will eventually be an iso.

Theorem 34. *Let (S, Ψ) be a sharp table, let $\overline{S} \in \mathsf{close}(S, \Psi)$ and let $\kappa\colon S \to \overline{S}$ be the connecting map. If κ is an isomorphism, then (S, Ψ) is closed.*

Lemma 35. *Consider a sequence of sharp tables $(S_i \stackrel{s_i}{\rightarrowtail} X, \Psi)_{i \in \mathbb{N}}$ such that $s_{i+1} \in \mathsf{close}(S_i, \Psi)$ for all i. Moreover, let $(\kappa_i\colon S_i \to S_{i+1})_{i \in \mathbb{N}}$ be the connecting maps (Definition 29). If the logical quotient $|X|_\Phi$ of X has finitely many subobjects, then κ_i is an isomorphism for some $i \in \mathbb{N}$.*

Corollary 36. *If the Φ-logical quotient $|X|_\Phi$ has finitely many subobjects, then the inner while loop of Algorithm 1 terminates.*

For the outer loop, we assume that $|X|_\Phi$ has finitely many quotients, ensuring that every sequence of counterexamples proposed by the teacher is finite.

Theorem 37. *If the Φ-logical quotient $|X|_\Phi$ has finitely many quotients and finitely many subobjects, then Algorithm 1 terminates.*

7   Future Work

We showed how duality plays a natural role in automata learning, through the central connection between states and tests. Based on this foundation, we proved correctness and termination of an abstract algorithm for coalgebra learning. The generality is not so much in the base category (which, for the algorithm, we take to be **Set**) but rather in the functor used; we only require a few mild conditions on the functor, and make no assumptions about its shape. The approach is thus considered *coalgebra learning* rather than automata learning.

Returning to automata, an interesting direction is to extend the present work to cover learning of, e.g., non-deterministic or alternating automata [5,9] for a regular language. This would require explicitly handling branching in the type of coalgebra. One promising direction would be to incorporate the forgetful logics of [19], which are defined within the same framework of coalgebraic logic as the current work. It is not difficult to define in this setting what it means for a table to be closed 'up to the branching part', stating, e.g., that even though the table is not closed, all the successors of rows are present as combinations of other rows.

Another approach would be to integrate monads into our framework, which are also used to handle branching within the theory of coalgebras [16]. It is an intriguing question whether the current approach, which allows to move beyond automata-like examples, can be combined with the CALF framework [13], which is very far in handling branching occurring in various kinds of automata.

Acknowledgments. We are grateful to Joshua Moerman, Nick Bezhanishvili, Gerco van Heerdt, Aleks Kissinger and Stefan Milius for valuable discussions and suggestions.

References

1. Adámek, J., Lücke, D., Milius, S.: Recursive coalgebras of finitary functors. ITA **41**(4), 447–462 (2007)
2. Adámek, J., Milius, S., Moss, L.S., Sousa, L.: Well-pointed coalgebras. Logical Methods Comput. Sci. **9**(3) (2013)
3. Adámek, J., Rosický, J.: Locally Presentable and Accessible Categories. Cambridge Tracts in Mathematics. Cambridge University Press, Cambridge (1994)
4. Angluin, D.: Learning regular sets from queries and counterexamples. Inf. Comput. **75**(2), 87–106 (1987)
5. Angluin, D., Eisenstat, S., Fisman, D.: Learning regular languages via alternating automata. In: Yang, Q., Wooldridge, M. (eds.) IJCAI 2015, pp. 3308–3314. AAAI Press (2015)
6. Barlocco, S., Kupke, C.: Angluin learning via logic. In: Artemov, S., Nerode, A. (eds.) LFCS 2018. LNCS, vol. 10703, pp. 72–90. Springer, Cham (2018). https:// doi.org/10.1007/978-3-319-72056-2_5
7. Blackburn, P., de Rijke, M., Venema, Y.: Modal Logic. Cambridge Tracts in Theoretical Computer Science, vol. 53. Cambridge University Press, Cambridge (2001)
8. Blok, A.: Interaction, observation and denotation. Master's thesis, ILLC Amsterdam (2012)
9. Bollig, B., Habermehl, P., Kern, C., Leucker, M.: Angluin-style learning of NFA. In: Boutilier, C. (ed.) Proceedings of the 21st International Joint Conference on Artificial Intelligence, IJCAI 2009, pp. 1004–1009 (2009)
10. Borceux, F.: Handbook of Categorical Algebra. Encyclopedia of Mathematics and its Applications, vol. 1. Cambridge University Press, Cambridge (1994)
11. van Heerdt, G.: An abstract automata learning framework. Master's thesis, Radboud Universiteit Nijmegen (2016)
12. van Heerdt, G., Sammartino, M., Silva, A.: CALF: categorical automata learning framework. In: Goranko, V., Dam, M. (eds.) 26th EACSL Annual Conference on Computer Science Logic, CSL 2017. LIPIcs, vol. 2, pp. 29:1–29:24. Schloss Dagstuhl - Leibniz-Zentrum fuer Informatik (2017)
13. van Heerdt, G., Sammartino, M., Silva, A.: Learning automata with side-effects. CoRR, abs/1704.08055 (2017)
14. Jacobs, B.: Introduction to Coalgebra: Towards Mathematics of States and Observation. Cambridge Tracts in Theoretical Computer Science, vol. 59. Cambridge University Press, Cambridge (2016)

15. Jacobs, B., Silva, A.: Automata learning: a categorical perspective. In: van Breugel, F., Kashefi, E., Palamidessi, C., Rutten, J. (eds.) Panangaden Festschrift. LNCS, vol. 8464, pp. 384–406. Springer, Cham (2014). https://doi.org/10.1007/978-3-319-06880-0_20

16. Jacobs, B., Silva, A., Sokolova, A.: Trace semantics via determinization. J. Comput. Syst. Sci. **81**(5), 859–879 (2015)

17. Jacobs, B., Sokolova, A.: Exemplaric expressivity of modal logics. J. Logic Comput. **20**(5), 1041–1068 (2009)

18. Klin, B.: Coalgebraic modal logic beyond sets. Electr. Notes Theor. Comput. Sci. **173**, 177–201 (2007)

19. Klin, B., Rot, J.: Coalgebraic trace semantics via forgetful logics. Logical Methods Comput. Sci. **12**(4) (2016)

20. Kupke, C., Kurz, A., Pattinson, D.: Algebraic semantics for coalgebraic logics. Electr. Notes Theor. Comput. Sci. **106**, 219–241 (2004)

21. Kupke, C., Pattinson, D.: Coalgebraic semantics of modal logics: an overview. Theor. Comput. Sci. **412**(38), 5070–5094 (2011)

22. Maler, O., Pnueli, A.: On the learnability of infinitary regular sets. Inf. Comput. **118**(2), 316–326 (1995)

23. Osius, G.: Categorical set theory: a characterization of the category of sets. J. Pure Appl. Algebra **4**(1), 79–119 (1974)

24. Pavlovic, D., Mislove, M., Worrell, J.B.: Testing semantics: connecting processes and process logics. In: Johnson, M., Vene, V. (eds.) AMAST 2006. LNCS, vol. 4019, pp. 308–322. Springer, Heidelberg (2006). https://doi.org/10.1007/11784180_24

25. Rutten, J.J.M.M.: Automata and coinduction (an exercise in coalgebra). In: Sangiorgi, D., de Simone, R. (eds.) CONCUR 1998. LNCS, vol. 1466, pp. 194–218. Springer, Heidelberg (1998). https://doi.org/10.1007/BFb0055624

26. Rutten, J.J.M.M.: Universal coalgebra: a theory of systems. Theor. Comput. Sci. **249**(1), 3–80 (2000)

27. Schröder, L.: Expressivity of coalgebraic modal logic: the limits and beyond. Theor. Comput. Sci. **390**(2–3), 230–247 (2008)

28. Taylor, P.: Practical Foundations of Mathematics. Cambridge University Press, Cambridge (1999)

29. Trnková, V.: On descriptive classification of set-functors. I. Comment. Math. Univ. Carolinae **12**(1), 143–174 (1971)

30. Vaandrager, F.W.: Model learning. Commun. ACM **60**(2), 86–95 (2017)

9

A Sound and Complete Logic for Algebraic Effects

Cristina Matache[(✉)] and Sam Staton

University of Oxford, Oxford, UK
cristina.matache@balliol.ox.ac.uk

Abstract. This work investigates three notions of program equivalence for a higher-order functional language with recursion and general algebraic effects, in which programs are written in continuation-passing style. Our main contribution is the following: we define a logic whose formulas express program properties and show that, under certain conditions which we identify, the induced program equivalence coincides with a contextual equivalence. Moreover, we show that this logical equivalence also coincides with an applicative bisimilarity. We exemplify our general results with the nondeterminism, probabilistic choice, global store and I/O effects.

1 Introduction

Logic is a fundamental tool for specifying the behaviour of programs. A general approach is to consider that a logical formula ϕ encodes a program property, and the satisfaction relation of the logic, $t \models \phi$, asserts that program t enjoys property ϕ. An example is Hennessy-Milner logic [12] used to model concurrency and nondeterminism. Other program logics include Hoare logic [13], which describes imperative programs with state, and more recently separation logic [28]. Both state and nondeterminism are examples of *computational effects* [25], which represent impure behaviour in a functional programming language. The logics mentioned so far concern languages with first-order functions, so as a natural extension, we are interested in finding a logic which describes higher-order programs with general effects.

The particular flavour of effects we consider is that of *algebraic effects* developed by Plotkin and Power [32–34]. This is a unified framework in which effectful computation is triggered by a set of operations whose behaviour is axiomatized by a set of equations. For example, nondeterminism is given by a binary choice operation $or(-, -)$ that satisfies the equations of a semilattice. Thus, general effectful programs have multiple possible execution paths, which can be visualized as an (effect) tree, with effect operations labelling the nodes. Consider the following function or_suc which has three possible return values, and the effect tree of (or_suc 2):

$$\text{or\_suc} = \lambda x\text{:nat.}$$
$$or(x, \ or(x+1, x+2))$$

$$(\text{or\_suc } 2) \longmapsto \begin{array}{c} \\ 2 \end{array} \begin{array}{c} or \\ \diagup \quad \diagdown \\ \end{array} \begin{array}{c} or \\ 3 \diagup \quad \diagdown \ 4 \end{array}$$

Apart from state and nondeterminism, examples of algebraic effects include probabilistic choice and input and output operations.

Apart from providing a specification language for programs, a logic can also be used to compare two different programs. This leads to a notion of program equivalence: two programs are equivalent when they satisfy exactly the same formulas in the logic.

Many other definitions of program equivalence for higher-order languages exist. An early notion is contextual equivalence [26], which asserts that two programs are equivalent if they have the same observable behaviour in all program contexts. However, this is hard to establish in practice due to the quantification over all contexts. Another approach, which relies on the existence of a suitable denotational model of the language, is checking equality of denotations. Yet another notion, meant to address the shortcomings of the previous two, is that of applicative bisimilarity [1].

Given the wide range of definitions of program equivalence, comparing them is an interesting question. For example, the equivalence induced by Hennessy-Milner logic is known to coincide with bisimilarity for CCS. Thus, we not only aim to find a logic describing general algebraic effects, but also to compare it to existing notions of program equivalence.

Program equivalence for general algebraic effects has been studied by Johann, Simpson and Voigtländer [17] who define a notion of contextual equivalence and a corresponding logical relation. Dal Lago, Gavazzo and Levy [7] provide an abstract treatment of applicative bisimilarity in the presence of algebraic effects. Working in a typed, call-by-value setting, Simpson and Voorneveld [38] propose a modal logic for effectful programs whose induced program equivalence coincides with applicative bisimilarity, but not with contextual equivalence (see counterexample in Sect. 5). Dal Lago, Gavazzo and Tanaka [8] propose a notion of applicative similarity that coincides with contextual equivalence for an untyped, call-by-name effectful calculus.

These papers provide the main starting point for our work. Our goal is to find a logic of program properties which characterizes contextual equivalence for a higher-order language with algebraic effects. We study a typed call-by-value language in which programs are written in continuation-passing style (CPS). CPS is known to simplify contextual equivalence, through the addition of control operators (e.g. [5]), but it also implies that all notions of program equivalence we define can only use continuations to test return values. Contextual equivalence and bisimilarity for lambda-calculi with control, but without general effects, have been studied extensively (e.g. [4,15,23,41]).

In CPS, functions receive as argument the continuation (which is itself a function) to which they pass their return value. Consider the function that adds two natural numbers. This usually has type $\text{nat} \to \text{nat} \to \text{nat}$, but its CPS version is defined as: $\text{addk} = \lambda(n\text{:nat}, m\text{:nat}, k\text{:nat}\to\text{R}). \ k \ (n+m)$ for some fixed return type R. The function or_suc becomes in CPS:

$$\texttt{or\_succ} = \lambda(x\texttt{:nat}, k\texttt{:nat}{\rightarrow}\texttt{R}).\ or(k\ x,\ or(\texttt{addk}\ (x,\ 1,\ k),\ \texttt{addk}\ (x,\ 2,\ k))).$$

A general translation of direct-style functions into CPS can be found in Sect. 5.

We fix a calculus named ECPS (Sect. 2), in which programs are not expected to return, except through a call to the continuation. Contextual equivalence is defined using a custom set of observations $\mathfrak{P}$, where the elements of $\mathfrak{P}$ are sets of effect trees. We consider a logic $\mathcal{F}$ whose formulas express properties of ECPS programs (Sect. 3). For example, $\texttt{or\_succ}$ satisfies the following formula:
$$\phi = (\{2\},\ (\{3\} \vee \{4\}) \mapsto \square) \mapsto \Diamond.$$

Here, $\Diamond$ is the set of all effect trees for which at least one execution path succeeds and $\square$ is the set of trees that always succeed. So $\texttt{or\_succ} \models_{\mathcal{F}} \phi$ says that, when given arguments 2 and a continuation that always succeeds for input 3 or 4, then $\texttt{or\_succ}$ *may* succeed. In other words, $\texttt{or\_succ}$ may 'return' 3 or 4 to the continuation. In contrast, $\texttt{or\_succ} \models_{\mathcal{F}} \phi' = (\{2\},\ (\{3\} \vee \{4\}) \mapsto \square) \mapsto \square$ says that the program $\texttt{or\_succ}$ *must* return 3 or 4 to the continuation. Thus $\texttt{or\_succ} \not\models_{\mathcal{F}} \phi'$ because the continuation k might diverge on 2.

Another example can be obtained by generalizing the $\texttt{or\_succ}$ function to take a function as a parameter, rather than using $\texttt{addk}$:

$$\texttt{or\_succ'} = \lambda(x : \texttt{nat},\ k : \texttt{nat}{\rightarrow}\texttt{R},\ f : (\texttt{nat, nat, nat}{\rightarrow}\texttt{R}){\rightarrow}\texttt{R}).$$
$$or(k\ x,\ or(f\ (x,1,k),\ f\ (x,2,k)))$$
$$\models_{\mathcal{F}} \left(\{2\},\ \{4\} \mapsto \Diamond,\ ((\{2\},\ \{2\},\ \{4\} \mapsto \Diamond) \mapsto \Diamond) \right) \mapsto \Diamond.$$

The formula above says that $\texttt{or\_succ'}$ may call f with arguments 2, 2 and k.

The main theorem concerning the logic $\mathcal{F}$ (Theorem 1) is that, under certain restrictions on the observations in $\mathfrak{P}$, logical equivalence coincides with contextual equivalence. In other words, $\mathcal{F}$ is sound and complete with respect to contextual equivalence. The proof of this theorem, outlined in Sect. 4, involves applicative bisimilarity as an intermediate step. Thus, we show in fact that three notions of program equivalence for ECPS are the same: logical equivalence, contextual equivalence and applicative bisimilarity. Due to space constraints, proofs are omitted but they can be found in [21].

2 Programming Language – ECPS

We consider a simply-typed functional programming language with general recursion, a datatype of natural numbers and general algebraic effects as introduced by Plotkin and Power [32]. We will refer to this language as ECPS because programs are written in continuation-passing style.

ECPS distinguishes between terms which can reduce further, named computations, and values, which cannot reduce. ECPS is a variant of both Plotkin's PCF [31] and Levy's Jump-With-Argument language [20], extended with algebraic effects. A fragment of ECPS is discussed in [18] in connection with logic.

Types	$A, A_1, B := (A_1, \ldots, A_n){\rightarrow}\texttt{R} \mid \texttt{nat}$	$(n \geq 0)$
Typing contexts	$\Gamma := \emptyset \mid \Gamma, x : A.$	

The only base type in ECPS is **nat**. The return type of functions, R, is fixed and is *not* a first-class type. Intuitively, we consider that functions are not expected to return. A type in direct style $A \to B$ becomes in ECPS: $(A, B \to R) \to R$. In the typing context $(\Gamma, x : A)$, the free variable x does not appear in Γ.

First, consider the pure fragment of ECPS, without effects, named CPS:

Values $\qquad v, w := \texttt{zero} \mid \texttt{succ}(v) \mid \lambda(x_1{:}A_1, \ldots, x_n{:}A_n).t \mid x \qquad (n \geq 0)$

Computations $\quad s, t := v(w_1, \ldots, w_n) \mid \texttt{case } v \texttt{ of } \{\texttt{zero} \Rightarrow s, \texttt{ succ}(x) \Rightarrow t\} \mid$
$\qquad\qquad\qquad (\texttt{rec } x.v)(w_1, \ldots, w_n).$

Variables, natural numbers and lambdas are values. Computations include function application and an eliminator for natural numbers. The expression **rec** $x.v$ is a recursive definition of the function v, which must be applied. If exactly one argument appears in a lambda abstraction or an application term, we will sometimes omit the parentheses around that argument.

There are two typing relations in CPS, one for values $\Gamma \vdash v : A$, which says that value v has type A in the context Γ, and one for computations $\Gamma \vdash t : R$. This says that t is well-formed given the context Γ. All computations have the same return type R. We also define the *order of a type* recursively, which roughly speaking counts the number of function arrows $\to$ in a type.

$$\frac{}{\Gamma, x : A \vdash x : A} \qquad \frac{\Gamma, \overrightarrow{x : A} \vdash t : R}{\Gamma \vdash \lambda(\overrightarrow{x{:}A}).t : (\overrightarrow{A}) \to R} \qquad \frac{}{\Gamma \vdash \texttt{zero} : \texttt{nat}} \qquad \frac{\Gamma \vdash v : \texttt{nat}}{\Gamma \vdash \texttt{succ}(v) : \texttt{nat}}$$

$$\frac{\Gamma \vdash v : (\overrightarrow{A}) \to R \quad (\Gamma \vdash w_i : A_i)_i}{\Gamma \vdash v\,(\overrightarrow{w}) : R} \qquad \frac{\Gamma, x : (\overrightarrow{A}) \to R \vdash v : (\overrightarrow{A}) \to R \quad (\Gamma \vdash w_i : A_i)_i}{\Gamma \vdash (\texttt{rec } x.v)(\overrightarrow{w}) : R}$$

$$\frac{\Gamma \vdash v : \texttt{nat} \quad \Gamma \vdash t : R \quad \Gamma, x : \texttt{nat} \vdash s : R}{\Gamma \vdash \texttt{case } v \texttt{ of } \{\texttt{zero} \Rightarrow t, \texttt{ succ}(x) \Rightarrow s\} : R}$$

$$ord(\texttt{nat}) = 0 \qquad\qquad ord((\,) \to R) = 1$$

$$ord((A_1, \ldots, A_n) \to R) = max_{1 \leq i \leq n}(ord(A_i)) + 1 \qquad (\text{if } n > 0)$$

To introduce algebraic effects into our language, we consider a new kind of context Σ, disjoint from Γ, which we call an *effect context*. The symbols σ appearing in Σ stand for effect operations and their type must have either order 1 or 2. For example, the binary choice operation $or : ((\,) \to R, (\,) \to R) \to R$ expects two thunked computations. The output operation $output : (\texttt{nat}, (\,) \to R) \to R$ expects a parameter and a continuation. An operation signifying success, which takes no arguments, is $\downarrow : (\,) \to R$. Roughly, Σ could be regarded as a countable algebraic signature.

We extend the syntax of CPS with effectful computations. The typing relations now carry a Σ context: $\Gamma \vdash_\Sigma v : A$ and $\Gamma \vdash_\Sigma t : R$. Otherwise, the typing judgements remain unchanged; we have a new rule for typing effect operations:

$$s, t := \ldots \mid \sigma(\overrightarrow{v}, \overrightarrow{k}) \qquad \frac{\sigma : (\overrightarrow{A}, \overrightarrow{B}) \to \mathrm{R} \in \Sigma \quad (\Gamma \vdash_{\Sigma} v_i : A_i)_i \quad (\Gamma \vdash_{\Sigma} k_j : B_j)_j}{\Gamma \vdash_{\Sigma} \sigma(\overrightarrow{v}, \overrightarrow{k}) : \mathrm{R}}$$

In ECPS, the only type with order 0 is $\mathtt{nat}$, so in fact $A_i = \mathtt{nat}$ for all i. Notice that the grammar does not allow function abstraction over a symbol from Σ and that σ is not a first-class term. So we can assume that Σ is fixed, as in the examples from Sect. 2.1.

As usual, we identify terms up to alpha-equivalence. Substitution of values for free variables that are not operations, $v[w/x]$ and $t[w/x]$, is defined in the standard way by induction on the structure of v and t. We use $\overline{n}$ to denote the term $\mathtt{succ}^n(\mathtt{zero})$. Let $(\vdash_{\Sigma})$ be the set of well-formed closed computations and $(\vdash_{\Sigma} A)$ the set of closed values of type A.

2.1 Operational Semantics

We define a family of relations on closed computation terms $(\longrightarrow) \subseteq (\vdash_{\Sigma}) \times (\vdash_{\Sigma})$ for any effect context Σ:

$$(\lambda(\overrightarrow{x{:}A}).t)\,(\overrightarrow{w}) \longrightarrow t[\overrightarrow{w}/\overrightarrow{x}]$$
$$(\mathtt{rec}\ x.v)\,(\overrightarrow{w}) \longrightarrow (v[(\lambda(\overrightarrow{y{:}A}).(\mathtt{rec}\ x.v)(\overrightarrow{y}))/x])\,(\overrightarrow{w})$$
$$\mathtt{case\ zero\ of\ \{zero} \Rightarrow s,\ \mathtt{succ}(x) \Rightarrow t\} \longrightarrow s$$
$$\mathtt{case\ succ}(v)\ \mathtt{of\ \{zero} \Rightarrow s,\ \mathtt{succ}(x) \Rightarrow t\} \longrightarrow t[v/x].$$

Observe that the reduction given by $\longrightarrow$ can either run forever or terminate with an effect operation. If the effect operation does not take any arguments of order 1 (i.e. continuations), the computation stops. If the reduction reaches $\sigma(\overrightarrow{v}, \overrightarrow{k})$, the intuition is that any continuation k_i may be chosen, and executed with the results of operation σ. Thus, repeatedly evaluating effect operations leads to the construction of an infinitely branching tree (similar to that in [32]), as we now explain, which we call an *effect tree*. A path in the tree represents a possible execution path of the program.

An effect tree, of possibly infinite depth and width, can contain:

- leaves labelled $\bot$, which signifies nontermination of $\longrightarrow$;
- leaves labelled $\sigma_{\overrightarrow{v}}$, where $\sigma : (\overrightarrow{A}) \to \mathrm{R} \in \Sigma$ and $(\vdash_{\Sigma} v_i : A_i)_i$;
- nodes labelled $\sigma_{\overrightarrow{v}}$, where $\sigma : (\overrightarrow{A}, \overrightarrow{B}) \to \mathrm{R} \in \Sigma$ and each $\vdash_{\Sigma} v_i : A_i$; such a node has an infinite number of children $t_0, t_1, \ldots$.

Denote the set of all effect trees by Trees_{Σ}. This set has a partial order: $tr_1 \leq tr_2$ if and only if tr_1 can be obtained by replacing subtrees of tr_2 by $\bot$. Every ascending chain $t_1 \leq t_2 \leq \ldots$ has a least upper bound $\bigsqcup_n t_n$. In fact Trees_{Σ} is the free pointed Σ-algebra [2] and therefore also has a coinductive property [9].

Next, we define a sequence of effect trees associated with each well-formed closed computation. Each element in the sequence can be seen as evaluating the computation one step further. Let $[\![-]\!]_{(-)} : (\vdash_{\Sigma}) \times \mathbb{N} \longrightarrow \mathit{Trees}_{\Sigma}$:

$$[\![t]\!]_0 = \bot$$

$$[\![t]\!]_{m+1} = \begin{cases} [\![s]\!]_m & \text{if } t \longrightarrow s \\ \sigma_{\overrightarrow{v}}\Big(\Big(\big([\![k_i\ (\overline{n_1}, \dots, \overline{n_{p_i}})]\!]_m\big)_{n_1,\dots,n_{p_i} \in \mathbb{N}}\Big)_i\Big) & \text{if } t = \sigma(\overrightarrow{v}, \overrightarrow{k}) \end{cases}$$

These are all the cases since well-formed computations do not get stuck. We define the function $[\![-]\!] : (\vdash_\Sigma) \longrightarrow \mathit{Trees}_\Sigma$ as the least upper bound of the chain $\{[\![t_n]\!]\}_{n\in\mathbb{N}}$: $[\![t]\!] = \bigsqcup_{n\in\mathbb{N}}[\![t]\!]_n$.

We now give examples of effect contexts Σ for different algebraic effects, and of some computations and their associated effect trees.

Example 1 (Pure functional computation). $\Sigma = \{\downarrow\ :\ ()\!\to\!\mathrm{R}\}$. Intuitively, $\downarrow$ is a top-level success flag, analogous to a 'barb' in process algebra. This is to ensure a reasonable contextual equivalence for CPS programs, which never actually return results. For example, $loop = (\mathbf{rec}\ f.\lambda().(f\ x))\ ()$ runs forever, and

$$\mathtt{test\_zero} = \lambda(y\text{:nat}).\ \mathtt{case}\ y\ \mathtt{of}\ \{\mathtt{zero} \Rightarrow\ \downarrow ()\,,\ \mathtt{succ}(x) \Rightarrow loop\}$$

is a continuation that succeeds just when it is passed zero. Generally, an effect tree for a pure computation is either $\downarrow$ if it succeeds or $\bot$ otherwise.

Example 2 (Nondeterminism). $\Sigma = \{or\ :\ (()\!\to\!\mathrm{R},\ ()\!\to\!\mathrm{R})\!\to\!\mathrm{R},\ \downarrow\ :\ ()\!\to\!\mathrm{R}\}$. Intuitively, $or(k_1, k_2)$ performs a nondeterministic choice between computations $k_1\ ()$ and $k_2\ ()$. Consider a continuation $\mathtt{test\_3} : \mathtt{nat}\!\to\!\mathrm{R}$ that diverges on 3 and succeeds otherwise. The program $\mathtt{or\_succ}$ from the introduction is in ECPS:

$$\mathtt{or\_succ} = \lambda(x\text{:nat}, k\text{:nat}\!\to\!\mathrm{R}).\ or(\lambda().\ k\ x,$$
$$\lambda().\ or(\lambda().k\ (\mathtt{succ}(x)),$$
$$\lambda().k\ (\mathtt{succ}(\mathtt{succ}(x))))))$$

$[\![\mathtt{or\_succ}\ (\overline{2},\ \mathtt{test\_3})]\!] =$

Example 3 (Probabilistic choice). $\Sigma = \{p\text{-}or\ :\ (()\!\to\!\mathrm{R},\ ()\!\to\!\mathrm{R})\!\to\!\mathrm{R},\ \downarrow\ :\ ()\!\to\!\mathrm{R}\}$. Intuitively, the operation $p\text{-}or(k_1, k_2)$ chooses between $k_1\ ()$ and $k_2\ ()$ with probability 0.5. Consider the following term which encodes the geometric distribution:

$$\mathtt{geom} = \lambda k\text{:nat}\!\to\!\mathrm{R}.$$
$$\big(\mathbf{rec}\ f.\ \lambda(n\text{:nat}, k'\text{:nat}\!\to\!\mathrm{R}).p\text{-}or(\lambda().k'\ n,\ \lambda().f\ (\mathtt{succ}(n), k')))\big)\ (\overline{1}, k).$$

The probability that $\mathtt{geom}$ passes a number $n > 0$ to its continuation is 2^{-n}. To test it, consider $k = (\lambda x\text{:nat}.\ \downarrow ())$; then $[\![\mathtt{geom}\ k]\!]$ is an infinite tree:

$[\![\mathtt{geom}\ k]\!] = $

Example 4 (Global store). $\mathbb{L}$ is a finite set of locations storing natural numbers and $\Sigma = \{lookup_l\ :\ (\mathtt{nat}\!\to\!\mathrm{R})\!\to\!\mathrm{R},\ update_l\ :\ (\mathtt{nat}, ()\!\to\!\mathrm{R})\!\to\!\mathrm{R}\ |\ l \in \mathbb{L}\}\cup\{\downarrow\ :\ ()\!\to\!\mathrm{R}\}$. Intuitively, $lookup_l(k)$ looks up the value at storage location l, if this is $\overline{n}$ it continues with $k\,(\overline{n})$. For $update_l(v,k)$ the intuition is: write the number v in location l then continue with the computation $k\,()$. For example:

$$[\![update_{l_0}(\overline{1},\ \lambda().lookup_{l_0}(\lambda x{:}\mathtt{nat}.\mathtt{case}\ x$$
$$\mathtt{of}\ \{\mathtt{zero} \Rightarrow\ \downarrow\ (),\ \mathtt{succ}(y) \Rightarrow loop\}))]\!] =$$

$$update_{l_0,\overline{1}}$$
$$|$$
$$lookup_{l_0}$$
$$\swarrow\ /\ \searrow$$
$$\downarrow\quad \bot\quad \bot\ \cdots$$

Only the second branch of $lookup_{l_0}$ can occur. The other branches are still present in the tree because $[\![-]\!]$ treats effect operations as uninterpreted syntax.

Example 5 (Interactive input/output). $\Sigma = \{\downarrow\ :\ ()\to\mathtt{R},\ output : (\mathtt{nat}, ()\to\mathtt{R})\to\mathtt{R},$ $input : (\mathtt{nat}\to\mathtt{R})\to\mathtt{R}\}$. Intuitively, the computation $input(k)$ accepts number $\overline{n}$ from the input channel and continues with $k\,(\overline{n})$. The computation $output(v,k)$ writes v to the output channel then continues with computation $k\,()$. Below is a computation that inputs a number $\overline{n}$ then outputs it immediately, and repeats.

$$[\![echo]\!] = [\![(\mathtt{rec}\ f.\ \lambda().$$
$$input(\lambda x{:}\mathtt{nat}.\ output(x,\ \lambda().f\ ()))) ()]\!] =$$

$$input$$
$$\diagup\ /\ \searrow$$
$$output_{\overline{0}}\quad output_{\overline{1}}\quad output_{\overline{2}}\ \cdots$$
$$|\qquad\qquad |\qquad\qquad |$$
$$[\![echo]\!]\quad [\![echo]\!]\quad [\![echo]\!]$$

2.2 Contextual Equivalence

Informally, two terms are contextually equivalent if they have the same *observable behaviour* in all program contexts. The definition of observable behaviour depends on the programming language under consideration. In ECPS, we can observe effectful behaviour such as interactive output values or the probability with which a computation succeeds. This behaviour is encoded by the effect tree of a computation. Therefore, we represent an ECPS observation as a set of effect trees P. A computation t exhibits observation P if $[\![t]\!] \in P$.

For a fixed set of effect operations Σ, we define the set $\mathfrak{P}$ of possible *observations*. The elements of $\mathfrak{P}$ are subsets of $Trees_\Sigma$. Observations play a similar role to the modalities from [38]. For our running examples of effects, $\mathfrak{P}$ is defined as follows:

Example 6 (Pure functional computation). Define $\mathfrak{P} = \{\Downarrow\}$ where $\Downarrow = \{\downarrow\}$. There are no effect operations so the $\Downarrow$ observation only checks for success.

Example 7 (Nondeterminism). Define $\mathfrak{P} = \{\Diamond, \Box\}$ where:

$$\Diamond = \{tr \in Trees_\Sigma \mid \text{at least one of the paths in } tr \text{ has a } \downarrow \text{ leaf}\}$$
$$\Box = \{tr \in Trees_\Sigma \mid \text{the paths in } tr \text{ are all finite and finish with a } \downarrow\}.$$

The intuition is that, if $[\![t]\!] \in \Diamond$, then computation t *may* succeed, whereas if $[\![t]\!] \in \Box$, then t *must* succeed.

Example 8 (Probabilistic choice). Define $\mathbb{P} : Trees_\Sigma \longrightarrow [0,1]$ to be the least function, by the pointwise order, such that:

$$\mathbb{P}(\downarrow) = 1 \qquad \mathbb{P}(p\text{-}or(tr_0, tr_1)) = \frac{1}{2}\mathbb{P}(tr_0) + \frac{1}{2}\mathbb{P}(tr_1).$$

Notice that $\mathbb{P}(\bot) = 0$. Then observations are defined as:

$$\mathbf{P}_{>q} = \{tr \in Trees_\Sigma \mid \mathbb{P}(tr) > q\} \qquad \mathfrak{P} = \{\mathbf{P}_{>q} \mid q \in \mathbb{Q},\ 0 \leq q < 1\}.$$

This means that $[\![t]\!] \in \mathbf{P}_{>q}$ if the probability that t succeeds is greater than q.

Example 9 (Global store). Define the set of states as the set of functions from storage locations to natural numbers: $State = \mathbb{L} \longrightarrow \mathbb{N}$. Given a state S, we write $[S\!\downarrow] \subseteq Trees_\Sigma$ for the set of effect trees that terminate when starting in state S. More precisely, $[-]$ is the least $State$-indexed family of sets satisfying the following:

$$\frac{-}{\downarrow \in [S\!\downarrow]} \qquad \frac{l \in \mathbb{L} \qquad tr_{S(l)} \in [S\!\downarrow]}{lookup_l(tr_0, tr_1, tr_2, \ldots) \in [S\!\downarrow]} \qquad \frac{l \in \mathbb{L} \qquad tr \in [S[l := n]\!\downarrow]}{update_{l,\overline{n}}(tr) \in [S\!\downarrow]}$$

The set of observations is: $\mathfrak{P} = \{[S\!\downarrow] \mid S \in State\}$.

Example 10 (Interactive input/output). An I/O-trace is a finite word w over the alphabet $\{?n \mid n \in \mathbb{N}\} \cup \{!n \mid n \in \mathbb{N}\}$. For example, ?1 !1 ?2 !2 ?3 !3. The set of observations is: $\mathfrak{P} = \{\langle W \rangle_{...},\ \langle W \rangle\!\downarrow \mid W$ an I/O-trace$\}$. Observations are defined as the least sets satisfying the following rules:

$$\frac{-}{tr \in \langle \epsilon \rangle_{...}} \qquad \frac{tr = \downarrow}{tr \in \langle \epsilon \rangle\!\downarrow} \qquad \frac{tr_n \in \langle W \rangle_{...}}{input(tr_0, tr_1, \ldots) \in \langle (?n)W \rangle_{...}} \qquad \frac{tr' \in \langle W \rangle_{...}}{output_{\overline{n}}(tr') \in \langle (!n)W \rangle_{...}}$$

and the analogous rules for $\langle (?n)W \rangle\!\downarrow$ and $\langle (!n)W \rangle\!\downarrow$. Thus, $[\![t]\!] \in \langle W \rangle_{...}$ if computation t produces I/O trace W, and $[\![t]\!] \in \langle W \rangle\!\downarrow$ if additionally t succeeds immediately after producing W.

Using the set of observations $\mathfrak{P}$, we can now define contextual equivalence as the greatest compatible and adequate equivalence relation between possibly open terms of the same type. Adequacy specifies a necessary condition for two *closed* computations to be related, namely producing the same observations.

Definition 1. *A well-typed relation* $\mathcal{R} = (\mathcal{R}_A^\flat, \mathcal{R}^c)$ *(i.e. a family of relations indexed by ECPS types where* $\mathcal{R}^c$ *relates computations) on possibly open terms is adequate if:*

$$\forall s, t.\ \vdash_\Sigma s\, \mathcal{R}^c\, t \implies \forall P \in \mathfrak{P}.\ [\![s]\!] \in P \iff [\![t]\!] \in P.$$

Relation $\mathcal{R}$ *is compatible if it is closed under the rules in [21, Page 57]. As an example, the rules for application and lambda abstraction are:*

$$\frac{\Gamma \vdash_\Sigma v\, \mathcal{R}_{(\overrightarrow{A}) \to R}^\flat\, v' \qquad (\Gamma \vdash_\Sigma w_i\, \mathcal{R}_{A_i}^\flat\, w_i')_i}{\Gamma \vdash_\Sigma v(\overrightarrow{w})\, \mathcal{R}^c\, v'(\overrightarrow{w'})} \qquad \frac{\Gamma, \overrightarrow{x : A} \vdash_\Sigma s\, \mathcal{R}^c\, t}{\Gamma \vdash_\Sigma \lambda(\overrightarrow{x{:}A}).s\, \mathcal{R}_{(\overrightarrow{A}) \to R}^\flat\, \lambda(\overrightarrow{x{:}A}).t}$$

Definition 2 (Contextual equivalence). *Let* $\mathbb{CA}$ *be the set of well-typed relations on possibly open terms that are both compatible and adequate. Define contextual equivalence* $\equiv_{ctx}$ *to be* $\bigcup \mathbb{CA}$.

Proposition 1. *Contextual equivalence* $\equiv_{ctx}$ *is an equivalence relation, and is moreover compatible and adequate.*

This definition of contextual equivalence, originally proposed in [11,19], can be easily proved equivalent to the traditional definition involving program contexts (see [21, §7]). As Pitts observes [30], reasoning about program contexts directly is inconvenient because they cannot be defined up to alpha-equivalence, hence we prefer using Definition 2.

For example, in the pure setting (Example 1), we have $\bar{0} \not\equiv_{ctx} \bar{1}$, because $\texttt{test\_zero}(\bar{0}) \not\equiv_{ctx} \texttt{test\_zero}(\bar{1})$; they are distinguished by the observation $\Downarrow$. In the state example, $lookup_{l_1}(k) \not\equiv_{ctx} lookup_{l_2}(k)$, because they are distinguished by the context $(\lambda k\text{:nat}{\rightarrow}\text{R}. [-])$ $(\texttt{test\_zero})$ and the observation $[S\downarrow]$ where $S(l_1) = \bar{0}$ and $S(l_2) = \bar{1}$. In the case of probabilistic choice (Example 3), $\texttt{geom}\ (\lambda x\text{:nat}. \downarrow ()) \equiv_{ctx} \downarrow ()$ because $(\texttt{geom}\ (\lambda x\text{:nat}. \downarrow ()))$ succeeds with probability 1 ('almost surely').

3   A Program Logic for ECPS – $\mathcal{F}$

This section contains the main contribution of the paper: a logic $\mathcal{F}$ of program properties for ECPS which characterizes contextual equivalence. Crucially, the logic makes use of the observations in $\mathfrak{P}$ to express properties of computations.

In $\mathcal{F}$, there is a distinction between formulas that describe values and those that describe computations. Each value formula is associated an ECPS type A. Value formulas are constructed from the basic formulas $(\phi_1, \ldots, \phi_n) \mapsto P$ and $\phi = \{n\}$, where $n \in \mathbb{N}$ and $P \in \mathfrak{P}$, as below. The indexing set I can be infinite, even uncountable. Computation formulas are simply the elements of $\mathfrak{P}$.

(VAL)
$$\frac{n \in \mathbb{N}}{\{n\} : \text{nat}} \quad \frac{\phi_1 : A_1 \ldots \phi_n : A_n \quad P \in \mathfrak{P}}{(\phi_1, \ldots, \phi_n) \mapsto P : (A_1, \ldots, A_n){\rightarrow}\text{R}} \quad \frac{(\phi_i : A)_{i \in I}}{\bigvee_{i \in I}\phi_i : A} \quad \frac{(\phi_i : A)_{i \in I}}{\bigwedge_{i \in I}\phi_i : A} \quad \frac{\phi : A}{\neg\phi : A}$$

The satisfaction relation $\models_{\mathcal{F}}$ relates a closed value $\vdash_\Sigma v : A$ to a value formula $\phi : A$ of the same type, or a closed computation t to an observation P. Relation $t \models_{\mathcal{F}} P$ tests the shape of the effect tree of t.

$$
\begin{aligned}
v \models_{\mathcal{F}} \{n\} &\iff v = \bar{n} \\
v \models_{\mathcal{F}} (\phi_1, \ldots, \phi_n) \mapsto P &\iff \text{for all closed values } w_1, \ldots, w_n \text{ such that} \\
&\qquad \forall i.\ w_i \models_{\mathcal{F}} \phi_i \text{ then } v(w_1, \ldots, w_n) \models_{\mathcal{F}} P \\
v \models_{\mathcal{F}} \bigvee_{i \in I}\phi_i &\iff \text{there exists } j \in I \text{ such that } v \models_{\mathcal{F}} \phi_j \\
v \models_{\mathcal{F}} \bigwedge_{i \in I}\phi_i &\iff \text{for all } j \in I,\ v \models_{\mathcal{F}} \phi_j \\
v \models_{\mathcal{F}} \neg\phi &\iff \text{it is false that } v \models_{\mathcal{F}} \phi \\
t \models_{\mathcal{F}} P &\iff [\![t]\!] \in P.
\end{aligned}
$$

Example 11. Consider the following formulas, where only ϕ_3 and ϕ_4 refer to the same effect context:

$$\phi_1 = \big((\{3\} \mapsto \Diamond) \mapsto \Diamond\big) \wedge \big((\{4\} \mapsto \Diamond) \mapsto \Diamond\big) \wedge \big((\{3\} \mapsto \Box \wedge \{4\} \mapsto \Box) \mapsto \Box\big)$$

$$\phi_2 = \big((\vee_{n>1}\{n\}) \mapsto \mathbf{P}_{>q}\big) \mapsto \mathbf{P}_{>q/2}$$

$$\phi_3 = \wedge_{S \in State}\big((\{S(l)\} \mapsto [S\!\downarrow]) \mapsto [S\!\downarrow]\big)$$

$$\phi_4 = \wedge_{S \in State} \wedge_{n \in \mathbb{N}} \big((\{n\}, () \mapsto [S[l_0 := n, l_1 := n+1]\!\downarrow]) \mapsto [S[l_0 := n]\!\downarrow]\big)$$

$$\phi_5 = \wedge_{k \in \mathbb{N}} \vee_{n_1,\ldots,n_k \in \mathbb{N}} \big(() \mapsto \langle ?n_1!n_1?n_2!n_2 \ldots ?n_k!n_k\rangle \ldots\big).$$

Given a function $v : (\mathbf{nat} \rightarrow \mathbf{R}) \rightarrow \mathbf{R}$, $v \models_{\mathcal{F}} \phi_1$ means that v is guaranteed to call its argument only with $\overline{3}$ or $\overline{4}$. The function $\mathbf{geom}$ from Example 3 satisfies ϕ_2 because with probability $1/2$ it passes to the continuation a number $n > 1$.

For example, the following satisfactions hold: $\lambda k{:}\mathbf{nat}{\rightarrow}\mathbf{R}.\ lookup_l(k) \models_{\mathcal{F}} \phi_3$ and $f = \lambda(x{:}\mathbf{nat}, k{:}(){\rightarrow}\mathbf{R}).\ update_{l_1}(\mathbf{succ}(x), k) \models_{\mathcal{F}} \phi_4$. The latter formula says that, either f always succeeds, or f evaluated with $\overline{n}$ changes the state from $S[l_0 := n]$ to $S[l_0 := n, l_1 := n+1]$ before calling its continuation. This is similar to a total correctness assertion $[S[l_0 := n]](-)[S[l_0 := n, l_1 := n+1]]$ from Hoare logic, for a direct style program. Formula ϕ_5 is satisfied by $\lambda().\mathbf{echo}$, where $\mathbf{echo}$ is the computation defined in Example 5.

Even though the indexing set I in $\wedge_{i \in I}$ and $\vee_{i \in I}$ may be uncountable, the sets of values and computations are countable. Since logical formulas are interpreted over values and computations, all conjunctions and disjunctions are logically equivalent to countable ones.

Definition 3 (Logical equivalence). *For any closed values $\vdash_\Sigma v_1 : A$ and $\vdash_\Sigma v_2 : A$, and for any closed computations $\vdash_\Sigma s_1$ and $\vdash_\Sigma s_2$:*

$$v_1 \equiv_{\mathcal{F}} v_2 \iff \forall \phi : A \text{ in } \mathcal{F}.\ (v_1 \models_{\mathcal{F}} \phi \iff v_2 \models_{\mathcal{F}} \phi)$$

$$s_1 \equiv_{\mathcal{F}} s_2 \iff \forall P \text{ in } \mathcal{F}.\ (s_1 \models_{\mathcal{F}} P \iff s_2 \models_{\mathcal{F}} P).$$

To facilitate equational reasoning, logical equivalence should be compatible, a property proved in the next section (Proposition 3). Compatibility allows substitution of related programs for a free variable that appears on both sides of a program equation. Notice that logical equivalence would not be changed if we added conjunction, disjunction and negation at the level of computation formulas. We have omitted such connectives for simplicity.

To state our main theorem, first define the open extension of a well-typed relation $\mathcal{R}$ on closed terms as: $\overrightarrow{x : A} \vdash_\Sigma t\ \mathcal{R}^\circ\ s$ if and only if for any closed values $(\vdash_\Sigma v_i : A_i)_i$, $t[\overrightarrow{v/x}]\ \mathcal{R}\ s[\overrightarrow{v/x}]$. Three sufficient conditions that we impose on the set of observations $\mathfrak{P}$ are defined below. The first one, consistency, ensures that contextual equivalence can distinguish at least two programs.

Definition 4 (Consistency). *A set of observations $\mathfrak{P}$ is consistent if there exists at least one observation $P_0 \in \mathfrak{P}$ such that:*

1. $P_0 \neq \textit{Trees}_\Sigma$ and
2. *there exists at least one computation* t_0 *such that* $[\![t_0]\!] \in P_0$.

Definition 5 (Scott-openness). *A set of trees* X *is Scott-open if:*

1. *It is upwards closed, that is:* $tr \in X$ *and* $tr \leq tr'$ *imply* $tr' \in X$.
2. *Whenever* $tr_1 \leq tr_2 \leq \ldots$ *is an ascending chain with least upper bound* $\bigsqcup tr_i \in X$, *then* $tr_j \in X$ *for some* j.

Definition 6 (Decomposability). *The set of observations* $\mathfrak{P}$ *is decomposable if for any* $P \in \mathfrak{P}$, *and for any* $tr \in P$:

$$\forall \sigma \in \Sigma. \left(tr = \sigma_{\overrightarrow{v}}(\overrightarrow{tr'}) \implies \right.$$
$$\left. \exists \overrightarrow{P'} \in \mathfrak{P} \cup \{\textit{Trees}_\Sigma\}. \ \overrightarrow{tr'} \in \overrightarrow{P'} \text{ and } \forall \overrightarrow{p'} \in \overrightarrow{P'}. \ \sigma_{\overrightarrow{v}}(\overrightarrow{p'}) \in P \right).$$

Theorem 1 (Soundness and Completeness of $\mathcal{F}$**).** *For a decomposable set of Scott-open observations* $\mathfrak{P}$ *that is consistent, the open extension of* $\mathcal{F}$-*logical equivalence coincides with contextual equivalence:* $(\equiv^\circ_{\mathcal{F}}) = (\equiv_{\mathrm{ctx}})$.

The proof of this theorem is outlined in Sect. 4. It is easy to see that for all running examples of effects the set $\mathfrak{P}$ is consistent. The proof that each $P \in \mathfrak{P}$ is Scott-open is similar to that for modalities from [38]. It remains to show that for all our examples $\mathfrak{P}$ is decomposable. Intuitively, decomposability can be understood as saying that logical equivalence is a congruence for the effect context Σ.

Example 12 (Pure functional computation). The only observation is $\Downarrow = \{\downarrow\}$. There are no trees in $\Downarrow$ whose root has children, so decomposability is satisfied.

Example 13 (Nondeterminism). Consider $tr \in \Diamond$. Either $tr = \downarrow$, in which case we are done, or $tr = or(tr'_0, tr'_1)$. It must be the case that either tr'_0 or tr'_1 have a $\downarrow$-leaf. Without loss of generality, assume this is the case for tr'_0. Then we know $tr'_0 \in \Diamond$ so we can choose $P'_0 = \Diamond, P'_1 = \textit{Trees}_\Sigma$. For any $\overrightarrow{p'} \in \overrightarrow{P'}$ we know $or(\overrightarrow{p'}) \in \Diamond$ because p'_0 has a $\downarrow$-leaf, so decomposability holds. The argument for $tr \in \square$ is analogous: $P'_0 = P'_1 = \square$.

Example 14 (Probabilistic choice). Consider $tr = p\text{-}or(tr'_0, tr'_1) \in \mathbf{P}_{>q}$. Choose: $q_0 = \frac{\mathbb{P}(tr'_0)}{\mathbb{P}(tr'_0) + \mathbb{P}(tr'_1)} \cdot 2q$ and $q_1 = \frac{\mathbb{P}(tr'_1)}{\mathbb{P}(tr'_0) + \mathbb{P}(tr'_1)} \cdot 2q$. From $\mathbb{P}(tr) = \frac{1}{2}(\mathbb{P}(tr'_0) + \mathbb{P}(tr'_1)) > q$ we can deduce that: $1 \geq \mathbb{P}(tr'_0) > q_0$ and $1 \geq \mathbb{P}(tr'_1) > q_1$. So we can choose $P'_0 = \mathbf{P}_{>q_0}, P'_1 = \mathbf{P}_{>q_1}$ to satisfy decomposability.

Example 15 (Global store). Consider a tree $tr = \sigma_{\overrightarrow{v}}(tr'_0, tr'_1, tr'_2, \ldots) \in [S\downarrow]$. If $\sigma = lookup_l$, then we know $tr'_{S(l)} \in [S\downarrow]$. In the definition of decomposability, choose $P'_{S(l)} = [S\downarrow]$ and $P'_{k \neq S(l)} = \textit{Trees}_\Sigma$ and we are done. If $\sigma_{\overrightarrow{v}} = update_{l,\overline{n}}$, then $tr'_0 \in [S[l := n]\downarrow]$. Choose $P'_0 = [S[l := n]\downarrow]$.

Example 16 (Interactive input/output). Consider an I/O trace $W \neq \epsilon$ and a tree $tr = \sigma_{\overrightarrow{v}}(tr'_0, tr'_1, tr'_2, \ldots) \in \langle W \rangle_{\ldots}$. If $\sigma = input$, it must be the case that $W = (?k)W'$ and $tr'_k \in \langle W' \rangle_{\ldots}$. We can choose $P'_k = \langle W' \rangle_{\ldots}$ and $P'_{m \neq k} = \langle \epsilon \rangle_{\ldots}$ and we are done. If $\sigma_{\overrightarrow{v}} = output_{\overline{n}}$, then $W = (!n)W'$ and $tr'_0 \in \langle W' \rangle_{\ldots}$. Choose $P'_0 = \langle W' \rangle_{\ldots}$ and we are done. The proof for $\langle W \rangle \downarrow$ is analogous.

4 Soundness and Completeness of the Logic $\mathcal{F}$

This section outlines the proof of Theorem 1, which says that $\mathcal{F}$-logical equivalence coincides with contextual equivalence. The full proof can be found in [21]. First, we define applicative bisimilarity for ECPS, similarly to the way Simpson and Voorneveld [38] define it for PCF with algebraic effects. Then, we prove in turn that $\mathcal{F}$-logical equivalence coincides with applicative bisimilarity, and that applicative bisimilarity coincides with contextual equivalence. Thus, three notions of program equivalence for ECPS are in fact the same.

Definition 7 (Applicative $\mathfrak{P}$-bisimilarity). *A collection of relations* $\mathcal{R}_A^{\mathfrak{v}} \subseteq (\vdash_\Sigma A)^2$ *for each type A and* $\mathcal{R}^{\mathfrak{c}} \subseteq (\vdash_\Sigma)^2$ *is an applicative $\mathfrak{P}$-simulation if:*

1. $v \, \mathcal{R}_{\mathrm{nat}}^{\mathfrak{v}} \, w \implies v = w$.
2. $s \, \mathcal{R}^{\mathfrak{c}} \, t \implies \forall P \in \mathfrak{P}. \, (\llbracket s \rrbracket \in P \implies \llbracket t \rrbracket \in P)$.
3. $v \, \mathcal{R}_{(\overrightarrow{A}) \to \mathrm{R}}^{\mathfrak{v}} \, u \implies \forall (\vdash_\Sigma w_i : A_i)_i. \, v(\overrightarrow{w}) \, \mathcal{R}^{\mathfrak{c}} \, u(\overrightarrow{w})$.

An applicative $\mathfrak{P}$-bisimulation is a symmetric simulation. Bisimilarity, *denoted by* $\sim$, *is the union of all bisimulations. Therefore, it is the greatest applicative $\mathfrak{P}$-bisimulation.*

Notice that applicative bisimilarity uses the set of observations $\mathfrak{P}$ to relate computations, just as contextual and logical equivalence do. It is easy to show that bisimilarity is an equivalence relation.

Proposition 2. *Given a decomposable set of Scott-open observations $\mathfrak{P}$, the open extension of applicative $\mathfrak{P}$-bisimilarity, $\sim^\circ$, is compatible.*

Proof (notes). This is proved using Howe's method [14], following the structure of the corresponding proof from [38]. Scott-openness is used to show that the observations P interact well with the sequence of trees $\llbracket - \rrbracket_{(-)}$ associated with each computation. For details see [21, §5.4]. □

Proposition 3. *Given a decomposable set of Scott-open observations $\mathfrak{P}$, applicative $\mathfrak{P}$-bisimilarity $\sim$ coincides with $\mathcal{F}$-logical equivalence $\equiv_{\mathcal{F}}$. Hence, the open extension of $\mathcal{F}$-logical equivalence $\equiv_{\mathcal{F}}^\circ$ is compatible.*

Proof (sketch). We define a new logic $\mathcal{V}$ which is almost the same as $\mathcal{F}$ except that the (VAL) rule is replaced by:

$$\frac{\vdash_\Sigma w_1 : A_1 \ldots \vdash_\Sigma w_n : A_n \quad P \in \mathfrak{P}}{(w_1, \ldots, w_n) \mapsto P : (A_1, \ldots, A_n) \to \mathrm{R}} \qquad v \models_{\mathcal{V}} (\overrightarrow{w}) \mapsto P \iff v(\overrightarrow{w}) \models_{\mathcal{V}} P.$$

That is, formulas of function type are now constructed using ECPS values. It is relatively straightforward to show that $\mathcal{V}$-logical equivalence coincides with applicative $\mathfrak{P}$-bisimilarity [21, Prop. 6.3.1]. However, we do not know of a similar direct proof for the logic $\mathcal{F}$. From Proposition 2, we deduce that $\mathcal{V}$-logical equivalence is compatible.

Next, we prove that the logics $\mathcal{F}$ and $\mathcal{V}$ are in fact equi-expressive, so they induce the same relation of logical equivalence on ECPS programs [21, Prop. 6.3.4]. Define a translation of formulas from $\mathcal{F}$ to $\mathcal{V}$, $(-)^\flat$, and one from $\mathcal{V}$ to $\mathcal{F}$, $(-)^\sharp$. The most interesting cases are those for formulas of function type:

$$((\phi_1, \ldots, \phi_n) \mapsto P)^\flat = \bigwedge \left\{ (w_1, \ldots, w_n) \mapsto P \mid w_1 \models_\mathcal{V} \phi_1^\flat, \ldots, w_n \models_\mathcal{V} \phi_n^\flat \right\}$$

$$((w_1, \ldots, w_n) \mapsto P)^\sharp = (\chi_{w_1}, \ldots, \chi_{w_n}) \mapsto P$$

where χ_{w_i} is the characteristic formula of w_i, that is $\chi_{w_i} = \bigwedge \{\phi \mid w_i \models_\mathcal{F} \phi\}$. Equi-expressivity means that the satisfaction relation remains unchanged under both translations, for example $v \models_\mathcal{V} \phi \iff v \models_\mathcal{F} \phi^\sharp$. Most importantly, the proof of equi-expressivity makes use of compatibility of $\equiv_\mathcal{V}$, which we established previously. For a full proof see [21, Prop. 6.2.3]). $\qquad\square$

Finally, to prove Theorem 1 we show that applicative $\mathfrak{P}$-bisimilarity coincides with contextual equivalence [21, Prop. 7.2.2]:

Proposition 4. *Consider a decomposable set $\mathfrak{P}$ of Scott-open observations that is consistent. The open extension of applicative $\mathfrak{P}$-bisimilarity $\sim^\circ$ coincides with contextual equivalence $\equiv_{ctx}$.*

Proof (sketch). Prove $(\equiv_{ctx}) \subseteq (\sim^\circ)$ in two stages: first we show it holds for closed terms by showing $\equiv_{ctx}$ for them is a bisimulation; we make use of consistency of $\mathfrak{P}$ in the case of natural numbers. Then we extend to open terms using compatibility of $\equiv_{ctx}$. The opposite inclusion follows immediately by compatibility and adequacy of $\sim^\circ$. $\qquad\square$

5 Related Work

The work closest to ours is that by Simpson and Voorneveld [38]. In the context of a direct-style language with algebraic effects, EPCF, they propose a modal logic which characterizes applicative bisimilarity but not contextual equivalence. Consider the following example from [19] (we use simplified EPCF syntax):

$$M = \lambda().?\mathtt{nat} \qquad N = \mathbf{let}\ y \Rightarrow ?\mathtt{nat}\ \mathbf{in}\ \lambda().\min(?\mathtt{nat}, y) \qquad (1)$$

where $?\mathtt{nat}$ is a computation, defined using *or*, which returns a natural number nondeterministically. Term M satisfies the formula $\Phi = \Diamond(true \mapsto \bigwedge_{n \in \mathbb{N}} \Diamond\{n\})$ in the logic of [38], which says that M may return a function which in turn may return any natural number. However, N does not satisfy Φ because it always returns a *bounded* number generator G. The bound on G is arbitrarily high so M and N are contextually equivalent, since a context can only test a finite number of outcomes of G.

EPCF can be translated into ECPS via a continuation-passing translation that preserves the shape of computation trees. The translation maps a value $\Gamma \vdash V : \tau$ to a value $\Gamma^* \vdash V^* : \tau^*$. An EPCF computation $\Gamma \vdash M : \tau$ becomes an ECPS value $\Gamma^* \vdash M^* : (\tau^* \to \mathrm{R}) \to \mathrm{R}$, which intuitively is waiting for a continuation k to pass its return result to (see [21, §4]). As an example, consider the cases for functions and application, where k stands for a continuation:

$$(\Gamma \vdash \lambda x{:}\tau.M : \tau \to \rho)^* = \Gamma^* \vdash \lambda(x{:}\tau^*, k{:}\rho^* \to \mathrm{R}).\,(M^*\ k) : (\tau^*, (\rho^* \to \mathrm{R})) \to \mathrm{R}$$
$$(\Gamma \vdash V\ W : \rho)^* = \Gamma^* \vdash \lambda k{:}\rho^* \to \mathrm{R}.\,V^*\ (W^*, k) : (\rho^* \to \mathrm{R}) \to \mathrm{R}.$$

This translation suggests that ECPS functions of type $(A_1, \ldots, A_n) \to \mathrm{R}$ can be regarded as continuations that never return. In EPCF the CPS-style algebraic operations can be replaced by direct-style generic effects [34], e.g. $input() : \mathtt{nat}$.

One way to understand this CPS translation is that it arises from the fact that $((-) \to \mathrm{R}) \to \mathrm{R}$ is a monad on the multicategory of values (in a suitable sense, e.g. [40]), which means that we can use the standard monadic interpretation of a call-by-value language. As usual, the algebraic structure on the return type R induces an algebraic structure on the entire monad (see e.g. [16], [24, §8]). We have not taken a denotational perspective in this paper, but for the reader with this perspective, a first step is to note that the quotient set $Q \stackrel{\mathrm{def}}{=} (Trees_\Sigma)/_{\equiv_{\mathfrak{P}}}$ is a Σ-algebra, where $(tr \equiv_{\mathfrak{P}} tr')$ if $\forall P \in \mathfrak{P}, (tr \in P \iff tr' \in P)$; decomposability implies that $(\equiv_{\mathfrak{P}})$ is a Σ-congruence. This thus induces a CPS monad $Q^{(Q^-)}$ on the category of cpos.

Note that the terms in (1) above are an example of programs that are not bisimilar in EPCF but become bisimilar when translated to ECPS. This is because in ECPS bisimilarity, like contextual and logical equivalence, uses continuations to test return results. Therefore, in ECPS we cannot test for all natural numbers, like formula Φ does. This example provides an intuition of why we were able to show that all three notions of equivalence coincide, while [38] was not.

The modalities in Simpson's and Voorneveld's logic are similar to the observations from $\mathfrak{P}$, because they also specify shapes of effect trees. Since EPCF computations have a return value, a modality is used to *lift* a formula about the return values to a computation formula. In contrast, in the logic $\mathcal{F}$ observations alone suffice to specify properties of computations. From this point of view, our use of observations is closer to that found in the work of Johann et al. [17]. This use of observations also leads to a much simpler notion of decomposability (Definition 6) than that found in [38].

It can easily be shown that for the running examples of effects, $\mathcal{F}$-logical equivalence induces the program equations which are usually used to axiomatize algebraic effects, for example the equations for global store from [33]. Thus our choice of observations is justified further.

A different logic for algebraic effects was proposed by Plotkin and Pretnar [35]. It has a modality for each effect operation, whereas observations in $\mathfrak{P}$ are determined by the behaviour of effects, rather than by the syntax of their operations. Plotkin and Pretnar prove that their logic is sound for establishing several notions of program equivalence, but not complete in general. Refinement types are yet another approach to specifying the behaviour of algebraic effects, (e.g. [3]). Several monadic-based logics for computational effects have been proposed, such as [10], [29], although without the focus on contextual equivalence.

A logic describing a higher-order language with local store is the Hoare logic of Yoshida, Honda and Berger [42]. Hoare logic has also been integrated into a type system for a higher-order functional language with dependent types, in the form of Hoare type theory [27]. Although we do not yet know how to deal with local state or dependent types in the logic $\mathcal{F}$, an advantage of our logic over the previous two is that we describe different algebraic effects in a uniform manner.

Another aspect worth noticing is that some (non-trivial) $\mathcal{F}$-formulas are not inhabited by any program. For example, there is no function $v : (()\rightarrow R)\rightarrow R$ satisfying: $\psi = (() \mapsto \langle !0 \rangle_{...}) \mapsto \langle !1 \rangle_{...} \wedge (() \mapsto \langle !1 \rangle_{...}) \mapsto \langle !0 \rangle_{...}$.

Formula ψ says that, if the first operation of a continuation is $output(\overline{0})$, this is replaced by $output(\overline{1})$ and vice-versa. But in ECPS, one cannot check whether an argument outputs something without also causing the output observation, and so the formula is never satisfied.

However, ψ could be inhabited if we extended ECPS to allow λ-abstraction over the symbols in the effect context Σ, and allowed such symbols to be *captured* during substitution (dynamic scoping). Consider the following example in an imaginary extended ECPS where we abstract over *output*:

$$h = \lambda(x{:}\mathbf{nat}, k{:}()\rightarrow R). \text{ case } x \text{ of } \{\mathbf{zero} \Rightarrow output(\overline{1}, k), \mathbf{succ}(y) \Rightarrow$$
$$\text{case } y \text{ of } \{\mathbf{zero} \Rightarrow output(\overline{0}, k), \mathbf{succ}(z) \Rightarrow k\ ()\}\}$$
$$v = \lambda f{:}()\rightarrow R. \left((\lambda output{:}(\mathbf{nat}, ()\rightarrow R)\rightarrow R.\ (f\ ()))\ h\right).$$

The idea is that during reduction of $(v\ f)$, the *output* operations in f are captured by $\lambda output$. Thus, $output(\overline{0})$ operations from $(f\ ())$ are replaced by $output(\overline{1})$ and vice-versa, and all other writes are skipped; so in particular $v \models_{\mathcal{F}} \psi$. This behaviour is similar to that of *effect handlers* [36]: computation $(f\ ())$ is being handled by handler h. We leave for future work the study of handlers in ECPS and of their corresponding logic.

6 Concluding Remarks

To summarize, we have studied program equivalence for a higher-order CPS language with general algebraic effects and general recursion (Sect. 2). Our main contribution is a logic $\mathcal{F}$ of program properties (Sect. 3) whose induced program equivalence coincides with contextual equivalence (Theorem 1; Sect. 4). Previous work on algebraic effects concentrated on logics that are sound for contextual equivalence, but not complete [35,38]. Moreover, $\mathcal{F}$-logical equivalence also coincides with applicative bisimilarity for our language. We exemplified our results for nondeterminism, probabilistic choice, global store and I/O. A next step would be to consider local effects (e.g. [22,33,37,39]) or normal form bisimulation (e.g. [6]).

Acknowledgements. This research was supported by an EPSRC studentship, a Balliol College Jowett scholarship, and the Royal Society. We would like to thank Niels Voorneveld for pointing out example (1), Alex Simpson and Ohad Kammar for useful discussions, and the anonymous reviewers for comments and suggestions.

References

1. Abramsky, S.: The lazy λ-calculus. In: Turner, D. (ed.) Research Topics in Functional Programming. Chapter 4, pp. 65–117. Addison Wesley, Boston (1990)
2. Abramsky, S., Jung, A.: Domain theory. In: Abramsky, S., Gabbay, D.M., Maibaum, T.S.E. (eds.) Handbook of Logic in Computer Science, Chap. 1, vol. 3, pp. 1–168. Oxford University Press, Oxford (1994)
3. Ahman, D., Plotkin, G.: Refinement types for algebraic effects. In: TYPES (2015)
4. Biernacki, D., Lenglet, S.: Applicative bisimulations for delimited-control operators. In: Birkedal, L. (ed.) FoSSaCS 2012. LNCS, vol. 7213, pp. 119–134. Springer, Heidelberg (2012). https://doi.org/10.1007/978-3-642-28729-9_8
5. Cartwright, R., Curien, P., Felleisen, M.: Fully abstract semantics for observably sequential languages. Inf. Comput. **111**(2), 297–401 (1994)
6. Dal Lago, U., Gavazzo, F.: Effectful normal form bisimulation. In: Proceedings of ESOP 2019 (2019)
7. Dal Lago, U., Gavazzo, F., Levy, P.: Effectful applicative bisimilarity: monads, relators, and Howe's method. In: LICS (2017)
8. Dal Lago, U., Gavazzo, F., Tanaka, R.: Effectful applicative similarity for call-by-name lambda calculi. In: ICTCS/CILC (2017)
9. Freyd, P.: Algebraically complete categories. In: Carboni, A., Pedicchio, M.C., Rosolini, G. (eds.) Category Theory. LNM, vol. 1488, pp. 95–104. Springer, Heidelberg (1991). https://doi.org/10.1007/BFb0084215
10. Goncharov, S., Schröder, L.: A relatively complete generic Hoare logic for order-enriched effects. In: LICS (2013)
11. Gordon, A.: Operational equivalences for untyped and polymorphic object calculi. In: Gordon, A., Pitts, A. (eds.) Higher Order Operational Techniques in Semantics, pp. 9–54. Cambridge University Press, Cambridge (1998)
12. Hennessy, M., Milner, R.: Algebraic laws for nondeterminism and concurrency. J. ACM **32**(1), 137–161 (1985)
13. Hoare, C.: An axiomatic basis for computer programming. Commun. ACM **12**(10), 576–580 (1969)
14. Howe, D.: Proving congruence of bisimulation in functional programming languages. Inf. Comput. **124**(2), 103–112 (1996)
15. Hur, C.K., Neis, G., Dreyer, D., Vafeiadis, V.: A logical step forward in parametric bisimulations. Technical report MPI-SWS-2014-003, January 2014
16. Hyland, M., Levy, P.B., Plotkin, G., Power, J.: Combining algebraic effects with continuations. Theoret. Comput. Sci. **375**, 20–40 (2007)
17. Johann, P., Simpson, A., Voigtländer, J.: A generic operational metatheory for algebraic effects. In: LICS (2010)
18. Lafont, Y., Reus, B., Streicher, T.: Continuations semantics or expressing implication by negation. Technical report 9321, Ludwig-Maximilians-Universität, München (1993)
19. Lassen, S.: Relational reasoning about functions and nondeterminism. Ph.D. thesis, University of Aarhus, BRICS, December 1998

20. Lassen, S.B., Levy, P.B.: Typed normal form bisimulation. In: Duparc, J., Henzinger, T.A. (eds.) CSL 2007. LNCS, vol. 4646, pp. 283–297. Springer, Heidelberg (2007). https://doi.org/10.1007/978-3-540-74915-8_23

21. Matache, C.: Program equivalence for algebraic effects via modalities. Master's thesis, University of Oxford, September 2018. https://arxiv.org/abs/1902.04645

22. Melliès, P.-A.: Local states in string diagrams. In: Dowek, G. (ed.) RTA 2014. LNCS, vol. 8560, pp. 334–348. Springer, Cham (2014). https://doi.org/10.1007/978-3-319-08918-8_23

23. Merro, M.: On the observational theory of the CPS-calculus. Acta Inf. **47**(2), 111–132 (2010)

24. Møgelberg, R.E., Staton, S.: Linear usage of state. Log. Meth. Comput. Sci. **10** (2014)

25. Moggi, E.: Notions of computation and monads. Inf. Comput. **93**(1), 55–92 (1991)

26. Morris, J.: Lambda calculus models of programming languages. Ph.D. thesis, MIT (1969)

27. Nanevski, A., Morrisett, J., Birkedal, L.: Hoare type theory, polymorphism and separation. J. Funct. Program. **18**(5–6), 865–911 (2008)

28. O'Hearn, P., Reynolds, J., Yang, H.: Local reasoning about programs that alter data structures. In: Fribourg, L. (ed.) CSL 2001. LNCS, vol. 2142, pp. 1–19. Springer, Heidelberg (2001). https://doi.org/10.1007/3-540-44802-0_1

29. Pitts, A.: Evaluation logic. In: Birtwistle, G. (ed.) IVth Higher Order Workshop, Banff 1990. Springer, Heidelberg (1991). https://doi.org/10.1007/978-1-4471-3182-3_11

30. Pitts, A.: Howe's method for higher-order languages. In: Sangiorgi, D., Rutten, J. (eds.) Advanced Topics in Bisimulation and Coinduction. Chapter 5, pp. 197–232. Cambridge University Press, Cambridge (2011)

31. Plotkin, G.: LCF considered as a programming language. Theor. Comput. Sci. **5**(3), 223–255 (1977)

32. Plotkin, G., Power, J.: Adequacy for algebraic effects. In: Honsell, F., Miculan, M. (eds.) FoSSaCS 2001. LNCS, vol. 2030, pp. 1–24. Springer, Heidelberg (2001). https://doi.org/10.1007/3-540-45315-6_1

33. Plotkin, G., Power, J.: Notions of computation determine monads. In: Nielsen, M., Engberg, U. (eds.) FoSSaCS 2002. LNCS, vol. 2303, pp. 342–356. Springer, Heidelberg (2002). https://doi.org/10.1007/3-540-45931-6_24

34. Plotkin, G., Power, J.: Algebraic operations and generic effects. Appl. Categ. Struct. **11**(1), 69–94 (2003)

35. Plotkin, G., Pretnar, M.: A logic for algebraic effects. In: LICS (2008)

36. Plotkin, G., Pretnar, M.: Handling Algebraic Effects. Log. Methods Comput. Sci. **9**(4) (2013)

37. Power, J.: Indexed Lawvere theories for local state. In: Models, Logics and Higher-Dimensional Categories, pp. 268–282. AMS (2011)

38. Simpson, A., Voorneveld, N.: Behavioural equivalence via modalities for algebraic effects. In: Ahmed, A. (ed.) ESOP 2018. LNCS, vol. 10801, pp. 300–326. Springer, Cham (2018). https://doi.org/10.1007/978-3-319-89884-1_11

39. Staton, S.: Instances of computational effects. In: Proceedings of LICS 2013 (2013)

40. Staton, S., Levy, P.B.: Universal properties for impure programming languages. In: Proceedings of POPL 2013 (2013)

41. Yachi, T., Sumii, E.: A sound and complete bisimulation for contextual equivalence in λ-calculus with call/cc. In: Igarashi, A. (ed.) APLAS 2016. LNCS, vol. 10017, pp. 171–186. Springer, Heidelberg (2016). https://doi.org/10.1007/978-3-319-47958-3_10

10

Path Category for Free Open Morphisms from Coalgebras with Non-deterministic Branching

Thorsten Wißmann[1]($^{(\boxtimes)}$)(iD), Jérémy Dubut[2,3], Shin-ya Katsumata[2], and Ichiro Hasuo[2,4]

[1] Friedrich-Alexander-Universität Erlangen-Nürnberg, Erlangen, Germany
`thorsten.wissmann@fau.de`
[2] National Institute of Informatics, Tokyo, Japan
`{dubut,s-katsumata,hasuo}@nii.ac.jp`
[3] Japanese-French Laboratory for Informatics, Tokyo, Japan
[4] SOKENDAI, Hayama, Kanagawa, Japan

Abstract. There are different categorical approaches to variations of transition systems and their bisimulations. One is coalgebra for a functor G, where a bisimulation is defined as a span of G-coalgebra homomorphism. Another one is in terms of path categories and open morphisms, where a bisimulation is defined as a span of open morphisms. This similarity is no coincidence: given a functor G, fulfilling certain conditions, we derive a path-category for pointed G-coalgebras and lax homomorphisms, such that the open morphisms turn out to be precisely the G-coalgebra homomorphisms. The above construction provides path-categories and trace semantics for free for different flavours of transition systems: (1) non-deterministic tree automata (2) regular nondeterministic nominal automata (RNNA), an expressive automata notion living in nominal sets (3) multisorted transition systems. This last instance relates to Lasota's construction, which is in the converse direction.

Keywords: Coalgebra · Open maps · Categories · Nominal sets

1 Introduction

Coalgebras [25] and *open maps* [16] are two main categorical approaches to transition systems and bisimulations. The former describes the branching type of systems as an endofunctor, a system becoming a coalgebra and bisimulations being spans of coalgebra homomorphisms. Coalgebra theory makes it easy to consider state space types in different settings, e.g. nominal sets [17,18] or algebraic categories [5,11,20]. The latter, open maps, describes systems as objects of

Table 1. Two approaches to categorical (bi)simulations

	worlds	data	systems	func. sim.	func. bisim.	(bi)simulation
this paper	open maps	$J\colon \mathbb{P} \longrightarrow \mathbb{M}$ Def. 2.4	$\mathbf{obj}\,(\mathbb{M})$	$\mathbf{mor}\,(\mathbb{M})$	open maps Def. 2.5	Z (with T, T' below)
	coalgebra	$G\colon \mathbb{C} \longrightarrow \mathbb{C}$ Def. 2.7	pointed G-coalg. Sec. 2.2	lax hom. Def. 2.8	coalg. hom. Def. 2.6	*Lasota's*

a category and the execution types as particular objects called paths. In this case, bisimulations are spans of open morphisms. Open maps are particularly adapted to extend bisimilarity to history dependent behaviors, e.g. true concurrency [7,8], timed systems [22] and weak (bi)similarity [9]. Coalgebra homomorphisms and open maps are then key concepts to describe bisimilarity categorically. They intuitively correspond to functional bisimulations, that is, those maps between states whose graph is a bisimulation.

We are naturally interested in the relationship between those two categorical approaches to transition systems and bisimulations. A reduction of open maps situations to coalgebra was given by Lasota using multi-sorted transition systems [19]. In this paper, we give the reduction in the other direction: from the category $\mathsf{Coalg}_l(TF)$ of pointed TF-coalgebras and lax homomorphisms, we construct the path-category Path and a functor $J : \mathsf{Path} \longrightarrow \mathsf{Coalg}_l(TF)$ such that Path-open morphisms coincide with strict homomorphisms, hence functional bisimulations. Here, T is a functor describing the branching behaviour and F describes the input type, i.e. the type of data that is processed (e.g. words or trees). This development is carried out with the case where T is a powerset-like functor, and covers transition systems allowing non-deterministic branching.

The key concept in the construction of Path are *F-precise maps*. Roughly speaking in set, a map $f\colon X \longrightarrow FY$ is F-precise if every $y \in Y$ is used precisely once in f, i.e. there is a unique x such that y appears in $f(x)$ and additionally y appears precisely once in $f(x)$. Such an F-precise map represents one deterministic step (of shape F). Then a path $P \in \mathsf{Path}$ is a finite sequence of deterministic steps, i.e. finitely many precise maps. J converts such a data into a pointed TF-coalgebra. There are many existing notions of paths and traces in coalgebra [4,12,13,21], which lack the notion of *precise* map, which is crucial for the present work.

Once we set up the situation $J\colon \mathsf{Path} \longrightarrow \mathsf{Coalg}_l(TF)$, we are on the framework of open map bisimulations. Our construction of Path using precise maps is justified by the characterisation theorem: Path-open morphisms and strict coalgebra homomorphisms coincide (Theorems 3.20 and 3.24). This coincidence relies on the concept of path-reachable coalgebras, namely, coalgebras such that every state can be reached by a path. Under mild conditions, path-reachability is equivalent to an existing notion in coalgebra, defined as the non-existence of a proper sub-coalgebra (Sect. 3.5). Additionally, this characterization produces a canonical trace semantics for free, given in terms of paths (Sect. 3.6).

We illustrate our reduction with several concrete situations: different classes of non-deterministic top-down tree automata using analytic functors (Sect. 4.1), Regular Nondeterministic Nominal Automata (RNNA), an expressive automata notion living in nominal sets (Sect. 4.2), multisorted transition systems, used in Lasota's work to construct a coalgebra situation from an open map situation (Sect. 4.3).

Notation. We assume basic categorical knowledge and notation (see e.g. [1,3]). The cotupling of morphisms $f\colon A \to C$, $g\colon B \to C$ is denoted by $[f,g]\colon A+B \to C$, and the unique morphsim to the terminal object is $!\colon X \to 1$ for every X.

2 Two Categorical Approaches for Bisimulations

We introduce the two formalisms involved in the present paper: the open maps (Sect. 2.1) and the coalgebras (Sect. 2.2). Those formalisms will be illustrated on the classic example of Labelled Transition Systems (LTSs).

Definition 2.1. *Fix a set A, called the alphabet. A labelled transition system is a triple (S,i,Δ) with S a set of states, $i \in S$ the initial state, and $\Delta \subseteq S \times A \times S$ the transition relation. When Δ is obvious from the context, we write $s \xrightarrow{a} s'$ to mean $(s,a,s') \in \Delta$.*

For instance, the tuple $(\{0, \cdots, n\}, 0, \{(k-1, a_k, k) \mid 1 \le k \le n\})$ is an LTS, and called the *linear system* over the word $a_1 \cdots a_n \in A^\star$. To relate LTSs, one considers functions that preserves the structure of LTSs:

Definition 2.2. *A morphism of LTSs from (S,i,Δ) to (S',i',Δ') is a function $f\colon S \longrightarrow S'$ such that $f(i) = i'$ and for every $(s,a,s') \in \Delta$, $(f(s),a,f(s')) \in \Delta'$. LTSs and morphisms of LTSs form a category, which we denote by LTS_A.*

Some authors choose other notions of morphisms (e.g. [16]), allowing them to operate between LTSs with different alphabets for example. The usual way of comparing LTSs is by using simulations and bisimulations [23]. The former describes what it means for a system to have at least the behaviours of another, the latter describes that two systems have exactly the same behaviours. Concretely:

Definition 2.3. *A simulation from (S,i,Δ) to (S',i',Δ') is a relation $R \subseteq S \times S'$ such that (1) $(i,i') \in R$, and (2) for every $s \xrightarrow{a} t$ and $(s,s') \in R$, there is $t' \in S'$ such that $s' \xrightarrow{a} t'$ and $(t,t') \in R$. Such a relation R is a bisimulation if $R^{-1} = \{(s',s) \mid (s,s') \in R\}$ is also a simulation.*

Morphisms of LTSs are functional simulations, i.e. functions between states whose graph is a simulation. So how to model (1) systems, (2) functional simulations and (3) functional bisimulations categorically? In the next two sections, we will describe known answers to this question, with open maps and coalgebra. In both cases, it is possible to capture similarity and bisimilarity of two LTSs T

and T'. Generally, a simulation is a (jointly monic) span of a functional bisimulation and a functional simulation, and a bisimulation is a simulation whose converse is also a simulation, as depicted in Table 1. Consequently, to understand similarity and bisimilarity on a general level, it is enough to understand functional simulations and bisimulations.

2.1   Open Maps

The categorical framework of open maps [16] assumes functional simulations to be already modeled as a category $\mathbb{M}$. For example, for $\mathbb{M} := \mathsf{LTS}_A$, objects are LTSs, and morphisms are functional simulations. Furthermore, the open maps framework assumes another category $\mathbb{P}$ of 'paths' or 'linear systems', together with a functor J that tells how a 'path' is to be understood as a system:

Definition 2.4 [16]. *An* open map situation *is given by categories* $\mathbb{M}$ *('systems' with 'functional simulations') and* $\mathbb{P}$ *('paths') together with a functor* $J \colon \mathbb{P} \to \mathbb{M}$.

For example with $\mathbb{M} := \mathsf{LTS}_A$, we pick $\mathbb{P} := (A^\star, \leq)$ to be the poset of words over A with prefix order. Here, the functor J maps a word $w \in A^\star$ to the linear system over w, and $w \leq v$ to the evident functional simulation $J(w \leq v) \colon Jw \longrightarrow Jv$.

In an open map situation $J \colon \mathbb{P} \longrightarrow \mathbb{M}$, we can abstractly represent the concept of a *run* in a system. A run of a path $w \in \mathbb{P}$ in a system $T \in \mathbb{M}$ is simply defined to be an $\mathbb{M}$-morphism of type $Jw \longrightarrow T$. With this definition, each $\mathbb{M}$-morphism $h \colon T \longrightarrow T'$ (i.e. functional simulation) inherently transfers runs: given a run $x \colon Jw \longrightarrow T$, the morphism $h \cdot x \colon Jw \longrightarrow T'$ is a run of w in T'. In the example open map situation $J \colon (A^\star, \leq) \longrightarrow \mathsf{LTS}_A$, a run of a path $w = a_1 \cdots a_n \in A^\star$ in an LTS $T = (S, i, \Delta)$ is nothing but a sequence of states $x_0, \dots, x_n \in S$ such that $x_0 = i$ and $x_{k-1} \xrightarrow{a_k} x_k$ holds for all $1 \leq k \leq n$.

We introduce the concept of open map [16]. This is an abstraction of the property posessed by *functional bisimulations*. For LTSs $T = (S, i, \Delta)$ and $T' = (S', i', \Delta')$, an LTS_A-morphism $h \colon T \longrightarrow T'$ is a functional bisimulation if the graph of h is a bisimulation. This implies the following relationship between runs in T and runs in T'. Suppose that $w \leq w'$ holds in $A^\star$, and a run x of w in T is given as in (1); here n, m are lengths of w, w' respectively. Then for any run y' of w' in T' extending $h \cdot x$ as in (2), there is a run x' of w' extending x, and moreover its image by h coincides with y' (that is, $h \cdot x' = y'$). Such x' is obtained by repetitively applying the condition of functional bisimulation.

$$\overbrace{\underbrace{\to i \xrightarrow{w_1} x_1 \xrightarrow{w_2} \cdots \xrightarrow{w_n} x_n}^{x} \xrightarrow{w'_{n+1}} x'_{n+1} \xrightarrow{w'_{n+2}} \cdots \xrightarrow{w'_m} x'_m}_{x'} \quad \text{(in } T\text{)} \quad (1)$$

$$\underbrace{\to i' \xrightarrow{w_1} h(x_1) \xrightarrow{w_2} \cdots \xrightarrow{w_n} h(x_n) \xrightarrow{w'_{n+1}} y'_{n+1} \xrightarrow{w_{n+2}} \cdots \xrightarrow{w'_m} y'_m}_{y'} \quad \text{(in } T'\text{)} \quad (2)$$

Observe that y' extending $h \cdot x$ can be represented as $y' \cdot J(w \leq w') = h \cdot x$, and x' extending x as $x' \cdot J(w \leq w') = x$. From these, we conclude that if an

LTS_A-morphism $h: T \longrightarrow T'$ is a functional bisimulation, then for any $w \le w'$ in $A^\star$ and run $x: Jw \longrightarrow T$ and $y': Jw' \longrightarrow T'$ such that $y' \cdot J(w \le w') = h \cdot x$, there is a run $x': Jw' \longrightarrow T$ such that $x' \cdot J(w \le w') = x$ and $h \cdot x' = y'$ (the converse also holds if all states of T are reachable). This necessary condition of functional bisimulation can be rephrased in any open map situation, leading us to the definition of open map.

Definition 2.5 [16]. *Let $J: \mathbb{P} \longrightarrow \mathsf{M}$ be an open map situation. An M-morphism $h: T \longrightarrow T'$ is said to be* open *if for every morphism $\Phi: w \longrightarrow w' \in \mathbb{P}$ making the square on the right commute, there is x' making the two triangles commute.*

$$
\begin{array}{ccc}
Jw & \xrightarrow{\;x\;} & T \\
{\scriptstyle J\Phi}\big\downarrow & {\scriptstyle \exists x' \nearrow} & \big\downarrow{\scriptstyle h} \\
Jw' & \xrightarrow{\;y'\;} & T'
\end{array}
$$

Open maps are closed under composition and stable under pullback [16].

2.2   Coalgebras

The theory of G-coalgebras is another categorical framework to study bisimulations. The type of systems is modelled using an endofunctor $G: \mathbb{C} \longrightarrow \mathbb{C}$ and a system is then a coalgebra for this functor, that is, a pair of an object S of $\mathbb{C}$ (modeling the state space), and of a morphism of type $S \longrightarrow GS$ (modeling the transitions). For example for LTSs, the transition relation is of type $\Delta \subseteq S \times A \times S$. Equivalently, this can be defined as a function $\Delta: S \longrightarrow \mathcal{P}(A \times S)$, where $\mathcal{P}$ is the powerset. In other words, the transition relation is a coalgebra for the Set-functor $\mathcal{P}(A \times \_)$. Intuitively, this coalgebra gives the one-step behaviour of an LTS: S describes the state space of the system, $\mathcal{P}$ describes the 'branching type' as being non-deterministic, $A \times S$ describe the 'computation type' as being linear, and the function itself lists all possible futures after one-step of computation of the system. Now, changing the underlying category or the endofunctor allows to model different types of systems. This is the usual framework of coalgebra, as described for example in [25].

Initial states are modelled coalgebraically by a pointing to the carrier $i: I \longrightarrow S$ for a fixed object I in $\mathbb{C}$, describing the 'type of initial states' (see e.g. [2, Sec. 3B]). For example, an initial state of an LTS is the same as a function from the singleton set $I := \{*\}$ to the state space S. This object I will often be the final object of $\mathbb{C}$, but we will see other examples later. In total, an *I-pointed G-coalgebra* is a $\mathbb{C}$-object S together with morphisms $\alpha: S \longrightarrow GS$ and $i: I \longrightarrow S$. E.g. an LTS is an I-pointed G-coalgebra for $I = \{*\}$ and $GX = \mathcal{P}(A \times X)$.

In coalgebra, functional bisimulations are the first class citizens to be modelled as homomorphisms. The intuition is that those preserve the initial state, and preserve and reflect the one-step relation.

Definition 2.6. *An I-pointed G-coalgebra homomorphism from $I \xrightarrow{i} S \xrightarrow{\alpha} GS$ to $I \xrightarrow{i'} S' \xrightarrow{\alpha'} GS'$ is a morphism $f: S \longrightarrow S'$ making the right-hand diagram commute.*

$$
\begin{array}{ccc}
I & \xrightarrow{\;i\;} S & \xrightarrow{\;\alpha\;} GS \\
& {\scriptstyle i'}\searrow \;\; \big\downarrow{\scriptstyle f} & \big\downarrow{\scriptstyle Gf} \\
& S' & \xrightarrow{\;\alpha'\;} GS'
\end{array}
$$

For instance, when $G = \mathcal{P}(A \times \_)$, one can easily see that a function f is a G-coalgebra homomorphism iff it is a functional bisimulation. Thus, if we want to capture functional simulations in LTSs, we need to weaken the condition of homomorphism to the inequality $Gf(\alpha(s)) \subseteq \alpha'(f(s))$ (instead of equality). To express this condition for general G-coalgebras, we introduce a partial order $\sqsubseteq_{X,Y}$ on each homset $\mathbb{C}(X, GY)$ in a functorial manner.

Definition 2.7. *A partial order on G-homsets is a functor $\sqsubseteq \colon \mathbb{C}^{\mathrm{op}} \times \mathbb{C} \longrightarrow \mathsf{Pos}$ such that $U \cdot \sqsubseteq = \mathbb{C}(\_, G\_)$; here, $U \colon \mathsf{Pos} \longrightarrow \mathsf{Set}$ is the forgetful functor from the category Pos of posets and monotone functions.*

The functoriality of $\sqsubseteq$ amounts to that $f_1 \sqsubseteq f_2$ implies $Gh \cdot f_1 \cdot g \sqsubseteq Gh \cdot f_2 \cdot g$.

Definition 2.8. *Given a partial order on G-homsets, an I-pointed lax G-coalgebra homomorphism $f \colon (S, \alpha, i) \longrightarrow (S', \alpha', i')$ is a morphism $f \colon S \longrightarrow S'$ making the right-hand diagram commute. The I-pointed G-coalgebras and lax homomorphisms form a category, denoted by $\mathsf{Coalg}_l(I, G)$.*

$$I \xrightarrow{\ i\ } S \xrightarrow{\ \alpha\ } GS$$
$$i' \searrow \quad \downarrow f \quad \sqsupseteq \quad \downarrow Gf$$
$$S' \xrightarrow[\alpha']{} GS'$$

Conclusion 2.9. In Set, with $I = \{*\}$, $G = \mathcal{P}(A \times \_)$, define the order $f \sqsubseteq g$ in $\mathsf{Set}(X, \mathcal{P}(A \times Y))$ iff for every $x \in X$, $f(x) \subseteq g(x)$. Then $\mathsf{Coalg}_l(\{*\}, \mathcal{P}(A \times \_)) = \mathsf{LTS}_A$. In particular, we have an open map situation

$$\mathbb{P} = (A^\star, \leq) \xrightarrow{\ J\ } \mathbb{M} = \mathsf{LTS}_A = \mathsf{Coalg}_l(\{*\}, \mathcal{P}(A \times \_))$$

and the open maps are precisely the coalgebra homomorphisms (for reachable LTSs). In this paper, we will construct a path category $\mathbb{P}$ for more general I and G, such that the open morphisms are precisely the coalgebra homomorphisms.

3   The Open Map Situation in Coalgebras

Lasota's construction [19] transforms an open map situation $J \colon \mathbb{P} \longrightarrow \mathbb{M}$ into a functor G (with a partial order on G-homsets), together with a functor $\mathsf{Beh} \colon \mathbb{M} \longrightarrow \mathsf{Coalg}_l(I, G)$ that sends open maps to G-coalgebra homomorphisms (see Sect. 4.3 for details). In this paper, we provide a construction in the converse direction for functors G of a certain shape.

As exemplified by LTSs, it is a common pattern that G is the composition $G = TF$ of two functors [12], where T is the branching type (e.g. partial, or non-deterministic) and F is the data type, or the 'linear behaviour' (words, trees, words modulo α-equivalence). If we instantiate our path-construction to $T = \mathcal{P}$ and $F = A \times \_$, we obtain the known open map situation for LTSs (Conclusion 2.9).

Fix a category $\mathbb{C}$ with pullbacks, functors $T, F \colon \mathbb{C} \longrightarrow \mathbb{C}$, an object $I \in \mathbb{C}$ and a partial order $\sqsubseteq^T$ on T-homsets. They determine a coalgebra situation $(\mathbb{C}, I, TF, \sqsubseteq)$ where $\sqsubseteq$ is the partial order on TF-homsets defined by $\sqsubseteq_{X,Y} = \sqsubseteq^T_{X,FY}$. Under some conditions on T and F, we construct a path-category $\mathsf{Path}(I, F+1)$ and an open map situation $\mathsf{Path}(I, F+1) \hookrightarrow \mathsf{Coalg}_l(I, TF)$ where TF-coalgebra homomorphisms and $\mathsf{Path}(I, F+1)$-open morphisms coincide.

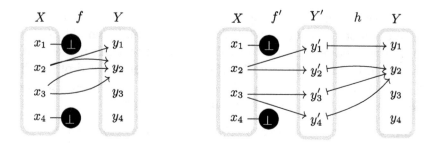

Fig. 1. A non-precise map f that factors through the F-precise $f' \colon X \longrightarrow Y' \times Y' + \{\bot\}$

3.1 Precise Morphisms

While the path category is intuitively clear for $FX = A \times X$, it is not for inner functors F that model tree languages. For example for $FX = A + X \times X$, a $\mathcal{P}F$-coalgebra models transition systems over binary trees with leaves labelled in A, instead of over words. Hence, the paths should be these kind of binary trees. We capture the notion of tree like shape ("every node in a tree has precisely one route to the root") by the following abstract definition:

Definition 3.1. *For a functor $F \colon \mathbb{C} \longrightarrow \mathbb{C}$, a morphism $s \colon S \longrightarrow FR$ is called F-precise if for all f, g, h the following implication holds:*

$$
\begin{array}{ccc}
S \xrightarrow{f} FC \\
s\downarrow \quad\quad \downarrow Fh \\
FR \xrightarrow{Fg} FD
\end{array}
\quad \overset{\exists d}{\Longrightarrow} \quad
\begin{array}{cc}
S \xrightarrow{f} FC \\
s\downarrow \quad \nearrow_{Fd} \\
FR
\end{array}
\;\&\;
\begin{array}{cc}
& C \\
d\nearrow & \downarrow h \\
R \xrightarrow{g} & D
\end{array}
$$

Remark 3.2. If F preserves weak pullbacks, then a morphism s is F-precise iff it fulfils the above definition for $g = \mathrm{id}$.

Example 3.3. Intuitively speaking, for a polynomial Set-functor F, a map $s \colon S \to FR$ is F-precise iff every element of R is mentioned precisely once in the definition of the map f. For example, for $FX = A \times X + \{\bot\}$, the case needed later for LTSs, a map $f \colon X \longrightarrow FY$ is precise iff for every $y \in Y$, there is a unique pair $(x, a) \in X \times A$ such that $f(x) = (a, y)$. For $FX = X \times X + \{\bot\}$ on Set, the map $f \colon X \longrightarrow FY$ in Fig. 1 is not F-precise, because y_2 is used three times (once in $f(x_2)$ and twice in $f(x_3)$), and y_3 and y_4 do not occur in f at all. However, $f' \colon X \longrightarrow FY'$ is F-precise because every element of Y' is used precisely once in f', and we have that $Fh \cdot f' = f$. Also note that f' defines a forest where X is the set of roots, which is closely connected to the intuition that, in the F-precise map f', from every element of Y', there is precisely one edge up to a root in X.

So when transforming a non-precise map into a precise map, one duplicates elements that are used multiple times and drops elements that are not used. We will cover functors F for which this factorization pattern provides F-precise maps. If F involves unordered structure, this factorization needs to make choices, and so we restrict the factorization to a class S of objects that have that choice-principle (see Example 4.5 later):

Definition 3.4. *Fix a class of objects $S \subseteq \mathbf{obj}\,\mathbb{C}$ closed under isomorphism. We say that F admits precise factorizations w.r.t. S if for every $f\colon S \to FY$ with $S \in S$, there exist $Y' \in S$, $h\colon Y' \to Y$ and $f'\colon S \to FY'$ F-precise with $Fh \cdot f' = f$.*

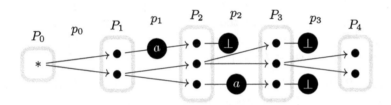

Fig. 2. A path of length 4 for $FX = \{a\} \times X + X \times X + \{\bot\}$ with $I = \{*\}$.

For $\mathbb{C} = \mathsf{Set}$, S contains all sets. However for the category of nominal sets, S will only contain the strong nominal sets (see details in Subsect. 4.2).

Remark 3.5. Precise morphisms are essentially unique. If $f_1\colon X \longrightarrow FY_1$ and $f_2\colon X \longrightarrow FY_2$ are F-precise and if there is some $h\colon Y_1 \longrightarrow Y_2$ with $Fh \cdot f_1 = f_2$, then h is an isomorphism. Consequently, if $f\colon S \longrightarrow FY$ with $S \in S$ is F-precise and F-admits precise factorizations, then $Y \in S$.

Functors admitting precise factorizations are closed under basic constructions:

Proposition 3.6. *The following functors admit precise factorizations w.r.t. S:*

1. *Constant functors, if $\mathbb{C}$ has an initial object 0 and $0 \in S$.*
2. *$F \cdot F'$ if $F\colon \mathbb{C} \longrightarrow \mathbb{C}$ and $F'\colon \mathbb{C} \longrightarrow \mathbb{C}$ do so.*
3. *$\prod_{i \in I} F_i$, if all $(F_i)_{i \in I}$ do so and S is closed under I-coproducts.*
4. *$\coprod_{i \in I} F_i$, if all $(F_i)_{i \in I}$ do so, $\mathbb{C}$ is I-extensive and S is closed under I-coproducts.*
5. *Right-adjoint functors, if and only if its left-adjoint preserves S-objects.*

Example 3.7. When $\mathbb{C}$ is infinitary extensive and S is closed under coproducts, every polynomial endofunctor $F\colon \mathbb{C} \longrightarrow \mathbb{C}$ admits precise factorizations w.r.t. S. This is in particular the case for $\mathbb{C} = S = \mathsf{Set}$. In this case, we shall see later (Sect. 4.1) that many other Set-functors, e.g. the bag functor $\mathcal{B}$, where $\mathcal{B}(X)$ is the set of finite multisets, have precise factorizations. In contrast, $F = \mathcal{P}$ does not admit precise factorizations, and if $f\colon X \longrightarrow \mathcal{P}Y$ is $\mathcal{P}$-precise, then $f(x) = \emptyset$ for all $x \in X$.

3.2   Path Categories in Pointed Coalgebras

We define a path for I-pointed TF-coalgebras as a tree according to F. Following the observation in Example 3.3, one layer of the tree is modelled by a F-precise morphism and hence a path in a TF-coalgebra is defined to be a finite sequence of $(F+1)$-precise maps, where the $\_+1$ comes from the dead states w.r.t. T; the argument is given later in Remark 3.23 when reachability is discussed. Since the $\_+1$ is not relevant yet, we define $\mathsf{Path}(I,F)$ in the following and will use $\mathsf{Path}(I,F+1)$ later. For simplicity, we write $\boldsymbol{X}_n$ for finite families $(X_k)_{0 \le k < n}$.

Definition 3.8. *The category* $\mathsf{Path}(I,F)$ *consists of the following. An object is* $(\boldsymbol{P}_{n+1}, \boldsymbol{p}_n)$ *for an* $n \in \mathbb{N}$ *with* $P_0 = I$ *and* $\boldsymbol{p}_n$ *a family of F-precise maps* $(p_k \colon P_k \longrightarrow FP_{k+1})_{k<n}$. *We say that* $(\boldsymbol{P}_{n+1}, \boldsymbol{p}_n)$ *is a path of length n. A morphism* $\phi_{n+1} \colon (\boldsymbol{P}_{n+1}, \boldsymbol{p}_n) \longrightarrow (\boldsymbol{Q}_{m+1}, \boldsymbol{q}_m)$, $m \ge n$, *is a family* $(\phi_k \colon P_k \longrightarrow Q_k)_{k \le n}$ *with* $\phi_0 = \mathrm{id}_I$ *and* $q_k \cdot \phi_k = F\phi_{k+1} \cdot p_k$ *for all* $0 \le k \le n$.

Example 3.9. Paths for $FX = A \times X + 1$ and $I = \{*\}$ singleton are as follows. First, a map $f \colon I \longrightarrow FX$ is precise iff (up-to isomorphism) either $X = I$ and $f(*) = (a, *)$ for some $a \in A$; or $X = \varnothing$ and $f(*) = \bot$. Then a path is isomorphic to an object of the form: $P_i = I$ for $i \le k$, $P_i = \varnothing$ for $i > k$, $p_i(*) = (a_i, *)$ for $i < k$, and $p_k(*) = \bot$. A path is the same as a word, plus some "junk", concretely, a word in $A^\star.\bot^\star$. For LTSs, an object in $\mathsf{Path}(I,F)$ with $FX = A \times X$ is simply a word in $A^\star$. For a more complicated functor, Fig. 2 depicts a path of length 4, which is a tree for the signature with one unary, one binary symbol, and a constant. The layers of the tree are the sets $\boldsymbol{P}_4$. Also note that since every p_i is F-precise, there is precisely one route to go from every element of a P_k to $*$.

Remark 3.10. The inductive continuation of Remark 3.5 is as follows. Given a morphism ϕ_{n+1} in $\mathsf{Path}(I,F)$, since ϕ_0 is an isomorphism, then ϕ_k is an isomorphism for all $0 \le k \le n$. If F admits precise factorizations and if $I \in \mathcal{S}$, then for every path $(\boldsymbol{P}_{n+1}, \boldsymbol{p}_n)$, all P_k, $0 \le k \le n$, are in $\mathcal{S}$.

Remark 3.11. If in Definition 3.4, the connecting morphism $h \colon Y' \longrightarrow Y$ uniquely exists, then it follows by induction that the hom-sets of $\mathsf{Path}(I,F)$ are at most singleton. This is the case for all polynomial functors, but not the case for the bag functor on sets (discussed in Subsect. 4.1).

Definition 3.12. *The* path poset $\mathsf{PathOrd}(I,F)$ *is the set* $\coprod_{0 \le n} \mathbb{C}(I, F^n 1)$ *equipped with the order: for* $u \colon I \longrightarrow F^n 1$ *and* $v \colon I \longrightarrow F^m 1$, *we define* $u \le v$ *if* $n \le m$ *and* $F^n(!) \cdot v = u$.

$$\begin{array}{ccc} & & F^n F^{m-n} 1 \\ & {}^{v}\nearrow & \downarrow {}^{F^n !} \\ I & \xrightarrow{\ u\ } & F^n 1 \end{array}$$

So $u \le v$ if u is the truncation of v to n levels. This matches the morphisms in $\mathsf{Path}(I,F)$ that witnesses that one path is prefix of another:

Proposition 3.13. *1. The functor* $\mathsf{Comp} \colon \mathsf{Path}(I,F) \longrightarrow \mathsf{PathOrd}(I,F)$ *defined by* $I = P_0 \xrightarrow{p_0} FP_1 \cdots \to F^n P_n \xrightarrow{F^n !} F^n 1$ *on* $(\boldsymbol{P}_{n+1}, \boldsymbol{p}_n)$ *is full, and reflects isos.*
2. If F admits precise factorizations w.r.t. $\mathcal{S}$ and $I \in \mathcal{S}$, then Comp is sujective.
3. If additionally h in Definition 3.4 is unique, then Comp has a right-inverse.

In particular, $\mathsf{PathOrd}(I, F)$ is $\mathsf{Path}(I, F)$ up to isomorphism. In the instances, it is often easier to characterize $\mathsf{PathOrd}(I, F)$. This also shows that $\mathsf{Path}(I, F)$ contains the elements – understood as morphisms from I – of the finite start of the final chain of F: $1 \xleftarrow{!} F1 \xleftarrow{F!} F^2 1 \xleftarrow{F^2!} F^3 1 \leftarrow \cdots$.

Example 3.14. When $FX = A \times X + 1$, $F^n 1$ is isomorphic to the set of words in $A^\star.\bot^\star$ of length n. Consequently, $\mathsf{PathOrd}(I, F)$ is the set of words in $A^\star.\bot^\star$, equipped with the prefix order. In this case, Comp is an equivalence of categories.

3.3　Embedding Paths into Pointed Coalgebras

The paths $(\boldsymbol{P}_{n+1}, \boldsymbol{p}_n)$ embed into $\mathsf{Coalg}_l(I, TF)$ as one expects it for examples like Fig. 2: one takes the disjoint union of the P_k, one has the pointing $I = P_0$ and the linear structure of F is embedded into the branching type T.

During the presentation of the results, we require T, F, and I to have certain properties, which will be introduced one after the other. The full list of assumptions is summarized in Table 2:

(Ax1) – The main theorem will show that coalgebra homomorphisms in $\mathsf{Coalg}_l(I, TF)$ are the open maps for the path category $\mathsf{Path}(I, F + 1)$. So from now on, we assume that $\mathbb{C}$ has finite coproducts and to use the results from the previous sections, we fix a class $\mathcal{S} \subseteq \mathbf{obj}\, \mathbb{C}$ such that $F + 1$ admits precise factorizations w.r.t. $\mathcal{S}$ and that $I \in \mathcal{S}$.

(Ax2) – Recall, that a family of morphisms $(e_i \colon X_i \longrightarrow Y)_{i \in I}$ with common codomain is called jointly epic if for $f, g \colon Y \longrightarrow Z$ we have that $f \cdot e_i = g \cdot e_i \, \forall i \in I$ implies $f = g$. For Set, this means, that every element $y \in Y$ is in the image of some e_i. Since we work with partial orders on T-homsets, we also need the generalization of this property if $f \sqsubseteq g$ are of the form $Y \longrightarrow TZ'$.

(Ax3) – In this section, we encode paths as a pointed coalgebra by constructing a functor $J \colon \mathsf{Path}(I, F+1) \hookrightarrow \mathsf{Coalg}_l(I, TF)$. For that we need to embed the linear behaviour $FX + 1$ into TFX. This is done by a natural transformation $[\eta, \bot] \colon \mathrm{Id} + 1 \longrightarrow T$, and we require that $\bot \colon 1 \longrightarrow T$ is a bottom element for $\sqsubseteq$.

Example 3.15. For the case where T is the powerset functor $\mathcal{P}$, η is given by the unit $\eta_X(x) = \{x\}$, and $\bot$ is given by empty sets $\bot_X(*) = \varnothing$.

Definition 3.16. *We have an inclusion functor* $J \colon \mathsf{Path}(I, F + 1) \hookrightarrow \mathsf{Coalg}_l(I, TF)$ *that maps a path* $(\boldsymbol{P}_{n+1}, \boldsymbol{p}_n)$ *to an I-pointed TF-coalgebra on* $\coprod \boldsymbol{P}_{n+1} := \coprod_{0 \le k \le n} P_k$. *The pointing is given by* $\mathrm{in}_0 \colon I = P_0 \longrightarrow \coprod \boldsymbol{P}_{n+1}$ *and the structure by:*

$$\coprod_{0 \le k < n} P_k + P_n \xrightarrow{[(F\mathrm{in}_{k+1}+1) \cdot p_k]_{0 \le k < n} +!} F \coprod \boldsymbol{P}_{n+1} + 1 \xrightarrow{[\eta, \bot]} TF \coprod \boldsymbol{P}_{n+1}.$$

Example 3.17. In the case of LTSs, a path, or equivalently a word $a_1 ... a_k.\bot....\bot \in A^\star.\bot^\star$, is mapped to the finite linear system over $a_1 ... a_k$ (see Sect. 2.1), seen as a coalgebra (see Sect. 2.2).

Proposition 3.18. *Given a morphism* $[x_k]_{k \leq n} \colon \coprod \boldsymbol{P}_{n+1} \longrightarrow X$ *for some system* (X, ξ, x_0) *and a path* $(\boldsymbol{P}_{n+1}, \boldsymbol{p}_n)$, *we have*

$$J(\boldsymbol{P}_{n+1}, \boldsymbol{p}_n) \xrightarrow{[x_k]_{k \leq n}} (X, \xi, x_0) \iff \forall k < n \colon \quad
\begin{array}{ccc}
P_k & \xrightarrow{\quad x_k \quad} & X \\
{\scriptstyle p_k}\downarrow & {\scriptstyle F x_{k+1}+1} \sqsubseteq \quad {\scriptstyle [\eta, \perp]_X} & \downarrow{\scriptstyle \xi} \\
F P_{k+1}+1 & \xrightarrow{\quad} FX + 1 & \xrightarrow{\quad} TFX.
\end{array}$$
$$\text{a run in } \mathsf{Coalg}_l(I, TF)$$

Also note that the pointing x_0 of the coalgebra is necessarily the first component of any run in it. In a run $[x_k]_{k \leq n}$, p_k corresponds to an edge from x_k to x_{k+1}.

Example 3.19. For LTSs, since the P_k are singletons, x_k just picks the kth state of the run. The right-hand side of this lemma describes that this is a run iff there is a transition from the kth state and the $(k+1)$−th state.

3.4   Open Morphisms Are Exactly Coalgebra Homomorphisms

In this section, we prove our main contribution, namely that $\mathsf{Path}(I, F + 1)$-open maps in $\mathsf{Coalg}_l(I, TF)$ are exactly coalgebra homomorphisms. For the first direction of the main theorem, that is, that coalgebra homomorphisms are open, we need two extra axioms:

(Ax4) – describing that the order on $\mathbb{C}(X, TY)$ is point-wise. This holds for the powerset because every set is the union of its singleton subsets.

(Ax5) – describing that $\mathbb{C}(X, TY)$ admits a choice-principle. This holds for the powerset because whenever $y \in h[x]$ for a map $h \colon X \longrightarrow Y$ and $x \subseteq X$, then there is some $\{x'\} \subseteq x$ with $h(x') = y$.

Theorem 3.20. *Under the assumptions of Table 2, a coalgebra homomorphism in* $\mathsf{Coalg}_l(I, TF)$ *is* $\mathsf{Path}(I, F + 1)$-*open.*

Table 2. Main assumptions on $F, T \colon \mathbb{C} \longrightarrow \mathbb{C}$, $\sqsubseteq^T$, $\mathcal{S} \subseteq \mathbf{obj}\,\mathbb{C}$

F	(Ax1)	$F + 1$ admits precise factorizations, w.r.t. $\mathcal{S}$ and $I \in \mathcal{S}$
T	(Ax2)	If $(e_i \colon X_i \longrightarrow Y)_{i \in I}$ jointly epic, then $f \cdot e_i \sqsubseteq g \cdot e_i$ for all $i \in I \Rightarrow f \sqsubseteq g$.
	(Ax3)	$[\eta, \perp] \colon \mathrm{Id} + 1 \longrightarrow T$, with $\perp_Y \cdot !_X \sqsubseteq f$ for all $f \colon X \longrightarrow TY$
	(Ax4)	For every $f \colon X \longrightarrow TY$, $X \in \mathcal{S}$, $f = \bigsqcup \{ [\eta, \perp]_Y \cdot f' \sqsubseteq f \mid f' \colon X \longrightarrow Y + 1 \}$

$$
\text{(Ax5)} \quad \forall A \in \mathcal{S} \qquad
\begin{array}{ccc}
A & \xrightarrow{\;x\;} & TX \\
{\scriptstyle y}\downarrow & \swarrow\!\!\!\diagup & \downarrow{\scriptstyle Th} \\
Y+1 & \xrightarrow{[\eta, \perp]_Y} & TY
\end{array}
\quad \overset{\exists x'}{\Longrightarrow} \quad
\begin{array}{c}
A \;\cdots\xrightarrow{\;\;x'\;\;} \; X+1 \;\; \xrightarrow[\text{ }]{} \; TX \\
{\scriptstyle y}\searrow \quad \downarrow{\scriptstyle h+1} \quad \uparrow \\
Y+1 \xrightarrow{[\eta,\perp]_Y} TY
\end{array}
$$

The converse is not true in general, because intuitively, open maps reflect runs, and thus only reflect edges of reachable states, as we have seen in Sect. 2.1. The notion of a state being reached by a path is the following:

Definition 3.21. *A system* (X, ξ, x_0) *is* path-reachable *if the family of runs* $[x_k]_{k \leq n} \colon J(\boldsymbol{P}_{n+1}, \boldsymbol{p}_n) \longrightarrow (X, \xi, x_0)$ *(of paths from* $\mathsf{Path}(I, F+1)$*) is jointly epic.*

Example 3.22. For LTSs, this means that every state in X is reached by a run, that is, there is a path from the initial state to every state of X.

Remark 3.23. In Definition 3.21, it is crucial that we consider $\mathsf{Path}(I, F+1)$ and not $\mathsf{Path}(I, F)$ for functors incorporating 'arities ≥ 2'. This does not affect the example of LTSs, but for $I = 1$, $FX = X \times X$ and $T = \mathcal{P}$ in Set, the coalgebra (X, ξ, x_0) on $X = \{x_0, y_1, y_2, z_1, z_2\}$ given by $\xi(x_0) = \{(y_1, y_2)\}$, $\xi(y_1) = \{(z_1, z_2)\}$, $\xi(y_2) = \xi(z_1) = \xi(z_2) = \emptyset$ is path-reachable for $\mathsf{Path}(I, F+1)$. There is no run of a length 2 path from $\mathsf{Path}(I, F)$, because y_2 has no successors, and so there is no path to z_1 or to z_2.

Theorem 3.24. *Under the assumptions of Table 2, if* (X, ξ, x_0) *is path-reachable, then an open morphism* $h \colon (X, \xi, x_0) \longrightarrow (Y, \zeta, y_0)$ *is a coalgebra homomorphism.*

3.5   Connection to Other Notions of Reachability

There is another concise notion for reachability in the coalgebraic literature [2].

Definition 3.25. *A* subcoalgebra *of* (X, ξ, x_0) *is a coalgebra homomorphism* $h \colon (Y, \zeta, y_0) \longrightarrow (X, \xi, x_0)$ *that is carried by a monomorphism* $h \colon X \rightarrowtail Y$*. Furthermore* (X, ξ, x_0) *is called* reachable *if it has no proper subcoalgebra, i.e. if any subcoalgebra* h *is an isomorphism.*

Under the following assumptions, this notion coincides with the path-based definition of reachability (Definition 3.21).

Assumption 3.26. For the present Subsect. 3.5, let $\mathbb{C}$ be cocomplete, have (epi,mono)-factorizations and wide pullbacks of monomorphisms.

The first direction follows directly from Theorem 3.20:

Proposition 3.27. *Every path-reachable* (X, ξ, x_0) *has no proper subcoalgebra.*

For the other direction it is needed that TF preserves arbitrary intersections, that is, wide pullbacks of monomorphisms. In Set, this means that for a family $(X_i \subseteq Y)_{i \in I}$ of subsets we have $\bigcap_{i \in I} TFX_i = TF \bigcap_{i \in I} X_i$ as subsets of TFY.

Proposition 3.28. *If, furthermore, for every monomorphism* $m \colon Y \longrightarrow Z$*, the function* $\mathbb{C}(-, Tm) \colon \mathbb{C}(X, TY) \longrightarrow \mathbb{C}(X, TZ)$ *reflects joins and if* TF *preserves arbitrary intersections, then a reachable coalgebra* (X, ξ, x_0) *is also path-reachable.*

All those technical assumptions are satisfied in the case of LTSs, and will also be satisfied in all our instances in Sect. 4.

3.6 Trace Semantics for Pointed Coalgebras

The characterization from Theorems 3.20 and 3.24 points out a natural way of defining a trace semantics for pointed coalgebras. Indeed, the paths category $\mathsf{Path}(I, F+1)$ provides a natural way of defining the runs of a system. A possible way to go from runs to trace semantics is to describe accepting runs as the subcategory $J'\colon \mathsf{Path}(I,F) \hookrightarrow \mathsf{Path}(I, F+1)$. We can define the *trace semantics* of a system (X, ξ, x_o) as the set:

$$\mathrm{tr}(X, \xi, x_0) = \{\mathsf{Comp}(\boldsymbol{P}_{n+1}, \boldsymbol{p}_n) \mid \exists \text{ run } [x_k]_{k\leq n}\colon JJ'(\boldsymbol{P}_{n+1}, \boldsymbol{p}_n) \longrightarrow (X, \xi, x_0)$$
$$\text{with } (\boldsymbol{P}_{n+1}, \boldsymbol{p}_n) \in \mathsf{Path}(I,F)\}$$

Since $\mathsf{Path}(I, F)$-open maps preserve and reflect runs, we have the following:

Corollary 3.29. $\mathrm{tr}\colon \mathsf{Coalg}_l(I, TF) \longrightarrow (\mathcal{P}(\mathsf{PathOrd}(I, F)), \subseteq)$ *is a functor and if* $f\colon (X, \xi, x_0) \longrightarrow (Y, \zeta, y_0)$ *is* $\mathsf{Path}(I, F+1)$-*open, then* $\mathrm{tr}(X, \xi, x_0) = \mathrm{tr}(Y, \zeta, y_0)$.

Let us look at two LTS-related examples (we will describe some others in the next section). First, for $FX = A \times X$. The usual trace semantics is given by all the words in $A^\star$ that are labelled of a run of a system. This trace semantics is obtained because $\mathsf{PathOrd}(I, F) = \coprod_{n\geq 0} A^n$ and because Comp maps every path to its underlying word. Another example is given for $FX = A \times X + \{\checkmark\}$, where $\checkmark$ marks final states. In this case, a path in $\mathsf{Path}(I, F)$ of length n is either a path that can still be extended or encodes less than n steps to an accepting state $\checkmark$. This obtains the trace semantics containing the set of accepted words, as in automata theory, plus the set of possibly infinite runs.

4 Instances

4.1 Analytic Functors and Tree Automata

In Example 3.7, we have seen that every polynomial Set-functors, in particular the functor $X \mapsto A \times X$, has precise factorizations with respect to all sets. This allowed us to see LTSs, modelled as $\{*\}$-pointed $\mathcal{P}(A \times \_)$-coalgebra, as an instance of our theory. This allowed us in particular to describe their trace semantics using our path category in Sect. 3.6. This can be extended to tree automata as follows. Assume given a signature Σ, that is, a collection $(\Sigma_n)_{n\in\mathbb{N}}$ of disjoint sets. When σ belongs to Σ_n, we say that n is the *arity of* σ or that σ is a *symbol of arity* n. A top-down non-deterministic tree automata as defined in [6] is then the same as a $\{*\}$-pointed $\mathcal{P}F$-coalgebra where F is the polynomial functor $X \mapsto \coprod_{\sigma\in\Sigma_n} X^n$. For this functor, $F^n(1)$ is the set of trees over $\Sigma \sqcup \{*(0)\}$ of depth at most $n+1$ such that a leaf is labelled by $*$ if and only if it is at depth $n + 1$. Intuitively, elements of $F^n(1)$ are partial runs of length n that can possibly be extended. Then, the trace semantics of a tree automata, seen as a pointed coalgebra, is given by the set of partial runs of the automata. In particular, this contains the set of accepted finite trees as those partial runs without any $*$, and the set of accepted infinite trees, encoded as the sequence of their truncations of depth n, for every n.

In the following, we would like to extend this to other kinds of tree automata by allowing some symmetries. For example, in a tree, we may not care about the order of the children. This boils down to quotient the set X^n of n-tuples, by some permutations of the indices. This can be done generally given a subgroup G of the permutation group $\mathfrak{S}_n$ on n elements by defining X^n/G as the quotient of X^n under the equivalence relation: $(x_1,\ldots,x_n) \equiv_G (y_1,\ldots,y_n)$ iff there is $\pi \in G$ such that for all i, $x_i = y_{\pi(i)}$. Concretely, this means that we replace the polynomial functor F by a so-called *analytic functor*:

Definition 4.1 [14,15]. *An* analytic Set*-functor is a functor of the form* $FX = \coprod_{\sigma\in\Sigma_n} X^n/G_\sigma$ *where for every* $\sigma \in \Sigma_n$, *we have a subgroup* G_σ *of the permutation group* $\mathfrak{S}_n$ *on* n *elements.*

Example 4.2. Every polynomial functor is analytic. The bag-functor is analytic, with $\Sigma = (\{*\})_{n\in\mathbb{N}}$ has one operation symbol per arity and $G_\sigma = \mathfrak{S}_{\mathsf{ar}(\sigma)}$ is the full permutation group on $\mathsf{ar}(\sigma)$ elements. It is the archetype of an analytic functor, in the sense that for every analytic functor $F\colon \mathsf{Set} \longrightarrow \mathsf{Set}$, there is a natural transformation into the bag functor $\alpha\colon F \longrightarrow \mathcal{B}$. If F is given by Σ and G_σ as above, then α_X is given by

$$FX = \coprod_{\sigma\in\Sigma_n} X^n/G_\sigma \twoheadrightarrow \coprod_{\sigma\in\Sigma_n} X^n/\mathfrak{S}_n \to \coprod_{n\in\mathbb{N}} X^n/\mathfrak{S}_n = \mathcal{B}X.$$

Proposition 4.3. *For an analytic* Set*-functor* F, *the following are equivalent* (1) *a map* $f\colon X \longrightarrow FY$ *is* F-precise, (2) $\alpha_Y \cdot f$ *is* $\mathcal{B}$-precise, (3) *every element of* Y *appears precisely once in the definition of* f, *i.e. for every* $y \in Y$, *there is exactly one* x *in* X, *such that* $f(x)$ *is the equivalence class of a tuple* $(y_1,\ldots,y_n)$ *where there is an index* i, *such that* $y_i = y$; *and furthermore this index is unique. So every analytic functor has precise factorizations w.r.t.* Set.

4.2 Nominal Sets: Regular Nondeterministic Nominal Automata

We derive an open map situation from the coalgebraic situation for *regular nondeterministic nominal automata (RNNAs)* [26]. They are an extension of automata to accept *words with binders*, consisting of literals $a \in \mathbb{A}$ and binders $|_a$ for $a \in \mathbb{A}$; the latter is counted as length 1. An example of such a word of length 4 is $a|_cbc$, where the last c is bound by $|_c$. The order of binders makes difference: $|_a|_bab \neq |_a|_bba$. RNNAs are coalgebraically represented in the category of nominal sets [10], a formalism about atoms (e.g. variables) that sit in more complex structures (e.g. lambda terms), and gives a notion of *binding*. Because the choice principles (Ax4) and (Ax5) are not satisfied by every nominal sets, we instead use the class of *strong nominal sets* for the precise factorization (Definition 3.4).

Definition 4.4 [10,24]. *Fix a countably infinite set* $\mathbb{A}$, *called the set of* atoms. *For the group* $\mathfrak{S}_f(\mathbb{A})$ *of finite permutations on the set* $\mathbb{A}$, *a group action* $(X,\cdot)$ *is a set* X *together with a group homomorphism* $\cdot\colon \mathfrak{S}_f(\mathbb{A}) \longrightarrow \mathfrak{S}_f(X)$, *written in* *infix notation. An element* $x \in X$ *is* supported by $S \subseteq \mathbb{A}$, *if for all* $\pi \in \mathfrak{S}_f(\mathbb{A})$ *with* $\pi(a) = a \; \forall a \in S$ *we have* $\pi \cdot x = x$. *A nominal set is a group action for* $\mathfrak{S}_f(\mathbb{A})$ *such that every* $x \in X$ *is finitely supported, i.e. supported by a finite* $S \subseteq \mathbb{A}$. *A map* $f: (X, \cdot) \longrightarrow (Y, \star)$ *is* equivariant *if for all* $x \in X$ *and* $\pi \in \mathfrak{S}_f(\mathbb{A})$ *we have* $f(\pi \cdot x) = \pi \star f(x)$. *The category of nominal sets and equivariant maps is denoted by* Nom. *A nominal set* $(X, \cdot)$ *is called* strong *if for all* $x \in X$ *and* $\pi \in \mathfrak{S}_f(\mathbb{A})$ *with* $\pi \cdot x = x$ *we have* $\pi(a) = a$ *for all* $a \in \mathsf{supp}(x)$.

Intuitively, the support of an element is the set of free literals. An equivariant map can forget some of the support of an element, but can never introduce new atoms, i.e. $\mathsf{supp}(f(x)) \subseteq \mathsf{supp}(x)$. The intuition behind strong nominal sets is that all atoms appear in a fixed order, that is, $\mathbb{A}^n$ is strong, but $\mathcal{P}_f(\mathbb{A})$ (the finite powerset) is not. We set $\mathcal{S}$ to be the class of strong nominal sets:

Example 4.5. The Nom-functor of unordered pairs admits precise factorizations w.r.t. strong nominal sets, but not w.r.t. all nominal sets.

In the application, we fix the set $I = \mathbb{A}^{\#n}$ of distinct n-tuples of atoms ($n \geq 0$) as the pointing. The hom-sets $\mathsf{Nom}(X, \mathcal{P}_{\mathsf{ufs}}Y)$ are ordered point-wise.

Proposition 4.6. *Uniformly finitely supported powerset* $\mathcal{P}_{\mathsf{ufs}}(X) = \{Y \subseteq X \mid \bigcup_{y \in Y} \mathsf{supp}(y) \text{ finite}\}$ *satisfies* (Ax2-5) *w.r.t.* $\mathcal{S}$ *the class of strong nominal sets.*[1]

As for F, we study an LTS-like functor, extended with the *binding functor* [10]:

Definition 4.7. *For a nominal set* X, *define the* α-equivalence relation $\sim_\alpha$ *on* $\mathbb{A} \times X$ *by:* $(a, x) \sim_\alpha (b, y) \Leftrightarrow \exists c \in \mathbb{A} \setminus \mathsf{supp}(x) \setminus \mathsf{supp}(y)$ *with* $(a\,c) \cdot x = (b\,c) \cdot y$. *Denote the quotient by* $[\mathbb{A}]X := \mathbb{A} \times X / \sim_\alpha$. *The assignment* $X \mapsto [\mathbb{A}]X$ *extends to a functor, called the* binding functor $[\mathbb{A}]$: Nom $\longrightarrow$ Nom.

RNNA are precisely $\mathcal{P}_{\mathsf{ufs}}F$-coalgebras for $FX = \{\checkmark\} + [\mathbb{A}]X + \mathbb{A} \times X$ [26]. In this paper we additionally consider initial states for RNNAs.

Proposition 4.8. *The binding functor* $[\mathbb{A}]$ *admits precise factorizations w.r.t. strong nominal sets and so does* $FX = \{\checkmark\} + [\mathbb{A}]X + \mathbb{A} \times X$.

An element in $\mathsf{PathOrd}(\mathbb{A}^{\#n}, F)$ may be regarded as a word with binders under a context $\boldsymbol{a} \vdash w$, where $\boldsymbol{a} \in \mathbb{A}^{\#n}$, all literals in w are bound or in $\boldsymbol{a}$, and w may end with $\checkmark$. Moreover, two word-in-contexts $\boldsymbol{a} \vdash w$ and $\boldsymbol{a}' \vdash w'$ are identified if their closures are α-equivalent, that is, $|_{a_1} \cdots |_{a_n} w = |_{a_1'} \cdots |_{a_n'} w'$. The trace semantics of a RNNA T contains all the word-in-contexts corresponding to runs in T. This trace semantics distinguishes whether words are concluded by $\checkmark$.

4.3 Subsuming Arbitrary Open Morphism Situations

Lasota [19] provides a translation of a small path-category $\mathbb{P} \hookrightarrow \mathbb{M}$ into a functor $\mathbb{F}: \mathsf{Set}^{\mathsf{obj}\,\mathbb{P}} \longrightarrow \mathsf{Set}^{\mathsf{obj}\,\mathbb{P}}$ defined by $\mathbb{F}(X_P)_P = \left(\prod_{Q \in \mathbb{P}} (\mathcal{P}(X_Q))^{\mathbb{P}(P,Q)}\right)_{P \in \mathbb{P}}$.

---

[1] There are two variants of powersets discussed in [26]. The finite powerset $\mathcal{P}_f$ also fulfils the axioms. However, *finitely supported* powerset $\mathcal{P}_{\mathsf{fs}}$ does not fulfil (Ax5).

So the hom-sets $\mathsf{Set}^{\mathbf{obj}\,\mathbb{P}}(X, \mathbb{F}Y)$ have a canonical order, namely the point-wise inclusion. This admits a functor Beh from $\mathbb{M}$ to $\mathbb{F}$-coalgebras and lax coalgebra homomorphisms, and Lasota shows that $f \in \mathbb{M}(X, Y)$ is $\mathbb{P}$-open iff $\mathsf{Beh}(f)$ is a coalgebra homomorphism. In the following, we show that we can apply our framework to $\mathbb{F}$ by a suitable decomposition $\mathbb{F} = TF$ and a suitable object I for the initial state pointing. As usual in open map papers, we require that $\mathbb{P}$ and $\mathbb{M}$ have a common initial object $0_{\mathbb{P}}$. Observe that we have $\mathbb{F} = T \cdot F$ where

$$T(X_P)_{P\in\mathbb{P}} = \big(\mathcal{P}(X_P)\big)_{P\in\mathbb{P}} \quad \text{and} \quad F(X_P)_{P\in\mathbb{P}} = \big(\textstyle\coprod_{Q\in\mathbb{P}}\mathbb{P}(P,Q) \times X_Q\big)_{P\in\mathbb{P}}.$$

Lasota considers coalgebras without pointing, but one indeed has a canonical pointing as follows. For $P \in \mathbb{P}$, define the characteristic family $\chi^P \in \mathsf{Set}^{\mathbf{obj}\,\mathbb{P}}$ by $\chi_Q^P = 1$ if $P = Q$ and $\chi_Q^P = \emptyset$ if $P \neq Q$. With this, we fix the pointing $I = \chi^{0_{\mathbb{P}}}$.

Proposition 4.9. *T, F and I satisfy the axioms from Table 2, with $\mathcal{S} = \mathsf{Set}^{\mathbf{obj}\,\mathbb{P}}$.*

The path category in $\mathsf{Coalg}_l(I, TF)$ from our theory can be described as follows.

Proposition 4.10. *An object of $\mathsf{Path}(I, F)$ is a sequence of composable $\mathbb{P}$-morphisms $0_{\mathbb{P}} \xrightarrow{m_1} P_1 \xrightarrow{m_2} P_2 \cdots \xrightarrow{m_n} P_n$.*

5 Conclusions and Further Work

We proved that coalgebra homomorphisms for systems with non-deterministic branching can be seen as open maps for a canonical path-category, constructed from the computation type F. This limitation to non-deterministic systems is unsurprising: as we have proved in Sect. 4.3 on Lasota's work [19], every open map situation can been encoded as a coalgebra situation with a powerset-like functor, so with non-deterministic branching. As a future work, we would like to extend this theory of path-categories to coalgebras for further kinds of branching, especially probabilistic and weighted. This will require (1) to adapt open maps to allow those kinds of branching (2) adapt the axioms from Table 2, by replacing the "+1" part of (Ax1) to something depending on the branching type.

References

1. Adámek, J., Herrlich, H., Strecker, G.E.: Abstract and concrete categories: the joy of cats. online and enhanced edition of the book published in 1990 by John Wiley and Sons (2004). http://katmat.math.uni-bremen.de/acc/acc.pdf
2. Adámek, J., Milius, S., Moss, L.S., Sousa, L.: Well-pointed coalgebras. Logical Methods Comput. Sci. **9**(3), 1–51 (2013)
3. Awodey, S.: Category Theory, 2nd edn. Oxford University Press, Inc., New York (2010)
4. Beohar, H., Küpper, S.: On path-based coalgebras and weak notions of bisimulation. In: 7th Conference on Algebra and Coalgebra in Computer Science, CALCO 2017, Ljubljana, Slovenia, 12–16 June 2017, pp. 6:1–6:17 (2017). https://doi.org/10.4230/LIPIcs.CALCO.2017.6

5. Bonchi, F., Silva, A., Sokolova, A.: The power of convex algebras. In: Meyer, R., Nestmann, U. (eds.) 28th International Conference on Concurrency Theory (CONCUR 2017), Dagstuhl, Germany, vol. 85, pp. 23:1–23:18 (2017). https://doi.org/10.4230/LIPIcs.CONCUR.2017.23

6. Comon, H., et al.: Tree Automata Techniques and Applications (2007). http://tata.gforge.inria.fr

7. Dubut, J., Goubault, É., Goubault-Larrecq, J.: Natural homology. In: Halldórsson, M.M., Iwama, K., Kobayashi, N., Speckmann, B. (eds.) ICALP 2015, Part II. LNCS, vol. 9135, pp. 171–183. Springer, Heidelberg (2015). https://doi.org/10.1007/978-3-662-47666-6_14

8. Fahrenberg, U., Legay, A.: History-preserving bisimilarity for higher-dimensional automata via open maps. Electron. Notes Theor. Comput. Sci. **298**, 165–178 (2013)

9. Fiore, M.P., Cattani, G.L., Winskel, G.: Weak bisimulation and open maps. In: 14th Annual IEEE Symposium on Logic in Computer Science (LICS 1999), pp. 67–76 (1999)

10. Gabbay, M., Pitts, A.M.: A new approach to abstract syntax involving binders. In: Longo, G. (ed.) Proceedings of the Fourteenth Annual IEEE Symposium on Logic in Computer Science, LICS 1999, pp. 214–224. IEEE Computer Society Press (1999)

11. Hansen, H.H., Klin, B.: Pointwise extensions of GSOS-defined operations. Math. Struct. Comput. Sci. **21**(1), 321–361 (2011)

12. Hasuo, I., Jacobs, B., Sokolova, A.: Generic trace semantics via coinduction. Logical Methods Comput. Sci. **3**(4), 1–36 (2007)

13. Jacobs, B., Sokolova, A.: Traces, executions and schedulers, coalgebraically. In: Kurz, A., Lenisa, M., Tarlecki, A. (eds.) CALCO 2009. LNCS, vol. 5728, pp. 206–220. Springer, Heidelberg (2009). https://doi.org/10.1007/978-3-642-03741-2_15

14. Joyal, A.: Une théorie combinatoire des séries formelles. Adv. Math. **42**(1), 1–82 (1981)

15. Joyal, A.: Foncteurs analytiques et espèces de structures. In: Labelle, G., Leroux, P. (eds.) Combinatoire énumérative. LNM, vol. 1234, pp. 126–159. Springer, Heidelberg (1986). https://doi.org/10.1007/BFb0072514

16. Joyal, A., Nielsen, M., Winskel, G.: Bisimulation from open maps. Inf. Comput. **127**, 164–185 (1996)

17. Kozen, D., Mamouras, K., Petrişan, D., Silva, A.: Nominal Kleene coalgebra. In: Halldórsson, M.M., Iwama, K., Kobayashi, N., Speckmann, B. (eds.) ICALP 2015, Part II. LNCS, vol. 9135, pp. 286–298. Springer, Heidelberg (2015). https://doi.org/10.1007/978-3-662-47666-6_23

18. Kurz, A., Petrisan, D., Severi, P., de Vries, F.: Nominal coalgebraic data types with applications to lambda calculus. Logical Methods Comput. Sci. **9**(4) (2013). https://doi.org/10.2168/LMCS-9(4:20)2013

19. Lasota, S.: Coalgebra morphisms subsume open maps. Theor. Comput. Sci. **280**(1), 123–135 (2002)

20. Milius, S.: A sound and complete calculus for finite stream circuits. In: Proceedings of the 25th Annual Symposium on Logic in Computer Science (LICS 2010), pp. 449–458 (2010)

21. Milius, S., Pattinson, D., Schröder, L.: Generic trace semantics and graded monads. In: Moss, L.S., Sobocinski, P. (eds.) Proceedings of 6th Conference on Algebra and Coalgebra in Computer Science, CALCO 2015. Leibniz International Proceedings in Informatics, vol. 35, pp. 253–269 (2015). http://www8.cs.fau.de/_media/research:papers:traces-gm.pdf

22. Nielsen, M., Hune, T.: Bisimulation and open maps for timed transition systems. Fundam. Inform. **38**, 61–77 (1999)
23. Park, D.: Concurrency and automata on infinite sequences. Theor. Comput. Sci. **104**, 167–183 (1981)
24. Pitts, A.M.: Nominal Sets: Names and Symmetry in Computer Science. Cambridge Tracts in Theoretical Computer Science, vol. 57. Cambridge University Press, Cambridge (2013)
25. Rutten, J.: Universal coalgebra: a theory of systems. Theor. Comput. Sci. **249**(1), 3–80 (2000)
26. Schröder, L., Kozen, D., Milius, S., Wißmann, T.: Nominal automata with name binding. In: Esparza, J., Murawski, A.S. (eds.) FoSSaCS 2017. LNCS, vol. 10203, pp. 124–142. Springer, Heidelberg (2017). https://doi.org/10.1007/978-3-662-54458-7_8

11

A Complete Normal-Form Bisimilarity for State

Dariusz Biernacki[1], Serguei Lenglet[2(✉)], and Piotr Polesiuk[1]

[1] University of Wrocław, Wrocław, Poland
{dabi,ppolesiuk}@cs.uni.wroc.pl
[2] Université de Lorraine, Nancy, France
serguei.lenglet@univ-lorraine.fr

Abstract. We present a sound and complete bisimilarity for an untyped λ-calculus with higher-order local references. Our relation compares values by applying them to a fresh variable, like normal-form bisimilarity, and it uses environments to account for the evolving store. We achieve completeness by a careful treatment of evaluation contexts comprising open stuck terms. This work improves over Støvring and Lassen's incomplete environment-based normal-form bisimilarity for the λρ-calculus, and confirms, in relatively elementary terms, Jaber and Tabareau's result, that the state construct is discriminative enough to be characterized with a bisimilarity without any quantification over testing arguments.

1 Introduction

Two terms are contextually equivalent if replacing one by the other in a bigger program does not change the behavior of the program. The quantification over program contexts makes contextual equivalence hard to use in practice and it is therefore common to look for more effective characterizations of this relation. In a calculus with local state, such a characterization has been achieved either through *logical relations* [1,5,15], which rely on types, denotational models [6,10,13], or coinductively defined *bisimilarities* [9,12,17–19].

Koutavas et al. [8] argue that to be sound w.r.t. contextual equivalence, a bisimilarity for state should accumulate the tested terms in an environment to be able to try them again as the store evolves. Such *environmental bisimilarities* usually compare terms by applying them to arguments built from the environment [12,17,19], and therefore still rely on some universal quantification over testing arguments. An exception is Støvring and Lassen's bisimilarity [18], which compares terms by applying them to a fresh variable, like one would do with a *normal-form* (or *open*) bisimilarity [11,16]. Their bisimilarity characterizes contextual equivalence in a calculus with control and state, but is not *complete* in a calculus with state only: there exist equivalent terms that are not related by the bisimilarity. Jaber and Tabareau [6] go further and propose a sound and complete *Kripke Open Bisimilarity* for a calculus with local state, which also compares terms by applying them to a fresh variable, but uses notions from Kripke logical relations, namely transition systems of invariants, to reason about heaps.

In this paper, we propose a sound and complete normal-form bisimilarity for a call-by-value λ-calculus with local references which relies on environments to handle heaps. We therefore improve over Støvring and Lassen's work, since our relation is complete, by following a different, potentially simpler, path than Jaber and Tabareau, since we use environments to represent possible worlds and do not rely on any external structures such as transition systems of invariants. Moreover, we do not need types and define our relation in an untyped calculus.

We obtain completeness by treating carefully normal forms that are not values, i.e., open stuck terms of the form $E[x\,v]$. First, we distinguish in the environment the terms which should be tested multiple times from the ones that should be run only once, namely the evaluation contexts like E in the above term. The latter are kept in a separate environment that takes the form of a stack, according to the idea presented by Laird [10] and by Jagadeesan et al. [7]. Second, we relate the so-called *deferred diverging* terms [5,6], i.e., open stuck terms which hide a diverging behavior in the evaluation context E, with the regular diverging terms.

It may be worth stressing that our congruence proof is based on the machinery we have developed before [3] and is simpler than Støvring and Lassen's one, in particular in how it accounts for the extensionality of functions.

We believe that this work makes a contribution to the understanding of how one should adjust the normal-form bisimulation proof principle when the calculus under consideration becomes less discriminative, assuming that one wishes to preserve completeness of the theory. In particular, it is quite straightforward to define a complete normal-form bisimilarity for the λ-calculus with first-class continuations and global store, with no need to refer to other notions than the ones already present in the reduction semantics. Similarly, in the $\lambda\mu\rho$-calculus (continuations and local references), one only needs to introduce environments to ensure soundness of the theory, but essentially nothing more is required to obtain completeness [18]. In this article we show which new ingredients are needed when moving from these two highly expressive calculi to the corresponding, less discriminative ones—with global or local references only—that do not offer access to the current continuation.

The rest of this paper is as follows. In Sect. 2, we study a simple calculus with global store to see how to reach completeness in that case. In particular, we show in Sect. 2.2 how we deal with deferred diverging terms. We remind in Sect. 2.3 the notion of *diacritical progress* [3] and the framework our bisimilarity and its proof of soundness are based upon. We sketch the completeness proof in Sect. 2.4. Section 2 paves the way for the main result of the paper, described in Sect. 3, where we turn to the calculus with local store. We define the bisimilarity in Sect. 3.2, prove its soundness and completeness in Sect. 3.3, and use it in Sect. 3.4 on examples taken from the literature. We conclude in Sect. 4, where we discuss related work and in particular compare our work to Jaber and Tabareau's. A companion report expands on the proofs [4].

2   Global Store

We first consider a calculus where terms share a global store and present how we deal with deferred diverging terms to get a complete bisimilarity.

2.1   Syntax, Semantics, and Contextual Equivalence

We extend the call-by-value λ-calculus with the ability to read and write a global memory. We let x, y, ... range over term variables and l range over references. A *store*, denoted by h, g, is a finite map from references to values; we write $\mathsf{dom}(h)$ for the domain of h, i.e., the set of references on which h is defined. We write $\emptyset$ for the empty store, $h \uplus g$ for the union of two stores, assuming $\mathsf{dom}(h) \cap \mathsf{dom}(g) = \emptyset$. The syntax of terms and contexts is defined as follows.

Terms:	$t, s ::= v \mid t\,t \mid l := t; t \mid\, !l$
Values:	$v, w ::= x \mid \lambda x.t$
Evaluation contexts:	$E, F ::= \square \mid E\,t \mid v\,E \mid l := E; t$

The term $l := t; s$ evaluates t (if possible) and stores the resulting value in l before continuing as s, while $!l$ reads the value kept in l. When writing examples and in the completeness proofs, we use natural numbers, booleans, the conditional if ... then ... else ..., local definitions let ... in ..., sequence ;, and unit () assuming the usual call-by-value encodings for these constructs.

A λ-abstraction $\lambda x.t$ binds x in t; we write $\mathsf{fv}(t)$ (respectively $\mathsf{fv}(E)$) for the set of free variables of t (respectively E). We identify terms up to α-conversion of their bound variables. A variable or reference is *fresh* if it does not occur in any other entities under consideration, and a store is fresh if it maps references to pairwise distinct fresh variables. A term or context is *closed* if it has no free variables. We write $\mathsf{fr}(t)$ for the set of references that occur in t.

The call-by-value semantics of the calculus is defined on *configurations* $\langle h \mid t \rangle$ such that $\mathsf{fr}(t) \subseteq \mathsf{dom}(h)$ and for all $l \in \mathsf{dom}(h)$, $\mathsf{fr}(h(l)) \subseteq \mathsf{dom}(h)$. We let c and d range over configurations. We write $t\{v/x\}$ for the usual capture-avoiding substitution of x by v in t, and we let f range over simultaneous substitutions $.\{v_1/x_1\} \dots \{v_n/x_n\}$. We write $h[l := v]$ for the operation updating the value of l to v. The reduction semantics $\rightarrow$ is defined by the following rules.

$$\langle h \mid (\lambda x.t)\,v \rangle \rightarrow \langle h \mid t\{v/x\} \rangle \qquad \langle h \mid\, !l \rangle \rightarrow \langle h \mid h(l) \rangle$$
$$\langle h \mid l := v; t \rangle \rightarrow \langle h[l := v] \mid t \rangle \qquad \langle h \mid E[t] \rangle \rightarrow \langle g \mid E[s] \rangle \text{ if } \langle h \mid t \rangle \rightarrow \langle g \mid s \rangle$$

The well-formedness condition on configurations ensures that a read operation $!l$ cannot fail. We write $\rightarrow^*$ for the reflexive and transitive closure of $\rightarrow$.

A term t of a configuration $\langle h \mid t \rangle$ which cannot reduce further is called a *normal form*. Normal forms are either values or *open-stuck terms* of the form $E[x\,v]$; closed normal forms can only be λ-abstractions. A configuration *terminates*, written $c \Downarrow$ if it reduces to a normal-form configuration; otherwise it *diverges*, written $c \Uparrow$, like configurations running $\Omega \stackrel{\text{def}}{=} (\lambda x.x\,x)\,(\lambda x.x\,x)$.

Contextual equivalence equates terms behaving the same in all contexts. A substitution f closes a term t if tf is closed; it closes a configuration $\langle h \mid t \rangle$ if it closes t and the values in h.

Definition 1. *t and s are contextually equivalent, written $t \equiv s$, if for all contexts E, fresh stores h, and closing substitutions f, $\langle h \mid E[t] \rangle f \Downarrow$ iff $\langle h \mid E[s] \rangle f \Downarrow$.*

Testing only evaluation contexts is not a restriction, as it implies the equivalence w.r.t. all contexts $\equiv_C$: one can show that $t \equiv_C s$ iff $\lambda x.t \equiv_C \lambda x.s$ iff $\lambda x.t \equiv \lambda x.s$.

2.2 Normal-Form Bisimulation

Informal Presentation. Two open terms are normal-form bisimilar if their normal forms can be decomposed into bisimilar subterms. For example in the plain λ-calculus, a stuck term $E[x\,v]$ is bisimilar to t if t reduces to a stuck term $F[x\,w]$ so that respectively E, F and v, w are bisimilar when they are respectively plugged with and applied to a fresh variable.

Such a requirement is too discriminating for many languages, as it distinguishes terms that should be equivalent. For instance in plain λ-calculus, given a closed value v, $t \stackrel{\text{def}}{=} x\,v$ is not normal form bisimilar to $s \stackrel{\text{def}}{=} (\lambda y.x\,v)\,(x\,v)$. Indeed, $\square$ is not bisimilar to $(\lambda y.x\,v)\,\square$ when plugged with a fresh z: the former produces a value z while the latter reduces to a stuck term $x\,v$. However, t and s are contextually equivalent, as for all closed value w, $t\{w/x\}$ and $s\{w/x\}$ behave like $w\,v$: if $w\,v$ diverges, then they both diverges, and if $w\,v$ evaluates to some value w', then they also evaluates to w'. Similarly, $x\,v\,\Omega$ and Ω are not normal-form bisimilar (one is a stuck term while the other is diverging), but they are contextually equivalent by the same reasoning.

The terms t and s are no longer contextually equivalent in a λ-calculus with store, since a function can count how many times it is applied and change its behavior accordingly. More precisely, t and s are distinguished by the context $l := 0; (\lambda x.\square)\,\lambda z.l :=!l + 1;$ if $!l = 1$ then 0 else Ω. But this counting trick is not enough to discriminate $x\,v\,\Omega$ and Ω, as they are still equivalent in a λ-calculus with store. Although $x\,v\,\Omega$ is a normal form, it is in fact always diverging when we replace x by an arbitrary closed value w, either because $w\,v$ itself diverges, or it evaluates to some w' and then $w'\,\Omega$ diverges. A stuck term which hides a diverging behavior has been called *deferred diverging* in the literature [5,6].

It turns out that being able to relate a diverging term to a deferred diverging term is all we need to change from the plain λ-calculus normal-form bisimilarity to get a complete equivalence when we add global store. We do so by distinguishing two cases in the clause for open-stuck terms: a configuration $\langle h \mid E[x\,v] \rangle$ is related to c either if c can reduce to a stuck configuration with related subterms, or if E is a diverging context, and we do not require anything of c. The resulting simulation is not symmetric as it relates a deferred diverging configuration with any configuration c (even converging one), but the corresponding notion of bisimulation equates such configuration only to either a configuration of the same kind or a diverging configuration such as $\langle h \mid \Omega \rangle$.

Progress. We define simulation using the notion of *diacritical progress* we developed in a previous work [2,3], which distinguishes between *active* and *passive* clauses. Roughly, passive clauses are between simulation states which should be considered equal, while active clauses are between states where actual progress is taking place. This distinction does not change the notions of bisimulation or bisimilarity, but it simplifies the soundness proof of the bisimilarity. It also allows for the definition of powerful *up-to techniques*, relations that are easier to use than bisimulations but still imply bisimilarity. For normal-form bisimilarity, our framework enables up-to techniques which respects η-expansion [3].

Progress is defined between objects called *candidate relations*, denoted by $\mathcal{R}$, $\mathcal{S}$, $\mathcal{T}$. A candidate relation $\mathcal{R}$ contains pairs of configurations, and a set of configurations written $\mathcal{R}\!\uparrow$, which we expect to be composed of diverging or deferred diverging configurations (for such relations we take $\mathcal{R}^{-1}\!\uparrow$ to be $\mathcal{R}\!\uparrow$). We extend $\mathcal{R}$ to stores, terms, values, and contexts with the following definitions.

$$\frac{\mathsf{dom}(h) = \mathsf{dom}(g) \quad \forall l, h(l) \; \mathcal{R}^{\mathsf{v}} \; g(l)}{h \; \mathcal{R}^{\mathsf{h}} \; g} \qquad \frac{\langle h \mid t \rangle \; \mathcal{R} \; \langle h \mid s \rangle \quad h \text{ fresh}}{t \; \mathcal{R}^{\mathsf{t}} \; s}$$

$$\frac{v \; x \; \mathcal{R}^{\mathsf{t}} \; w \; x \quad x \text{ fresh}}{v \; \mathcal{R}^{\mathsf{v}} \; w} \qquad \frac{E[x] \; \mathcal{R}^{\mathsf{t}} \; F[x] \quad x \text{ fresh}}{E \; \mathcal{R}^{\mathsf{c}} \; F} \qquad \frac{\langle h \mid E[x] \rangle \in \mathcal{R}\!\uparrow \quad x, h \text{ fresh}}{E \in \mathcal{R}\!\uparrow^{\mathsf{c}}}$$

We use these extensions to define progress as follows.

Definition 2. *A candidate relation $\mathcal{R}$ progresses to $\mathcal{S}$, $\mathcal{T}$ written $\mathcal{R} \rightarrowtail \mathcal{S}, \mathcal{T}$, if $\mathcal{R} \subseteq \mathcal{S}$, $\mathcal{S} \subseteq \mathcal{T}$, and*

1. *$c \; \mathcal{R} \; d$ implies*
   - *if $c \rightarrow c'$, then $d \rightarrow^* d'$ and $c' \; \mathcal{T} \; d'$;*
   - *if $c = \langle h \mid v \rangle$, then $d \rightarrow^* \langle g \mid w \rangle$, $h \; \mathcal{S}^{\mathsf{h}} \; g$, and $v \; \mathcal{S}^{\mathsf{v}} \; w$;*
   - *if $c = \langle h \mid E[x \, v] \rangle$, then either*
     - *$d \rightarrow^* \langle g \mid F[x \, w] \rangle$, $h \; \mathcal{T}^{\mathsf{h}} \; g$, $E \; \mathcal{T}^{\mathsf{c}} \; F$, and $v \; \mathcal{T}^{\mathsf{v}} \; w$, or*
     - *$E \in \mathcal{T}\!\uparrow^{\mathsf{c}}$.*
2. *$c \in \mathcal{R}\!\uparrow$ implies $c \neq \langle h \mid v \rangle$ for all h and v and*
   - *if $c \rightarrow c'$, then $c' \in \mathcal{T}\!\uparrow$;*
   - *if $c = \langle h \mid E[x \, v] \rangle$, then $E \in \mathcal{T}\!\uparrow^{\mathsf{c}}$.*

A normal-form simulation is a candidate relation $\mathcal{R}$ such that $\mathcal{R} \rightarrowtail \mathcal{R}, \mathcal{R}$, and a bisimulation is a candidate relation $\mathcal{R}$ such that $\mathcal{R}$ and $\mathcal{R}^{-1}$ are simulations. Normal-form bisimilarity $\approx$ is the union of all normal-form bisimulations.

We test values and contexts by applying or plugging them with a fresh variable x, and running them in a fresh store; with a global memory, the value represented by x may access any reference and assign it an arbitrary value, hence the need for a fresh store. The stores of two bisimilar value configurations must have the same domain, as it would be easy to distinguish them otherwise by testing the content of the references that would be in one store but not in the other.

The main novelty compared to usual definitions of normal-form bisimilarity [3,11] is the set of (deferred) diverging configurations used in the stuck terms clause. We detect that E in a configuration $\langle h \mid E[x\,v]\rangle$ is (deferred) diverging by running $\langle h' \mid E[y]\rangle$ where y and h' are fresh; this configuration may then diverge or evaluate to an other deferred diverging configuration $\langle h \mid E'[x\,v]\rangle$.

Like in the plain λ-calculus [3], $\mathcal{R}$ progresses towards $\mathcal{S}$ in the value clause and $\mathcal{T}$ in the others; the former is passive while the others are active. Our framework prevents some up-to techniques from being applied after a passive transition. In particular, we want to forbid the application of bisimulation up to context as it would be unsound: we could deduce that $v\,x$ and $w\,x$ are equivalent for all v and w just by building a candidate relation containing v and w.

Example 1. To prove that $\langle h \mid x\,v\,\Omega\rangle \approx \langle h \mid \Omega\rangle$ holds for all v and h, we prove that $\mathcal{R} \overset{\text{def}}{=} \{(\langle h \mid x\,v\,\Omega\rangle, \langle h \mid \Omega\rangle), \{\langle g \mid y\,\Omega\rangle \mid y, g \text{ fresh}\}\}$ is a bisimulation. Indeed, $\langle h \mid x\,v\,\Omega\rangle$ is stuck with $\langle g \mid y\,\Omega\rangle \in \mathcal{R}\!\uparrow$ for fresh y and g, and we have $\langle g \mid y\,\Omega\rangle \to \langle g \mid y\,\Omega\rangle$. Conversely, the transition $\langle h \mid \Omega\rangle \to \langle h \mid \Omega\rangle$ is matched by $\langle h \mid x\,v\,\Omega\rangle \to^* \langle h \mid x\,v\,\Omega\rangle$ and the resulting terms are in $\mathcal{R}$.

2.3   Soundness

In this framework, proving that $\approx$ is sound is a consequence that a form of bisimulation up to context is valid, a result which itself may require to prove that other up-to techniques are valid. We distinguish the techniques which can be used in passive clauses (called *strong* up-to techniques), from the ones which cannot. An up-to technique (resp. strong up-to technique) is a function f such that $\mathcal{R} \rightarrowtail \mathcal{R}, f(\mathcal{R})$ (resp. $\mathcal{R} \rightarrowtail f(\mathcal{R}), f(\mathcal{R})$) implies $\mathcal{R} \subseteq \approx$. To show that a given f is an up-to technique, we rely on a notion of *respectfulness*, which is simpler to prove and gives sufficient conditions for f to be an up-to technique.

We briefly recall the notions we need from our previous work [2]. We extend $\subseteq$ and $\cup$ to functions argument-wise (e.g., $(f \cup g)(\mathcal{R}) = f(\mathcal{R}) \cup g(\mathcal{R})$), and given a set $\mathfrak{F}$ of functions, we also write $\mathfrak{F}$ for the function defined as $\bigcup_{f \in \mathfrak{F}} f$. We define f^ω as $\bigcup_{n \in \mathbb{N}} f^n$. We write id for the identity function on relations, and $\widehat{f}$ for $f \cup \text{id}$. A function f is monotone if $\mathcal{R} \subseteq \mathcal{S}$ implies $f(\mathcal{R}) \subseteq f(\mathcal{S})$. We write $\mathcal{P}_{fin}(\mathcal{R})$ for the set of finite subsets of $\mathcal{R}$, and we say f is continuous if it can be defined by its image on these finite subsets, i.e., if $f(\mathcal{R}) \subseteq \bigcup_{\mathcal{S} \in \mathcal{P}_{fin}(\mathcal{R})} f(\mathcal{S})$. The up-to techniques we use are defined by inference rules with a finite number of premises, so they are trivially continuous.

Definition 3. *A function f evolves to g, h, written $f \rightsquigarrow g, h$, if for all $\mathcal{R}$ and $\mathcal{T}$, $\mathcal{R} \rightarrowtail \mathcal{R}, \mathcal{T}$ implies $f(\mathcal{R}) \rightarrowtail g(\mathcal{R}), h(\mathcal{T})$. A function f strongly evolves to g, h, written $f \rightsquigarrow_{\mathbf{s}} g, h$, if for all $\mathcal{R}, \mathcal{S}$, and $\mathcal{T}$, $\mathcal{R} \rightarrowtail \mathcal{S}, \mathcal{T}$ implies $f(\mathcal{R}) \rightarrowtail g(\mathcal{S}), h(\mathcal{T})$.*

Evolution can be seen as progress for functions on relations. Evolution is more restrictive than strong evolution, as it requires $\mathcal{R}$ such that $\mathcal{R} \rightarrowtail \mathcal{R}, \mathcal{T}$.

Definition 4. *A set $\mathfrak{F}$ of continuous functions is* respectful *if there exists $\mathfrak{G}$ such that $\mathfrak{G} \subseteq \mathfrak{F}$ and*

- *for all $f \in \mathfrak{G}$, we have $f \rightsquigarrow_{\mathbf{s}} \widehat{\mathfrak{G}}^\omega, \widehat{\mathfrak{F}}^\omega$;*
- *for all $f \in \mathfrak{F}$, we have $f \rightsquigarrow \widehat{\mathfrak{G}}^\omega \circ \widehat{\mathfrak{F}} \circ \widehat{\mathfrak{G}}^\omega, \widehat{\mathfrak{F}}^\omega$.*

$$\frac{c \; \mathcal{R} \; d \quad v \; \mathcal{R}^v \; w}{c\{v/x\} \; \mathsf{subst}(\mathcal{R}) \; d\{w/x\}} \qquad \frac{c \in \mathcal{R}{\uparrow}}{c\{v/x\} \in \mathsf{subst}(\mathcal{R}){\uparrow}} \qquad \frac{\langle h \mid t \rangle \; \mathcal{R} \; \langle g \mid s \rangle \quad E \; \mathcal{R}^c \; F}{\langle h \mid E[t] \rangle \; \mathsf{plug}_c(\mathcal{R}) \; \langle g \mid F[s] \rangle}$$

$$\frac{\langle h \mid t \rangle \in \mathcal{R}{\uparrow}}{\langle h \mid E[t] \rangle \in \mathsf{plug}_{\uparrow}(\mathcal{R}){\uparrow}} \qquad \frac{c \to^* c' \quad d \to^* d' \quad c' \; \mathcal{R} \; d'}{c \; \mathsf{red}(\mathcal{R}) \; d}$$

$$\frac{c \in \mathcal{R}{\uparrow}}{c \; \mathsf{div}(\mathcal{R}) \; d} \qquad \frac{E \in \mathcal{R}{\uparrow}^c}{\langle h \mid E[t] \rangle \in \mathsf{plugdiv}(\mathcal{R}){\uparrow}}$$

Fig. 1. Up-to techniques for the calculus with global store

In words, a function is in a respectful set $\mathfrak{F}$ if it evolves towards a combination of functions in $\mathfrak{F}$ after active clauses, and in $\mathfrak{S}$ after passive ones. When checking that f is regular (second case), we can use a regular function at most once after a passive clause. The (possibly empty) subset $\mathfrak{S}$ intuitively represents the strong up-to techniques of $\mathfrak{F}$. If $\mathfrak{S}_1$ and $\mathfrak{S}_2$ are subsets of $\mathfrak{F}$ which verify the conditions of the definition, then $\mathfrak{S}_1 \cup \mathfrak{S}_2$ also does, so there exists the largest subset of $\mathfrak{F}$ which satisfies the conditions, written $\mathsf{strong}(\mathfrak{F})$.

Lemma 1. *Let $\mathfrak{F}$ be a respectful set.*

- *If $f \in \mathfrak{F}$, then f is an up-to technique. If $f \in \mathsf{strong}(\mathfrak{F})$, then f is a strong up-to technique.*
- *For all $f \in \mathfrak{F}$, we have $f(\approx) \subseteq \approx$.*

Showing that f is in a respectful set $\mathfrak{F}$ is easier than proving it is an up-to technique. Besides, proving that a bisimulation up to context is respectful implies that $\approx$ is preserved by contexts thanks to the last property of Lemma 1.

The up-to techniques for the calculus with global store are given in Fig. 1. The techniques subst and plug allow to prove that $\approx$ is preserved by substitution and by evaluation contexts. The remaining ones are auxiliary techniques which are used in the respectfulness proof: red relies on the fact that the calculus is deterministic to relate terms up to reduction steps. The technique div allows to relate a diverging configuration to any other configuration, while $\mathsf{plugdiv}$ states that if E is a diverging context, then $\langle h \mid E[t] \rangle$ is a diverging configuration for all h and t. We distinguish the technique plug_c from $\mathsf{plug}_{\uparrow}$ to get a more fine-grained classification, as plug_c is the only one which is not strong.

Lemma 2. *The set $\mathfrak{F} \overset{\mathrm{def}}{=} \{\mathsf{subst}, \mathsf{plug}_m, \mathsf{red}, \mathsf{div}, \mathsf{plugdiv} \mid m \in \{c, \uparrow\}\}$ is respectful, with $\mathsf{strong}(\mathfrak{F}) = \mathfrak{F} \setminus \{\mathsf{plug}_c\}$.*

We omit the proof, as it is similar but much simpler than for the calculus with local store of Sect. 3. We deduce that $\approx$ is sound using Lemma 1.

Theorem 1. *For all t, s, and fresh store h, if $\langle h \mid t \rangle \approx \langle h \mid s \rangle$, then $t \equiv s$.*

2.4 Completeness

We prove the reverse implication by building a bisimulation which contains $\equiv$.

Theorem 2. *For all t, s, if $t \equiv s$, then for all fresh stores h, $\langle h \mid t \rangle \approx \langle h \mid s \rangle$.*

Proof (Sketch). It suffices to show that the candidate $\mathcal{R}$ defined as

$$\{(\langle h \mid t \rangle, \langle g \mid s \rangle) \mid \forall E, h_E, \text{ closing } \int, \langle h \uplus h_E \mid E[t] \rangle \int \Downarrow \; \Rightarrow \; \langle g \uplus h_E \mid E[s] \rangle \int \Downarrow\}$$
$$\cup \, \{\langle h \mid t \rangle \mid \forall E, h_E, \text{ closing } \int, \langle h \uplus h_E \mid E[t] \rangle \int \Uparrow\}$$

is a simulation. We proceed by case analysis on the behavior of $\langle h \mid t \rangle$. The details are in the report [4]; we sketch the proof in the case when $\langle h \mid t \rangle \, \mathcal{R} \, \langle g \mid s \rangle$, $t = E[x \, v]$, and E is not deferred diverging.

A first step is to show that $\langle g \mid s \rangle$ also evaluates to an open-stuck configuration with x in function position. To do so, we consider a fresh l and we define $\int$ such that $\int(y)$ sets l at 1 when it is first applied if $y = x$, and at 2 if $y \neq x$. Then $\langle h \uplus l := 0 \mid t \rangle \int$ sets l at 1, which should also be the case of $\langle g \uplus l := 0 \mid s \rangle \int$, and it is possible only if $\langle g \mid s \rangle \rightarrow^* \langle g' \mid F[x \, w] \rangle$ for some g', F, and w.

We then have to show that $E \, \mathcal{R}^c \, F$, $v \, \mathcal{R}^v \, w$, and $h \, \mathcal{R}^h \, g'$. We sketch the proof for the contexts, as the proofs for the values and the stores are similar. Given h_f a fresh store, y a fresh variable, E' a context, $h_{E'}$ a store, $\int$ a closing substitution, we want $\langle h_f \uplus h_{E'} \mid E'[E[y]] \rangle \int \Downarrow$ iff $\langle h_f \uplus h_{E'} \mid E'[F[y]] \rangle \int \Downarrow$.

Let l be a fresh reference. Assuming $\mathsf{dom}(h) = \{l_1 \ldots l_n\}$, given a term t, we write $\bigcup_i l_i := h; t$ for $l_1 := h(l_1); \ldots l_n := h(l_n); t$. We define

$$\int_x \overset{\text{def}}{=} \begin{cases} x \mapsto \lambda a. \text{if } !l = 0 \text{ then } l := 1; \bigcup_i l_i := h_f \uplus h_{E'}; \int(y) \text{ else } \int(x) \, a \\ \\ z \mapsto \int'(z) \quad \text{if } z \neq x \end{cases}$$

The substitution $\int_x$ behaves like $\int$ except that when $\int_x(x)$ is applied for the first time, it replaces its argument by $\int(y)$ and sets the store to $h_f \uplus h_{E'}$. Therefore $\langle h \uplus l := 0 \mid E'[t] \rangle \int_x \rightarrow^* \langle h_f \uplus h_{E'} \uplus l := 1 \mid E'[E[y]] \rangle \int_x$, but this configuration then behaves like $\langle h_f \uplus h_{E'} \mid E'[E[y]] \rangle \int$. Similarly, $\langle g \uplus l := 0 \mid E'[s] \rangle \int_x$ evaluates to a configuration equivalent to $\langle h_f \uplus h_{E'} \mid E'[F[y]] \rangle \int$, and since $\langle h \uplus l := 0 \mid E'[t] \rangle \int_x \Downarrow$ implies $\langle g \uplus l := 0 \mid E'[s] \rangle \int_x \Downarrow$, we can conclude from there.

3 Local Store

We adapt the ideas of the previous section to a calculus where terms create their own local store. To be able to deal with local resources, the relation we define mixes principles from normal-form and environmental bisimilarities.

3.1 Syntax, Semantics, and Contextual Equivalence

In this section, the terms no longer share a global store, but instead must create
local references before storing values. We extend the syntax of Sect. 2 with a
construct to create a new reference.

Terms: $t, s ::= \ldots \mid$ new $l := v$ in t

Reference creation new $l := v$ in t binds l in t; we identify terms up to α-
conversion of their references. We write $\mathsf{fr}(t)$ and $\mathsf{fr}(E)$ for the set of free references of t or E, and a term or context is *reference-closed* if its set of free references
is empty. Following [18] and in contrast with [5,6], references are not values, but
we can still give access to a reference l by passing $\lambda x.!l$ and $\lambda x.l := x; \lambda y.y$.

As before, the semantics is defined on configurations $\langle h \mid t \rangle$ verifying $\mathsf{fr}(t) \subseteq$
$\mathsf{dom}(h)$ and for all $l \in \mathsf{dom}(h)$, $\mathsf{fr}(h(l)) \subseteq \mathsf{dom}(h)$. We add to the rules of Sect. 2
the following one for reference creation.

$$\langle h \mid \text{new } l := v \text{ in } t \rangle \rightarrow \langle h \uplus l := v \mid t \rangle$$

We remind that $\uplus$ is defined for disjoint stores only, so the above rule assumes
that $l \notin \mathsf{dom}(h)$, which is always possible using α-conversion.

We define contextual equivalence on reference-closed terms as we expect programs to allocate their own store.

Definition 5. *Two reference-closed terms t and s are contextually equivalent,
written $t \equiv s$, if for all reference-closed evaluation contexts E and closing sub-
stitutions $\int$, $\langle \emptyset \mid E[t] \rangle \int \Downarrow$ iff $\langle \emptyset \mid E[s] \rangle \int \Downarrow$.*

3.2 Bisimilarity

With local stores, an external observer no longer has direct access to the stored
values. In presence of such information hiding, a sound bisimilarity relies on an
environment to accumulate terms which should be tested in different stores [8].

Example 2. Let $f_1 \stackrel{\text{def}}{=} \lambda x.\text{if } !l = \text{true then } l := \text{false}; \text{true else false}$ and $f_2 \stackrel{\text{def}}{=}$
$\lambda x.\text{true}$. If we compare new $l := \text{true}$ in f_1 and f_2 only once in the empty store,
they would be seen as equivalent as they both return true, however f_1 modify
its store, so running f_1 and f_2 a second time distinguishes them.

Environments generally contain only values [17], except in $\lambda\mu\rho$ [18], where
plugged evaluation contexts are kept in the environment when comparing open-
stuck configurations. In contrast with $\lambda\mu\rho$, our environment collects values, and
we use a *stack* for registering contexts [7,10]. Unlike values, contexts are therefore
tested only once, following a last-in first-out ordering. The next example shows
that considering contexts repeatedly would lead to an overly-discriminating
bisimilarity. For the stack discipline of testing contexts in action see Example 8
in Sect. 3.4.

Example 3. With the same f_1 and f_2 as in Example 2, the terms $t \overset{\text{def}}{=}$ new $l :=$ true in f_1 $(x\ \lambda y.y)$ and $s \overset{\text{def}}{=} f_2$ $(x\ \lambda y.y)$ are contextually equivalent. Roughly, for all closing substitution $\int$, t and s either both diverge (if $\int(x)\ \lambda y.y$ diverges), or evaluate to true, since $\int(x)$ cannot modify the value in l. Testing $f_1\ \square$ and $f_2\ \square$ twice would discriminate them and wrongfully distinguish t and s.

Remark 1. The bisimilarity for $\lambda\mu\rho$ runs evaluation contexts several times and is still complete because of the μ operator, which, like call/cc, captures evaluation contexts, and may then execute them several times.

We let $\mathcal{E}$ range over sets of pairs of values, and ϵ over sets of values. Similarly, we write Σ for a stack of pairs of evaluation contexts and σ for a stack of evaluation contexts. We write $\odot$ for the empty stack, :: for the operator putting an element on top of a stack, and $+\!\!+$ for the concatenation of two stacks. The projection operator π_1 transforms a set or stack of pairs into respectively a set or stack of single elements by taking the first element of each pair. A candidate relation $\mathcal{R}$ can be composed of:

- quadruples $(\mathcal{E}, \Sigma, c, d)$, written $\mathcal{E}, \Sigma \vdash c\ \mathcal{R}\ d$, meaning that c and d are related under $\mathcal{E}$ and Σ;
- quadruples $(\mathcal{E}, \Sigma, h, g)$, written $\mathcal{E}, \Sigma \vdash h\ \mathcal{R}\ g$, meaning that the elements of $\mathcal{E}$ and the top of Σ should be related when run with the stores h and g;
- triples (ϵ, σ, c), written $\epsilon, \sigma \vdash c \in \mathcal{R}\uparrow$, meaning that either c is (deferred) diverging, or σ is non-empty and contains a (deferred) diverging context;
- triples (ϵ, σ, h), written $\epsilon, \sigma \vdash h \in \mathcal{R}\uparrow$, meaning that σ is non-empty and contains a (deferred) diverging context.

Definition 6. *A candidate relation $\mathcal{R}$ progresses to $\mathcal{S}$, $\mathcal{T}$ written $\mathcal{R} \rightarrowtail \mathcal{S}, \mathcal{T}$, if $\mathcal{R} \subseteq \mathcal{S}$, $\mathcal{S} \subseteq \mathcal{T}$, and*

1. $\mathcal{E}, \Sigma \vdash c\ \mathcal{R}\ d$ *implies*
   - *if $c \rightarrow c'$, then $d \rightarrow^* d'$ and $\mathcal{E}, \Sigma \vdash c'\ \mathcal{T}\ d'$;*
   - *if $c = \langle h \mid v \rangle$, then either*
     - *$d \rightarrow^* \langle g \mid w \rangle$, and $\mathcal{E} \cup \{(v,w)\}, \Sigma \vdash h\ \mathcal{S}\ g$, or*
     - *$\Sigma \neq \odot$ and $\pi_1(\mathcal{E}) \cup \{v\}, \pi_1(\Sigma) \vdash h \in \mathcal{S}\uparrow$;*
   - *if $c = \langle h \mid E[x\ v] \rangle$, then either*
     - *$d \rightarrow^* \langle g \mid F[x\ w] \rangle$, and $\mathcal{E} \cup \{(v,w)\}, (E,F) :: \Sigma \vdash h\ \mathcal{S}\ g$, or*
     - *$\pi_1(\mathcal{E}) \cup \{v\}, E :: \pi_1(\Sigma) \vdash h \in \mathcal{S}\uparrow$.*
2. $\mathcal{E}, \Sigma \vdash h\ \mathcal{R}\ g$ *implies*
   - *if $v\ \mathcal{E}\ w$, then $\mathcal{E}, \Sigma \vdash \langle h \mid v\ x \rangle\ \mathcal{S}\ \langle g \mid w\ x \rangle$ for a fresh x;*
   - *if $\Sigma = (E,F) :: \Sigma'$, then $\mathcal{E}, \Sigma' \vdash \langle h \mid E[x] \rangle\ \mathcal{S}\ \langle g \mid F[x] \rangle$ for a fresh x.*
3. $\epsilon, \sigma \vdash c \in \mathcal{R}\uparrow$ *implies*
   - *if $c \rightarrow c'$, then $\epsilon, \sigma \vdash c' \in \mathcal{T}\uparrow$;*
   - *if $c = \langle h \mid v \rangle$, then $\sigma \neq \odot$ and $\epsilon \cup \{v\}, \sigma \vdash h \in \mathcal{S}\uparrow$;*
   - *if $c = \langle h \mid E[x\ v] \rangle$, then $\epsilon \cup \{v\}, E :: \sigma \vdash h \in \mathcal{S}\uparrow$.*
4. $\epsilon, \sigma \vdash h \in \mathcal{R}\uparrow$ *implies that $\sigma \neq \odot$ and*
   - *if $v \in \epsilon$, then $\epsilon, \sigma \vdash \langle h \mid v\ x \rangle \in \mathcal{S}\uparrow$ for a fresh x;*
   - *if $\sigma = E :: \sigma'$, then $\epsilon, \sigma' \vdash \langle h \mid E[x] \rangle \in \mathcal{S}\uparrow$ for a fresh x.*

A normal-form simulation is a candidate relation $\mathcal{R}$ such that $\mathcal{R} \rightarrowtail \mathcal{R}, \mathcal{R}$, and a bisimulation is a candidate relation $\mathcal{R}$ such that $\mathcal{R}$ and $\mathcal{R}^{-1}$ are simulations. Normal-form bisimilarity $\approx$ is the union of all normal-form bisimulations.

When $\mathcal{E}, \Sigma \vdash c \mathcal{R} d$, we reduce c until we get a value v or a stuck term $E[x\,v]$. At that point, either d also reduces to a normal form of the same kind, or we test (the first projection of) the stack Σ for divergence, assuming it is not empty. In the former case, we add the values to $\mathcal{E}$ and the evaluation contexts at the top of Σ, getting a judgment of the form $\mathcal{E}', \Sigma' \vdash h \mathcal{R} g$, which then tests the environment and the stack by running either terms in $\mathcal{E}'$ or at the top of Σ'.

Example 4. We sketch the bisimulation proof for the terms t and s of Example 3. Because $\langle \emptyset \mid t \rangle \rightarrow^* \langle l := \mathsf{true} \mid f_1 (x\,\lambda y.y) \rangle$ and $\langle \emptyset \mid s \rangle = \langle \emptyset \mid f_2 (x\,\lambda y.y) \rangle$, we need to define $\mathcal{R}$ such that $\{(\lambda y.y, \lambda y.y)\}, (f_1 \square, f_2 \square) :: \odot \vdash l := \mathsf{true}\ \mathcal{R}\ \emptyset$. Testing the equal values in the environment is easy with up-to techniques. For the contexts on the stack, we need $\{(\lambda y.y, \lambda y.y)\}, \odot \vdash \langle l := \mathsf{true} \mid f_1 z \rangle\ \mathcal{R}\ \langle \emptyset \mid f_2 z \rangle$ for a fresh z. Since $\langle l := \mathsf{true} \mid f_1 z \rangle \rightarrow^* \langle l := \mathsf{false} \mid \mathsf{true} \rangle$ and $\langle \emptyset \mid f_2 z \rangle \rightarrow^* \langle \emptyset \mid \mathsf{true} \rangle$, we need $\{(\lambda y.y, \lambda y.y), (\mathsf{true}, \mathsf{true})\}, \odot \vdash l := \mathsf{false}\ \mathcal{R}\ \emptyset$, which is simple to check.

Example 5. In contrast, we show that $t' \overset{\text{def}}{=} \mathsf{new}\ l := \mathsf{true}\ \mathsf{in}\ f_1 (x\,\lambda y.l := y; y)$ and $s' \overset{\text{def}}{=} f_2 (x\,\lambda y.y)$ are not bisimilar. We would need to build $\mathcal{R}$ such that $\{(\lambda y.l := y; y, \lambda y.y)\}, (f_1 \square, f_2 \square) :: \odot \vdash l := \mathsf{true}\ \mathcal{R}\ \emptyset$. Testing the values in the environment, we want $\{(\lambda y.l := y; y, \lambda y.y), (z, z)\}, (f_1 \square, f_2 \square) :: \odot \vdash l := z\ \mathcal{R}\ \emptyset$ for a fresh z. Executing the contexts on the stack, we get a stuck term of the form $\mathsf{if}\ z\ \mathsf{then}\ l := \mathsf{false}; \mathsf{true}\ \mathsf{else}\ \mathsf{false}$ and a value true, which cannot be related, because the former is not deferred diverging.

The terms t' and s' are therefore not bisimilar, and they are indeed not contextually equivalent, since t' gives access to its private reference by passing $\lambda y.l := y; y$ to x. The function represented by x can then change the value of l to false and break the equivalence.

The last two cases of the bisimulation definition aim at detecting a deferred diverging context. The judgment $\epsilon, \sigma \vdash h \in \mathcal{R}\!\uparrow$ roughly means that if $\sigma = E_n :: \ldots E_1 :: \odot$, then the configuration $\langle h' \mid E_1[\ldots E_n[x]] \rangle$ diverges for all fresh x and all h' obtained by running a term from $\mathcal{E}$ with the store h. As a result, when $\epsilon, \sigma \vdash h \in \mathcal{R}\!\uparrow$, we have two possibilities: either we run a term from $\mathcal{E}$ in h to potentially change h, or we run the context at the top of σ (which cannot be empty in that case) to check if it is diverging. In both cases, we get a judgment of the form $\epsilon, \sigma' \vdash c \in \mathcal{R}\!\uparrow$. In that case, either c diverges and we are done, or it terminates, meaning that we have to look for divergence in σ'.

Example 6. We prove that $\langle \emptyset \mid x\,v\,\Omega \rangle$ and $\langle \emptyset \mid \Omega \rangle$ are bisimilar. We define $\mathcal{R}$ such that $\emptyset, \odot \vdash \langle \emptyset \mid x\,v\,\Omega \rangle\ \mathcal{R}\ \langle \emptyset \mid \Omega \rangle$, for which we need $\{v\}, \square\ \Omega :: \odot \vdash \emptyset \in \mathcal{R}\!\uparrow$, which itself holds if $\{v\}, \odot \vdash \langle \emptyset \mid y\,\Omega \rangle \in \mathcal{R}\!\uparrow$.

Finally, only the two clauses where a reduction step takes place are active; all the others are passive, because they are simply switching from one judgment to

$$\frac{\mathcal{E}, \Sigma \vdash c \, \mathcal{R} \, d \qquad v \, \mathcal{E} \, w \qquad x \notin \mathsf{fv}(v) \cup \mathsf{fv}(w)}{\mathcal{E}\{(v,w)/x\}, \Sigma\{(v,w)/x\} \vdash c\{v/x\} \, \mathsf{subst_c}(\mathcal{R}) \, d\{w/x\}}$$

$$\frac{\mathcal{E}, \Sigma_1 \mathbin{+\mkern-8mu+} (E_1, F_1) :: (E_2, F_2) :: \Sigma_2 \vdash \langle h \mid t \rangle \, \mathcal{R} \, \langle g \mid s \rangle}{\mathcal{E}, \Sigma_1 \mathbin{+\mkern-8mu+} (E_2[E_1], F_2[F_1]) :: \Sigma_2 \vdash \langle h \mid t \rangle \, \mathsf{ccomp}(\mathcal{R}) \, \langle g \mid s \rangle}$$

$$\frac{\mathcal{E}, (E, F) :: \Sigma \vdash \langle h \mid t \rangle \, \mathcal{R} \, \langle g \mid s \rangle}{\mathcal{E}, \Sigma \vdash \langle h \mid E[t] \rangle \, \mathsf{plug}(\mathcal{R}) \, \langle g \mid F[s] \rangle} \qquad \frac{c \to^* c' \qquad d \to^* d' \qquad \mathcal{E}, \Sigma \vdash c' \, \mathcal{R} \, d'}{\mathcal{E}, \Sigma \vdash c \, \mathsf{red}(\mathcal{R}) \, d}$$

$$\frac{\epsilon, \sigma \vdash \langle h \mid t \rangle \in \mathcal{R}{\uparrow} \qquad \pi_1(\mathcal{E}) = \epsilon \qquad \pi_1(\Sigma) = \sigma}{\mathcal{E}, \Sigma \vdash \langle h \mid t \rangle \, \mathsf{div}(\mathcal{R}) \, \langle g \mid s \rangle} \qquad \frac{\mathcal{E}, \Sigma \vdash c \, \mathcal{R} \, d \qquad \mathcal{E}' \subseteq \mathcal{E}}{\mathcal{E}', \Sigma \vdash c \, \mathsf{weak}(\mathcal{R}) \, d}$$

$$\frac{\mathcal{E}, \Sigma_1 \mathbin{+\mkern-8mu+} \Sigma_2 \vdash \langle h \mid t \rangle \, \mathcal{R} \, \langle g \mid s \rangle \qquad \mathsf{fr}(E) \subseteq \mathsf{dom}(h')}{\mathcal{E}, \Sigma_1 \mathbin{+\mkern-8mu+} (E, E) :: \Sigma_2 \vdash \langle h \uplus h' \mid t \rangle \, \mathsf{refl}(\mathcal{R}) \, \langle g \uplus h' \mid s \rangle}$$

Fig. 2. Selected up-to techniques for the calculus with local store

the other without any real progress taking place. For example, when comparing value configurations, we go from a configuration judgment $\mathcal{E}, \Sigma \vdash c \, \mathcal{R} \, d$ to a store judgment $\mathcal{E}, \Sigma \vdash h \, \mathcal{R} \, g$ or a diverging store judgment $\mathcal{E}, \Sigma \vdash h \in \mathcal{R}{\uparrow}$. In a (diverging) store judgment, we simply decide whether we reduce a term from the store of from the stack, going back to a (diverging) configuration judgment. Actual progress is made only when we start reducing the chosen configuration.

3.3 Soundness and Completeness

We briefly discuss the up-to techniques we need to prove soundness. We write $\mathcal{E}\{(v,w)/x\}$ for the environment $\{(v'\{v/x\}, w'\{w/x\}) \mid v' \, \mathcal{E} \, w'\}$, and we also define $\Sigma\{(x,w)/x\}$, $\epsilon\{v/x\}$, and $\sigma\{v/x\}$ as expected. To save space, Fig. 2 presents the up-to techniques for the configuration judgment only; see the report [4] for the other judgments.

As in Sect. 2.3, the techniques subst and plug allow to reason up to substitution and plugging into an evaluation context, except that the substituted values and plugged contexts must be taken from respectively the environment and the top of the stack. The technique div relates a diverging configuration to any configuration, like in the calculus with global store. The technique ccomp allows to merge successive contexts in the stack into one. The weakening technique weak, originally known as bisimulation up to environment [17], is an usual technique for environmental bisimulations. Making the environment smaller creates a weaker judgment, as having less testing terms means a less discriminating candidate relation. Bisimulation up to reduction red is also standard and allows for a big-step reasoning by ignoring reduction steps. Finally, the technique refl allows to introduce identical contexts in the stack, but also values in the environment or terms in configurations (see the report [4]).

We denote by $\mathsf{subst_c}$ the up to substitution technique restricted to the configuration and diverging configuration judgments, and by $\mathsf{subst_s}$ the restriction to the store and diverging store judgments.

Lemma 3. *The set $\mathfrak{F} \stackrel{\mathsf{def}}{=} \{\mathsf{subst}_m, \mathsf{plug}, \mathsf{ccomp}, \mathsf{div}, \mathsf{weak}, \mathsf{red}, \mathsf{refl} \mid m \in \{\mathsf{c}, \mathsf{s}\}\}$ is respectful, with $\mathsf{strong}(\mathfrak{F}) = \{\mathsf{subst_s}, \mathsf{ccomp}, \mathsf{div}, \mathsf{weak}, \mathsf{red}, \mathsf{refl}\}$.*

In contrast with Sect. 2.3 and our previous work [3], $\mathsf{subst_c}$ is *not* strong, because values are taken from the environment. Indeed, with $\mathsf{subst_c}$ strong, from $\{(v, w)\}, \odot \vdash \emptyset \; \mathcal{R} \; \emptyset$, we could derive $\{(v, w)\}, \odot \vdash \langle \emptyset \mid x \, y \rangle \; \mathsf{refl}(\mathcal{R}) \; \langle \emptyset \mid x \, y \rangle$ and then $\{(v, w)\}, \odot \vdash \langle \emptyset \mid v \, x \rangle \; \mathsf{subst_c}(\mathsf{refl}(\mathcal{R})) \; \langle \emptyset \mid w \, x \rangle$ for any v and w, which would be unsound.

The respectfulness proofs are in the report [4]. Using refl, plug, $\mathsf{subst_c}$, and Lemma 1 we prove that $\approx$ is preserved by evaluation contexts and substitution, from which we deduce it is sound w.r.t. contextual equivalence.

Theorem 3. *For all t and s, if $\emptyset, \odot \vdash \langle \emptyset \mid t \rangle \approx \langle \emptyset \mid s \rangle$, then $t \equiv s$.*

To establish completeness, we follow the proof of Theorem 2, i.e., we construct a candidate relation $\mathcal{R}$ that contains $\equiv$ and prove it is a simulation by case analysis on the behavior of the related terms.

Theorem 4. *For all t and s, if $t \equiv s$, then $\emptyset, \odot \vdash \langle \emptyset \mid t \rangle \approx \langle \emptyset \mid s \rangle$.*

The main difference is that the contexts and closing substitutions are built from the environment using compatible closures [17], to take into account the private resources of the related terms. We discuss the proof in the report [4].

3.4 Examples

Example 7. We start by the so-called awkward example [5,6,15]. Let

$$v \stackrel{\mathsf{def}}{=} \lambda f. l := 0; f\,(); l := 1; f\,(); !l \qquad w \stackrel{\mathsf{def}}{=} \lambda f. f\,(); f\,(); 1.$$

We equate new $l := 0$ in v and w, building the candidate $\mathcal{R}$ incrementally, starting from $\{(v, w)\}, \odot \vdash l := 0 \; \mathcal{R} \; \emptyset$.

Running v and w with a fresh variable f, we obtain $\langle l := 0 \mid E_1[f\,()] \rangle$ and $\langle \emptyset \mid E_2[f\,()] \rangle$ with $E_1 \stackrel{\mathsf{def}}{=} \square; l := 1; f\,(); !l$ and $F_1 \stackrel{\mathsf{def}}{=} \square; f\,(); 1$. Ignoring the identical unit arguments (using refl), we need $\{(v, w)\}, (E_1, F_1) :: \odot \vdash l := 0 \; \mathcal{R} \; \emptyset$; from that point, we can either test v and w again, resulting into an extra pair (E_1, F_1) on the stack, or run $\langle l := 0 \mid E_1[g] \rangle$ and $\langle \emptyset \mid F_1[g] \rangle$ for a fresh g instead.

In the latter case, we get $\langle l := 1 \mid E_2[g\,()] \rangle$ and $\langle \emptyset \mid F_2[g\,()] \rangle$, with $E_2 \stackrel{\mathsf{def}}{=} \square; !l$ and $F_2 \stackrel{\mathsf{def}}{=} \square; 1$, so we want $\{(v, w)\}, (E_2, F_2) :: \odot \vdash l := 1 \; \mathcal{R} \; \emptyset$ (ignoring again the units). From there, testing v and w produces $\{(v, w)\}, (E_1, F_1) :: (E_2, F_2) :: \odot \vdash l := 0 \; \mathcal{R} \; \emptyset$, while executing $\langle l := 1 \mid E_2[x] \rangle$ and $\langle \emptyset \mid F_2[x] \rangle$ for a fresh x gives us $\langle l := 1 \mid 1 \rangle$ and $\langle \emptyset \mid 1 \rangle$. This analysis suggests that $\mathcal{R}$ should be composed only of judgments of the form $\{(v, w)\}, \Sigma \vdash l := n \; \mathcal{R} \; \emptyset$ such that $n \in \{0, 1\}$ and

- Σ is an arbitrary stack composed only of pairs (E_1, F_1) or (E_2, F_2);
- if $\Sigma = (E_2, F_2) :: \Sigma'$, then $n = 1$.

We can check that such a candidate is a bisimulation, and it ensures that when l is read (when E_2 is executed), it contains the value 1.

Example 8. As a variation on the awkward example, let

$$v \stackrel{\text{def}}{=} \lambda f.l := !l + 1; f\ (); l := !l - 1; !l > 0 \qquad w \stackrel{\text{def}}{=} \lambda f.f\ (); \text{true}.$$

We show that $\langle \emptyset \mid \text{new } l := 1 \text{ in } v \rangle$ and $\langle \emptyset \mid w \rangle$ are bisimilar. Let $E \stackrel{\text{def}}{=} \square; l := !l - 1; !l > 0$ and $F \stackrel{\text{def}}{=} \square; \text{true}$. We write $(E, F)^n$ for the stack $\odot$ if $n = 0$ and $(E, F) :: (E, F)^{n-1}$ otherwise. Then the candidate $\mathcal{R}$ verifying $\{(v, w)\}, (E, F)^n \vdash l := n + 1 \mathcal{R} \emptyset$ for any n is a bisimulation. Indeed, running v and w increases the value stored in l and adds a pair (E, F) on the stack. If $n > 0$, we can run a copy of E and F, thus decreasing the value in l by 1, and then returning true in both cases.

Example 9. This deferred divergence example comes from Dreyer et al. [5]. Let

$$v_1 \stackrel{\text{def}}{=} \lambda x.\text{if } !l \text{ then } \Omega \text{ else } k := \text{true}; \lambda y.y \qquad w_1 \stackrel{\text{def}}{=} \lambda x.\Omega$$

$$v_2 \stackrel{\text{def}}{=} \lambda f.f\ v_1; \text{if } !k \text{ then } \Omega \text{ else } l := \text{true}; \lambda y.y \qquad w_2 \stackrel{\text{def}}{=} \lambda f.f\ w_1; \lambda y.y$$

We prove that new $l := \text{false}$ in new $k := \text{false}$ in v_2 is equivalent to w_2. Informally, if f in w_2 applies its argument w_1, the term diverges. Divergence also happens in v_2 but in a delayed fashion, as v_1 first sets k to true, and the continuation $t \stackrel{\text{def}}{=} \text{if } !k \text{ then } \Omega \text{ else } l := \text{true}; \lambda y.y$ then diverges. Similarly, if f stores w_1 or v_1 to later apply it, then divergence also occurs in both cases: in that case t sets l to true, and when v_1 is later applied, it diverges.

To build a candidate $\mathcal{R}$, we execute $\langle l := \text{false}; k := \text{false} \mid v_2\ f \rangle$ and $\langle \emptyset \mid w_2\ f \rangle$ for a fresh f, which gives us $\langle l := \text{false}; k := \text{false} \mid E[f\ v_1] \rangle$ and $\langle \emptyset \mid F[f\ w_1] \rangle$ with $E \stackrel{\text{def}}{=} \square; t$ and $F \stackrel{\text{def}}{=} \square; \lambda y.y$. We consider $\{(v_2, w_2), (v_1, w_1)\}, (E, F) :: \emptyset \vdash l := \text{false}; k := \text{false } \mathcal{R} \emptyset$, for which we have several checks to do. The interesting one is running $\langle l := \text{false}; k := \text{false} \mid v_1\ x \rangle$ and $\langle \emptyset \mid w_1\ x \rangle$, as we get $\langle l := \text{false}; k := \text{true} \mid \lambda y.y \rangle$ and $\langle \emptyset \mid \Omega \rangle$. In that case, we are showing that the stack contains divergence, by establishing that $\{v_2, v_1, \lambda y.y\}, E :: \emptyset \vdash l := \text{false}; k := \text{true} \in \mathcal{R}\uparrow$, and indeed, we have $\langle l := \text{false}; k := \text{true} \mid E[x] \rangle \rightarrow^* \langle l := \text{false}; k := \text{true} \mid \Omega \rangle$ for a fresh x. In the end, the relation $\mathcal{R}$ verifying

$$\{(v_2, w_2), (v_1, w_1)\}, (E, F)^n \vdash l := \text{false}; k := \text{false } \mathcal{R} \emptyset$$

$$\{(v_2, w_2), (v_1, w_1)\}, (E, F)^n \vdash \langle l := \text{false}; k := \text{true} \mid \lambda y.y \rangle \mathcal{R} \langle \emptyset \mid \Omega \rangle$$

$$\{v_2, v_1, \lambda y.y\}, E^n \vdash l := \text{false}; k := \text{true} \in \mathcal{R}\uparrow$$

$$\{v_2, v_1, \lambda y.y\}, E^n \vdash \langle l := \text{false}; k := \text{true} \mid \Omega \rangle \in \mathcal{R}\uparrow$$

$$\{(v_2, w_2), (v_1, w_1)\}, (E, F)^n \vdash l := \text{true}; k := \text{false } \mathcal{R} \emptyset$$

$$\{(v_2, w_2), (v_1, w_1)\}, (E, F)^n \vdash \langle l := \text{true}; k := \text{false} \mid \Omega \rangle \mathcal{R} \langle \emptyset \mid \Omega \rangle$$

for all n is a bisimulation up to refl and red.

4   Related Work and Conclusion

Related Work. As pointed out in Sect. 1, the other bisimilarities defined for state either feature universal quantification over testing arguments [9,12,17,19], or are complete only for a more expressive language [18]. Kripke logical relations [1,5] also involve quantification over arguments when testing terms of a functional type. Finally, denotational models [10,13] can also be used to prove program equivalence, by showing that the denotations of two terms are equal. However, computing such denotations is difficult in general, and the automation of this task is so far restricted to a language with first-order references [14].

The work most closely related to ours is Jaber and Tabareau's Kripke Open Bisimulation (KOB) [6]. A KOB tests functional terms with fresh variables and not with related values like a regular logical relation would do. To relate two given configurations, one has to provide a World Transition System (WTS) which states the invariants the heaps of the configurations should satisfy and how to go from one invariant to the other during the evaluation. Similarly, the bisimulations for the examples of Sect. 3.4 state properties which could be seen as invariants about the stores at different points of the evaluation.

The difficulty for KOB as well as with our bisimilarity is to come up with the right invariants about the heaps, expressed either as a WTS or as a bisimulation. We believe that choosing a technique over the other is just a matter of preference, depending on whether one is more comfortable with game semantics or with coinduction. It would be interesting to see if there is a formal correspondence between KOB and our bisimilarity; we leave this question as a future work.

Conclusion. We define a sound and complete normal-form bisimilarity for higher-order local state, with an environment to be able to run terms in different stores. We distinguish in the environment values which should be tested several times from the contexts which should be executed only once. The other difficulty is to relate deferred and regular diverging terms, which is taken care of by the specific judgments about divergence. The lack of quantification over arguments make the bisimulation proofs quite simple.

A future work would be to make these proofs even simpler by defining appropriate up-to techniques. The techniques we use in Sect. 3.3 to prove soundness turn out to be not that useful when establishing the equivalences of Sect. 3.4, except for trivial ones such as up to reduction or reflexivity. The difficulty in defining the candidate relations for the examples of Sect. 3.4 is in finding the right property relating the stack Σ to the store, so maybe an up-to technique could make this task easier.

As pointed out in Sect. 1, our results can be seen as an indication of what kind of additional infrastructure in a complete normal-form bisimilarity is required when the considered syntactic theory becomes less discriminative—in our case, when control operators vanish from the picture, and mutable state is the only extension of the λ-calculus. A question one could then ask is whether we can find a less expressive calculus—maybe the plain λ-calculus itself—for which a suitably enhanced normal-form bisimilarity is still complete.

Acknowledgements. We thank Guilhem Jaber and the anonymous reviewers for their comments. This work was supported by the National Science Centre, Poland, grant no. 2014/15/B/ST6/00619 and by COST Action EUTypes CA15123.

References

1. Ahmed, A., Dreyer, D., Rossberg, A.: State-dependent representation independence. In: Pierce, B.C. (ed.) Proceedings of the Thirty-Fifth Annual ACM Symposium on Principles of Programming Languages, pp. 340–353. ACM Press, January 2009
2. Aristizábal, A., Biernacki, D., Lenglet, S., Polesiuk, P.: Environmental bisimulations for delimited-control operators with dynamic prompt generation. Logical Methods Comput. Sci. **13**(3) 2017
3. Biernacki, D., Lenglet, S., Polesiuk, P.: Proving soundness of extensional normal-form bisimilarities. In: Silva, A. (ed.) Proceedings of the 33rd Annual Conference on Mathematical Foundations of Programming Semantics (MFPS XXXIII), Ljubljana, Slovenia. Electronic Notes in Theoretical Computer Science, vol. 336, pp. 41–56, June 2017
4. Biernacki, D., Lenglet, S., Polesiuk, P.: A complete normal-form bisimilarity for state. Research report RR-9251, Inria, Nancy, France, January 2019
5. Dreyer, D., Neis, G., Birkedal, L.: The impact of higher-order state and control effects on local relational reasoning. J. Funct. Program. **22**(4–5), 477–528 (2012)
6. Jaber, G., Tabareau, N.: Kripke open bisimulation – a marriage of game semantics and operational techniques. In: Feng, X., Park, S. (eds.) APLAS 2015. LNCS, vol. 9458, pp. 271–291. Springer, Cham (2015)
7. Jagadeesan, R., Pitcher, C., Riely, J.: Open bisimulation for aspects. Trans. Aspect-Oriented Softw. Dev. **5**, 72–132 (2009)
8. Koutavas, V., Levy, P.B., Sumii, E.: From applicative to environmental bisimulation. In: Mislove, M., Ouaknine, J. (eds.) Proceedings of the 27th Annual Conference on Mathematical Foundations of Programming Semantics (MFPS XXVII), Pittsburgh, PA, USA. ENTCS, vol. 276, pp. 215–235, May 2011
9. Koutavas, V., Wand, M.: Small bisimulations for reasoning about higher-order imperative programs. In: Morrisett, J.G., Jones, S.L.P. (eds.) POPL 2006, Charleston, SC, USA, pp. 141–152. ACM Press (2006)
10. Laird, J.: A fully abstract trace semantics for general references. In: Arge, L., Cachin, C., Jurdziński, T., Tarlecki, A. (eds.) ICALP 2007. LNCS, vol. 4596, pp. 667–679. Springer, Heidelberg (2007)
11. Lassen, S.B.: Eager normal form bisimulation. In: Panangaden, P. (ed.) LICS 2005, Chicago, IL, pp. 345–354. IEEE Computer Society Press (2005)
12. Madiot, J.-M., Pous, D., Sangiorgi, D.: Bisimulations up-to: beyond first-order transition systems. In: Baldan, P., Gorla, D. (eds.) CONCUR 2014. LNCS, vol. 8704, pp. 93–108. Springer, Heidelberg (2014)
13. Murawski, A.S., Tzevelekos, N.: Game semantics for good general references. In: Proceedings of the 26th Annual IEEE Symposium on Logic in Computer Science, LICS 2011, pp. 75–84. IEEE Computer Society, June 2011
14. Murawski, A.S., Tzevelekos, N.: Algorithmic games for full ground references. Formal Methods Syst. Des. **52**(3), 277–314 (2018)
15. Pitts, A., Stark, I.: Operational reasoning for functions with local state. In: Gordon, A., Pitts, A. (eds.) Higher Order Operational Techniques in Semantics, pp. 227–273. Publications of the Newton Institute, Cambridge University Press (1998)

16. Sangiorgi, D.: The lazy lambda calculus in a concurrency scenario. In: Scedrov, A. (ed.) LICS 1992, Santa Cruz, California, pp. 102–109. IEEE Computer Society (1992)
17. Sangiorgi, D., Kobayashi, N., Sumii, E.: Environmental bisimulations for higher-order languages. ACM Trans. Program. Lang. Syst. **33**(1), 1–69 (2011)
18. Støvring, K., Lassen, S.B.: A complete, co-inductive syntactic theory of sequential control and state. In: Felleisen, M. (ed.) SIGPLAN Notices, POPL 2007, Nice, France, vol. 42, no. 1, pp. 161–172. ACM Press (2007)
19. Sumii, E.: A complete characterization of observational equivalence in polymorphic λ-calculus with general references. In: Grädel, E., Kahle, R. (eds.) CSL 2009. LNCS, vol. 5771, pp. 455–469. Springer, Heidelberg (2009)

12

Equational Theories and Monads from Polynomial Cayley Representations

Maciej Piróg$^{(\boxtimes)}$, Piotr Polesiuk, and Filip Sieczkowski

University of Wrocław, Wrocław, Poland
mpirog@cs.uni.wroc.pl

Abstract. We generalise Cayley's theorem for monoids by providing an explicit formula for a (multi-sorted) equational theory represented by the type $PX \to X$, where P is an arbitrary polynomial endofunctor with natural coefficients. From the computational perspective, examples of effects given by such theories include backtracking nondeterminism (obtained with the original Cayley representation $X \to X$), finite mutable state (obtained with $n \to X$, for a constant n), and their different combinations (via $n \times X \to X$ or $X^n \to X$). Moreover, we show that monads induced by such theories are implementable using the type formers available in programming languages based on a polymorphic λ-calculus, both as compositions of algebraic datatypes and as continuation-like monads. We give a set-theoretic model of the latter in terms of Barr-dinatural transformations. We also introduce CayMon, a tool that takes a polynomial as an input and generates the corresponding equational theory together with the two implementations of the induced monad in Haskell.

1 Introduction

The relationship between universal algebra and monads has been studied at least since Linton [13] and Eilenberg and Moore [4], while the relationship between monads and the general theory of computational effects (exceptions, mutable state, nondeterminism, and such) has been observed by Moggi [14]. By transitivity, one can study computational effects using concepts from universal algebra, which is the main theme of Plotkin and Power's prolific research programme (see [10, 20–24] among many others).

The simplest possible case of this approach is to describe an effect via a finitary equational theory: a finite set of operations (of finite arities), together with a finite set of equations. One such example is the theory of monoids:

Operations: $\gamma, \quad \varepsilon$

Equations: $\gamma(x, \varepsilon) = x, \quad \gamma(\varepsilon, x) = x, \quad \gamma(\gamma(x, y), z) = \gamma(x, \gamma(y, z))$

The above reads that the signature of the theory consists of two operations: binary γ and nullary ε. The equations state that γ is associative, with ε being its left and right unit.[1] One can also read this theory as a specification of backtracking nondeterminism, in which the order of results matters, where γ is an operation that creates a new computation as a choice between two subcomputations, while ε denotes failure. The connection between the equational theory and the computational effect becomes apparent when we consider the monad of free monoids (that is, the list monad), which is in fact used to form backtracking computations in programming; see, for example, Bird's pearl [1].

This suggests a simple recipe for computational effects: it is enough to come up with an equational theory, and out of the hat comes the induced monad of free algebras that implements the corresponding effect. Such an approach is indeed possible in the category **Set**, where every finitary equational theory admits a free monad, constructed by quotienting terms over the signature by the congruence induced by the equations. However, if we want to implement this monad in a programming language, the situation is not so simple, since in most programming languages (in particular, those without higher inductive types) we cannot generally express this kind of quotients. For instance, to describe a variant of nondeterminism that does not admit duplicate results, we may extend the theory of monoids with an equation stating that γ is idempotent, that is, $\gamma(x, x) = x$. But, unlike in the case of general monoids, the monad induced by the theory of idempotent monoids seems to be no longer directly expressible in, say, Haskell. This means that there is no implementation that satisfies all the equations of the theory "on the nose"—one informal argument is that the representations of $\gamma(x, x)$ and x should be the same whatever the type of x, and this would require a decidable equality test on every type, which is not possible.

Thus, both from the practical viewpoint of programming and as a question on the general nature of equational theories, it makes sense to ask which theories are "simple" enough to induce monads expressible using only the basic type formers, such as (co)products, function spaces, algebraic datatypes, universal and existential quantification. This question seems difficult in general, and to our knowledge there is little work that addresses it. In this paper, we focus on a small piece of this problem: we study a certain subset of such implementable equational theories, and conjecture some novel extensions.

The monads that we consider arise from Cayley representations. The overall idea is that if a theory has an expressible, well-behaved (in a sense that we make precise in the paper) Cayley representation, the induced monad also has an expressible implementation. The well-known Cayley theorem for monoids states that every monoid with a carrier X embeds in the monoid of endofunctions $X \to X$. In this paper, we generalise this result: given a polynomial **Set**-endofunctor P with natural coefficients, we provide an explicit formula for an equational theory such that its every algebra with a carrier X embeds in a certain algebra with the carrier given by $PX \to X$. Then, we show that the monad of

---

[1] Although one usually writes γ as an infix operation, we use a "functional" syntax, since, in the following, the arity of corresponding operations may vary.

free algebras of such a theory can be implemented as a continuation-like monad with the endofunctor given at a set A as:

$$\forall X.(A \to PX \to X) \to PX \to X \tag{1}$$

This type is certainly expressible in programming languages based on polymorphic λ-calculi, such as Haskell.

However, before we can give the details of this construction, we need to address some technical issues. It is easy to notice that there may be more than one "Cayley representation" of a given theory: for example, a monoid X embeds not only in $X \to X$, but also in a "smaller" monoid $X \overset{\gamma}{\rightsquigarrow} X$, by which we mean the monoid of functions of the type $X \to X$ of the shape $a \mapsto \gamma(b, a)$, where $b \in X$. The same monoid X embeds also in a "bigger" monoid $X^2 \to X$, in which we interpret the operations as $\gamma(f, g) = (x, y) \mapsto f(g(x, y), y)$ and $\varepsilon = (x, y) \mapsto x$. What makes $X \to X$ special is that instantiating (1) with $PX = X$ gives a monad that is *isomorphic* to the list monad (note that in this case, the type (1) is simply the Church representation of lists). At the same time, we cannot use $X \overset{\gamma}{\rightsquigarrow} X$ instead of $X \to X$, since (1) quantifies over sets, and thus there is no natural candidate for γ. Moreover, even though we may use the instantiation $PX = X^2$, this choice yields a *different* monad (which we describe in more detail in Sect. 5.4). To sort this out, in Sect. 2, we introduce the notion of *tight Cayley representation*. This notion gives rise to the monad of the following shape, which is a strict generalisation of (1), where R is a **Set**-bifunctor of mixed variance:

$$\forall X.(A \to R(X, X)) \to R(X, X) \tag{2}$$

Formally, all our constructions are set-theoretic—to focus the presentation, the connection with programming languages and type theory is left implicit. Thus, the second issue that we discuss in Sect. 2 is the meaning of the universal quantifier $\forall$ in (1). It is known [27] that polymorphic functions of this shape enjoy a form of dinaturality proposed by Michael Barr (see Paré and Román [16]), called by Mulry *strong* dinaturality [15]. We model the universally quantified types above as collections of Barr-dinatural transformations, and prove that if R is a tight representation, the collection (2) is always a set.

In Sect. 4, we give the formula that defines an equational theory given a polynomial functor P. In general, the theories we construct can be multi-sorted, which is useful for avoiding a combinatory explosion of the induced theories, hence a brief discussion of such theories in Sect. 3. We show that $PX \to X$ is indeed a tight representation of the generated theory. Then, in Sect. 5, we study a number of examples in order to discover what effects are denoted by the generated theories. It turns out that each theory can be seen as a (rather complex, for nontrivial polynomial functors) composition of backtracking nondeterminism and finite mutable state. Moreover, in Sect. 6, we show that the corresponding monads can be implemented not only as continuation-like monads (1), but also in "direct style", using algebraic datatypes.

Since they are parametrised by a polynomial, both the equational theory and its representation consist of many indexed components, so it is not necessarily trivial to get much intuition simply by looking at the formulas. To facilitate this, we have implemented a tool, called **CayMon**, that generates the theory from a given polynomial, and produces two implementations in Haskell: as a composition of algebraic datatypes and as a continuation-like ("Cayley") monad (1). The tool can be run in a web browser, and is available at http://pl-uwr.bitbucket. io/caymon.

2   Tight Cayley Representations

In this section, we take a more abstract view on the concept of "Cayley representation". In the literature (for example, [2,5,17,25]), authors usually define Cayley representations of different forms of algebraic structures in terms of embeddings. This means that given an object X, there is a homomorphism $\sigma : X \to Y$ to a different object Y, and moreover σ has a retraction (not necessarily a homomorphism) $\rho : Y \to X$ (meaning $\rho \cdot \sigma = \mathrm{id}$). One important fact, which is usually left implicit, is that the construction of Y from X is in some sense functorial. Since we are interested in coming up with representations for many different equational theories, we first identify sufficient properties of such a representation needed to carry out the construction of the monad (2) sketched in the introduction. In particular, we introduce the notion of *tight Cayley representation*, which characterises the functoriality and naturality conditions for the components of the representation.

As for notation, we use $A \to B$ to denote both the type of a morphism in a category, and the set of all functions from A to B (the exponential object in **Set**). Also, for brevity, we write the application of a bifunctor to two arguments, e.g., $G(X, Y)$, without parentheses, as GXY. We begin with the following definition:

Definition 1 (see [16]). *Let $\mathscr{C}, \mathscr{D}$ be categories, and $G, H : \mathscr{C}^{\mathrm{op}} \times \mathscr{C} \to \mathscr{D}$ be functors. Then, a collection of $\mathscr{D}$-morphisms $\theta_X : GXX \to HXX$ indexed by $\mathscr{C}$-objects is called a Barr-dinatural transformation if it is the case that for all objects A in $\mathscr{D}$, objects X, Y in $\mathscr{C}$, morphisms $f_1 : A \to GXX$, $f_2 : A \to GYY$ in $\mathscr{D}$, and a morphism $g : X \to Y$ in $\mathscr{C}$,*

$$
\begin{array}{ccc}
 & GXX & \\
{}^{f_1}\nearrow & & \searrow^{GXg} \\
A & & GXY \\
{}_{f_2}\searrow & & \nearrow_{GgY} \\
 & GYY &
\end{array}
\quad commutes, \; then \quad
\begin{array}{ccc}
GXX & \xrightarrow{\;\theta_X\;} & HXX \\
{}^{f_1}\nearrow & & \searrow^{HXg} \\
A & & HXY \\
{}_{f_2}\searrow & & \nearrow_{HgY} \\
GYY & \xrightarrow{\;\theta_Y\;} & HYY
\end{array}
\quad commutes.
$$

An important property of Barr-dinaturality is that the component-wise composition gives a well-behaved notion of vertical composition of two such transformations. The connection between Barr-dinatural transformations and Cayley representations is suggested by the fact, shown by Paré and Román [16], that the collection of such transformations of type $H \to H$ for the **Set**-bifunctor $H(X, Y) = X \to Y$ is isomorphic to the set of natural numbers. The latter, equipped with addition and zero (or the former with composition and the identity transformation, respectively), is simply the free monoid with a single generator, that is, an instance of (1) with $PX = X$ and $A = 1$.

For the remainder of this section, assume that $\mathscr{T}$ is a category, while $F :$ **Set** $\to \mathscr{T}$ is a functor with a right adjoint $U : \mathscr{T} \to$ **Set**. Intuitively, $\mathscr{T}$ is a category of algebras of some theory, and U is the forgetful functor. Then, the monad generated by the theory is given by the composition UF. For a function $f : A \to UX$, we write $\widehat{f} = Uf' : UFA \to UX$, where $f' : FA \to X$ is the contraposition of f via the adjunction (intuitively, the unique homomorphism induced by the freeness of the algebra FA).

Definition 2. *A* tight Cayley representation *of $\mathscr{T}$ with respect to $F \dashv U$ consists of the following components:*

*(a) A bifunctor $R : $ **Set**$^{\mathrm{op}} \times$ **Set** $\to$ **Set**,*
(b) For each set X, an object $\mathbb{R}X$ in $\mathscr{T}$, such that $U\mathbb{R}X = RXX$,
(c) For all sets A, X, Y and functions $f_1 : A \to RXX$, $f_2 : A \to RYY$, $g : X \to Y$, it is the case that

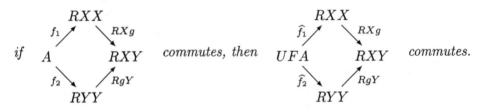

(d) For each object M in $\mathscr{T}$, a morphism $\sigma_M : M \to \mathbb{R}(UM)$ in $\mathscr{T}$, such that $U\sigma_M : UM \to R(UM)(UM)$ is Barr-dinatural in M,
(e) A Barr-dinatural transformation $\rho_M : R(UM)(UM) \to UM$, such that $\rho_M \cdot U\sigma_M = \mathrm{id}$,
(f) For each set X, a set of indices I_X and a family of functions $\mathrm{run}_{X,i} : RXX \to X$, where $i \in I_X$, such that $R(RXX)\mathrm{run}_X$ is a jointly monic family, and the following diagram commutes for all X and $i \in I_X$:

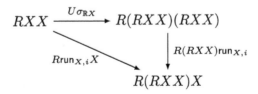

Note that the condition (c) states that the objects $\mathbb{R}$ are, in a sense, natural. Intuitively, understanding an object $\mathbb{R}X$ as an algebra, the condition states that the algebraic structure of $\mathbb{R}X$ does not really depend on the set X. The condition (f) may seem rather complicated: the intuition behind the technical formulation is that RXY behaves like a form of a function space (after all, we are interested in abstract *Cayley* representations), and $\mathrm{run}_{X,i}$ is an application to an argument specified by i, as in the example below. In such a case, the joint monicity becomes the extensional equality of functions.

Example 3. Let us check how Cayley representation for monoids fits the definition above: (a) The bifunctor is $RXY = X \to Y$. (b) The $\mathscr{T}$-object for a monoid M is the monoid $M \to M$ with $\gamma(f,g) = f \circ g$ and $\varepsilon = \text{id}$. (c) Given some elements $a, b, \ldots, c \in A$, we need to see that $g \circ f_1(a) \circ f_1(b) \circ \cdots \circ f_1(c) = f_2(a) \circ f_2(b) \circ \cdots \circ f_2(c) \circ g$. Fortunately, the assumption, which in this case becomes $g \circ f_1(a) = f_2(a) \circ g$ for all $a \in A$, allows us to "commute" g from one side of the chain of function compositions to the other. (d) $\sigma_M(a) = b \mapsto \gamma(a,b)$. It is easy to verify that it is a homomorphism. The Barr-dinaturality condition: assuming $f(m) = n$ for some $m \in M$ and $n \in N$, and a homomorphism $f : M \to N$, it is the case that, omitting the U functor, $RfN(\sigma_N(n)) = RfN(\sigma_N(f(m))) = b \mapsto \gamma(f(m), f(b)) = b \mapsto f(\gamma(m,b)) = RMf(\sigma_M(m))$, where the equalities can be explained respectively as: assumption in the definition of Barr-dinaturality, unfolding definitions, homomorphism, unfolding definitions. (e) $\rho_M(f) = f(\varepsilon)$. It is easy to show that it is Barr-dinatural; note that we need to use the fact that $\mathscr{T}$-morphisms (that is, monoid homomorphisms) preserve ε. (f) We define $I_X = X$, while $\text{run}_{X,i}(f) = f(i)$.

The first main result of this paper states that given a tight representation of $\mathscr{T}$ with respect to $F \dashv U$, the monad given by the composition UF can be alternatively defined using a continuation-like monad constructed with sets of Barr-dinatural transformations:

Theorem 4. *For a tight Cayley representation R with respect to $F \dashv U$, elements of the set UFA are in 1-1 correspondence with Barr-dinatural transformations of the type $(A \to RXX) \to RXX$. In particular, this means that the latter form a set. Moreover, this correspondence gives a monad isomorphism between UF and the evident continuation-like structure on (2), given by the unit $(\eta_A(a))_X(f) = f(a)$ and the Kleisli extension $(f^*(k))_X(g) = k_X(a \mapsto (f(a))_X(g))$.*

We denote the set of all Barr-dinatural transformations from the bifunctor $(X,Y) \mapsto A \to RXY$ to R as $\forall X.(A \to RXX) \to RXX$. This gives us a monad similar in shape to the continuation monad, or, more generally, Kock's codensity monad [12] embodied using the formula for right Kan extensions as ends. One important difference with the codensity monad (except, of course, the fact that we have bifunctors on the right-hand sides of arrows) is that we use Barr-dinatural transformations instead of the usual dinatural transformations [3]. Indeed, if we use ends instead of $\forall$, the end $\int_X (A \to RXX) \to RXX$ is given as the collection of all dinatural transformations of the given shape. It is known, however, that even in the simple case when $A = 1$ and $RXY = X \to Y$, this collection is too big to be a set (see the discussion in [16]), hence such end does not exist.

3   Multi-sorted Equational Theories with a Main Sort

The equational theories that we generate in Sect. 4 are multi-sorted, which is useful for trimming down the combinatorial complexity of the result. This turns

out to be, in our view, essential in understanding what computational effects
they actually represent. In this section, we give a quick overview of what kind
of equational theories we work with, and discuss the construction of their free
algebras.

We need to discuss the free algebras here, since we want the freeness to be
with respect to a forgetful functor to **Set**, rather than to the usual category of
sorted sets; compare [26]. This is because we want the equational theories to
generate monads on **Set**, as described in the previous section. In particular, we
are interested in theories in which one of the sorts is chosen as the *main* one, and
work with the functor that forgets not only the structure, but also the carriers
of all the other sorts, only preserving the main one. Luckily, this functor can be
factored as a composition of two forgetful functors, each with an obvious left
adjoint.

In detail, assume a finite set of sorts $S = \{\Omega, K_1, \ldots, K_d\}$ for some $d \in \mathbb{N}$,
where Ω is the main sort. The category of sorted sets is simply the category
$\mathbf{Set}^{|S|}$, where $|S|$ is the discrete category generated by the set S. More explicitly,
the objects of $\mathbf{Set}^{|S|}$ are tuples of sets (one for each sort), while morphisms are
tuples of functions. Given an S-sorted finitary theory $\mathfrak{T}$, we denote the category
of its algebras as $\mathfrak{T}$-Alg. To see that the forgetful functor from $\mathfrak{T}$-Alg to **Set** has
a left adjoint, consider the following composition of adjunctions:

$$\mathbf{Set} \underset{(X, A_1, \ldots, A_d) \,\mapsto\, X}{\overset{X \,\mapsto\, (X, \emptyset, \ldots, \emptyset)}{\rightleftarrows}} \mathbf{Set}^{|S|} \underset{\text{carriers}}{\overset{\text{free}}{\rightleftarrows}} \mathfrak{T}\text{-Alg}$$

This means that the free algebra for each sort has the carrier given by the set
of terms of the given sort (with variables appearing only at positions intended
for the main sort Ω) quotiented by the congruence induced by the equations.
This kind of composition of adjunctions is similar to [18], but in this case the
compound right adjoints of the theories given in the next section are monadic.

4   Theories from Polynomial Cayley Representations

In this section, we introduce algebraic theories that are tightly Cayley-
represented by $PX \to X$ for a polynomial functor P. Notation-wise, whenever
we write $i \leq k$ for a fixed $k \in \mathbb{N}$, we mean that i is a natural number in
the range $1, \ldots, k$, and use $[x_i]_{i \leq k}$ to denote a sequence $x_1, \ldots, x_k$. The latter
notation is used also in arguments of functions and operations, so $f([x_i]_{i \leq k})$
means $f(x_1, \ldots, x_k)$, while $f(x, [y_i]_{i \leq k})$ means $f(x, y_1, \ldots, y_k)$. We sometimes
use double indexing; for example, by $\prod_{i=1}^{k} \prod_{j=1}^{t_i} X_{i,j} \to Y$ for some $[t_i]_{i \leq k}$,
we mean the type $X_{1,1} \times \cdots \times X_{1,t_1} \times \cdots \times X_{k,1} \times \cdots \times X_{k,t_k} \to Y$. This
is matched by a double-nested notation in arguments, that is, $f([[x_i^j]_{j \leq t_i}]_{i \leq k})$
means $f(x_1^1, \ldots, x_1^{t_1}, \ldots, x_k^1, \ldots, x_k^{t_k})$. Also, whenever we want to repeat an argument k-times, we write $[x]_k$; for example, $f([x]_3)$ means $f(x, x, x)$. Because we
use a lot of sub- and superscripts as indices, we do not use the usual notation for

exponentiation. This means that x^i always denotes some x at index i, while a k-fold product of some type X, ordinarily denoted X^k, is written as $\prod^k X$. We use the $[\![\text{-}]\!]$ brackets to denote the interpretation of sorts and operations in an algebra (that is, a model of the theory). If the algebra is clear from the context, we skip the brackets in the interpretation of operations.

For the rest of the paper, let $d \in \mathbb{N}$ (the number of monomials in the polynomial) and sequences of natural numbers $[c_i]_{i \leq d}$ and $[e_i]_{i \leq d}$ (the coeffcients and exponents respectively) define the following polynomial endofunctor on **Set**:

$$PX = \sum_{i=1}^{d} c_i \times \prod^{e_i} X, \tag{3}$$

where c_i is an overloaded notation for the set $\{1, \ldots, c_i\}$. With this data, we define the following equational theory:

Definition 5. *Assuming d, $[c_i]_{i \leq d}$, and $[e_i]_{i \leq d}$ as above, we define the following equational theory $\mathfrak{T}$:*

- *Sorts:*

$$\Omega \qquad \text{(main sort)}$$
$$K_i, \text{ for all } i \leq d$$

- *Operations:*

$$\text{cons} : \prod_{i=1}^{d} \prod^{c_i} K_i \to \Omega$$
$$\pi_i^j : \Omega \to K_i, \text{ for } i \leq d \text{ and } j \leq c_i$$
$$\varepsilon_i^j : K_i, \text{ for } i \leq d \text{ and } j \leq e_i$$
$$\gamma_i^j : K_j \times \prod^{e_j} K_i \to K_i, \text{ for } i, j \leq d$$

- *Equations:*

$$\pi_i^j(\text{cons}([[x_i^j]_{j \leq c_i}]_{i \leq d})) = x_i^j \qquad \text{(beta-}\pi)$$
$$\text{cons}([[\pi_i^j(x)]_{j \leq c_i}]_{i \leq d}) = x \qquad \text{(eta-}\pi)$$
$$\gamma_i^j(\varepsilon_j^k, [x_t]_{t \leq e_j}) = x_k \qquad \text{(beta-}\varepsilon)$$
$$\gamma_i^i(x, [\varepsilon_i^j]_{j \leq e_i}) = x \qquad \text{(eta-}\varepsilon)$$
$$\gamma_i^j(\gamma_j^k(x, [y_t]_{t \leq e_k}), [z_s]_{s \leq e_j}) = \gamma_i^k(x, [\gamma_i^j(y_t, [z_s]_{s \leq e_j})]_{t \leq e_k}) \qquad \text{(assoc-}\gamma)$$

Thus, in the theory $\mathfrak{T}$, there is a main sort Ω, which we think of as corresponding to the entire functor, and one sort K_i for each "monomial" $\prod^{e_i} X$. Then, we can think of Ω as a tuple containing elements of each sort, where each sort K_i has exactly c_i occurrences. The fact that Ω is a tuple, which is witnessed by the cons and π operations equipped with the standard equations for tupling and projections, is not too surprising—one should keep in mind that $\mathfrak{T}$ is a theory represented by the type $PX \to X$, which can be equivalently given as the *product* of function spaces $c_i \times \prod^{e_i} X \to X$ for all $i \leq d$.

Each operation γ_i^j can be used to compose an element of K_j and e_j elements of K_i to obtain an element of K_i. The ε constants can be seen as selectors: in (beta-ε), ε_j^k in the first argument of γ_i^j selects the k-th argument of the sort K_i, while the (eta-ε) equation states that composing a value of K_i with the successive selectors of K_i gives back the original value. The equation (assoc-γ) states that the composition of values is associative in an appropriate sense. In Sect. 5, we provide a reading of the theory $\mathfrak{T}$ as a specification of a computational effect for different choices of d, c_i, and e_i.

Remark 6. If it is the case that $e_i = e_j$ for some $i, j \leq d$, then the sorts K_i and K_j are isomorphic. This means that in every algebra of such a theory, there is an isomorphism of sorts $\varphi : [\![K_i]\!] \to [\![K_j]\!]$, given by $\varphi(x) = \gamma_j^i(x, [\varepsilon_j^k]_{k \leq e_i})$. This suggests an alternative setting, in which instead of having a single $c_i \times \prod^{e_i} X$ comoponent, we can have c_i components of the shape $\prod^{e_i} X$. In such a setting, the equational theory $\mathfrak{T}$ in Definition 5 would be slightly simpler—specifically, there would be no need for double-indexing in the types of cons and π. On the downside, this would obfuscate the connection with computational effects described in Sect. 5 and some conjured extensions in Sect. 7.

The theory $\mathfrak{T}$ has a tight Cayley representation using functions from P, as detailed in the following theorem. This gives us the second main result of this paper: by Theorem 4, the theory $\mathfrak{T}$ is the equational theory of the monad (1). The notation in_i means the i-th inclusion of the coproduct in the functor P.

Theorem 7. *The equational theory $\mathfrak{T}$ from Definition 5 is tightly Cayley-represented by the following data:*

- *The bifunctor $RXY = PX \to Y$,*
- *For a set X, the following algebra:*
  - *Carriers of sorts:*

$$[\![\Omega]\!] = RXX$$
$$[\![K_i]\!] = \prod^{e_i} X \to X$$

  - *Interpretation of operations:*

$$[\![\text{cons}]\!]([[f_k^j]_{j \leq c_k}]_{k \leq d})(\text{in}_i(c, [x_t]_{t \leq e_i})) = f_i^c([x_t]_{t \leq e_i})$$
$$[\![\pi_i^j]\!](f)([x_t]_{t \leq e_i}) = f(\text{in}_i(j, [x_t]_{t \leq e_i}))$$
$$[\![\varepsilon_i^j]\!]([x_t]_{t \leq e_i}) = x_j$$
$$[\![\gamma_i^j]\!](f, [g_k]_{k \leq e_j})([x_t]_{t \leq e_i}) = f([g_k([x_t]_{t \leq e_i})]_{k \leq e_j})$$

- *The homomorphism σ_M for the main sort and sorts K_i:*

$$\sigma_M^\Omega(m)(\text{in}_i(c, [x_t]_{t \leq e_i})) = \text{cons}([[\gamma_k^i(\pi_i^c(m), [\pi_k^j(x_t)]_{t \leq e_i})]_{j \leq e_k}]_{k \leq d})$$
$$\sigma_M^i(s)([x_t]_{t \leq e_i}) = \text{cons}([[\gamma_k^i(s, [\pi_k^j(x_t)]_{t \leq e_i})]_{j \leq e_k}]_{k \leq d})$$

– *The transformation ρ_M:*

$$\rho_M(f) = \text{cons}([[\pi_k^j(f(\text{in}_k(j, [\text{cons}([w_r^f]_{r<k}, [\varepsilon_k^t]_{c_k}, [w_r^f]_{k<r\leq d})]_{t\leq e_k})))]_{j\leq c_k}]_{k\leq d})$$
$$\text{where } w_r^f = [\pi_r^c(f(\text{in}_r(c, [\varepsilon_r^j]_{j\leq e_r})))]_{c\leq c_r}$$

– *The set of indices $I_X = PX$ and the functions* $\text{run}_{X,i}(f) = f(i)$.

In the representing algebra, it is the case that each $[\![K_i]\!]$ represents one monomial, as mentioned in the description of $\mathfrak{T}$, while $[\![\Omega]\!]$ is the appropriate tuple of representations of monomials, which is encoded as a single function from a coproduct (in our opinion, this encoding turns out to be much more readable on paper), while cons and π are indeed given by tupling and projections. For each $i \leq d$, the function ε_i^j simply returns its j-th argument, while γ is interpreted as the usual composition of multi-argument functions.

Homomorphisms between multi-sorted algebras are defined as operation-preserving functions for each sort, so σ is defined for the sort Ω and for each sort K_i. In general, the point of Cayley representations is to encode an element m of an algebra M using its possible behaviours with other elements of the algebra. It is no different here: for each sort K_i at the c-th occurrence in the tuple, the function σ^Ω packs (using cons) all possible compositions (by means of γ) of values of K_i with the "components" of m (extracted using π). The same happens for each $s \in [\![K_i]\!]$ in $\sigma_M^i(s)$, but there is no need to unpack s, as it is already a value of a single sort.

The transformation ρ_M is a bit more complicated. The argument f is, in general, a function from a coproduct to M, but we cannot simply apply f to one value $\text{in}_i(\ldots)$ for some sort K_i, as we would obviously lose the information about the components in different sorts. This is why we need to apply f to all possible sorts with ε in the right place to ensure that we recover the original value. We extract the information about particular sorts from such values, and combine them using cons. Interestingly, the elements of w_r^f could actually be replaced by any expression of the appropriate sort that is preserved by homomorphisms, assuming that f is also preserved. This is needed to ensure that ρ is Barr-dinatural (the fact that f is preserved by homomorphisms is exactly the assumption in the definition of Barr-dinaturality). For example, if $e_r > 0$ for some $r \leq d$, one can define w_r^f simply as $[\varepsilon_r^j]_{c_r}$ for some $j \leq e_r$. The complicated expression in the definition of w_r^f is a way to produce values also for sorts K_r with $e_r = 0$, which do not have any ε constants.

5 Effects Modeled by Polynomial Representations

Now we describe what kind of computational effects are captured by the theories introduced in the previous section. It turns out that they all are different compositions of finite mutable state and backtracking nondeterminism. These compositions include the two most basic ones: when the state is *local* for each nondeterministic branch, and when it is *global* to the entire computation.

In the following, if there is only one object of a given kind, we skip the indices. For example, if for some i, it is the case that $e_i = 1$, we write ε_i instead of ε_i^1. If $d = 1$, we skip the subscripts altogether.

5.1 Backtracking Nondeterminism via Monoids

We recover the original Cayley theorem for monoids instantiating Theorem 7 with $PX = X$, that is, $d = 1$ and $c_1 = e_1 = 1$. In this case, we obtain two sorts, Ω and K, while the equations (beta-π) and (eta-π) instantiate respectively as follows:

$$\pi(\mathsf{cons}(x)) = x, \quad \mathsf{cons}(\pi(x)) = x$$

This means that both sorts are isomorphic, so one can think of this theory as being single-sorted. Of course, this is always the case if $d = 1$ and $c_1 = 1$. Since $e_1 = 1$, the operation γ is binary and there is a single ε constant. The equations (beta-ε) and (eta-ε) say, respectively, that ε is the left and right unit of γ, that is:

$$\gamma(\varepsilon, x) = x, \quad \gamma(x, \varepsilon) = x$$

Interestingly, the two unit laws for monoids are symmetrical, but in general the (beta-ε) and (eta-ε) equations are not. One should note that the symmetry is already broken when one implements free monoids (that is, lists) in a programming language: in the usual right-nested implementation, the "beta" rule is part of the definition of the **append** function, while the "eta" rule is a theorem. The (assoc-γ) equation instantiates as the associativity of γ:

$$\gamma(\gamma(x, y), z) = \gamma(x, \gamma(y, z))$$

5.2 Finite Mutable State

For $n \in \mathbb{N}$, if we take $PX = n$, that is, $d = 1$, $c_1 = n$ and $e_1 = 0$, we obtain the equational theory of a single mutable cell in which the set of possible states is $\{1, \ldots, n\}$. There are two sorts in the theory: Ω and K. The sort K does not have any interesting structure on its own, as there are no constants ε, and the equation (eta-ε) instantiates to

$$\gamma(x) = x,$$

which means that γ is necessarily an identity. The fact that this theory is indeed the theory of state becomes apparent when we identify Ω as a sort of computations that require some initial state to proceed, and K as computations that produce a final state. Then, the operations $\pi^j : \Omega \to K$ ($j \leq n$) are the "update" operations, where π^j sets the current state to j, while $\mathsf{cons} : \prod^n K \to \Omega$ is the "lookup" operation, in which the j-th argument is the computation to be executed if the current state is j. The equations (beta-π), for all $j \leq n$, and (eta-π) state respectively:

$$\pi^j(\mathsf{cons}([x_i]_{i \leq n})) = x_j, \quad \mathsf{cons}([\pi^i(x)]_{i \leq n}) = x$$

These equations embody the natural behaviour rules for this limited form of state. The former reads that setting the current state to j and then proceeding with the computation x_i if the current state is i is the same thing as simply proceeding with x_j (note that x_j is of the sort K, hence it does not use the information that the current state has just been updated to j, so there is no need to keep the π^j operation on the right-hand side of the equation). The latter states that if the current state is i and we set the current state to i, it is the same thing as not changing the state at all (note that x does not depend on the current state, as it is the same in every argument of cons).

Interestingly, the presentations of equational theories for state in the literature (for example, [7,23]) are all single-sorted. Such a setting can be recovered by defining the following macro-operations on the sort Ω:

$$\mathsf{put}^j : \Omega \to \Omega \qquad\qquad \mathsf{get} : \textstyle\prod^n \Omega \to \Omega$$

$$\mathsf{put}^j(x) = \mathsf{cons}([\pi^j(x)]_n) \qquad \mathsf{get}([x_i]_{i \leq n}) = \mathsf{cons}([\pi^i(x_i)]_{i \leq n})$$

The trick here is that the get operation does not change the state (by setting the new state to the current one), while put does not depend on the current state (by having the same computation in every argument of cons). The usual four equations for the interaction of put and get can be obtained by unfolding the definitions and using the (beta-π) and (eta-π) equations:

$$\mathsf{put}^j(\mathsf{put}^k(x)) = \mathsf{put}^k(x) \qquad\qquad \mathsf{put}^j(\mathsf{get}([x_i]_{i \leq n})) = \mathsf{put}^j(x_j)$$

$$\mathsf{get}([\mathsf{get}([x_i]_{i \leq n})]_n) = \mathsf{get}([x_i]_{i \leq n}) \qquad \mathsf{get}([\mathsf{put}^i(x_i)]_{i \leq n}) = \mathsf{get}([x_i]_{i \leq n})$$

The connection with the implementation of state in programming becomes evident when we take a closer look at the endofunctor of the induced monad from Theorem 4. Consider the following informal calculation:

$$
\begin{aligned}
&\forall X.(A \to n \to X) \to n \to X \\
\cong\ &\forall X.n \to (A \to n \to X) \to X &&\text{(flipping the arguments)} \\
\cong\ &n \to \forall X.(A \to n \to X) \to X &&\text{($\forall$ commutes with arrows)} \\
\cong\ &n \to \forall X.(A \times n \to X) \to X &&\text{(Curry)} \\
\cong\ &n \to A \times n &&\text{(Church)}
\end{aligned}
$$

This means that not only do we prove that the equational theory corresponds to the usual state monad, but we can actually *derive* the implementation of state as the endofunctor $A \mapsto (n \to A \times n)$.

5.3   Backtracking with Local State

We obtain one way to combine nondeterminism with state using the functor $PX = n \times X$, for $n \in \mathbb{N}$, that is, $d = 1$, $c_1 = n$ and $e_1 = 1$. It has two sorts, Ω and K, which play roles similar to those detailed in the previous section. However, this time K additionally has the structure of a monoid. This gives us the theory of backtracking with *local* state, which means that whenever we make a choice using the γ operation, the computations in each argument carry separate, non-interfering states. In particular, in a computation $\gamma(x, y)$, both subcomputations x and y start with the same state, which is the initial state of the entire computation. This non-interference is guaranteed simply by the system of sorts: the arguments of γ are of the sort K, which means that the stateful computations inside the arguments begin with π, which sets a new state.

We can also obtain a single-sorted theory, similar to the case of the pure state. To the put and get macro-operations, we add choice and failure as follows:

$$\text{choose} : \Omega \times \Omega \to \Omega \qquad\qquad \text{fail} : \Omega$$
$$\text{choose}(x, y) = \text{cons}([\gamma(\pi^j(x), \pi^j(y))]_{j \leq n}) \qquad \text{fail} = \text{cons}([\varepsilon]_n)$$

Then, the locality of state can be summarised by the following equality, which is easy to show using the (beta-π) and (eta-π) equations:

$$\text{put}^k(\text{choose}(x, y)) = \text{choose}(\text{put}^k(x), \text{put}^k(y))$$

5.4 Backtracking with Global State

Another way to compose nondeterminism and state is by using *global* state, which is obtained for $n \in \mathbb{N}$ and $PX = X^n$, that is, $d = 1$, $c_1 = 1$, and $e_1 = n$. As in the case of pure backtracking nondeterminism, it means that the sorts Ω and K are isomorphic. The intuitive understanding of the expression $\gamma(x, [y_i]_{i \leq n})$ is: first perform the computation x, and then the computation y_i, where i is the final state of the computation x. The operation ε^j is: fail, but set the current state to j. In this case, the equations (beta-ε) instantiate to the following for all $j \leq n$:

$$\gamma(\varepsilon^j, [y_i]_{i \leq n}) = y_j$$

It states that if the first computation fails but sets the state to j, the next step is to try the computation y_j. Note that there is no other way to give a new state than via failure, but this can be circumvented using $\gamma(x, [\varepsilon^k]_n)$ to set the state to k after performing x. The (eta-ε) instantiates to:

$$\gamma(x, [\varepsilon^j]_{j \leq n}) = x$$

This reads that if we execute x and then set the current state to the resulting state of x, it is the same as just executing x.

6 Direct-Style Implementation

Free algebras of the theory $\mathfrak{T}$ from Definition 5 can also be presented as terms of a certain shape. They are best described as terms built using the operations from $\mathfrak{T}$ that are well-typed according to the following typing rules, where the types are called Ω, K_i, and P_i for $i \leq d$. The type of the entire term is Ω, and VAR(x) means that x is a variable.

$$\frac{[[t_i^j : K_i]_{j \leq c_i}]_{i \leq d}}{\mathsf{cons}([[t_i^j]_{j \leq c_i}]_{i \leq d}) : \Omega} \qquad \varepsilon_i^j : K_i \qquad \frac{t : P_j \quad [w_k : K_i]_{k \leq e_j}}{\gamma_i^j(t, [w_k]_{k \leq e_j}) : K_i} \qquad \frac{\mathrm{VAR}(x)}{\pi_i^j(x) : P_i}$$

Note that even though variables appear as arguments to the operations π, they are not of the type Ω. This means that the entire term cannot be a variable, as it is always constructed with cons as the outermost operation. Each argument of cons is a term of the type K_i for an appropriate i, which is built out of the operations ε and γ. Note that the first argument of γ is always a variable wrapped in π, while all the other arguments are again terms of the type K_i. Overall, such terms can be captured as the following endofunctors on **Set**, where W^i represents terms of the type K_i, while W^Ω represents terms of the type Ω. By $\mu Y.GY$ we mean the carrier of the initial algebra of an endofunctor G.

$$W^i X = \mu Y . e_i + \sum_{j=1}^{d} \left(\sum^{c_i} X \right) \times \prod^{e_j} Y$$
$$W^\Omega X = \prod_{i=1}^{d} \prod^{c_i} W^i X$$

Clearly, e_i in the definition of W^i represents the ε_i constants, while the second component of the coproduct is a choice between the γ_i operations with appropriate arguments.

It is the case that every term of the sort Ω can be normalised to a term of the type Ω by a term-rewriting system obtained by orienting the "beta" and "assoc" equations left to right, and eta-expanding variables at the top-level:

$$\pi_i^j(\mathsf{cons}([[x_i^j]_{j \leq c_i}]_{i \leq d})) \rightsquigarrow x_i^j$$
$$\gamma_i^j(\varepsilon_j^k, [x_t]_{t \leq e_j}) \rightsquigarrow x_k$$
$$\gamma_i^j(\gamma_j^k(x, [y_t]_{t \leq e_k}), [z_s]_{s \leq e_j}) \rightsquigarrow \gamma_i^k(x, [\gamma_i^j(y_t, [z_s]_{s \leq e_j})]_{t \leq e_k})$$
$$x \rightsquigarrow \mathsf{cons}([[\gamma_i^i(\pi_i^j(x), [\varepsilon_i^k]_{k \leq e_i})]_{j \leq c_i}]_{i \leq d})$$

This term rewriting system gives rise to a natural implementation of the monadic structure, where the "beta" and "assoc" rules normalise the two-level term structure, thus implementing the monadic multiplication, while the eta-expansion rule implements the monadic unit.

7   Discussion

The idea for employing Cayley representations to explore implementations of monads induced by equational theories is inspired by Hinze [8], who suggested a connection between codensity monads, Church representation of lists, and the Cayley theorem for monoids. We note that Hinze's discussion is informal, but he suggests using ends, which, as we discuss in Sect. 2, is not sound.

Most of related work follows one of two main paths: it either concentrates on algebraic explanation of monads already used in programming and semantics (for example, $[11, 19, 23]$), or on the general connection between different kinds of algebraic theories and computational effects, but without much interest in whether it leads to structures implementable in a programming language. Some exceptions are the construction of the sum of a theory and a free theory [9] or the sum of ideal monads [6]. What we propose in Sect. 4 is a form of a "functional combinatorics": given a type, what kind of algebra describes the possible values?

As our approach veers off the main paths of the recent work on effects, there are many possible directions of future work. One interesting direction would be to generalise **Set**, the base category used throughout this paper, to more abstract categories. After all, we want to talk about structures definable only in terms of (co)products, exponentials, and quantifiers—which are all constructions whose universal properties are singled out and explored using (co)cartesian (or even monoidal) closed categories. However, the current development relies heavily on the particular properties of **Set**, such as extensional equality of functions, which appears in disguise in the condition (f) in Definition 2.

One can also try to extend the type used as a Cayley representation. For example, we could consider the polynomial P in (3) to range over the space of all sets, that is, allow the coefficients c_i to vary over sets rather than natural numbers. In the Cayley representation, it would be enough to consider functions from c_i in place of c_i-fold products. We would immediately gain expressiveness, as the obtained state monad would no longer need to be defined only for a finite set of possible states. On the flip side, this would make the resulting theory infinitary – which, of course, is not uncommon in the field of algebraic treatment of computational effects. However, we decide to stick to the simplest possible setting in this paper, which greatly simplifies the presentation, but still gives us some novel observations, like the fact that the theory of finite state is simply the theory of 2-sorted tuples in Sect. 5.2, or the novel theory of backtracking nondeterminism with global state in Sect. 5.4. Other future extensions that we believe are worth exploring include iterating the construction to obtain a from of a distributive tensor (compare Rivas *et al.*'s [25] "double" representation of near-semirings) or quantifying over more variables, leading to less interaction between sorts.

Acknowledgements. We thank the reviewers for their insightful comments and suggestions.

References

1. Bird, R.: Functional pearl: a program to solve Sudoku. J. Funct. Program. **16**(6), 671–679 (2006). http://dx.doi.org/10.1017/S0956796806006058
2. Bloom, S.L., Ésik, Z., Manes, E.G.: A Cayley theorem for Boolean algebras. Am. Math. Monthly **97**(9), 831–833 (1990). http://dx.doi.org/10.2307/2324751
3. Dubuc, E., Street, R.: Dinatural transformations. In: MacLane, S., et al. (eds.) Reports of the Midwest Category Seminar IV, pp. 126–137. Springer, Heidelberg (1970). https://doi.org/10.1007/BFb0060443

4. Eilenberg, S., Moore, J.C.: Adjoint functors and triples. Illinois J. Math. **9**(3), 381–398 (1965). https://projecteuclid.org:443/euclid.ijm/1256068141
5. Ésik, Z.: A Cayley theorem for ternary algebras. Int. J. Algebra Comput. **8**, 311–316 (1998)
6. Ghani, N., Uustalu, T.: Coproducts of ideal monads. ITA **38**(4), 321–342 (2004). https://doi.org/10.1051/ita:2004016
7. Gibbons, J., Hinze, R.: Just do it: simple monadic equational reasoning. In: Chakravarty, M.M.T., Hu, Z., Danvy, O. (eds.) Proceeding of the 16th ACM SIGPLAN international conference on Functional Programming, ICFP 2011, Tokyo, Japan, 19–21 September 2011, pp. 2–14. ACM (2011). http://doi.acm.org/10.1145/2034773.2034777
8. Hinze, R.: Kan extensions for program optimisation *Or*: Art and Dan explain an old trick. In: Gibbons, J., Nogueira, P. (eds.) MPC 2012. LNCS, vol. 7342, pp. 324–362. Springer, Heidelberg (2012). https://doi.org/10.1007/978-3-642-31113-0_16
9. Hyland, M., Plotkin, G.D., Power, J.: Combining effects: sum and tensor. Theor. Comput. Sci. **357**(1–3), 70–99 (2006). https://doi.org/10.1016/j.tcs.2006.03.013
10. Hyland, M., Power, J.: The category theoretic understanding of universal algebra: Lawvere theories and monads. Electron. Notes Theor. Comput. Sci. **172**, 437–458 (2007). https://doi.org/10.1016/j.entcs.2007.02.019
11. Jaskelioff, M., Moggi, E.: Monad transformers as monoid transformers. Theor. Comput. Sci. **411**(51–52), 4441–4466 (2010). https://doi.org/10.1016/j.tcs.2010.09.011
12. Kock, A.: Continuous Yoneda representation of a small category (1966). Aarhus University preprint. http://home.math.au.dk/kock/CYRSC.pdf
13. Linton, F.: Some aspects of equational categories. In: Eilenberg, S., Harrison, D.K., MacLane, S., Röhrl, H. (eds.) Proceedings of the Conference on Categorical Algebra, pp. 84–94. Springer, Heidelberg (1966). https://doi.org/10.1007/978-3-642-99902-4_3
14. Moggi, E.: Notions of computation and monads. Inf. Comput. **93**(1), 55–92 (1991). https://doi.org/10.1016/0890-5401(91)90052-4
15. Mulry, P.S.: Strong monads, algebras and fixed points. London Mathematical Society Lecture Note Series, pp. 202–216. Cambridge University Press, New York (1992)
16. Paré, R., Román, L.: Dinatural numbers. J. Pure Appl. Algebra **128**(1), 33–92 (1998). http://www.sciencedirect.com/science/article/pii/S0022404997000364
17. Piróg, M.: Eilenberg-Moore monoids and backtracking monad transformers. In: Atkey, R., Krishnaswami, N.R. (eds.) Proceedings of 6th Workshop on Mathematically Structured Functional Programming, MSFP@ETAPS 2016, Eindhoven, Netherlands, 8th April 2016. EPTCS, vol. 207, pp. 23–56 (2016). https://doi.org/10.4204/EPTCS.207.2
18. Piróg, M., Schrijvers, T., Wu, N., Jaskelioff, M.: Syntax and semantics for operations with scopes. In: Proceedings of the 33rd Annual ACM/IEEE Symposium on Logic in Computer Science. LICS 2018, pp. 809–818. ACM, New York (2018). http://doi.acm.org/10.1145/3209108.3209166
19. Piróg, M., Staton, S.: Backtracking with cut via a distributive law and left-zero monoids. J. Funct. Program. **27**, e17 (2017). https://doi.org/10.1017/S0956796817000077
20. Plotkin, G.: Adequacy for algebraic effects with state. In: Fiadeiro, J.L., Harman, N., Roggenbach, M., Rutten, J. (eds.) CALCO 2005. LNCS, vol. 3629, pp. 51–51. Springer, Heidelberg (2005). https://doi.org/10.1007/11548133_3

21. Plotkin, G., Power, J.: Adequacy for algebraic effects. In: Honsell, F., Miculan, M. (eds.) FoSSaCS 2001. LNCS, vol. 2030, pp. 1–24. Springer, Heidelberg (2001). https://doi.org/10.1007/3-540-45315-6_1
22. Plotkin, G.D., Power, J.: Semantics for algebraic operations. Electron. Notes Theor. Comput. Sci. **45**, 332–345 (2001). https://doi.org/10.1016/S1571-0661(04)80970-8
23. Plotkin, G., Power, J.: Notions of computation determine monads. In: Nielsen, M., Engberg, U. (eds.) FoSSaCS 2002. LNCS, vol. 2303, pp. 342–356. Springer, Heidelberg (2002). https://doi.org/10.1007/3-540-45931-6_24
24. Plotkin, G.D., Power, J.: Computational effects and operations: an overview. Electron. Notes Theor. Comput. Sci. **73**, 149–163 (2004). http://dx.doi.org/10.1016/j.entcs.2004.08.008
25. Rivas, E., Jaskelioff, M., Schrijvers, T.: From monoids to near-semirings: the essence of MonadPlus and alternative. In: Falaschi, M., Albert, E. (eds.) Proceedings of the 17th International Symposium on Principles and Practice of Declarative Programming, Siena, Italy, 14–16 July 2015. pp. 196–207. ACM (2015). http://doi.acm.org/10.1145/2790449.2790514
26. Tarlecki, A.: Some nuances of many-sorted universal algebra: a review. Bull. EATCS **104**, 89–111 (2011)
27. Vene, V., Ghani, N., Johann, P., Uustalu, T.: Parametricity and strong dinaturality (2006). https://www.ioc.ee/~tarmo/tday-voore/vene-slides.pdf

13

Rewriting Abstract Structures: Materialization Explained Categorically

Andrea Corradini[1], Tobias Heindel[2], Barbara König[3], Dennis Nolte[3(✉)], and Arend Rensink[4]

[1] Università di Pisa, Pisa, Italy
andrea@di.unipi.it
[2] University of Hawaii, Honolulu, USA
heindel@hawaii.edu
[3] Universität Duisburg-Essen, Duisburg, Germany
{barbara_koenig,dennis.nolte}@uni-due.de
[4] University of Twente, Enschede, Netherlands
arend.rensink@utwente.nl

Abstract. The paper develops an abstract (over-approximating) semantics for double-pushout rewriting of graphs and graph-like objects. The focus is on the so-called materialization of left-hand sides from abstract graphs, a central concept in previous work. The first contribution is an accessible, general explanation of how materializations arise from universal properties and categorical constructions, in particular partial map classifiers, in a topos. Second, we introduce an extension by enriching objects with annotations and give a precise characterization of strongest post-conditions, which are effectively computable under certain assumptions.

1 Introduction

Abstract interpretation [12] is a fundamental static analysis technique that applies not only to conventional programs but also to general infinite-state systems. Shape analysis [30], a specific instance of abstract interpretation, pioneered an approach for analyzing pointer structures that keeps track of information about the "heap topology", e.g., out-degrees or existence of certain paths. One central idea of shape analysis is *materialization*, which arises as companion operation to summarizing distinct objects that share relevant properties. Materialization, a.k.a. partial concretization, is also fundamental in verification approaches based on separation logic [5,6,24], where it is also known as rearrangement [26], a special case of frame inference. Shape analysis—construed in a wide sense—has been adapted to graph transformation [29], a general purpose modelling language for systems with dynamically evolving topology, such as network protocols and cyber-physical systems. Motivated by earlier work of shape analysis for graph transformation [1, 2, 4, 27, 28, 31], we want to put the materialization operation on a new footing, widening the scope of shape analysis.

A natural abstraction mechanism for transition systems with graphs as states "summarizes" all graphs over a specific *shape graph*. Thus a single graph is used as abstraction for all graphs that can be mapped homomorphically into it. Further annotations on shape graphs, such as cardinalities of preimages of its nodes and general first-order formulas, enable fine-tuning of the granularity of abstractions. While these natural abstraction principles have been successfully applied in previous work [1, 2, 4, 27, 28, 31], their companion materialization constructions are notoriously difficult to develop, hard to understand, and are redrawn from scratch for every single setting. Thus, we set out to explain materializations based on mathematical principles, namely universal properties (in the sense of category theory). In particular, partial map classifiers in the topos of graphs (and its slice categories) cover the purely structural aspects of materializations; this is related to final pullback complements [13], a fundamental construction of graph rewriting [7, 25]. Annotations of shape graphs are treated orthogonally via op-fibrations.

The first milestones of a general framework for shape analysis of graph transformation and more generally rewriting of objects in a topos are the following:

▷ A rewriting formalism for graph abstractions that lifts the rule-based rewriting from single graphs to *abstract graphs*; it is developed for (abstract) objects in a topos.

▷ We characterize the materialization operation for abstract objects in a topos in terms of partial map classifiers, giving a sound and complete description of all occurrences of right-hand sides of rules obtained by rewriting an abstract object.   → Sect. 3

▷ We decorate abstract objects with annotations from an ordered monoid and extend abstract rewriting to abstract objects with annotations. For the specific case of graphs, we consider global annotations (counting the nodes and edges in a graph), local annotations (constraining the degree of a node), and path annotations (constraining the existence of paths between certain nodes).   → Sect. 4

▷ We show that abstract rewriting with annotations is sound and, with additional assumptions, complete. Finally, we derive strongest post-conditions for the case of graph rewriting with annotations.   → Sect. 5

Related work: The idea of shape graphs together with shape constraints was pioneered in [30] where the constraints are specified in a three-valued logic. A similar approach was proposed in [31], using first-order formulas as constraints. In partner abstraction [3, 4], cluster abstraction [1, 2], and neighbourhood abstraction [28] nodes are clustered according to local criteria, such as their neighbourhood and the resulting graph structures are enriched with counting constraints, similar to our constraints. The idea of counting multiplicities of nodes and edges is also found in canonical graph shapes [27]. The uniform treatment of monoid annotations was introduced in previous work [9, 10, 20], in the context of type systems and with the aim of studying decidability and closure properties, but not for abstract rewriting.

2 Preliminaries

This paper presupposes familiarity with category theory and the topos structure of graphs. Some concepts (in particular elementary topoi, subobject and partial map classifiers, and slice categories) are defined in the full version of this paper [8], which also contains all the proofs.

The rewriting formalism for graphs and graph-like structures that we use throughout the paper is the double-pushout (DPO) approach [11]. Although it was originally introduced for graphs [16], it is well-defined in any category $\mathbf{C}$. However, certain standard results for graph rewriting require that the category $\mathbf{C}$ has "good" properties. The category of graphs is an elementary topos—an extremely rich categorical structure—but weaker conditions on $\mathbf{C}$, for instance adhesivity, have been studied [14, 15, 21].

Definition 1 (Double-pushout rewriting). *A production in $\mathbf{C}$ is a span of monos $L \hookleftarrow I \rightarrowtail R$ in $\mathbf{C}$; the objects L and R are called left- and right-hand side, respectively. A match of a production $p\colon L \hookleftarrow I \rightarrowtail R$ to an object X of $\mathbf{C}$ is a mono $m_L\colon L \rightarrowtail X$ in $\mathbf{C}$. The production p rewrites X to Y at m_L (resp. the match m_L to the co-match $m_R\colon R \to Y$) if the production and the match (and the co-match) extend to a diagram in $\mathbf{C}$, shown to the right, such that both squares are pushouts.*

$$
\begin{array}{ccccc}
L & \longleftarrow & I & \longrightarrow & R \\
m_L \downarrow & (\mathrm{PO}) & \downarrow & (\mathrm{PO}) & \downarrow m_R \\
X & \longleftarrow & C & \longrightarrow & Y
\end{array}
$$

In this case, we write $X \xRightarrow{p,m_L} Y$ (resp. $(L \xrightarrow{m_L} X) \xRightarrow{p} (R \xrightarrow{m_R} Y)$). We also write $X \xRightarrow{p,m_L}$ if there exists an object Y such that $X \xRightarrow{p,m_L} Y$ and $X \xRightarrow{p} Y$ if the specific match m_L is not relevant.

Given a production p and a match m_L, if there exist arrows $X \leftarrow C$ and $C \leftarrow I$ that make the left-hand square of the diagram in Definition 1 a pushout square, then the *gluing condition* is satisfied.

If $\mathbf{C}$ is an adhesive category (and thus also if it is a topos [22]) and the production consists of monos, then all remaining arrows of double-pushout diagrams of rewriting are monos [21] and the result of rewriting—be it the object Y or the co-match m_R—is unique (up to a canonical isomorphism).

2.1 Subobject Classifiers and Partial Map Classifiers of Graphs

A standard category for graph rewriting that is also a topos is the category of edge-labelled, directed graphs that we shall use in examples, as recalled in the next definition. Note that due to the generality of the categorical framework, our results also hold for various other forms of graphs, such as node-labelled graphs, hypergraphs, graphs with scopes or graphs with second-order edges.

Definition 2 (Category of graphs). *Let Λ be a fixed set of edge labels. A (Λ-labelled) graph is a tuple $G = (V_G, E_G, src_G, tgt_G, \ell_G)$ where V_G is a finite set of nodes, E_G is a finite set of edges, $src_G, tgt_G\colon E_G \to V_G$ are the source and target mappings and $\ell_G\colon E_G \to \Lambda$ is the labelling function.*

Let G, H be two Λ-labelled graphs. A graph morphism $\varphi \colon G \to H$ consists of two functions $\varphi_V \colon V_G \to V_H$, $\varphi_E \colon E_G \to E_H$, such that for each edge $e \in E_G$ we have $src_H(\varphi_E(e)) = \varphi_V(src_G(e))$, $tgt_H(\varphi_E(e)) = \varphi_V(tgt_G(e))$ and $\ell_H(\varphi_E(e)) = \ell_G(e)$. If φ_V, φ_E are both bijective, φ is an isomorphism. The category having (Λ-labelled) graphs as objects and graph morphisms as arrows is denoted by **Graph**.

We shall often write φ instead of φ_V or φ_E to avoid clutter. The graph morphisms in our diagrams will be indicated by black and white nodes and thick edges. In the category **Graph**, where the objects are labelled graphs over the label alphabet Λ, the subobject classifier **true** is displayed to the right where every Λ-labelled edge represents several edges, one for each $\lambda \in \Lambda$.

The subobject classifier $\mathbf{true} \colon 1 \rightarrowtail \Omega$ from the terminal object $\mathbf{1}$ to Ω allows us to single out a subgraph X of a graph Y, by mapping Y to Ω in such a way that all elements of X are mapped to the image of **true**.

Given arrows α, m as in the diagram in Definition 3, we can construct the most general pullback, called final pullback complement [7,13].

Definition 3 (Final pullback complement). *A pair of arrows $I \xrightarrow{\gamma} F \xrightarrow{\beta} G$ is a* final pullback complement *(FPBC) of another pair $I \xrightarrow{\alpha} L \xrightarrow{m} G$ if*

- *they induce a pullback square*
- *for each pullback square $G \xleftarrow{m} L \xleftarrow{\alpha'} I' \xrightarrow{\gamma'} F' \xrightarrow{\beta'} G$ and arrow $f \colon I' \to I$ such that $\alpha \circ f = \alpha'$, there exists a unique arrow $f' \colon F' \to F$ such that $\beta \circ f' = \beta'$ and $\gamma \circ f = f' \circ \gamma'$ both hold (see the diagram to the right).*

Final pullback complements and subobject classifiers are closely related to partial map classifiers (see [13, Corollary 4.6]): a category has FPBCs (over monos) and a subobject classifier if and only if it has a partial map classifier. These exist in all elementary topoi.

Proposition 4 (Final pullback complements, subobject and partial map classifiers). *Let* **C** *be a category with finite limits. Then the following are equivalent:*

(1) **C** *has a subobject classifier $\mathbf{true} \colon 1 \rightarrowtail \Omega$ and final pullback complements for each pair of arrows $I \xrightarrow{\alpha} L \xrightarrow{m} G$ with m mono;*

(2) **C** *has a partial map classifier $(F : \mathbf{C} \to \mathbf{C}, \eta : Id \xrightarrow{\cdot} F)$.*

2.2 Languages

The main theme of the paper is "simultaneous" rewriting of entire sets of objects of a category by means of rewriting a single *abstract* object that represents a collection of structures—the *language* of the abstract object. The simplest example of an abstract structure is a plain object of a category to which we associate the language of objects that can be mapped to it; the formal definition is as follows (see also [10]).

Definition 5 (Language of an object). *Let A be an object of a category* **C**. *Given another object X, we write X --→ A whenever there exists an arrow from X to A. We define the* language[1] *of A, denoted by* $\mathcal{L}(A)$, *as* $\mathcal{L}(A) = \{X \in$ **C** $\mid X$ --→ $A\}$.

Whenever $X \in \mathcal{L}(A)$ holds, we will say that X is *abstracted by* A, and A is called the *abstract object*. In the following we will also need to characterize a class of (co-)matches which are represented by a given (co-)match (which is a mono).

Definition 6 (Language of a mono). *Let* $\varphi\colon L \rightarrowtail A$ *be a mono in* **C**. *The* language *of* φ *is the set of monos* m *with source* L *that factor* φ *such that the square on the right is a pullback:*

$$\mathcal{L}(\varphi) = \{m\colon L \rightarrowtail X \mid \exists(\psi\colon X \to A)$$
$$\text{such that square (1) is a pullback}\}.$$

$$
\begin{array}{ccc}
L & \overset{m}{\rightarrowtail} & X \\
id_L \downarrow & \text{(PB)} & \downarrow \psi \\
L & \underset{\varphi}{\rightarrowtail} & A
\end{array}
\qquad (1)
$$

Intuitively, for any arrow $(L \overset{m}{\to} X) \in \mathcal{L}(\varphi)$ we have $X \in \mathcal{L}(A)$ and X has a distinguished subobject L which corresponds precisely to the subobject $L \rightarrowtail A$. In fact ψ restricts and co-restricts to an isomorphism between the images of L in X and A. For graphs, no nodes or edges in X outside of L are mapped by ψ into the image of L in A.

3 Materialization

Given a production $p : L \hookleftarrow I \rightarrowtail R$, an abstract object A, and a (possibly non-monic) arrow $\varphi\colon L \to A$, we want to transform the abstract object A in order to characterize all successors of objects in $\mathcal{L}(A)$, i.e., those obtained by rewriting via p at a match compatible with φ. (Note that φ is not required to be monic, because a monic image of the left-hand side of p in an object of $\mathcal{L}(A)$ could be mapped non-injectively to A.) Roughly, we want to lift DPO rewriting to the level of abstract objects.

For this, it is necessary to use the materialization construction, defined categorically in Sect. 3.1, that enables us to concretize an instance of a left-hand side in a given abstract object. This construction is refined in Sect. 3.2 where we restrict to materializations that satisfy the gluing condition and can thus be rewritten via p. Finally in Sect. 3.3 we present the main result about materializations showing that we can fully characterize the co-matches obtained by rewriting.

---

[1] Here we assume that **C** is essentially small, so that a language can be seen as a set instead of a proper class of objects.

3.1 Materialization Category and Existence of Materialization

From now on we assume $\mathbf{C}$ to be an elementary topos. We will now define the materialization, which, given an arrow $\varphi\colon L \to A$, characterizes all objects X, abstracted over A, which contain a (monic) occurrence of the left-hand side compatible with φ.

Definition 7 (Materialization). *Let $\varphi\colon L \to A$ be an arrow in $\mathbf{C}$. The materialization category for φ, denoted $\mathbf{Mat}_\varphi$, has as*

objects *all factorizations $L \rightarrowtail X \to A$ of φ whose first factor $L \rightarrowtail X$ is a mono, and as*
arrows *from a factorization $L \rightarrowtail X \to A$ to another one $L \rightarrowtail Y \to A$, all arrows $f\colon X \to Y$ in $\mathbf{C}$ such that the diagram to the right is made of a commutative triangle and a pullback square.*

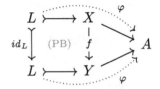

If $\mathbf{Mat}_\varphi$ has a terminal object it is denoted by $L \rightarrowtail \langle\varphi\rangle \to A$ and is called the materialization of φ.

Sometimes we will also call the object $\langle\varphi\rangle$ the materialization of φ, omitting the arrows.

Since we are working in a topos by assumption, the slice category over A provides us with a convenient setting to construct materializations. Note in particular that in the diagram in Definition 7 above, the span $X \leftarrowtail L \rightarrowtail L$ is a partial map from X to L in the slice category over A. Hence the materialization $\langle\varphi\rangle$ corresponds to the partial map classifier for L in this slice category.

Proposition 8 (Existence of materialization). *Let $\varphi\colon L \to A$ be an arrow in $\mathbf{C}$, and let $\eta_\varphi\colon \varphi \to F(\varphi)$, with $F(\varphi)\colon \bar{A} \to A$, be the partial map classifier of φ in the slice category $\mathbf{C}\downarrow A$ (which also is a topos).[2] Then $L \xrightarrow{\eta_\varphi} \bar{A} \xrightarrow{F(\varphi)} A$ is the materialization of φ, hence $\langle\varphi\rangle = \bar{A}$.*

As a direct consequence of Propositions 4 and 8 (and the fact that final pullback complements in the slice category correspond to those in the base category [25]), the terminal object of the materialization category can be constructed for each arrow of a topos by taking final pullback complements.

Corollary 9 (Construction of the materialization). *Let $\varphi\colon L \to A$ be an arrow of $\mathbf{C}$ and let $\mathrm{true}_A\colon A \rightarrowtail A \times \Omega$ be the subobject classifier (in the slice category $\mathbf{C} \downarrow A$) from $id_A\colon A \to A$ to the projection $\pi_1\colon A \times \Omega \to A$. Then the terminal object $L \xrightarrow{\eta_\varphi} \langle\varphi\rangle \xrightarrow{\psi} A$ in the materialization category consists of the arrows η_φ and $\psi = \pi_1 \circ \chi_{\eta_\varphi}$, where $L \xrightarrow{\eta_\varphi} \langle\varphi\rangle \xrightarrow{\chi_{\eta_\varphi}} A \times \Omega$ is the final pullback complement of $L \xrightarrow{\varphi} A \xrightarrow{\mathrm{true}_A}\rightarrowtail A \times \Omega$.*

$$
\begin{array}{ccc}
L & \xrightarrow{\ \eta_\varphi\ } & \langle\varphi\rangle \\
{\scriptstyle\varphi}\downarrow & \text{(FPBC)} & \downarrow{\scriptstyle\chi_{\eta_\varphi}} \quad {\scriptstyle\psi} \\
A & \xrightarrow[\mathrm{true}_A]{} & A \times \Omega \xrightarrow[\pi_1]{} A
\end{array}
$$

---

[2] This is by the Fundamental Theorem of topos theory [17, Theorem 2.31].

Example 10. We construct the materialization $L \overset{\eta_\varphi}{\rightarrowtail} \langle\varphi\rangle \overset{\psi}{\rightarrow} A$ for the following morphism $\varphi\colon L \to A$ of graphs with a single (omitted) label:

φ:

In particular, the materialization is obtained as a final pullback complement as depicted to the right (compare with the corresponding diagram in Corollary 9). Note that edges which are not in the image of η_φ resp. $\mathbf{true}_A$ are dashed.

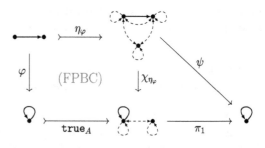

This construction corresponds to the usual intuition behind materialization: the left-hand side and the edges that are attached to it are "pulled out" of the given abstract graph.

We can summarize the result of our constructions in the following proposition:

Proposition 11 (Language of the materialization). *Let $\varphi\colon L \to A$ be an arrow in $\mathbf{C}$ and let $L \overset{\eta_\varphi}{\rightarrowtail} \langle\varphi\rangle \to A$ be the corresponding materialization. Then we have*

$$\mathcal{L}(L \overset{\eta_\varphi}{\rightarrowtail} \langle\varphi\rangle) = \{L \overset{m_L}{\rightarrowtail} X \mid \exists\psi\colon (X \to A).\ (\varphi = \psi \circ m_L)\}.$$

3.2 Characterizing the Language of Rewritable Objects

A match obtained through the materialization of the left-hand side of a production from a given object may not allow a DPO rewriting step because of the gluing condition. We illustrate this problem with an example.

Example 12. Consider the materialization $L \rightarrowtail \langle\varphi\rangle \to A$ from Example 10 and the production $L \hookleftarrow I \rightarrowtail R$ shown in the diagram to the right. It is easy to see that the pushout complement of morphisms $I \rightarrowtail L \rightarrowtail \langle\varphi\rangle$ does not exist.

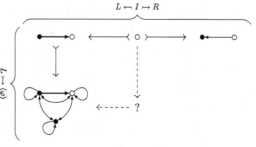

Nevertheless there exist factorizations $L \rightarrowtail X \to A$ abstracted by $\langle\varphi\rangle$ that could be rewritten using the production.

In order to take the existence of pushout complements into account, we consider a subcategory of the materialization category.

Definition 13 (Materialization subcategory of rewritable objects). *Let $\varphi\colon L \to A$ be an arrow of $\mathbf{C}$ and let $\varphi_L\colon I \rightarrowtail L$ be a mono (corresponding to the left leg of a production). The* materialization subcategory of rewritable objects *for φ and φ_L, denoted $\mathbf{Mat}_\varphi^{\varphi_L}$, is the full subcategory of $\mathbf{Mat}_\varphi$ containing as objects all factorizations $L \stackrel{m}{\rightarrowtail} X \to A$ of φ, where m is a mono and $I \stackrel{\varphi_L}{\rightarrowtail} L \stackrel{m}{\rightarrowtail} X$ has a pushout complement.*

Its terminal element, if it exists, is denoted by $L \stackrel{n_L}{\rightarrowtail} \langle\!\langle \varphi, \varphi_L \rangle\!\rangle \to A$ and is called the rewritable materialization.

We show that this subcategory of the materialization category has a terminal object.

Proposition 14 (Construction of the rewritable materialization). *Let $\varphi\colon L \to A$ be an arrow and let $\varphi_L\colon I \rightarrowtail L$ be a mono of $\mathbf{C}$. Then the* rewritable materialization *of φ w.r.t. φ_L exists and can be constructed as the following factorization $L \stackrel{n_L}{\rightarrowtail} \langle\!\langle \varphi, \varphi_L \rangle\!\rangle \stackrel{\psi \circ \alpha}{\longrightarrow} A$ of φ. In the left diagram, F is obtained as the final pullback complement of $I \stackrel{\varphi_L}{\rightarrowtail} L \rightarrowtail \langle \varphi \rangle$, where $L \rightarrowtail \langle \varphi \rangle \stackrel{\psi}{\to} A$ is the materialization of φ (Definition 7). Next in the right diagram $L \stackrel{n_L}{\rightarrowtail} \langle\!\langle \varphi, \varphi_L \rangle\!\rangle \stackrel{\beta}{\leftarrowtail} F$ is the pushout of the span $L \stackrel{\varphi_L}{\leftarrowtail} I \rightarrowtail F$ and α is the resulting mediating arrow.*

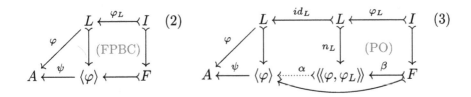

Example 15. We come back to the running example (Example 12) and, as in Proposition 14, determine the final pullback complement $I \rightarrowtail F \rightarrowtail \langle \varphi \rangle$ of $I \stackrel{\varphi_L}{\rightarrowtail} L \rightarrowtail \langle \varphi \rangle$ (see diagram below left) and obtain $\langle\!\langle \varphi, \varphi_L \rangle\!\rangle$ by taking the pushout over $L \leftarrowtail I \rightarrowtail F$ (see diagram below right).

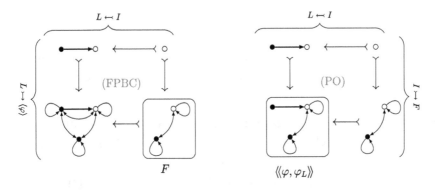

It remains to be shown that $L \rightarrowtail \langle\!\langle \varphi, \varphi_L \rangle\!\rangle \to A$ represents every factorization which can be rewritten. As before we obtain a characterization of the rewritable objects, including the match, as the language of an arrow.

Proposition 16 (Language of the rewritable materialization). *Assume there is a production* $p\colon L \xleftarrow{\varphi_L} I \xrightarrow{\varphi_R} R$ *and let* $L \xrightarrow{n_L} \langle\!\langle \varphi, \varphi_L \rangle\!\rangle$ *be the match for the rewritable materialization for* φ *and* φ_L. *Then we have*

$$\mathcal{L}(L \xrightarrow{n_L} \langle\!\langle \varphi, \varphi_L \rangle\!\rangle) = \{L \xrightarrow{m_L} X \mid \exists \psi\colon (X \to A). \ (\varphi = \psi \circ m_L \ \wedge \ X \xRightarrow{p,m_L})\}.$$

3.3   Rewriting Materializations

In the next step we will now rewrite the rewritable materialization $\langle\!\langle \varphi, \varphi_L \rangle\!\rangle$ with the match $L \xrightarrow{n_L} \langle\!\langle \varphi, \varphi_L \rangle\!\rangle$, resulting in a co-match $R \rightarrowtail B$. In particular, we will show that this co-match represents all co-matches that can be obtained by rewriting an object X of $\mathcal{L}(A)$ at a match compatible with φ. We first start with an example.

Example 17. We can rewrite the materialization $L \rightarrowtail \langle\!\langle \varphi, \varphi_L \rangle\!\rangle \to A$ as follows:

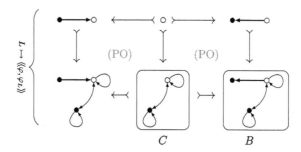

Proposition 18 (Rewriting abstract matches). *Let a match* $n_L\colon L \rightarrowtail \tilde{A}$ *and a production* $p\colon L \leftarrowtail I \rightarrowtail R$ *be given. Assume that* $\tilde{A}$ *is rewritten along the match* n_L, *i.e.,* $(L \xrightarrow{n_L} \tilde{A}) \xRightarrow{p} (R \xrightarrow{n_R} B)$. *Then*

$$\mathcal{L}(R \xrightarrow{n_R} B) = \{R \xrightarrow{m_R} Y \mid \exists (L \xrightarrow{m_L} X) \in \mathcal{L}(L \xrightarrow{n_L} \tilde{A}). \ ((L \xrightarrow{m_L} X) \xRightarrow{p} (R \xrightarrow{m_R} Y))\}$$

If we combine Propositions 16 and 18, we obtain the following corollary that characterizes the co-matches obtained from rewriting a match compatible with $\varphi\colon L \to A$.

Corollary 19 (Co-match language of the rewritable materialization). *Let* $\varphi\colon L \to A$ *and a production* $p\colon L \xleftarrow{\varphi_L} I \xrightarrow{\varphi_R} R$ *be given. Assume that* $\langle\!\langle \varphi, \varphi_L \rangle\!\rangle$ *is obtained as the rewritable materialization of* φ *and* φ_L *with match* $L \xrightarrow{n_L} \langle\!\langle \varphi, \varphi_L \rangle\!\rangle$ *(see Proposition 14). Furthermore let* $(L \xrightarrow{n_L} \langle\!\langle \varphi, \varphi_L \rangle\!\rangle) \xRightarrow{p} (R \xrightarrow{n_R} B)$. *Then*

$$\mathcal{L}(R \xrightarrow{n_R} B) = \{R \xrightarrow{m_R} Y \mid \exists (L \xrightarrow{m_L} X), (X \xrightarrow{\psi} A). \ (\varphi = \psi \circ m_L \ \wedge$$
$$(L \xrightarrow{m_L} X) \xRightarrow{p} (R \xrightarrow{m_R} Y))\}$$

This result does not yet enable us to construct post-conditions for languages of objects. The set of co-matches can be fully characterized as the language of a mono, which can only be achieved by fixing the right-hand side R and thus ensuring that exactly one occurrence of R is represented. However, as soon as we forget about the co-match, this effect is gone and can only be retrieved by adding annotations, which will be introduced next.

4 Annotated Objects

We now endow objects with annotations, thus making object languages more expressive. In particular we will use ordered monoids in order to annotate objects. Similar annotations have already been studied in [20] in the context of type systems and in [10] with the aim of studying decidability and closure properties, but not for abstract rewriting.

Definition 20 (Ordered monoid). *An* ordered monoid $(\mathcal{M}, +, \leq)$ *consists of a set* $\mathcal{M}$, *a partial order* $\leq$ *and a binary operation* $+$ *such that* $(\mathcal{M}, +)$ *is a monoid with unit* 0 *(which is the bottom element wrt.* $\leq$*) and the partial order is compatible with the monoid operation. In particular* $a \leq b$ *implies* $a + c \leq b + c$ *and* $c + a \leq c + b$ *for all* $a, b, c \in \mathcal{M}$. *An ordered monoid is* commutative *if* $+$ *is commutative.*

A tuple $(\mathcal{M}, +, -, \leq)$, *where* $(\mathcal{M}, +, \leq)$ *is an ordered monoid and* $-$ *is a binary operation on* $\mathcal{M}$, *is called an* ordered monoid with subtraction.

We say that subtraction is well-behaved *whenever for all* $a, b \in \mathcal{M}$ *it holds that* $a - a = 0$ *and* $(a - b) + b = a$ *whenever* $b \leq a$.

For now subtraction is just any operation, without specific requirements. Later we will concentrate on specific subtraction operations and demand that they are well-behaved.

In the following we will consider only commutative monoids.

Definition 21 (Monotone maps and homomorphisms). *Let* $\mathcal{M}_1$, $\mathcal{M}_2$ *be two ordered monoids. A map* $h: \mathcal{M}_1 \to \mathcal{M}_2$ *is called* monotone *if* $a \leq b$ *implies* $h(a) \leq h(b)$ *for all* $a, b \in \mathcal{M}_1$. *The category of ordered monoids with subtraction and monotone maps is called* **Mon**.

A monotone map h *is called a* homomorphism *if* $h(0) = 0$ *and* $h(a + b) = h(a) + h(b)$. *If* $\mathcal{M}_1, \mathcal{M}_2$ *are ordered monoids with subtraction, we say that* h preserves subtraction *if* $h(a - b) = h(a) - h(b)$.

Example 22. Let $n \in \mathbb{N} \backslash \{0\}$ and take $\mathcal{M}_n = \{0, 1, \ldots, n, *\}$ (zero, one, $\ldots$, n, many) with $0 \leq 1 \leq \cdots \leq n \leq *$ and addition as (commutative) monoid operation with the proviso that $a + b = *$ if the sum is larger than n. In addition $a + * = *$ for all $a \in \mathcal{M}_n$. Subtraction is truncated subtraction where $a - b = 0$ if $a \leq b$. Furthermore $* - a = *$ for all $a \in \mathbb{N}$. It is easy to see that subtraction is well-behaved.

Given a set S and an ordered monoid (with subtraction) $\mathcal{M}$, it is easy to check that also $\mathcal{M}^S$ is an ordered monoid (with subtraction), where the elements are functions from S to $\mathcal{M}$ and the partial order, the monoidal operation and the subtraction are taken pointwise.

The following path monoid is useful if we want to annotate a graph with information over which paths are present. Note that due to the possible fusion of nodes and edges caused by the abstraction, a path in the abstract graph does not necessarily imply the existence of a corresponding path in a concrete graph. Hence annotations based on such a monoid, which provide information about the existence of paths, can yield useful additional information.

Example 23. Given a graph G, we denote by $E_G^+ \subseteq V_G \times V_G$ the transitive closure of the edge relation $\overrightarrow{E_G} = \{(src_G(e), tgt_G(e)) \mid e \in E_G\}$. The *path monoid* $\mathcal{P}_G$ of G has the carrier set $\mathcal{P}(E_G^+)$. The partial order is simply inclusion and the monoid operation is defined as follows: given $P_0, P_1 \in \mathcal{P}_G$, we have

$$P_0 + P_1 = \{(v_0, v_n) \mid \exists v_1, \ldots, v_{n-1} \colon (v_i, v_{i+1}) \in P_{j_i},$$
$$j_0 \in \{0, 1\}, j_{i+1} = 1 - j_i, i \in \{0, \ldots, n-1\} \text{ and } n \in \mathbb{N}\}.$$

That is, new paths can be formed by concatenating alternating path fragments from P_0, P_1. It is obvious to see that $+$ is commutative and one can also show associativity. $P = \emptyset$ is the unit. Subtraction simply returns the first parameter: $P_0 - P_1 = P_0$.

We will now formally define annotations for objects via a functor from a given category to **Mon**.

Definition 24 (Annotations for objects). *Given a category* $\mathbf{C}$ *and a functor* $\mathcal{A} \colon \mathbf{C} \to \mathbf{Mon}$, *an annotation based on* $\mathcal{A}$ *for an object* $X \in \mathbf{C}$ *is an element* $a \in \mathcal{A}(X)$. *We write* $\mathcal{A}_\varphi$, *instead of* $\mathcal{A}(\varphi)$, *for the action of functor* $\mathcal{A}$ *on a* $\mathbf{C}$-*arrow* φ. *We assume that for each object* X *there is a standard annotation based on* $\mathcal{A}$ *that we denote by* s_X, *thus* $s_X \in \mathcal{A}(X)$.

It can be shown quite straightforwardly that the forgetful functor mapping an annotated object $X[a]$, with $a \in \mathcal{A}(X)$, to X is an op-fibration (or co-fibration [19]), arising via the Grothendieck construction.

Our first example is an annotation of graphs with global multiplicities, counting nodes and edges, where the action of the functor is to sum up those multiplicities.

Example 25. Given $n \in \mathbb{N} \backslash \{0\}$, we define the functor $\mathcal{B}^n \colon \mathbf{Graph} \to \mathbf{Mon}$: For every graph G, $\mathcal{B}^n(G) = \mathcal{M}_n^{V_G \cup E_G}$. For every graph morphism $\varphi \colon G \to H$ and $a \in \mathcal{B}^n(G)$, we have $\mathcal{B}_\varphi^n(a) \in \mathcal{M}_n^{V_H \cup E_H}$ with:

$$\mathcal{B}_\varphi^n(a)(y) = \sum_{\varphi(x)=y} a(x), \quad \text{where } x \in (V_G \cup E_G) \text{ and } y \in (V_H \cup E_H).$$

Therefore an annotation based on a functor $\mathcal{B}^n$ associates every item of a graph with a number (or the top value $*$). We will call such annotations *multiplicities*. Furthermore the action of the functor on a morphism transforms a multiplicity by summing up (in $\mathcal{M}_n$) the values of all items of the source graph that are mapped to the same item of the target graph.

For a graph G, its *standard multiplicity* $s_G \in \mathcal{B}^n(G)$ is defined as the function which maps every node and edge of G to 1.

As another example we consider local annotations which record the out-degree of a node and where the action of the functor is to take the supremum instead of the sum.

Example 26. Given $n \in \mathbb{N}\backslash\{0\}$, we define the functor $\mathcal{S}^n :$ **Graph** $\rightarrow$ **Mon** as follows: For every graph G, $\mathcal{S}^n(G) = \mathcal{M}_n^{V_G}$. For every graph morphism $\varphi\colon G \rightarrow H$ and $a \in \mathcal{S}^n(G)$, we have $\mathcal{S}_\varphi^n(a) \in \mathcal{M}_n^{V_H}$ with:

$$\mathcal{S}_\varphi^n(a)(w) = \bigvee_{\varphi(v)=w} a(v), \quad \text{where } v \in V_G \text{ and } w \in V_H.$$

For a graph G, its *standard annotation* $s_G \in \mathcal{S}^n(G)$ is defined as the function which maps every node of G to its out-degree (or $*$ if the out-degree is larger than n).

Finally, we consider annotations based on the path monoid (see Example 23).

Example 27. We define the functor $\mathcal{T}\colon$ **Graph** $\rightarrow$ **Mon** as follows: For every graph G, $\mathcal{T}(G) = \mathcal{P}_G$. For every graph morphism $\varphi\colon G \rightarrow H$ and $P \in \mathcal{T}(G)$, we have $\mathcal{T}_\varphi(P) \in \mathcal{P}_H$ with:

$$\mathcal{T}_\varphi(P) = \{(\varphi(v), \varphi(w)) \mid (v, w) \in P\}.$$

For a graph G, its *standard annotation* $s_G \in \mathcal{T}(G)$ is the transitive closure of the edge relation, i.e., $s_G = E_G^+$.

In the following we will consider only annotations satisfying certain properties in order to achieve soundness and completeness.

Definition 28 (Properties of annotations). *Let $\mathcal{A} :$ **C** $\rightarrow$ **Mon** be an annotation functor, together with standard annotations. In this setting we say that*

- *the* homomorphism property *holds if whenever φ is a mono, then $\mathcal{A}_\varphi$ is a monoid homomorphism, preserving also subtraction.*
- *the* adjunction property *holds if whenever $\varphi\colon A \rightarrowtail B$ is a mono, then*
  - $\mathcal{A}_\varphi\colon \mathcal{A}(A) \rightarrow \mathcal{A}(B)$ *has a right adjoint $red_\varphi\colon \mathcal{A}(B) \rightarrow \mathcal{A}(A)$, i.e., red_φ is monotone and satisfies $a \leq red_\varphi(\mathcal{A}_\varphi(a))$ for $a \in \mathcal{A}(A)$ and $\mathcal{A}_\varphi(red_\varphi(b)) \leq b$ for $b \in \mathcal{A}(B)$.[3]*

---

[3] This amounts to saying that the forgetful functor is a bifibration when we restrict to monos, see [19, Lem. 9.1.2].

- red_φ is a monoid homomorphism that preserves subtraction.
- it holds that $red_\varphi(s_B) = s_A$, where s_A, s_B are standard annotations.

Furthermore, assuming that $\mathcal{A}_\varphi$ has a right adjoint red_φ, we say that

- *the* pushout property *holds, whenever for each pushout as shown in the diagram to the right, with all arrows monos where $\eta = \psi_1 \circ \varphi_1 = \psi_2 \circ \varphi_2$, it holds that for every $d \in \mathcal{A}(D)$:*

$$d = \mathcal{A}_{\psi_1}(red_{\psi_1}(d)) + (\mathcal{A}_{\psi_2}(red_{\psi_2}(d)) - \mathcal{A}_\eta(red_\eta(d))).$$

We say that the pushout property for standard annotations *holds if we replace d by s_D, $red_\eta(d)$ by s_A, $red_{\psi_1}(d)$ by s_B and $red_{\psi_2}(d)$ by s_C.*

- *the* Beck-Chevalley property *holds if whenever the square shown to the right is a pullback with φ_1, ψ_2 mono, then it holds for every $b \in \mathcal{A}(B)$ that*

$$\mathcal{A}_{\varphi_2}(red_{\varphi_1}(b)) = red_{\psi_2}(\mathcal{A}_{\psi_1}(b)).$$

Note that the annotation functor from Example 25 satisfies all properties above, whereas the functors from Examples 26 and 27 satisfy both the homomorphism property and the pushout property for standard annotations, but do not satisfy all the remaining requirements [8].

We will now introduce a more flexible notion of language, by equipping the abstract objects with two annotations, establishing lower and upper bounds.

Definition 29 (Doubly annotated object). *Given a topos $\mathbf{C}$ and a functor $\mathcal{A}: \mathbf{C} \to \mathbf{Mon}$, a* doubly annotated object $A[a_1, a_2]$ *is an object A of $\mathbf{C}$ with two annotations $a_1, a_2 \in \mathcal{A}(A)$. An arrow $\varphi: A[a_1, a_2] \to B[b_1, b_2]$, also called a* legal arrow, *is a $\mathbf{C}$-arrow $\varphi: A \to B$ such that $\mathcal{A}_\varphi(a_1) \geq b_1$ and $\mathcal{A}_\varphi(a_2) \leq b_2$.*

The language *of a doubly annotated object $A[a_1, a_2]$ (also called the language of objects which are abstracted by $A[a_1, a_2]$) is defined as follows:*

$$\mathcal{L}(A[a_1, a_2]) = \{X \in \mathbf{C} \mid \text{there exists a legal arrow } \varphi: X[s_X, s_X] \to A[a_1, a_2]\}$$

Note that legal arrows are closed under composition [9]. Examples of doubly annotated objects are given in Example 36 for global annotations from Example 25 (providing upper and lower bounds for the number of nodes resp. edges in the preimage of a given element). Graph elements without annotation are annotated by $[0, *]$ by default.

Definition 30 (Isomorphism property). *An annotation functor $\mathcal{A}: \mathbf{C} \to \mathbf{Mon}$, together with standard annotations, satisfies the* isomorphism property *if the following holds: whenever $\varphi: X[s_X, s_X] \to Y[s_Y, s_Y]$ is legal, then φ is an isomorphism, i.e., $\mathcal{L}(Y[s_Y, s_Y])$ contains only Y itself (and objects isomorphic to Y).*

5   Abstract Rewriting of Annotated Objects

We will now show how to actually rewrite annotated objects. The challenge is both to find suitable annotations for the materialization and to "rewrite" the annotations.

5.1   Abstract Rewriting and Soundness

We first describe how the annotated rewritable materialization is constructed and then we investigate its properties.

Definition 31 (Construction of annotated rewritable materialization).
Let $p\colon L \xleftarrow{\varphi_L} I \xrightarrow{\varphi_R} R$ be a production and let $A[a_1, a_2]$ be a doubly annotated object. Furthermore let $\varphi\colon L \to A$ be an arrow.

We first construct the factorization $L \xrightarrow{n_L} \langle\!\langle \varphi, \varphi_L \rangle\!\rangle \xrightarrow{\psi} A$, obtaining the rewritable materialization $\langle\!\langle \varphi, \varphi_L \rangle\!\rangle$ from Definition 13. Next, let M contain all maximal[4] elements of the set

$$\{(a_1', a_2') \in \mathcal{A}(\langle\!\langle \varphi, \varphi_L \rangle\!\rangle)^2 \mid \mathcal{A}_{n_L}(s_L) \le a_2', a_1 \le \mathcal{A}_\psi(a_1'), \mathcal{A}_\psi(a_2') \le a_2\}.$$

Then the doubly annotated objects $\langle\!\langle \varphi, \varphi_L \rangle\!\rangle[a_1', a_2']$ with $(a_1', a_2') \in M$ are the annotated rewritable materializations for $A[a_1, a_2]$, φ and φ_L.

Note that in general there can be several such materializations, differing by the annotations only, or possibly none. The definition of M ensures that the upper bound a_2' of the materialization covers the annotations arising from the left-hand side. We cannot use a corresponding condition for the lower bound, since the materialization might contain additional structures, hence the arrow n_L is only "semi-legal". A more symmetric condition will be studied in Sect. 5.2.

Proposition 32 (Annotated rewritable materialization is terminal).
Given a production $p\colon L \xleftarrow{\varphi_L} I \xrightarrow{\varphi_R} R$, let $L \xrightarrow{m_L} X$ be the match of L in an object X such that $X \xRightarrow{p, m_L}$, i.e., X can be rewritten. Assume that X is abstracted by $A[a_1, a_2]$, witnessed by ψ. Let $\varphi = \psi \circ m_L$ and let $L \xrightarrow{n_L} \langle\!\langle \varphi, \varphi_L \rangle\!\rangle \xrightarrow{\psi'} A$ the the corresponding rewritable materialization. Then there exists an arrow ζ_A and a pair of annotations $(a_1', a_2') \in M$ for $\langle\!\langle \varphi, \varphi_L \rangle\!\rangle$ (as described in Definition 31) such that the diagram below commutes and the square is a pullback in the underlying category. Furthermore the triangle consists of legal arrows. This means in particular that ζ_A is legal.

$$
\begin{array}{ccc}
L[s_L, s_L] & \xmapsto{\;\;m_L\;\;} X[s_X, s_X] & \xrightarrow{\;\;\psi\;\;} A[a_1, a_2] \\
{\scriptstyle id_L}\downarrow & \text{(PB)} \quad\;\; \downarrow{\scriptstyle \zeta_A} & \;\nearrow{\scriptstyle \psi'} \\
L[s_L, s_L] & \xmapsto[\;\;n_L\;\;]{} \langle\!\langle \varphi, \varphi_L \rangle\!\rangle[a_1', a_2'] &
\end{array}
$$

---

[4] "Maximal" means maximality with respect to the interval order $(a_1, a_2) \sqsubseteq (a_1', a_2') \iff a_1' \le a_1, a_2 \le a_2'$.

Having performed the materialization, we will now show how to rewrite anno-tated objects. Note that we cannot simply take pushouts in the category of anno-tated objects and legal arrows, since this would result in taking the supremum of annotations, when instead we need the sum (subtracting the annotation of the interface I, analogous to the inclusion-exclusion principle).

Definition 33 (Abstract rewriting step $\rightsquigarrow$). *Let $p\colon L \xleftarrow{\varphi_L} I \xrightarrow{\varphi_R} R$ be a production and let $A[a_1, a_2]$ be an annotated abstract object. Furthermore let $\varphi\colon L \to A$ be a match of a left-hand side, let $n_L\colon L \rightarrowtail \langle\!\langle \varphi, \varphi_L \rangle\!\rangle$ be the match obtained via materialization and let $(a'_1, a'_2) \in M$ (as in Definition 31).*

Then $A[a_1, a_2]$ can be transformed to $B[b_1, b_2]$ via p if there are arrows such that the two squares below are pushouts in the base category and b_1, b_2 are defined as:

$$b_i = \mathcal{A}_{\varphi_B}(c_i) + (\mathcal{A}_{n_R}(s_R) - \mathcal{A}_{n_R \circ \varphi_R}(s_I)) \qquad \text{for } i \in \{1, 2\}$$

where c_1, c_2 are maximal annotations such that:

$$a'_1 \le \mathcal{A}_{\varphi_A}(c_1) + (\mathcal{A}_{n_L}(s_L) - \mathcal{A}_{n_L \circ \varphi_L}(s_I)) \quad \mathcal{A}_{\varphi_A}(c_2) + (\mathcal{A}_{n_L}(s_L) - \mathcal{A}_{n_L \circ \varphi_L}(s_I)) \le a'_2$$

$$
\begin{array}{ccccc}
L[s_L, s_L] & \xleftarrow{\ \varphi_L\ } & I[s_I, s_I] & \xrightarrow{\ \varphi_R\ } & R[s_R, s_R] \\
{\scriptstyle n_L}\big\downarrow & & {\scriptstyle n_I}\big\downarrow & & \big\downarrow{\scriptstyle n_R} \\
\langle\!\langle \varphi, \varphi_L \rangle\!\rangle[a'_1, a'_2] & \xleftarrow{\ \varphi_A\ } & C[c_1, c_2] & \xrightarrow{\ \varphi_B\ } & B[b_1, b_2]
\end{array}
$$

In this case we write $A[a_1, a_2] \overset{p,\varphi}{\rightsquigarrow} B[b_1, b_2]$ and say that $A[a_1, a_2]$ makes an abstract rewriting step to $B[b_1, b_2]$.

We will now show soundness of abstract rewriting, i.e., whenever an object X is abstracted by $A[a_1, a_2]$ and X is rewritten to Y, then there exists an abstract rewriting step from $A[a_1, a_2]$ to $B[b_1, b_2]$ such that Y is abstracted by $B[b_1, b_2]$.

Assumption: In the following we will require that the homomorphism property as well as the pushout property for standard annotations hold (cf. Definition 28).

Proposition 34 (Soundness for $\rightsquigarrow$). *Relation $\rightsquigarrow$ is sound in the follow-ing sense: Let $X \in \mathcal{L}(A[a_1, a_2])$ (witnessed via a legal arrow $\psi\colon X[s_X, s_X] \to A[a_1, a_2]$) where $X \overset{p,m_L}{\Longrightarrow} Y$. Then there exists an abstract rewriting step $A[a_1, a_2] \overset{p,\psi \circ m_L}{\rightsquigarrow} B[b_1, b_2]$ such that $Y \in \mathcal{L}(B[b_1, b_2])$.*

5.2   Completeness

The conditions on the annotations that we imposed so far are too weak to guar-antee completeness, that is the fact that every object represented by $B[b_1, b_2]$ can be obtained by rewriting an object represented by $A[a_1, a_2]$. This can be clearly seen by the fact that the requirements hold also for the singleton monoid and, as discussed before, the graph structure of B is insufficient to characterize the successor objects or graphs.

Hence we will now strengthen our requirements in order to obtain completeness.

Assumption: In addition to the assumptions of Sect. 5.1, we will need that subtraction is well-behaved and that the adjunction property, the pushout property, the Beck-Chevalley property (Definition 28) and the isomorphism property (Definition 30) hold.

The global annotations from Example 25 satisfy all these properties. In particular, given an injective graph morphism $\varphi \colon G \rightarrowtail H$ the right adjoint $red_\varphi \colon \mathcal{M}_n^{V_H \cup E_H} \to \mathcal{M}_n^{V_G \cup E_G}$ to $\mathcal{B}_\varphi^n$ is defined as follows: given an annotation $b \in \mathcal{M}_n^{V_H \cup E_H}$, $red_\varphi(b)(x) = b(\varphi(x))$, i.e., red_φ simply provides a form of reindexing.

We will now modify the abstract rewriting relation and allow only those abstract annotations for the materialization that reduce to the standard annotation of the left-hand side.

Definition 35 (Abstract rewriting step $\hookrightarrow$). *Given $\varphi \colon L \to A$, assume that $B[b_1, b_2]$ is constructed from $A[a_1, a_2]$ via the construction described in Definitions 31 and 33, with the modification that the set of annotations from which the set of maximal annotations M of the materialization $\langle\!\langle \varphi, \varphi_L \rangle\!\rangle$ are taken, is replaced by:*

$$\{(a_1', a_2') \in \mathcal{A}(\langle\!\langle \varphi, \varphi_L \rangle\!\rangle)^2 \mid red_{n_L}(a_i') = s_L, i \in \{1, 2\}, a_1 \le \mathcal{A}_\psi(a_1'), \mathcal{A}_\psi(a_2') \le a_2\}.$$

In this case we write $A[a_1, a_2] \stackrel{p,\varphi}{\hookrightarrow} B[b_1, b_2]$.

Due to the adjunction property we have $\mathcal{A}_{n_L}(s_L) = \mathcal{A}_{n_L}(red_{n_L}(a_2')) \le a_2'$ and hence the set M of annotations of Definition 35 is a subset of the corresponding set of Definition 33.

Example 36. We give a small example of an abstract rewriting step (a more extensive, worked example can be found in the full version [8]). Elements without annotation are annotated by $[0, *]$ by default and those with annotation $[0, 0]$ are omitted. Furthermore elements in the image of the match and co-match are annotated by the standard annotation $[1, 1]$ to specify the concrete occurrence of the left-hand and right-hand side.

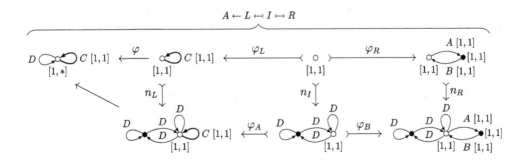

The variant of abstract rewriting introduced in Definition 35 can still be proven to be sound, assuming the extra requirements stated above.

Proposition 37 (Soundness for $\hookrightarrow$). *Relation $\hookrightarrow$ is sound in the sense of Proposition 34.*

Using the assumptions we can now show completeness.

Proposition 38 (Completeness for $\hookrightarrow$). *If $A[a_1, a_2] \overset{p,\varphi}{\hookrightarrow} B[b_1, b_2]$ and $Y \in \mathcal{L}(B[b_1, b_2])$, then there exists $X \in \mathcal{L}(A[a_1, a_2])$ (witnessed via a legal arrow $\psi\colon X[s_X, s_X] \to A[a_1, a_2]$) such that $X \overset{p,m_L}{\Longrightarrow} Y$ and $\varphi = \psi \circ m_L$.*

Finally, we can show that annotated graphs of this kind are expressive enough to construct a strongest post-condition. If we would allow several annotations for objects, as in [9], we could represent the language with a single (multiply) annotated object.

Corollary 39 (Strongest post-condition). *Let $A[a_1, a_2]$ be an annotated object and let $\varphi\colon L \to A$. We obtain (several) abstract rewriting steps $A[a_1, a_2] \overset{p,\varphi}{\hookrightarrow} B[b_1, b_2]$, where we always obtain the same object B. (B is dependent on φ, but not on the annotation.) Now let $N = \{(b_1, b_2) \mid A[a_1, a_2] \overset{p,\varphi}{\hookrightarrow} B[b_1, b_2]\}$. Then*

$$\bigcup_{(b_1, b_2) \in N} \mathcal{L}(B[b_1, b_2]) = \{Y \mid \exists (X \in \mathcal{L}(A[a_1, a_2]), \text{ witnessed by } \psi), (L \overset{m_L}{\hookrightarrow} X).$$
$$(\varphi = \psi \circ m_L \wedge X \overset{p,m_L}{\Longrightarrow} Y)\}$$

6 Conclusion

We have described a rewriting framework for abstract graphs that also applies to objects in any topos, based on existing work for graphs [1,2,4,27,28,31]. In particular, we have given a blueprint for materialization in terms of the universal property of partial map classifiers. This is a first theoretical milestone towards shape analysis as a general static analysis method for rule-based systems with graph-like objects as states. Soundness and completeness results for the rewriting of abstract objects with annotations in an ordered monoid provide an effective verification method for the special case of graphs We plan to implement the materialization construction and the computation of rewriting steps of abstract graphs in a prototype tool.

The extension of annotations with logical formulas is the natural next step, which will lead to a more flexible and versatile specification language, as described in previous work [30,31]. The logic can possibly be developed in full generality using the framework of nested application conditions [18,23] that applies to objects in adhesive categories. This logical approach might even reduce the proof obligations for annotation functors. Another topic for future work is the integration of widening or similar approximation techniques, which collapse abstract objects and ideally lead to finite abstract transition systems that (over-)approximate the typically infinite transitions systems of graph transformation systems.

References

1. Backes, P.: Cluster abstraction of graph transformation systems. Ph.D. thesis, Saarland University (2015)
2. Backes, P., Reineke, J.: Analysis of infinite-state graph transformation systems by cluster abstraction. In: D'Souza, D., Lal, A., Larsen, K.G. (eds.) VMCAI 2015. LNCS, vol. 8931, pp. 135–152. Springer, Heidelberg (2015). https://doi.org/10.1007/978-3-662-46081-8_8
3. Bauer, J.: Analysis of communication topologies by partner abstraction. Ph.D. thesis, Saarland University (2006)
4. Bauer, J., Wilhelm, R.: Static analysis of dynamic communication systems by partner abstraction. In: Nielson, H.R., Filé, G. (eds.) SAS 2007. LNCS, vol. 4634, pp. 249–264. Springer, Heidelberg (2007). https://doi.org/10.1007/978-3-540-74061-2_16
5. Calcagno, C., Distefano, D., O'Hearn, P.W., Yang, H.: Compositional shape analysis by means of bi-abduction. J. ACM **58**(6), 26:1–26:66 (2011)
6. Chang, B.-Y.E., Rival, X.: Relational inductive shape analysis. In: Proceedings of POPL 2008, pp. 247–260. ACM (2008)
7. Corradini, A., Heindel, T., Hermann, F., König, B.: Sesqui-pushout rewriting. In: Corradini, A., Ehrig, H., Montanari, U., Ribeiro, L., Rozenberg, G. (eds.) ICGT 2006. LNCS, vol. 4178, pp. 30–45. Springer, Heidelberg (2006). https://doi.org/10.1007/11841883_4
8. Corradini, A., Heindel, T., König, B., Nolte, D., Rensink, A.: Rewriting abstract structures: materialization explained categorically (2019). arXiv:1902.04809
9. Corradini, A., König, B., Nolte, D.: Specifying graph languages with type graphs. In: de Lara, J., Plump, D. (eds.) ICGT 2017. LNCS, vol. 10373, pp. 73–89. Springer, Cham (2017). https://doi.org/10.1007/978-3-319-61470-0_5
10. Corradini, A., König, B., Nolte, D.: Specifying graph languages with type graphs. J. Log. Algebraic Methods Program. (to appear)
11. Corradini, A., Montanari, U., Rossi, F., Ehrig, H., Heckel, R., Löwe, M.: Algebraic approaches to graph transformation–part I: basic concepts and double pushout approach, Chap. 3. In: Rozenberg, G. (ed.) Handbook of Graph Grammars and Computing by Graph Transformation: Foundations, vol. 1. World Scientific (1997)
12. Cousot, P.: Abstract interpretation. ACM Comput. Surv. **28**(2), 324–328 (1996). https://dl.acm.org/citation.cfm?id=234740
13. Dyckhoff, R., Tholen, W.: Exponentiable morphisms, partial products and pullback complements. J. Pure Appl. Algebra **49**(1–2), 103–116 (1987)
14. Ehrig, H., Golas, U., Hermann, F., et al.: Categorical frameworks for graph transformation and HLR systems based on the DPO approach. Bull. EATCS **3**(102), 111–121 (2013)
15. Ehrig, H., Habel, A., Padberg, J., Prange, U.: Adhesive high-level replacement categories and systems. In: Ehrig, H., Engels, G., Parisi-Presicce, F., Rozenberg, G. (eds.) ICGT 2004. LNCS, vol. 3256, pp. 144–160. Springer, Heidelberg (2004). https://doi.org/10.1007/978-3-540-30203-2_12
16. Ehrig, H., Pfender, M., Schneider, H.J.: Graph-grammars: an algebraic approach. In: 14th Annual Symposium on Switching and Automata Theory, Iowa City, Iowa, USA, 15–17 October 1973, pp. 167–180 (1973)
17. Freyd, P.: Aspects of topoi. Bull. Aust. Math. Soc. **7**(1), 1–76 (1972)
18. Habel, A., Pennemann, K.-H.: Nested constraints and application conditions for high-level structures. In: Kreowski, H.-J., Montanari, U., Orejas, F., Rozenberg,

G., Taentzer, G. (eds.) Formal Methods in Software and Systems Modeling. LNCS, vol. 3393, pp. 293–308. Springer, Heidelberg (2005). https://doi.org/10.1007/978-3-540-31847-7_17

19. Jacobs, B.: Categorical Logic and Type Theory. Studies in Logic and the Foundation of Mathematics, vol. 141. Elsevier, Amsterdam (1999)

20. König, B.: Description and verification of mobile processes with graph rewriting techniques. Ph.D. thesis, Technische Universität München (1999)

21. Lack, S., Sobociński, P.: Adhesive and quasiadhesive categories. RAIRO - Theor. Inform. Appl. **39**(3), 511–545 (2005)

22. Lack, S., Sobociński, P.: Toposes are adhesive. In: Corradini, A., Ehrig, H., Montanari, U., Ribeiro, L., Rozenberg, G. (eds.) ICGT 2006. LNCS, vol. 4178, pp. 184–198. Springer, Heidelberg (2006). https://doi.org/10.1007/11841883_14

23. Lambers, L., Orejas, F.: Tableau-based reasoning for graph properties. In: Giese, H., König, B. (eds.) ICGT 2014. LNCS, vol. 8571, pp. 17–32. Springer, Cham (2014). https://doi.org/10.1007/978-3-319-09108-2_2

24. Li, H., Rival, X., Chang, B.-Y.E.: Shape analysis for unstructured sharing. In: Blazy, S., Jensen, T. (eds.) SAS 2015. LNCS, vol. 9291, pp. 90–108. Springer, Heidelberg (2015). https://doi.org/10.1007/978-3-662-48288-9_6

25. Löwe, M.: Graph rewriting in span-categories. In: Ehrig, H., Rensink, A., Rozenberg, G., Schürr, A. (eds.) ICGT 2010. LNCS, vol. 6372, pp. 218–233. Springer, Heidelberg (2010). https://doi.org/10.1007/978-3-642-15928-2_15

26. O'Hearn, P.W.: A primer on separation logic (and automatic program verification and analysis). In: Software Safety and Security: Tools for Analysis and Verification. NATO Science for Peace and Security Series, vol. 33, pp. 286–318 (2012)

27. Rensink, A.: Canonical graph shapes. In: Schmidt, D. (ed.) ESOP 2004. LNCS, vol. 2986, pp. 401–415. Springer, Heidelberg (2004). https://doi.org/10.1007/978-3-540-24725-8_28

28. Rensink, A., Zambon, E.: Neighbourhood abstraction in GROOVE. In: Proceedings of GraBaTs 2010 (Workshop on Graph-Based Tools). Electronic Communications of the EASST, vol. 32 (2010)

29. Rozenberg, G. (ed.): Handbook of Graph Grammars and Computing by Graph Transformation: Foundations, vol. 1. World Scientific, Singapore (1997)

30. Sagiv, M., Reps, T., Wilhelm, R.: Parametric shape analysis via 3-valued logic. TOPLAS (ACM Trans. Program. Lang. Syst.) **24**(3), 217–298 (2002)

31. Steenken, D., Wehrheim, H., Wonisch, D.: Sound and complete abstract graph transformation. In: Simao, A., Morgan, C. (eds.) SBMF 2011. LNCS, vol. 7021, pp. 92–107. Springer, Heidelberg (2011). https://doi.org/10.1007/978-3-642-25032-3_7

Permissions

List of Contributors

Mnacho Echenim and Nicolas Peltier
Univ. Grenoble Alpes, CNRS, LIG, 38000
Grenoble, France

Radu Iosif
Univ. Grenoble Alpes, CNRS, VERIMAG,
38000 Grenoble, France

**Aurore Alcolei, Pierre Clairambault and
Olivier Laurent**
Universitéde Lyon, ENS de Lyon, CNRS,
UCB Lyon 1, LIP, Lyon, France

Cristina Matache and Sam Staton
University of Oxford, Oxford, UK

Christophe Lucasand
ENS–Lyon, Lyon, France

Matteo Mio
CNRS and ENS–Lyon, Lyon, France

Stefan Milius and Henning Urbat
Friedrich-Alexander-Universität Erlangen-
Nürnberg, Erlangen, Germany

Jakob Piribauer and Christel Baier
Technische Universität Dresden, Dresden,
Germany

Dariusz Biernacki and Piotr Polesiuk
University of Wrocław, Wrocław, Poland

Jurriaan Rot
Radboud University, Nijmegen, Netherlands

**Maciej Piróg, Piotr Polesiuk and Filip
Sieczkowski**
University of Wroclaw, Wroclaw, Poland

Fabio Zanasi
University College London, London, UK

Rob van Glabbeek
Data61, CSIRO, Sydney, Australia
Computer Science and Engineering,
University of New South Wales, Sydney,
Australia

Helmut Seidl and Raphaela Palenta
Fakultät für Informatik, TU München,
Munich, Germany

Sebastian Manet
FB3 - Informatik, Universität Bremen, Bremen,
Germany

Thorsten Wißmann
Friedrich-Alexander-Universität Erlangen-
Nürnberg, Erlangen, Germany

Jérémy Dubut
National Institute of Informatics, Tokyo,
Japan
Japanese-French Laboratory for Informatics,
Tokyo, Japan

Shin-ya Katsumata
National Institute of Informatics, Tokyo, Japan

Ichiro Hasuo
National Institute of Informatics, Tokyo,
Japan
SOKENDAI, Hayama, Kanagawa, Japan

Dietrich Kuske
Technische Universität Ilmenau, Ilmenau,
Germany

Bart Jacobs and Aleks Kissinger
Radboud University, Nijmegen, The
Netherlands

Andrea Corradini
Università d1i Pisa, Pisa, Italy

Tobias Heindel
University of Hawaii, Honolulu, USA

Barbara König and Dennis Nolte
Universität Duisburg-Essen, Duisburg,
Germany

Arend Rensink
University of Twente, Enschede, Netherlands

Index

End Page Sample